Constructing
Windows Dialogs

Constructing
Windows Dialogs

Steve Rimmer

Windcrest®/ McGraw-Hill

New York   San Francisco   Washington, D.C.   Auckland   Bogotá
Caracas   Lisbon   London   Madrid   Mexico City   Milan
Montreal   New Delhi   San Juan   Singapore
Sydney   Tokyo   Toronto

2 3 4 5 6 7 8 9 0   DOH / DOH   9 9 8 7 6 5 4

Library of Congress Cataloging-in-Publication Data
Rimmer, Steve.
    Constructing Windows dialogs / by Steve Rimmer.
        p.   cm.
    Includes index.
    ISBN 0-07-053009-2
    1. Windows (Computer programs) 2. Microsoft Windows (Computer
file) 3. User interfaces (Computer systems) I. Title.
QA76.76.W56R57   1994
005.265—dc20   93-46908
                                                       CIP

Editorial team: Brad J. Schepp, Acquisitions Editor
                Kellie Hagan, Book Editor
                Robert E. Ostrander, Executive Editor
Production team: Katherine G. Brown, Director
                Wanda S. Ditch, Desktop Operator
                Nancy K. Mickley, Proofreading
                Jodi L. Tyler, Indexer
Design team: Jaclyn J. Boone, Designer
                Brian Allison, Associate Designer   0530092
Marble paper background by Douglas M. Parks, Blue Ridge Summit, Pa. 17214 WK2

This one's for Megan too, as perhaps they all are, and for a view that stretches well into morning.

Contents

Introduction

"My reality check just bounced."

There are facilities built into Windows that the Windows software development kit documentation never even hints at. Some of it is so obscure and so well undocumented that reference to it can be found only deep in the Internet—scrambled, encrypted, and written in Sanskrit. Some of these things are truly astounding, too. None are much use, of course, but they're astounding nonetheless.

One of the things that makes writing Windows applications so mind-numbingly difficult is the same three books of function references, object descriptions, and other important information that Windows developers ultimately come to live by. Having all this land on your desk at once can be a bit daunting. It's rather like being given a large box of car parts and a set of wrenches and being told to put the car in question back together.

The first useful question might be what sort of car is involved. Windows won't tell you this. It also won't tell you whether all the parts are for the same car, or whether any of the wrenches can be expected to fit the nuts.

Another thing that makes writing Windows applications a lot like training elephants to levitate, only more so, is that there are all sorts of things that aren't documented in the aforementioned books but also aren't quite astounding and obscure enough to be left buried in encrypted files on the Internet. They're things you'll genuinely need to know if your applications are to work, and look sophisticated and professional. The object in Fig. I-1 is a Borland button.

Figure I-1

 A Borland button (the check mark is bright green).

You'll have encountered lots of these if you've used any applications written by Borland. If you've used one of Borland's language packages, you might have stumbled across what's involved in using these things in your own applications. Then again, you might not have. They're available in Borland's languages, but there's very little said in the documentation to suggest how to go about using them.

Windows applications are, in one form or another, lots of nested dialogs—a principal window calls dependent windows that in turn call more dependent windows, and so on. You could regard a complex Windows application as being the user interface elements—all the buttons and check boxes and scroll bars and such generated by Windows—and then the smarts of the application, which might display a graphic, process words, or calculate fractals. The latter part is, by definition, your problem. The former part is your problem too, but it should really be the province of Windows.

This book is about creating the former part—the user interface of a Windows application—in a way that works well, looks professional, and can be accomplished before the sun begins to go nova. In fact, it's really about a lot of tricks and poorly documented techniques that professional application developers have found through experimentation, blind dumb luck, or a lot of hours spent nagging Microsoft or reading Sanskrit on the Internet.

Windows dialogs in their simplest sense are just that—simple. However, they're not very interesting looking and they're exceedingly restrictive. Every time you attempt to create something that doesn't

look like it belongs back in the mid-'80s, Windows' basic dialogs seem determined to run out of steam. In some cases this will be merely cosmetic, although, with Windows itself being largely cosmetic, the value of appearance shouldn't be discounted lightly. In others it will mean that things you want to do flat out can't be done.

In looking at commercial Windows software, it will become apparent early on that there's a lot you can do with Windows' dialogs and controls that isn't defined in the basic structure of the Windows Software Development Kit. Some of these facilities are things that have always been in Windows, but that Microsoft never said much about. Others are resources that are provided by other parties, such as Borland—things that Borland never said much about. Still others are things you'll have to bolt onto your Windows applications, assuming you can figure out how to do so. In many cases the bolts involved are themselves things that Microsoft never explained.

Other authors in a more litigious mood have intimated that Microsoft has left so much of Windows undocumented to give its own applications an advantage over those written by third-party developers. After a while you might begin to believe this yourself. The salient aspect, however, is that there are things you'll need to know in order to go from writing hexadecimal calculator programs to polished Windows applications.

This book will provide you with a lot of it. More to the point, however, it will provide you with as many of the useful bits as possible while not burdening you with a lot of other information that is perhaps astounding, but of little practical use. By definition, this book is somewhat incomplete. In its incompleteness, however, it will be considerably easier to use than many of the more encyclopedic references for Windows software authors.

The later chapters of this book will illustrate example applications that deal with most of the interesting aspects of working with Windows dialogs and related matters. You'll require Borland C++ for Windows to compile them—I used version 3.1 to develop the code in this book. You'll also require at least version 3.1 of Windows to use many of the elements presented herein.

The companion disk for this book includes the source code for each of the demonstration Windows applications presented in this book. You'll also find a compiled version of PLAY.DLL—its use is described in detail in chapter 5. Finally, you'll find two shareware applications: Graphic Workshop for Windows to help you with the graphics that will turn up throughout this book, and Multimedia Workshop for Windows to assist in finding suitable crash-test dummies for the multimedia functions that will also turn up in chapter 5. See the README.TXT file on the companion disk for more information.

I hope you have as much fun with the lore and arcana of this book as I had scaring it all up. If buying it all wrapped up in a single package lacks the adventure of reading Sanskrit on the Internet, it's a lot more likely to help you meet your deadlines and brave the dark, fog-shrouded recesses of Windows suitably armed. (Along with its many poorly documented features, Windows' poorly documented fog-shrouded recesses are also the stuff of legends.)

Steve Rimmer
BBS: 1-905-729-4601*
CIS: 70451,2734

*This number should be changing some time in the summer of 1994. If you call and don't
  get through, listen for the phone company's recording announcing the new number.

What to click and why

"If the only tool you have is a hammer, everything will begin to look like a nail."

If the only object you have is a window, everything will begin to look rectangular. Under Windows, the only object you have is a window, whether or not it's immediately apparent. Buttons, check boxes, scroll bars—all of these are windows in disguise, or combinations of windows. In fact, they're windows of a special nature. They're controls.

The Zen and philosophy of Windows has been the subject of several less than stellar books by Microsoft Press, and of innumerable discussions. However, if you regard Windows as being an assemblage of discrete components, it's easy to see what it's really up to. It consists of:

> ➤ A pretty good graphics package

> ➤ A workable memory manager

> ➤ A multitasking facility of questionable design

> ➤ Some useful peripheral interface facilities

> ➤ A gargantuan user interface

> ➤ Three and a half tons of books

Actually, the last item might be somewhat in error as I write this, although by the time it hits the streets the average mean weight of the documentation required to successfully create applications for the Windows environment should have more or less approached this value.

It's actually the next to last item of the foregoing list that this book will help you out with. For the most part, making your software do whatever it's been written for—managing a spreadsheet, searching a database, computing a fractal, or designing the perfect compound bow to plug groundhogs with—will typically be a tiny fraction of the work required to make it into a successful, genuinely user-friendly Windows application. The rest of the work will be involved in getting the Windows user interface integrated into your software.

Software authors usually come to think of a user interface as that which mediates between an application and its users. Software authors who've worked with Windows for a while often come to appreciate that an application is something to be attached to the Windows user interface so that there's a reason to click on all the colorful buttons and scroll bars.

Potential Windows software authors who can't see the sense in this— perhaps because there isn't any—need only call Microsoft's technical support desk for help with a Microsoft application. The first question asked of you will almost certainly be about a Windows control, rather than a function of the software in question.

Actually, this is probably incorrect. The first question will most likely be "Will you hold?" Saying "no" doesn't work.

The importance of understanding how to manipulate the Windows user interface is two-fold. Being able to do so will make your applications easier to work with, and more intuitive for users who are confronted with a steep learning curve just coming to grips with what your applications do. Secondly, using the controls and interface features of Windows creatively will make your applications look slick, distinctive, and leading-edge.

If you have a choice between making your software easy to work with and making it look leading-edge, go for the latter. This is a very cynical view of software design, but it certainly helps sell a lot of applications.

Figure 1-1 illustrates three Windows buttons. The leftmost is a conventional Microsoft button. The middle one is a Borland BWCC button, a custom control available to applications written in Borland's language implementations. The rightmost one is a custom button created by a control library to be discussed later in this book.

The Microsoft button is consistent with every other Microsoft button under Windows, and this is why Microsoft would prefer that everyone used buttons like it. However, it's also somewhat dull. The Borland button clearly has the same function as its Microsoft forbearer, but it's more eye-catching. The check mark is bright green.

Figure 1-1

Three Windows buttons: a conventional button control, a Borland button, and a panic button.

The only drawback to Borland buttons and the other custom Borland controls is that they're becoming more commonplace. The widespread use of Borland's languages has seen the red and green Borland buttons become almost as common as Microsoft's original Windows buttons.

The custom button in Fig. 1-1 looks unlike any other button in a Windows application, and if you don't like the look of this one you're free to create any other sort of custom buttons you wish. Later in this book you'll see how to write a dynamic link library to supply custom controls for any Windows applications you write.

Here's another example of how knowing the secret facilities of Windows dialogs and controls can make your software more interesting. Figures 1-2A and 1-2B illustrate the About boxes from Microsoft Word and Graphic Workshop for Windows. The former is, of course, Microsoft's fairly expensive high-end Windows word processor. The latter is a $40 shareware package—you'll find a copy on the companion disk for this book.

You can have unicorns and other mythical regalia in shareware, but Microsoft clearly feels it's beneath them. At least, they usually do. You might want to try the following experiment with the Windows Notepad application to see another example of what you can do with dialogs. There's a secret screen in the Notepad About dialog.

❶ Run the Notepad application.

❷ Select Help from the menu, and then select the About Notepad item from the Help menu.

❸ Hold down the Shift and Ctrl keys and double click on the Notepad icon in the About dialog. Click on OK to close the dialog.

❹ Open the About dialog a second time and hold down Shift and Ctrl while double clicking on the Notepad icon. A waving Microsoft flag will appear. Click on OK when you get tired of it.

❺ Open the About dialog a third time and hold down Shift and Ctrl while double clicking on the Notepad icon. A waving Microsoft employee will appear, along with scrolling credits. Click on OK to return to Notepad.

Figure 1-2A

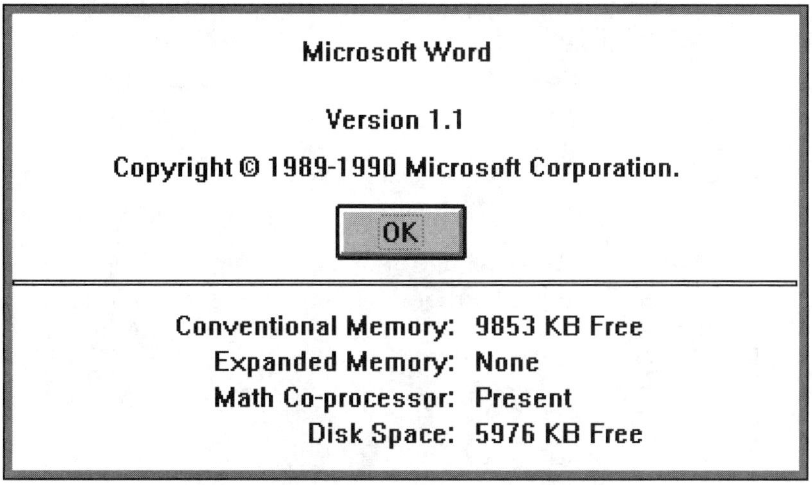

Microsoft Word

Version 1.1

Copyright © 1989-1990 Microsoft Corporation.

OK

Conventional Memory: 9853 KB Free
Expanded Memory: None
Math Co-processor: Present
Disk Space: 5976 KB Free

The About dialog for Word for Windows.

Legend has it that many of Microsoft's applications have these secret screens in them, accessible to the enlightened.

The ability to create custom controls and sophisticated dialogs offers a lot more than secret screens and gaudy buttons for your Windows applications. A complete understanding of how to work with the Windows user interface will allow you to better implement the features of your software. Unfortunately, a lot of what's involved is a bit obscure and poorly documented.

Here's an example—this is something that will be discussed in detail in the next chapter of this book. The background of the Graphic Workshop About box back in Fig. 1-2 is gray. By default, Windows dialogs have white backgrounds. Being able to change the color of a dialog can be very useful—as well as somewhat fashionable at the moment. It's not obvious how to do it, though.

Figure 1-2B

The About dialog for Graphic Workshop. Unicorns are in short supply in some applications.

In fact, as it turns out Windows will send the message handler for a dialog, the WM_CTLCOLOR message, before the dialog itself is created and once for each control in it. If the result of this message is a brush handle, it will use the brush so referenced to paint the background of the window involved. Remember that all Windows phenomena, including dialogs and controls, are really just windows. In effect, all you need do to make the background of a dialog gray is to return a brush handle to a gray brush when a WM_CTLCOLOR message appears.

Finding this out, however, can be a bit laborious. It's alluded to in the Windows development books, but only very obliquely. There are

dozens of issues like this in even the most trivial applications of the Windows user interface.

To some extent, this book will provide you with a single reference for all the best tricks in making Windows' controls and dialogs into something that suits your particular application. You'll probably be amazed at just how flexible Windows really can be—that, and how little of its flexibility is easily accessible to programmers who don't work for Microsoft.

⇨ A few Windows basics

The programs in this book are written in the C language, which is really the native language of Windows, as much as anything is. We'll get into a few of the dialect variations of C that pertain to Windows later in this chapter. An understanding of C is essential to use the examples to be presented throughout the following chapters.

This book won't teach you how to program in C—there are a number of very good books about the C language, and about the C language under Windows. If you're new to C you might want to put this book aside for a while and read an entry-level text on C programming.

Creating software involves a fairly linear tradeoff between the work and expertise involved in doing so and the functionality of the final application you generate. At one end of the spectrum, you can create applications for Windows in assembly language. Doing so, you can create software that gets the absolute last drop of performance from the platform it runs on, but at the expense of an almost unspeakable level of complexity in its creation. Assembly language programming forces you to work in something approaching the native language of a computer, which is very different from anything human beings would use to think or communicate in. It provides no resources more elaborate than simple numeric and data manipulation instructions.

The other end of the spectrum is a higher-level language, such as Microsoft's engagingly cute Visual Basic. With a syntax and command structure approaching stilted English, Visual Basic is easy to work with even for someone who knows relatively little about computers. It's really

not a serious programming language, however—the list of Windows facilities it can't access directly is several times longer than those it can, and Visual Basic applications offer less than stellar performance. You can extend the capabilities of Visual Basic by providing it with extra functions, called DLLs (dynamic link libraries), but these can't themselves be written in Visual Basic. They're typically written in C.

The C language offers the best tradeoff between the yawning chasm of assembly language and the padded cell of Visual Basic. It's by no means English-like, but neither does it require that you express yourself directly in the language of a computer. In addition, the C language development tools you'll be using in this book will allow you to cheat when need be—you can write Windows applications in C and enhance the performance of any time-crucial elements with assembly language subroutines.

The C language was originally developed in the late sixties for mainframe computers by two computer scientists at Bell Labs, Brian Kernighan and Dennis Ritchie. Should you be curious about where its name came from, it's said to have evolved from an earlier language called B, which in turn derived from an assembler. The assembler was called A. The original dialect of C, still used to some extent by many DOS programmers, is properly called "Kernighan and Ritchie C."

The Windows environment is many times more complex than a mainframe computer of the mid-sixties, and Kernighan and Ritchie C begins to exhibit a few holes when it turns up in Windows. These mostly have to do with assigning things to other things they might not be compatible with, and passing arguments to functions. They stem from the observation that under Windows not all simple objects are necessarily the same size, and that assigning them to places they shouldn't go will usually prove fatal.

On a PC, a short integer is always sixteen bits wide. That's what's defined if you declare:

```
int i;
```

A pointer under Windows can be sixteen or 32 bits wide, depending on what it's intended to point to. Specifically, pointers that point to objects allocated on the stack as local variables in a function, on the

local heap, or as static data are sixteen bits wide. Pointers that point to objects in the global memory heap are 32 bits wide.

I'll say a lot more about local and global memory later in this book when it turns up in real life. If the distinction is somewhat unclear as yet, do what experienced software authors do in a situation like this. Ignore it.

A pointer under Windows consists of one sixteen-bit number for the segment that the pointer addresses and a second sixteen-bit number for the offset into this segment. Pointers that point to local variables or static data reference the common data segment of your application, and by convention they're allowed to omit a segment component. Any sixteen-bit pointer is assumed to reference the common data segment. The common data segment contains an application's stack, static data, and any local memory allocated through LocalAlloc or the C language malloc function.

Pointers that are sixteen bits wide are called *near* pointers. Pointers that require an explicit segment component, and are thus 32 bits wide, are called *far* pointers. There's a lot more to pointers under Windows than I've touched on here, but really intense pointer sorcery won't turn up in this book.

A Windows C language compiler will attempt to take care of a lot of the confusion over pointers for you, and it will let you ignore everything else with the best of them if you use it correctly. Here's an example of how this works.

The function BigUglyFrogs does something inexplicable with a string—its exact purpose can be safely left to the dark wiles of imagination for the moment. It can be declared like this:

```
char *BigUglyFrogs(char *string)

{
    /* some code goes here */
    return(string);
}
```

This has declared a function that expects a pointer to a string as its argument, and can be expected to return a pointer to a string when

whatever it's up to has been completed. In a simpler environment this would be an end to the matter. Under C as it exists in Windows, it has merely begun to remove the lid of a barrel of frogs so big and so ugly as to defy easy description.

Conventional Windows applications are written in the medium C language memory model. This means that all pointers are implicitly defined as being near unless you tell C otherwise. In turn, this means that, by default, pointers are sixteen bits wide, and they refer to things in the common data segment of your application.

In the previous declaration of BigUglyFrogs, then, both the string it expects to have passed to it and the string it returns a pointer to will be represented by near pointers. Both objects must exist in the common data segment for this to work. Here's a perfectly respectable call to BigUglyFrogs:

```
static char uglyfrog[]="This is a big, ugly frog";
char *p;

p=BigUglyFrogs(uglyfrog);
```

In this case, the object uglyfrog is declared as static data, and can be referenced by a near pointer. Your C compiler knows this, and will pass a near pointer to BigUglyFrogs when it makes the function call. The frogs might be ugly, but the call will be managed correctly.

The following example won't fare quite as well. This bit of code uses a function called FixedGlobalAlloc, which for the moment can be thought of as the equivalent of the C language malloc function, but for allocating blocks of global memory. It returns a far pointer to an allocated block of memory. I'll discuss the FixedGlobalAlloc call in detail later in this book when we deal with the correct application of bad memory-management techniques.

```
char far *p,far *s;
static char uglyfrog[]="This is a big, ugly frog";

if((s=FixedGlobalAlloc(lstrlen(uglyfrog)+1)) != NULL) {
    lstrcpy(s,uglyfrog);
    p=BigUglyFrogs(s);
    FixedGlobalFree(s);
}
```

Actually, there's no need to call FixedGlobalFree to free the buffer allocated by FixedGlobalAlloc in this example, as Windows will have thrown a protected-mode fault when BigUglyFrogs was called and thus terminated this application.

The problem here is that s is a far pointer and BigUglyFrogs is expecting a near pointer. The pointer passed to BigUglyFrogs as it appears to the function will be meaningless, and anything written to it by the function will appear at some unpredictable location in the common data segment, perhaps overwriting your application's stack. This is very messy.

The solution to this probably seems pretty obvious, and so it is. You need only rewrite BigUglyFrogs to use far pointers:

```
char far *BigUglyFrogs(char far *string)
{
    /* some code goes here */
    return(string);
}
```

Unfortunately, having done this, any argument passed to BigUglyFrogs absolutely must be a far pointer. The first invocation of this function, in which its argument was a pointer to a string declared as static data, would be equally as disastrous as passing a far pointer to a version of the function that was written to expect near pointers. When it's running in protected mode, Windows loathes any attempt by an application to address memory it doesn't own. The result of doing so will be another altercation with the protected-mode fault dialog.

It might seem that the only way around this problem is to have two versions of any function that involves the use of pointers, and then to be very, very careful how you call them. Clearly this would be a serious inconvenience. In fact, there's a much simpler way to deal with the issue. If there's any chance that a function will be asked to deal with both near and far pointers, it should be written to use far pointers, and C should be instructed to transform any near pointers it encounters to far pointers. The mechanism for doing this is called *prototyping*.

A prototype is a declaration of how a function should be called. Prototypes are typically stowed in a header file that can be included

in the applications that will use them. The WINDOWS.H header file, for example, includes prototypes for all the callable functions provided by Windows, among other things. Here's a prototype for BigUglyFrogs:

```
char far *BigUglyFrogs(char far *string);
```

As long as C encounters this declaration prior to any calls to the BigUglyFrogs function, it will make sure that the pointers involved are handled correctly. It will also complain if you attempt to pass arguments of the wrong type, or the wrong number of arguments, to BigUglyFrogs. This will prevent you from accidentally passing an integer, rather than a pointer, to this function, for example.

This prototype has also told C that BigUglyFrogs returns a pointer. Left without prototypes, C assumes that all functions return short integers.

With the profusion of pointer types and sizes under C, and the hundreds of intrinsic function calls that Windows itself provides, prototyping is all but essential. Programmers who began working with C under DOS, or in a simpler environment, might still consider the creation of a prototype for every function declared to be a cosmic waste of effort and memory that could better be used for playing video games. If you agree with this sentiment, you're free to tell your compiler not to insist on prototypes. Windows will find a way to make you regret your foolishness—it probably has a specially written DLL dedicated to the task.

The extended version of C that Windows applications are usually written in is referred to as ANSI C. The prototype checking in ANSI C is very strict. It will make sure not only that you're passing a pointer to a function that expects one, for example, but that the pointer points to the sort of object your prototype says it should.

As an aside, you can use C++ to compile the programs in this book. The C++ language is a further extension of C. Because it's a superset of ANSI C, you can simply ignore the ++ part and use a C++ compiler to compile C programs. There are certainly some advantages to C++ if you're working on a large application with many programmers. Since this book is about small examples of C

language code with relatively few function calls, however, the examples are in C rather than in C++.

You're free either to mix the C language functions to be discussed herein with a C++ program or to add the C++ trappings to them if you're particularly enamored of C++.

A few good objects

Windows is replete with specialized data types, and it's worth having an overview of them before you actually start looking at some working code.

As was touched on earlier, every visible object under Windows is implemented as a window. Windows are referred to in an application by *window handles*, which are actually just unsigned integers and serve as indexes into an internal table of data structures that Windows maintains to corral the parameters of its screen objects. It's not necessary to know what's in the data structures a window handle references. A window handle is defined as an object of the type HWND.

Whenever it's appropriate to reference a window, you'll be provided with the HWND associated with it. At least, this is almost always true. There are two special cases of HWNDs that are useful when no specific window handle is applicable. An HWND with the value zero, a *null handle*, implicitly refers to the top window on your screen, whatever its actual window handle is. An HWND with the value 0xffff implicitly refers to all the windows open in your system. It's used in certain fairly exotic message-handling applications.

Windows regards anything that can be drawn on or printed to— including your monitor and your printer—as a device. To some extent, the same techniques are used for output to any device, regardless of whether it's glass and vacuum or lasers and carbon. A device is referred to by a *device context handle*, or HDC.

You can fetch an HDC for your current screen device in a number of ways, but, as you'll see presently, most screen updating will be done when Windows says it's ready, which is when it sends a WM_PAINT message to a window. There's a convenient mechanism provided to fetch an HDC when this happens.

I discussed far pointers at some length in the foregoing section of this chapter. Windows calls for a lot of pointers of varying types. To help keep your pointers straight, it specifies a number of defined pointer types. For example, a char far * pointer is defined as LPSTR, that is, a long pointer to a string. There's also LPINT, a long pointer to an array of integers. Near pointers are defined as PSTR and PINT, although you probably won't use them this way.

Windows defines a number of other specialized simple data types. Some of the ones you might want to keep in mind are:

BOOL An integer used to hold Boolean status

BYTE A char

WORD An unsigned short integer

DWORD An unsigned long integer

Windows makes extensive use of handles. A *handle* is an indirect reference to something. Handles are actually stored in WORD objects.

Traditionally, a handle is a pointer to a pointer—under Windows it's an index into a list of pointers. The reason handles are used is that they allow you to reference an object in memory without forcing Windows to keep it in the same place all the time. For example, consider allocating a block of memory like this:

```
char *p;
p=malloc(1000);
```

Having done so, there will be a 1,000-byte block of memory fixed in your address space. If previously allocated memory below it is subsequently freed up, there will be an immovable object in the midst of two otherwise useful blocks of heap space.

In handle-based memory management, the memory manager is free to move allocated blocks around. Prior to using one, you must "lock" it in order to derive a pointer to it and to keep it from moving, and then "unlock" it again when you're done. For the time it's not locked, Windows is free to move it to best use its available heap space.

Actually, in managing global memory this way, Windows is free to move unlocked buffers out of memory entirely and store them as temporary disk files. Locking a buffer that was previously "spilled" to disk will cause it to be reloaded.

In reality, Windows' handles are a very complex subject, as different sorts of objects turn out to be referenced by different types of handles. Some are really table indices and some are "magic cookie" handles that only Windows itself understands. For the purposes of this book, a handle is a mysterious entity that your applications can pass around, but that they need never attempt to understand. This is a bit unadventurous, but it works.

Windows defines a specific data type called HANDLE. There are also a number of specific handle types:

HSTR A handle to a string

HICON A handle to an icon

HDC A handle to a device context

HMENU A handle to a menu

HPEN A handle to a pen

HFONT A handle to a font

HBRUSH A handle to a brush

HBITMAP A handle to a bitmap

HCURSOR A handle to a cursor

HRGN A handle to a region

HPALETTE A handle to a palette

Some of these objects will turn up in the applications discussed later in this book.

Note that while these handles are really all defined as being of the type HANDLE in WINDOWS.H, they're by no means interchangeable. For example, while an icon is really a bitmap of a sort, you shouldn't pass an HICON handle to a function that expects an HBITMAP.

There are a number of other object types that will turn up throughout the code in this book—Windows is replete with dedicated data structures and defined objects.

 # A very brief introduction to resources

One of the things unique to Windows programming that turns up early on in this book is the idea of *resources*. The Resource Workshop application that accompanies Borland C++ for Windows is integral to working with the software in this book. It's important to understand a bit about how resources—the result of compiling an RC file—work in a Windows application. Knowing how to make resources dance is about half the work involved in understanding Windows' dialogs.

Long ago and far away when the universe was a simpler place—and everything ran under DOS—an application's EXE file was just a large chunk of machine code and a few rudimentary data objects to allow DOS to load and execute your programs. Things got a great deal more complicated when applications began to migrate to Windows. As a result, EXE files got a lot more complicated too.

In simple DOS applications, a typical example of software consists of some executable code and some data. Data might include text strings, numeric constants, and perhaps graphics. In an old-style DOS EXE file, all the code and data was more or less tossed into a blender and

poured onto your hard drive, there to run or void your warrantee, as fate decided.

Windows applications usually have a lot more data to worry about, and Windows likes to be able to manage its EXE files a lot more rigidly than DOS did. To this end, then, a Windows EXE file consists of blocks of code and bits of structured data. The data objects are stored as discrete entities called *resources*. A Windows application includes a *resource list*, which is a collection of structured data objects stored in such a way as to allow Windows to fetch a particular object from an application's EXE file when it's required.

Here's a simple example of why this is done. Back in Fig. 1-2, the About box for Graphic Workshop included a graphic of a unicorn. The unicorn is stored as a bitmap resource in Graphic Workshop's EXE file. This means that it lives on disk and will be called into memory only when it's required, that is, when the About dialog is displayed. As soon as it's no longer required in memory, it will be discarded. The result of handling it this way is to allow it to be part of the Graphic Workshop program without actually occupying any memory most of the time.

Most of the structured data of a Windows application works this way. Resources include dialog definitions, bitmaps, menus, keyboard accelerators, text string tables, and so on. Windows is forever fetching things from its applications' EXE files, using them, and throwing them away. This slows down Windows and the applications that run under it, but it allows Windows to do in sixteen megabytes of memory what would otherwise require three or four times this much real estate.

When you compile a Windows application under Borland C++, then, the compiler compiles your C language source file and uses it to create the code portion of the final EXE file. It also compiles your RC file, which becomes the resource list.

As will turn up later in this book, Resource Workshop can also disassemble a Windows EXE file to the extent of unpacking all the resources in its resource list back into an RC file. This allows you to see how other applications have managed things in some cases. It also means that you can often send Resource Workshop on raiding parties

to abduct resources from other Windows software—at least to the extent that doing so wouldn't prove unethical or likely to get you sued.

The result of compiling an RC file is a RES file, which is what the linker in Borland C++ actually links into your final EXE file. It's worth noting that there are two ways to come by a RES file; it can be created automatically by Resource Workshop when you select Save Project from its File menu, or it can be generated by Borland C++ when you compile an application. The latter will take place if Borland C++ observes that the file time stamp of an RC file in your project is newer than that of the corresponding RES file.

You can avoid a whole plethora of awkward problems by not setting up Resource Workshop to create RES files when it saves an RC file.

The C compiler from hell

The programs in this book are written using Borland's C++ for Windows 3.1. Just prior to shipping this manuscript, I received the beta for Borland C++ for Windows version 4.0. It came on a CD-ROM, took an hour to install, and occupied over 70 megabytes of hard disk space. The beta even had a nickname—Predator. While the origin of the name is unclear, it seems intuitively appropriate; in writing Windows applications, you might feel a bit like a light lunch even if you're still working in the comfortable surroundings of version 3.1.

If you compile the applications in this book using the PRJ files provided with them, your compiler will be correctly set up. Should you have cause to create your own PRJ files or to modify the ones included here, note the following:

> ➤ The applications in this book should be compiled under the medium memory model.

> ➤ The dynamic link libraries in this book should be compiled under the large memory model.

> ➤ The default char type should always be set to unsigned.

➤ The PRJ files all assume that Borland C++ for Windows has been installed on drive C in a subdirectory called \BC, and that the source code for the programs in this book resides in \BC\DIALOG. The compiler's header and library files are assumed to be in \BC\INCLUDE and \BC\LIB respectively. You must change the directory entries for the projects if your directory structure differs from this.

➤ The PRJ files are set up to use the classic editor configuration, that is, WordStar controls. You might want to change this if you're used to a different set of commands.

Creating Windows applications in C—contending with system calls and message handlers, resource scripts and dialog templates, FARPROCs, HWNDs, HDCs, LPSTRs, and perhaps a few objects too sinister to have names—can seem a bit like juggling chainsaws in the dark. In fact, it's not quite as complex as it seems because you needn't deal with it all at once. You can use the software author's refuge discussed earlier in this chapter. You can ignore it, or part of it—at least until it's convenient to deal with some of the nastier bits.

The example programs that will turn up throughout the rest of this book represent a very convenient place to begin to confront all the complexities of writing Windows software—or of dealing with some of the more exotic elements of the craft if you're already comfortable with far pointers and resource scripts. They're working applications, with all the difficult parts done. Once you get them compiled and running, and you understand more or less what they're up to, you can use them in two ways.

First, you can meddle with them as they stand and see what happens. Second, you can swipe the functions of interest from these programs and pour them into your own. (The quickest way to write your own applications is to either modify or abstract someone else's.)

The second approach is a lot less noble than the first, and less Zen-like than taking polecats to the movies, but it's the sort of thing that makes deadlines work and allows the real world to continue to revolve. In buying this book, you bought the right to pursue this

second approach and look anyone you care to in the eye while you're doing it.

Over the next few chapters you'll find the techniques, information, and mystical secrets to make your Windows applications professional, intuitive, and state of the art. You might well be amazed at what you can make Windows do. Windows will be amazed too—it's full of capabilities it never knew it had.

Simple dialogs

CHAPTER 2

"The phrase political will, *like the phrase* technical support, *is a contradiction in terms."*

nstalling Borland's C++ compiler for Windows is in itself a mighty undertaking, but clicking the BCW application into existence for the first time is singularly frightening. It's a bit like being given a large block of stone, a chisel, and a sketch of the statue it's to become and being told "Call us when you're done."

Windows C language development environments aren't necessarily badly documented per se. They're just vast beyond all imagination. Learning to use Borland's C++ for Windows from scratch makes the prospect of learning an application package, like CorelDRAW, seem pretty tame by comparison. In addition to figuring out how to work the language itself, you have to learn to write Windows applications. Even trivial Windows applications are pretty complex.

One way to look at a Windows application—and there are, in fact, two ways to do so—is as a series of dialogs. The principal window of such an application is itself a dialog, and every window spawned from it is also a dialog. This structure can be a bit restrictive for some exotic applications, but it makes creating the vast majority of Windows programs relatively simple, as it makes Windows itself do most of the work for you.

The alternative, by the way, is to create a Window through the classic approach of calling CreateWindow and adding other objects to it as child windows. Because this is a book about dialogs, I won't touch on this approach here. In addition, it's tedious, time-consuming, and rarely actually called for. You can accomplish the same results either way in most cases, but creating an application entirely from dialogs is usually a lot easier.

In writing books like this one, most authors are cautioned to be wary of Windows gurus—those small, troll-like creatures of the darkness with watery eyes from too many hours spent before a monitor and chronic carpal tunnel syndrome caused by typing continuously since birth. These parties will look at the foregoing notion as nearly

blasphemous. They would also argue that if software is hard to write it ought to be hard to use as well. We'll ignore them for the present.

This chapter will discuss a fairly simple Windows application structured as a dialog for its main window and a number of subsidiary dialogs for its functions, such as they are. While it's conventional as demonstration programs go in that it does nothing useful as it stands, seeing how it does nothing useful will illustrate much of what you need to know about how to work with dialogs and Windows applications in general. This program is called DEMO1.

Figure 2-1A illustrates the principal dialog of DEMO1, followed by the subsidiary dialogs of its various functions (Figs. 2-1B through 2-1H). Despite some of the objects in these dialogs looking a bit peculiar, they're all standard Windows control classes.

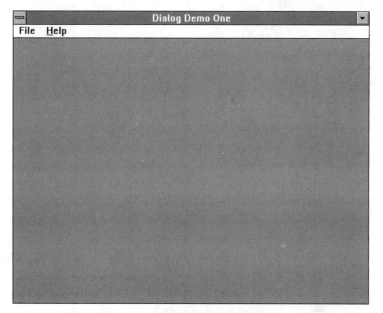

Figure 2-1A

The principal dialog of the DEMO1 application.

Figure 2-1B

The Buttons dialog of DEMO1.

Figure 2-1C

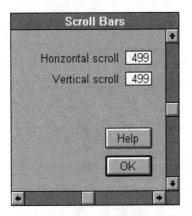

The Scroll Bars dialog of DEMO1.

Figure 2-1D

The Adjust Colour dialog of DEMO1.

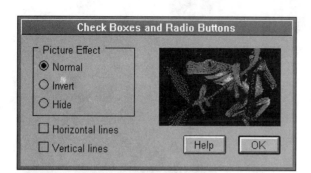

Figure 2-1E

The Check Boxes and Radio Buttons dialog of DEMO1.

Figure 2-1F

The Bitmap dialog of DEMO1.

Figure 2-1G

The List dialog of DEMO1.

Figure 2-1H

The Combo Box dialog of DEMO1.

You can see what this program does by compiling the source code for DEMO1 from the companion disk for this book. It should initially appear as a green window.

Making your windows green—or, in fact, making them any other color you like—is one of the things that this chapter will get into in detail. Figure 2-2 is the complete C language source code for DEMO1. In addition to DEMO1.CPP, you'll need DEMO1.RC, as shown in Fig. 2-3. Suitable DEF and project files for DEMO1 are included with the source code on the companion disk for this book.

Figure 2-2   *The DEMO1.CPP source code.*

```
/*
    Dialog Demo 1
    Copyright (c) 1993 Alchemy Mindworks Inc.
*/

#include <windows.h>
```

```
#include <stdio.h>
#include <stdlib.h>
#include <ctype.h>
#include <alloc.h>
#include <string.h>
#include <dos.h>
#include <time.h>

#define say(s)      MessageBox(NULL,s,"Yo...",MB_OK | MB_ICONSTOP);
#define saynumber(f,s)    {char b[128]; sprintf((LPSTR)b,(LPSTR)f,s); \
     MessageBox(NULL,b,"Debug Message",MB_OK | MB_ICONSTOP); }

#define STRINGSIZE          129         /* how big is a string? */

#ifndef IDHELP
#define IDHELP              998
#endif

#define MESSAGE_STRING      101         /* message box object */

#define FILE_BUTTONS        101
#define FILE_SCROLLBARS     102
#define FILE_COLOURS        103
#define FILE_CHECKBOXES     104
#define FILE_BITMAP         105
#define FILE_LISTBOX        106
#define FILE_COMBOBOX       107
#define FILE_EXIT           199

#define HELPM_INDEX         901
#define HELPM_USING         905
#define HELPM_ABOUT         999

#define COLOUR_REDSET       101
#define COLOUR_GREENSET     102
#define COLOUR_BLUESET      103
#define COLOUR_REDVAL       201
#define COLOUR_GREENVAL     202
#define COLOUR_BLUEVAL      203
#define COLOUR_REDTEXT      301
#define COLOUR_GREENTEXT    302
#define COLOUR_BLUETEXT     303

#define BUTTON_BASE         201
#define BUTTON_BASECOUNT    9

#define BITMAP16            "Bitmap16"
#define BITMAP256           "Bitmap256"

#define SCROLL_HORZTEXT     101
#define SCROLL_VERTTEXT     102
#define SCROLL_HORZVAL      201
#define SCROLL_VERTVAL      202
```

2-2 *Continued*

```
#define SCROLL_MAX          999

#define CHECK_NORMAL        101
#define CHECK_INVERT        102
#define CHECK_HIDE          103
#define CHECK_TITLE         105
#define CHECK_HORZ          201
#define CHECK_VERT          202

#define CHECK_LEFT          184
#define CHECK_TOP           16
#define CHECK_BITMAP        MENUBITMAP

#define LIST_LIST           101
#define LIST_TEXT           "ListText"
#define LIST_END            "ENDMARKER"
#define LIST_SELECT         102
#define LIST_TSELECT        103
#define LIST_BITMAP         "ListBitmap"

#define COMBO_COMBO         101
#define COMBO_TEXT          "ListText"
#define COMBO_SELECT        102
#define COMBO_TSELECT       103
#define COMBO_BITMAP        "ListBitmap"

#define HELPFILE            "DEMO.HLP"

#define DIALOG_KEY          "DialogDemo"

#define DINGBATS            "WingDings"

#define MENUBITMAP          "BitmapMenu"
#define SYS_BITMAP          300

#define MESSAGE_ABOUT       0
#define MESSAGE_HELP        1

#define BACKGROUND          RGB(0,128,0)
#define DARKBACKGROUND      RGB(128,128,0)

#define TEXTCOLOUR          RGB(255,255,0)
#define DARKTEXTCOLOUR      RGB(0,0,0)

#define RGB_RED             0
#define RGB_GREEN           1
#define RGB_BLUE            2
#define RGB_SIZE            3

#define CreateControlFont()    if(ControlFontName[0]) \
            controlfont=CreateFont(16,0,0,0,0,0,0,0,\
```

```
                      ANSI_CHARSET,OUT_DEFAULT_PRECIS,CLIP_DEFAULT_PRECIS,\
                      DEFAULT_QUALITY,DEFAULT_PITCH ¦ FF_DONTCARE,\
                      ControlFontName)

#define SetControlFont(hwnd,id) {HWND dlgH;\
              if(controlfont != NULL) {\
                  dlgH=GetDlgItem(hwnd,id);\
                  SendMessage(dlgH,WM_SETFONT,(WORD)controlfont,FALSE);\
              }\
              }

#define DestroyControlFont()    if(controlfont != NULL) DeleteObject(controlfont)

#define CheckOn(item)      SendDlgItemMessage(hwnd,item,BM_SETCHECK,1,0L);
#define CheckOff(item)     SendDlgItemMessage(hwnd,item,BM_SETCHECK,0,0L);
#define ItemOn(item)     { dlgH=GetDlgItem(hwnd,item); EnableWindow(dlgH,TRUE); }
#define ItemOff(item)    { dlgH=GetDlgItem(hwnd,item); EnableWindow(dlgH,FALSE); }
#define IsItemChecked(item)    SendDlgItemMessage(hwnd,item,BM_GETCHECK,0,0L)
#define ItemName(item,string)    { dlgH=GetDlgItem(hwnd,item); \
     SetWindowText(dlgH,(LPSTR)string); }
#define GetItemName(item,string) { dlgH=GetDlgItem(hwnd,item); \
     GetWindowText(dlgH,(LPSTR)string,BIGSTRINGSIZE); }

#ifndef max
#define max(a,b)              (((a)>(b))?(a):(b))
#endif
#ifndef min
#define min(a,b)              (((a)<(b))?(a):(b))
#endif

/* prototypes */
DWORD FAR PASCAL SelectProc(HWND hwnd,WORD message,WORD wParam,LONG lParam);
DWORD FAR PASCAL AboutDlgProc(HWND hwnd,WORD message,WORD wParam,LONG lParam);
DWORD FAR PASCAL ColourDlgProc(HWND hwnd,WORD message,WORD wParam,LONG lParam);
DWORD FAR PASCAL ButtonDlgProc(HWND hwnd,WORD message,WORD wParam,LONG lParam);
DWORD FAR PASCAL MessageDlgProc(HWND hwnd,WORD message,WORD wParam,LONG lParam);
DWORD FAR PASCAL BitmapDlgProc(HWND hwnd,WORD message,WORD wParam,LONG lParam);
DWORD FAR PASCAL ScrollDlgProc(HWND hwnd,WORD message,WORD wParam,LONG lParam);
DWORD FAR PASCAL CheckDlgProc(HWND hwnd,WORD message,WORD wParam,LONG lParam);
DWORD FAR PASCAL ListDlgProc(HWND hwnd,WORD message,WORD wParam,LONG lParam);
DWORD FAR PASCAL ComboDlgProc(HWND hwnd,WORD message,WORD wParam,LONG lParam);

void DrawImage(HDC hdc,int x,int y,HBITMAP image);
void DoMessage(HWND hwnd,LPSTR message);
void DoColours(HWND hwnd);
void DoButtons(HWND hwnd);
void DoBitmap(HWND hwnd);
void DoScrollbars(HWND hwnd);
void DoCheck(HWND hwnd);
void DoListbox(HWND hwnd);
void DoCombo(HWND hwnd);
void SetHelpSize(HWND hwnd);
void DoHelp(HWND hwnd,LPSTR keyword);
```

2-2 *Continued*

```
void MakeHelpPathName(LPSTR szFileName);
void CentreWindow(HWND hwnd);

int GetDeviceBits(HWND hwnd);
int GetBitmapDimensions(LPSTR name,LPINT x,LPINT y,LPINT bits);

LPSTR FetchString(unsigned int n);

/* globals*/
char szAppName[]="DialogDemoOne";
char ControlFontName[STRINGSIZE+1]="Arial";

LPSTR messagehook;
HANDLE hInst;
HFONT controlfont=NULL;

#pragma warn -par
int PASCAL WinMain(HANDLE hInstance,HANDLE hPrevInstance,
     LPSTR lpszCmdParam,int nCmdShow)
{
    FARPROC dlgProc;
    int r=0;

    hInst=hInstance;

    dlgProc=MakeProcInstance((FARPROC)SelectProc,hInst);
    r=DialogBox(hInst,"MainScreen",NULL,dlgProc);

    FreeProcInstance(dlgProc);

    return(r);
}

DWORD FAR PASCAL SelectProc(HWND hwnd,WORD message,WORD wParam,LONG lParam)
{
    HMENU hmenu;
    FARPROC lpfnDlgProc;
    PAINTSTRUCT ps;
    static HICON hIcon;
    static HBRUSH hBrush;
    static HBITMAP hBitmap;
    char b[129];
    POINT point;

    switch(message) {
        case WM_CTLCOLOR:
            if(HIWORD(lParam)==CTLCOLOR_STATIC ||
               HIWORD(lParam)==CTLCOLOR_DLG) {
                SetBkColor(wParam,DARKBACKGROUND);
                SetTextColor(wParam,TEXTCOLOUR);
```

```
                ClientToScreen(hwnd,&point);
                UnrealizeObject(hBrush);
                SetBrushOrg(wParam,point.x,point.y);

                return((DWORD)hBrush);

            }
        if(HIWORD(lParam)==CTLCOLOR_BTN) {
                SetBkColor(wParam,DARKBACKGROUND);
                SetTextColor(wParam,TEXTCOLOUR);

                ClientToScreen(hwnd,&point);
                UnrealizeObject(hBrush);
                SetBrushOrg(wParam,point.x,point.y);

                return((DWORD)hBrush);
            }
        break;
    case WM_SYSCOMMAND:
        switch(wParam & 0xfff0) {
            case SC_CLOSE:
                SendMessage(hwnd,WM_COMMAND,FILE_EXIT,0L);
                break;
        }
        switch(wParam) {
            case SYS_BITMAP:
                SendMessage(hwnd,WM_COMMAND,FILE_BITMAP,0L);
                break;
        }
        break;
    case WM_INITDIALOG:
        hBrush=CreateSolidBrush(BACKGROUND);
        SetHelpSize(hwnd);

        GetProfileString(DIALOG_KEY,"ControlFont",
            ControlFontName,b,STRINGSIZE);
        if(lstrlen(b)) lstrcpy(ControlFontName,b);
        CreateControlFont();

        hIcon=LoadIcon(hInst,szAppName);
        SetClassWord(hwnd,GCW_HICON,(WORD)hIcon);
        CentreWindow(hwnd);

        hmenu=GetSystemMenu(hwnd,FALSE);
        hBitmap=LoadBitmap(hInst,MENUBITMAP);
        AppendMenu(hmenu,MF_SEPARATOR,NULL,NULL);
        AppendMenu(hmenu,MF_BITMAP,SYS_BITMAP,(LPSTR)(LONG)hBitmap);
        break;
    case WM_PAINT:
        BeginPaint(hwnd,&ps);
        EndPaint(hwnd,&ps);
        break;
    case WM_COMMAND:
```

31

2-2 *Continued*

```
switch(wParam) {
    case HELPM_INDEX:
        MakeHelpPathName(b);
        WinHelp(hwnd,b,HELP_INDEX,NULL);
        break;
    case HELPM_USING:
        WinHelp(hwnd,"",HELP_HELPONHELP,NULL);
        break;
    case HELPM_ABOUT:
        if((lpfnDlgProc=MakeProcInstance((FARPROC)
          AboutDlgProc,hInst)) != NULL) {
            DialogBox(hInst,"AboutBox",hwnd,lpfnDlgProc);
            FreeProcInstance(lpfnDlgProc);
        }
        break;
    case FILE_BUTTONS:
        DoButtons(hwnd);
        break;
    case FILE_COLOURS:
        DoColours(hwnd);
        break;
    case FILE_BITMAP:
        DoBitmap(hwnd);
        break;
    case FILE_SCROLLBARS:
        DoScrollbars(hwnd);
        break;
    case FILE_CHECKBOXES:
        DoCheck(hwnd);
        break;
    case FILE_LISTBOX:
        DoListbox(hwnd);
        break;
    case FILE_COMBOBOX:
        DoCombo(hwnd);
        break;
    case FILE_EXIT:
        MakeHelpPathName(b);
        WinHelp(hwnd,b,HELP_QUIT,NULL);

        if(hBrush != NULL) DeleteObject(hBrush);
        DeleteObject(hBitmap);
        FreeResource(hIcon);
        DestroyControlFont();
        PostQuitMessage(0);
        break;
    }
    break;
}
return(FALSE);
}
```

```
void DoCombo(HWND hwnd)
{
    FARPROC lpfnDlgProc;

    if((lpfnDlgProc=MakeProcInstance((FARPROC)ComboDlgProc,hInst)) != NULL) {
        DialogBox(hInst,"ComboBox",hwnd,lpfnDlgProc);
        FreeProcInstance(lpfnDlgProc);
    }
}

DWORD FAR PASCAL ComboDlgProc(HWND hwnd,WORD message,WORD wParam,LONG lParam)
{
    PAINTSTRUCT ps;
    HWND dlgH;
    HDC hdc;
    HANDLE handle;
    HBITMAP hBitmap;
    RECT rect;
    LPSTR p;
    long l;
    char b[129];
    int i,x,y;

    switch(message) {
        case WM_INITDIALOG:
            if((handle=LoadResource(hInst,
              FindResource(hInst,COMBO_TEXT,RT_RCDATA))) != NULL) {

                if((p=(LPSTR)LockResource(handle))!=NULL) {
                    for(b[0]=0;;) {
                        for(i=0;p[i] >= 32 && i < 129;++i) b[i]=p[i];
                        b[i++]=0;
                        if(!lstrcmp(b,LIST_END)) break;
                        p+=i;
                        while(*p==10) ++p;
                        SendDlgItemMessage(hwnd,COMBO_COMBO,CB_INSERTSTRING,
                            -1,(LONG)b);
                    }
                    UnlockResource(handle);
                }
                FreeResource(handle);
            }

            SendDlgItemMessage(hwnd,COMBO_COMBO,CB_SETCURSEL,0,0L);

            SetControlFont(hwnd,IDOK);
            SetControlFont(hwnd,IDHELP);
            SetControlFont(hwnd,COMBO_COMBO);
            SetControlFont(hwnd,COMBO_SELECT);
            SetControlFont(hwnd,COMBO_TSELECT);

            CentreWindow(hwnd);
```

33

2-2   *Continued*

```
            break;
        case WM_PAINT:
            hdc=BeginPaint(hwnd,&ps);

            if(GetBitmapDimensions(COMBO_BITMAP,&x,&y,&i)) {
                GetClientRect(hwnd,&rect);
                if((hBitmap=LoadResource(hInst,FindResource(hInst,
                  COMBO_BITMAP,RT_BITMAP))) != NULL) {
                    DrawImage(hdc,rect.right-rect.left-x,0,hBitmap);
                    FreeResource(hBitmap);
                }
            }

            EndPaint(hwnd,&ps);
            break;
        case WM_COMMAND:
            switch(wParam) {
                case IDHELP:
                    DoHelp(hwnd,(LPSTR)"Combobox");
                    break;
                case COMBO_COMBO:
                    switch(HIWORD(lParam)) {
                        case CBN_DBLCLK:
                            SendMessage(hwnd,WM_COMMAND,IDOK,0L);
                            break;
                        case CBN_SELCHANGE:
                            if((l=SendDlgItemMessage(hwnd,COMBO_COMBO,
                              CB_GETCURSEL,0,0L)) != LB_ERR) {
                                SendDlgItemMessage(hwnd,COMBO_COMBO,
                                  CB_GETLBTEXT,(unsigned int)l,(LONG)(LPSTR)b);
                                ItemName(COMBO_SELECT,b);
                            }
                            break;
                    }
                    break;
                case IDOK:
                    EndDialog(hwnd,wParam);
                    break;
            }
            break;
    }
    return(FALSE);
}

void DoListbox(HWND hwnd)
{
    FARPROC lpfnDlgProc;

    if((lpfnDlgProc=MakeProcInstance((FARPROC)ListDlgProc,hInst)) != NULL) {
        DialogBox(hInst,"ListBox",hwnd,lpfnDlgProc);
```

```
            FreeProcInstance(lpfnDlgProc);
    }
}

DWORD FAR PASCAL ListDlgProc(HWND hwnd,WORD message,WORD wParam,LONG lParam)
{
    PAINTSTRUCT ps;
    HWND dlgH;
    HDC hdc;
    HANDLE handle;
    HBITMAP hBitmap;
    RECT rect;
    LPSTR p;
    long l;
    char b[129];
    int i,x,y;

    switch(message) {
        case WM_INITDIALOG:
            if((handle=LoadResource(hInst,FindResource(hInst,
                LIST_TEXT,RT_RCDATA))) != NULL) {

                if((p=(LPSTR)LockResource(handle))!=NULL) {
                    for(b[0]=0;;) {
                        for(i=0;p[i] >= 32 && i < 129;++i) b[i]=p[i];
                        b[i++]=0;
                        if(!lstrcmp(b,LIST_END)) break;
                        p+=i;
                        while(*p==10) ++p;
                        SendDlgItemMessage(hwnd,
                            LIST_LIST,LB_INSERTSTRING,-1,(LONG)b);
                    }

                    UnlockResource(handle);
                }
                FreeResource(handle);
            }

            SetControlFont(hwnd,IDOK);
            SetControlFont(hwnd,IDHELP);
            SetControlFont(hwnd,LIST_LIST);
            SetControlFont(hwnd,LIST_SELECT);
            SetControlFont(hwnd,LIST_TSELECT);

            CentreWindow(hwnd);

            break;
        case WM_PAINT:
            hdc=BeginPaint(hwnd,&ps);

            if(GetBitmapDimensions(LIST_BITMAP,&x,&y,&i)) {
                GetClientRect(hwnd,&rect);
                if((hBitmap=LoadResource(hInst,FindResource(hInst,
```

2-2 *Continued*

```
                LIST_BITMAP,RT_BITMAP))) != NULL) {
                    DrawImage(hdc,rect.right-rect.left-x,0,hBitmap);
                    FreeResource(hBitmap);
                }
            }

            EndPaint(hwnd,&ps);
            break;
        case WM_COMMAND:
            switch(wParam) {
                case IDHELP:
                    DoHelp(hwnd,(LPSTR)"Listbox");
                    break;
                case LIST_LIST:
                    switch(HIWORD(lParam)) {
                        case LBN_DBLCLK:
                            SendMessage(hwnd,WM_COMMAND,IDOK,0L);
                            break;
                        case LBN_SELCHANGE:
                            if((l=SendDlgItemMessage(hwnd,LIST_LIST,
                                LB_GETCURSEL,0,0L)) != LB_ERR) {
                                SendDlgItemMessage(hwnd,LIST_LIST,
                                    LB_GETTEXT,(unsigned int)l,(LONG)(LPSTR)b);
                                ItemName(LIST_SELECT,b);
                            }
                            break;
                    }
                    break;
                case IDOK:
                    EndDialog(hwnd,wParam);
                    break;
            }
            break;
    }

    return(FALSE);
}

void DoCheck(HWND hwnd)
{
    FARPROC lpfnDlgProc;

    if((lpfnDlgProc=MakeProcInstance((FARPROC)CheckDlgProc,hInst)) != NULL) {
        DialogBox(hInst,"CheckBox",hwnd,lpfnDlgProc);
        FreeProcInstance(lpfnDlgProc);
    }
}

DWORD FAR PASCAL CheckDlgProc(HWND hwnd,WORD message,WORD wParam,LONG lParam)
{
    static HBRUSH hBrush;
```

```
PAINTSTRUCT ps;
HBITMAP hBitmap;
HPEN hPen;
POINT point;
HDC hdc;
int i,x,y;

switch(message) {
    case WM_INITDIALOG:
        hBrush=CreateSolidBrush(DARKBACKGROUND);

        SetControlFont(hwnd,CHECK_NORMAL);
        SetControlFont(hwnd,CHECK_INVERT);
        SetControlFont(hwnd,CHECK_HIDE);
        SetControlFont(hwnd,CHECK_HORZ);
        SetControlFont(hwnd,CHECK_VERT);
        SetControlFont(hwnd,CHECK_TITLE);
        SetControlFont(hwnd,IDOK);
        SetControlFont(hwnd,IDHELP);

        CheckOn(CHECK_NORMAL);

        CentreWindow(hwnd);

        break;
    case WM_CTLCOLOR:
        if(HIWORD(lParam)==CTLCOLOR_STATIC ||
           HIWORD(lParam)==CTLCOLOR_DLG) {
            SetBkColor(wParam,DARKBACKGROUND);
            SetTextColor(wParam,DARKTEXTCOLOUR);

            ClientToScreen(hwnd,&point);
            UnrealizeObject(hBrush);
            SetBrushOrg(wParam,point.x,point.y);

            return((DWORD)hBrush);

        }
        if(HIWORD(lParam)==CTLCOLOR_BTN) {
            SetBkColor(wParam,DARKBACKGROUND);
            SetTextColor(wParam,DARKTEXTCOLOUR);

            ClientToScreen(hwnd,&point);
            UnrealizeObject(hBrush);
            SetBrushOrg(wParam,point.x,point.y);

            return((DWORD)hBrush);
        }

        break;
    case WM_PAINT:
        hdc=BeginPaint(hwnd,&ps);
```

37

2-2 *Continued*

```
        if(GetBitmapDimensions(CHECK_BITMAP,&x,&y,&i)) {
            if((hBitmap=LoadResource(hInst,FindResource(hInst,
              CHECK_BITMAP,RT_BITMAP))) != NULL) {
                DrawImage(hdc,CHECK_LEFT,CHECK_TOP,hBitmap);
                FreeResource(hBitmap);

                if(IsItemChecked(CHECK_HIDE)) {
                    SelectObject(hdc,hBrush);
                    SelectObject(hdc,GetStockObject(NULL_PEN));
                    Rectangle(hdc,CHECK_LEFT,CHECK_TOP,
                              CHECK_LEFT+x+1,
                              CHECK_TOP+y+1);
                    SelectObject(hdc,GetStockObject(NULL_BRUSH));
                }
                if(IsItemChecked(CHECK_INVERT)) {
                    SelectObject(hdc,GetStockObject(WHITE_BRUSH));
                    SelectObject(hdc,GetStockObject(NULL_PEN));
                    SetROP2(hdc,R2_NOT);
                    Rectangle(hdc,CHECK_LEFT,CHECK_TOP,
                              CHECK_LEFT+x+1,
                              CHECK_TOP+y+1);
                }
                if(IsItemChecked(CHECK_HORZ)) {
                    hPen=CreatePen(PS_SOLID,2,DARKBACKGROUND);
                    SelectObject(hdc,hPen);
                    for(i=0;i<=y;i+=4) {
                        MoveTo(hdc,CHECK_LEFT,CHECK_TOP+i);
                        LineTo(hdc,CHECK_LEFT+x,CHECK_TOP+i);
                    }
                    DeleteObject(hPen);
                }
                if(IsItemChecked(CHECK_VERT)) {
                    hPen=CreatePen(PS_SOLID,2,DARKBACKGROUND);
                    SelectObject(hdc,hPen);
                    for(i=0;i<=x;i+=4) {
                        MoveTo(hdc,CHECK_LEFT+i,CHECK_TOP);
                        LineTo(hdc,CHECK_LEFT+i,CHECK_TOP+y);
                    }
                    DeleteObject(hPen);
                }
            }
        }

    EndPaint(hwnd,&ps);
    break;
case WM_COMMAND:
    switch(wParam) {
        case IDHELP:
            DoHelp(hwnd,(LPSTR)"Checkboxes");
            break;
        case CHECK_NORMAL:
```

```
                            CheckOn(CHECK_NORMAL);
                            CheckOff(CHECK_INVERT);
                            CheckOff(CHECK_HIDE);
                            InvalidateRect(hwnd,NULL,FALSE);
                            break;
                    case CHECK_HIDE:
                            CheckOff(CHECK_NORMAL);
                            CheckOff(CHECK_INVERT);
                            CheckOn(CHECK_HIDE);
                            InvalidateRect(hwnd,NULL,FALSE);
                            break;
                    case CHECK_INVERT:
                            CheckOff(CHECK_NORMAL);
                            CheckOn(CHECK_INVERT);
                            CheckOff(CHECK_HIDE);
                            InvalidateRect(hwnd,NULL,FALSE);
                            break;
                    case CHECK_HORZ:
                    case CHECK_VERT:
                            if(IsItemChecked(wParam)) {
                                CheckOff(wParam);
                            }
                            else {
                                CheckOn(wParam);
                            }
                            InvalidateRect(hwnd,NULL,FALSE);
                            break;
                    case IDOK:
                            if(hBrush != NULL) DeleteObject(hBrush);
                            EndDialog(hwnd,wParam);
                            break;
                }
                break;
        }

        return(FALSE);
}

void DoScrollbars(HWND hwnd)
{
        FARPROC lpfnDlgProc;

        if((lpfnDlgProc=MakeProcInstance((FARPROC)ScrollDlgProc,hInst)) != NULL) {
            DialogBox(hInst,"ScrollBox",hwnd,lpfnDlgProc);
            FreeProcInstance(lpfnDlgProc);
        }
}

DWORD FAR PASCAL ScrollDlgProc(HWND hwnd,WORD message,WORD wParam,LONG lParam)
{
        static HBRUSH hBrush;
        PAINTSTRUCT ps;
        POINT point;
```

2-2 *Continued*

```
HWND dlgH;
char b[33];
int n,jump,pos;

switch(message) {
    case WM_INITDIALOG:
        hBrush=CreateSolidBrush(DARKBACKGROUND);

        SetScrollRange(hwnd,SB_HORZ,0,SCROLL_MAX,TRUE);
        SetScrollPos(hwnd,SB_HORZ,SCROLL_MAX/2,TRUE);
        n=GetScrollPos(hwnd,SB_HORZ);

        dlgH=GetDlgItem(hwnd,SCROLL_HORZVAL);
        sprintf(b,"  %d",n);
        SetWindowText(dlgH,b);
        EnableWindow(dlgH,TRUE);

        SetScrollRange(hwnd,SB_VERT,0,SCROLL_MAX,TRUE);
        SetScrollPos(hwnd,SB_VERT,SCROLL_MAX/2,TRUE);
        n=GetScrollPos(hwnd,SB_VERT);

        dlgH=GetDlgItem(hwnd,SCROLL_VERTVAL);
        sprintf(b,"  %d",n);
        SetWindowText(dlgH,b);
        EnableWindow(dlgH,TRUE);

        SetControlFont(hwnd,SCROLL_HORZVAL);
        SetControlFont(hwnd,SCROLL_VERTVAL);
        SetControlFont(hwnd,SCROLL_HORZTEXT);
        SetControlFont(hwnd,SCROLL_VERTTEXT);
        SetControlFont(hwnd,IDHELP);
        SetControlFont(hwnd,IDOK);

        CentreWindow(hwnd);
        break;
    case WM_CTLCOLOR:
        if(HIWORD(lParam)==CTLCOLOR_STATIC ||
           HIWORD(lParam)==CTLCOLOR_DLG) {
            n=GetDlgCtrlID((HWND)LOWORD(lParam));
            if(n==SCROLL_HORZVAL || n==SCROLL_VERTVAL)
                return(FALSE);

            SetBkColor(wParam,DARKBACKGROUND);
            SetTextColor(wParam,DARKTEXTCOLOUR);

            ClientToScreen(hwnd,&point);
            UnrealizeObject(hBrush);
            SetBrushOrg(wParam,point.x,point.y);

            return((DWORD)hBrush);
```

```
        }
        if(HIWORD(lParam)==CTLCOLOR_BTN) {
            SetBkColor(wParam,DARKBACKGROUND);
            SetTextColor(wParam,DARKTEXTCOLOUR);

            ClientToScreen(hwnd,&point);
            UnrealizeObject(hBrush);
            SetBrushOrg(wParam,point.x,point.y);

            return((DWORD)hBrush);
        }

        break;
    case WM_VSCROLL:
        pos=GetScrollPos(hwnd,SB_VERT);
        jump=SCROLL_MAX/10;
        switch(wParam) {
            case SB_LINEUP:
                pos-=1;
                break;
            case SB_LINEDOWN:
                pos+=1;
                break;
            case SB_PAGEUP:
                pos-=jump;
                break;
            case SB_PAGEDOWN:
                pos+=jump;
                break;
            case SB_THUMBPOSITION:
                pos=LOWORD(lParam);
                break;
        }

        if(pos < 0 ) pos=0;
        else if(pos >= SCROLL_MAX) pos=SCROLL_MAX;

        if(pos != GetScrollPos(hwnd,SB_VERT)) {
            SetScrollPos(hwnd,SB_VERT,pos,TRUE);
            sprintf(b,"  %d",pos);
            ItemName(SCROLL_VERTVAL,b);
            InvalidateRect(hwnd,NULL,FALSE);
        }
        break;
    case WM_HSCROLL:
        pos=GetScrollPos(hwnd,SB_HORZ);
        jump=SCROLL_MAX/10;
        switch(wParam) {
            case SB_LINEUP:
                pos-=1;
                break;
            case SB_LINEDOWN:
                pos+=1;
```

2-2 *Continued*

```
                    break;
                case SB_PAGEUP:
                    pos-=jump;
                    break;
                case SB_PAGEDOWN:
                    pos+=jump;
                    break;
                case SB_THUMBPOSITION:
                    pos=LOWORD(lParam);
                    break;
            }

            if(pos < 0 ) pos=0;
            else if(pos >= SCROLL_MAX) pos=SCROLL_MAX;

            if(pos != GetScrollPos(hwnd,SB_HORZ)) {
                SetScrollPos(hwnd,SB_HORZ,pos,TRUE);
                sprintf(b,"  %d",pos);
                ItemName(SCROLL_HORZVAL,b);
                InvalidateRect(hwnd,NULL,FALSE);
            }
            break;
        case WM_PAINT:
            BeginPaint(hwnd,&ps);
            EndPaint(hwnd,&ps);
            break;
        case WM_COMMAND:
            switch(wParam) {
                case IDHELP:
                    DoHelp(hwnd,(LPSTR)"Scrollbars");
                    break;
                case IDOK:
                    if(hBrush != NULL) DeleteObject(hBrush);
                    EndDialog(hwnd,wParam);
                    break;
            }
            break;
    }

    return(FALSE);
}

void DoBitmap(HWND hwnd)
{
    FARPROC lpfnDlgProc;

    if((lpfnDlgProc=MakeProcInstance((FARPROC)BitmapDlgProc,hInst)) != NULL) {
        DialogBox(hInst,"BitmapBox",hwnd,lpfnDlgProc);
        FreeProcInstance(lpfnDlgProc);
    }
}
```

```
DWORD FAR PASCAL BitmapDlgProc(HWND hwnd,WORD message,WORD wParam,LONG lParam)
{
    PAINTSTRUCT ps;
    HBITMAP hBitmap;
    HMENU hmenu;
    HDC hdc;
    LPSTR p;
    static char *bitsize[2]={ BITMAP16,BITMAP256 };
    int i,j,x,y;

    switch(message) {
        case WM_INITDIALOG:
            if(GetDeviceBits(hwnd) <= 4) p=bitsize[0];
            else p=bitsize[1];

            if(GetBitmapDimensions(p,&x,&y,&i)) {
                i=(GetSystemMetrics(SM_CXSCREEN)-x)/2;
                j=(GetSystemMetrics(SM_CYSCREEN)-y)/2;
                SetWindowPos(hwnd,NULL,i,j,
                    x,y+GetSystemMetrics(SM_CYCAPTION),SWP_NOZORDER);
            }
            hmenu=GetSystemMenu(hwnd,FALSE);
            AppendMenu(hmenu,MF_SEPARATOR,NULL,NULL);
            AppendMenu(hmenu,MF_STRING,IDHELP,FetchString(MESSAGE_HELP));
            break;
        case WM_PAINT:
            hdc=BeginPaint(hwnd,&ps);
            if(GetDeviceBits(hwnd) <= 4) p=bitsize[0];
            else p=bitsize[1];

            if((hBitmap=LoadResource(hInst,
              FindResource(hInst,p,RT_BITMAP))) != NULL) {
                DrawImage(hdc,0,0,hBitmap);
                FreeResource(hBitmap);
            }

            EndPaint(hwnd,&ps);
            break;
        case WM_SYSCOMMAND:
            switch(wParam & 0xfff0) {
                case SC_CLOSE:
                    SendMessage(hwnd,WM_COMMAND,IDOK,0L);
                    break;
            }
            switch(wParam) {
                case IDHELP:
                    SendMessage(hwnd,WM_COMMAND,IDHELP,0L);
                    break;
            }
            break;
        case WM_COMMAND:
            switch(wParam) {
                case IDHELP:
```

2-2 *Continued*

```
                    DoHelp(hwnd,(LPSTR)"Bitmaps");
                    break;
                case IDOK:
                    EndDialog(hwnd,wParam);
                    break;
            }
            break;
    }

    return(FALSE);
}

void DoButtons(HWND hwnd)
{
    FARPROC lpfnDlgProc;

    if((lpfnDlgProc=MakeProcInstance((FARPROC)ButtonDlgProc,hInst)) != NULL) {
        DialogBox(hInst,"ButtonBox",hwnd,lpfnDlgProc);
        FreeProcInstance(lpfnDlgProc);
    }
}

DWORD FAR PASCAL ButtonDlgProc(HWND hwnd,WORD message,WORD wParam,LONG lParam)
{
    static HBRUSH hBrush;
    static HFONT hFont;
    PAINTSTRUCT ps;
    POINT point;
    HWND dlgH;
    int i;

    switch(message) {
        case WM_INITDIALOG:
            hBrush=CreateSolidBrush(DARKBACKGROUND);
            if((hFont=CreateFont(32,0,0,0,0,0,0,0,
                SYMBOL_CHARSET,OUT_DEFAULT_PRECIS,CLIP_DEFAULT_PRECIS,
                DEFAULT_QUALITY,DEFAULT_PITCH | FF_DONTCARE,
                DINGBATS)) != NULL) {
                  for(i=0;i<BUTTON_BASECOUNT;++i) {
                    dlgH=GetDlgItem(hwnd,BUTTON_BASE+i);
                    SendMessage(dlgH,WM_SETFONT,(WORD)hFont,FALSE);
                  }
            }

            SetControlFont(hwnd,IDHELP);
            SetControlFont(hwnd,IDOK);

            CentreWindow(hwnd);

            break;
        case WM_CTLCOLOR:
```

```
              if(HIWORD(lParam)==CTLCOLOR_STATIC ||
                 HIWORD(lParam)==CTLCOLOR_DLG) {
                  SetBkColor(wParam,BACKGROUND);
                  SetTextColor(wParam,TEXTCOLOUR);

                  ClientToScreen(hwnd,&point);
                  UnrealizeObject(hBrush);
                  SetBrushOrg(wParam,point.x,point.y);

                  return((DWORD)hBrush);

              }
              if(HIWORD(lParam)==CTLCOLOR_BTN) {
                  SetBkColor(wParam,BACKGROUND);
                  SetTextColor(wParam,BACKGROUND);

                  ClientToScreen(hwnd,&point);
                  UnrealizeObject(hBrush);
                  SetBrushOrg(wParam,point.x,point.y);

                  return((DWORD)hBrush);
              }
              break;
          case WM_PAINT:
              BeginPaint(hwnd,&ps);
              EndPaint(hwnd,&ps);
              break;
          case WM_COMMAND:
              switch(wParam) {
                  case IDHELP:
                      DoHelp(hwnd,(LPSTR)"Buttons");
                      break;
                  case IDOK:
                      if(hFont != NULL) DeleteObject(hFont);
                      if(hBrush != NULL) DeleteObject(hBrush);
                      EndDialog(hwnd,wParam);
                      break;
                  default:
                      DoMessage(hwnd,FetchString(wParam));
                      break;
              }
              break;
      }

      return(FALSE);
}

void DoColours(HWND hwnd)
{
    FARPROC lpfnDlgProc;

    if((lpfnDlgProc=MakeProcInstance((FARPROC)ColourDlgProc,hInst)) != NULL) {
        DialogBox(hInst,"ColourBox",hwnd,lpfnDlgProc);
```

2-2   *Continued*

```
        FreeProcInstance(lpfnDlgProc);
    }
}

DWORD FAR PASCAL ColourDlgProc(HWND hwnd,WORD message,WORD wParam,LONG lParam)
{
    static HBRUSH hBrush[RGB_SIZE+1];
    static COLORREF colour=DARKBACKGROUND;
    PAINTSTRUCT ps;
    POINT point;
    HWND dlgH;
    HDC hdc;
    char b[33];
    int n,w;

    switch(message) {
        case WM_INITDIALOG:
            hBrush[RGB_RED]=CreateSolidBrush(RGB(255,0,0));
            hBrush[RGB_GREEN]=CreateSolidBrush(RGB(0,255,0));
            hBrush[RGB_BLUE]=CreateSolidBrush(RGB(0,0,255));
            hBrush[RGB_SIZE]=CreateSolidBrush(colour);

            dlgH=GetDlgItem(hwnd,COLOUR_REDSET);
            SetScrollRange(dlgH,SB_CTL,0,255,TRUE);
            SetScrollPos(dlgH,SB_CTL,GetRValue(colour),TRUE);
            n=GetScrollPos(dlgH,SB_CTL);

            dlgH=GetDlgItem(hwnd,COLOUR_REDVAL);
            sprintf(b," %d",n);
            SetWindowText(dlgH,b);
            EnableWindow(dlgH,TRUE);

            dlgH=GetDlgItem(hwnd,COLOUR_GREENSET);
            SetScrollRange(dlgH,SB_CTL,0,255,TRUE);
            SetScrollPos(dlgH,SB_CTL,GetGValue(colour),TRUE);
            n=GetScrollPos(dlgH,SB_CTL);

            dlgH=GetDlgItem(hwnd,COLOUR_GREENVAL);
            sprintf(b," %d",n);
            SetWindowText(dlgH,b);
            EnableWindow(dlgH,TRUE);

            dlgH=GetDlgItem(hwnd,COLOUR_BLUESET);
            SetScrollRange(dlgH,SB_CTL,0,255,TRUE);
            SetScrollPos(dlgH,SB_CTL,GetBValue(colour),TRUE);
            n=GetScrollPos(dlgH,SB_CTL);

            dlgH=GetDlgItem(hwnd,COLOUR_BLUEVAL);
            sprintf(b," %d",n);
            SetWindowText(dlgH,b);
            EnableWindow(dlgH,TRUE);
```

```
                    SetControlFont(hwnd,COLOUR_REDTEXT);
                    SetControlFont(hwnd,COLOUR_GREENTEXT);
                    SetControlFont(hwnd,COLOUR_BLUETEXT);

                    SetControlFont(hwnd,COLOUR_REDVAL);
                    SetControlFont(hwnd,COLOUR_GREENVAL);
                    SetControlFont(hwnd,COLOUR_BLUEVAL);
                    SetControlFont(hwnd,IDHELP);
                    SetControlFont(hwnd,IDOK);

                    CentreWindow(hwnd);

                    break;
            case WM_CTLCOLOR:
                if(HIWORD(lParam)==CTLCOLOR_SCROLLBAR) {
                    SetBkColor(wParam,GetSysColor(COLOR_CAPTIONTEXT));
                    SetTextColor(wParam,GetSysColor(COLOR_WINDOWFRAME));
                    w=GetWindowWord(LOWORD(lParam),GWW_ID);
                    switch(w) {
                        case COLOUR_REDSET:
                            ClientToScreen(hwnd,&point);
                            UnrealizeObject(hBrush[RGB_RED]);
                            SetBrushOrg(wParam,point.x,point.y);
                            return((DWORD)hBrush[RGB_RED]);
                        case COLOUR_GREENSET:
                            ClientToScreen(hwnd,&point);
                            UnrealizeObject(hBrush[RGB_GREEN]);
                            SetBrushOrg(wParam,point.x,point.y);
                            return((DWORD)hBrush[RGB_GREEN]);
                        case COLOUR_BLUESET:
                            ClientToScreen(hwnd,&point);
                            UnrealizeObject(hBrush[RGB_BLUE]);
                            SetBrushOrg(wParam,point.x,point.y);
                            return((DWORD)hBrush[RGB_BLUE]);
                    }
                }
                else if(HIWORD(lParam)==CTLCOLOR_DLG) {
                    SetBkColor(wParam,BACKGROUND);
                    SetTextColor(wParam,TEXTCOLOUR);

                    ClientToScreen(hwnd,&point);
                    UnrealizeObject(hBrush[RGB_RED]);
                    SetBrushOrg(wParam,point.x,point.y);

                    return((DWORD)hBrush[RGB_SIZE]);
                }
                break;
            case WM_HSCROLL:
                w=GetWindowWord(HIWORD(lParam),GWW_ID);

                dlgH=GetDlgItem(hwnd,w);
                n=GetScrollPos(dlgH,SB_CTL);
                switch(wParam) {
```

2-2 *Continued*

```
            case SB_LINEUP:
                n-=1;
                break;
            case SB_LINEDOWN:
                n+=1;
                break;
            case SB_PAGEUP:
                n-=10;
                break;
            case SB_PAGEDOWN:
                n+=10;
                break;
            case SB_THUMBPOSITION:
                n=LOWORD(lParam);
                break;
        }

        if(n < 0) n=0;
        else if(n > 255) n=255;

        if(n != GetScrollPos(dlgH,SB_CTL)) {
            SetScrollPos(dlgH,SB_CTL,n,TRUE);
            switch(w) {
                case COLOUR_REDSET:
                    dlgH=GetDlgItem(hwnd,COLOUR_REDVAL);
                    sprintf(b," %d",n);
                    SetWindowText(dlgH,b);
                    colour=RGB(n,GetGValue(colour),GetBValue(colour));
                    break;
                case COLOUR_GREENSET:
                    dlgH=GetDlgItem(hwnd,COLOUR_GREENVAL);
                    sprintf(b," %d",n);
                    SetWindowText(dlgH,b);
                    colour=RGB(GetRValue(colour),n,GetBValue(colour));
                    break;
                case COLOUR_BLUESET:
                    dlgH=GetDlgItem(hwnd,COLOUR_BLUEVAL);
                    sprintf(b," %d",n);
                    SetWindowText(dlgH,b);
                    colour=RGB(GetRValue(colour),GetGValue(colour),n);
                    break;
            }
            DeleteObject(hBrush[RGB_SIZE]);
                        hdc=GetDC(hwnd);
            hBrush[RGB_SIZE]=CreateSolidBrush(colour);

            ReleaseDC(hwnd,hdc);

            InvalidateRect(hwnd,NULL,TRUE);
        }
        return(FALSE);
```

```
        case WM_PAINT:
            BeginPaint(hwnd,&ps);
            EndPaint(hwnd,&ps);
            break;
        case WM_COMMAND:
            switch(wParam) {
                case IDHELP:
                    DoHelp(hwnd,(LPSTR)"Colours");
                    break;
                case IDOK:
                    if(hBrush[RGB_RED] != NULL)
                        DeleteObject(hBrush[RGB_RED]);
                    if(hBrush[RGB_GREEN] != NULL)
                        DeleteObject(hBrush[RGB_GREEN]);
                    if(hBrush[RGB_BLUE] != NULL)
                        DeleteObject(hBrush[RGB_BLUE]);
                    if(hBrush[RGB_SIZE] != NULL)
                        DeleteObject(hBrush[RGB_SIZE]);
                    EndDialog(hwnd,wParam);
                    break;

            }
            break;
    }

    return(FALSE);
}

void DoMessage(HWND hwnd,LPSTR message)
{
    FARPROC lpfnDlgProc;

    messagehook=message;

    if((lpfnDlgProc=MakeProcInstance((FARPROC)MessageDlgProc,hInst)) != NULL) {
        DialogBox(hInst,"MessageBox",hwnd,lpfnDlgProc);
        FreeProcInstance(lpfnDlgProc);
    }
}

DWORD FAR PASCAL MessageDlgProc(HWND hwnd,WORD message,WORD wParam,LONG lParam)
{
    static HBRUSH hBrush;
    POINT point;
    HWND dlgH;

    switch(message) {
        case WM_INITDIALOG:
            hBrush=CreateSolidBrush(DARKBACKGROUND);
            ItemName(MESSAGE_STRING,messagehook);
            CentreWindow(hwnd);
            SetControlFont(hwnd,MESSAGE_STRING);
            SetControlFont(hwnd,IDOK);
            return(FALSE);
```

2-2 *Continued*

```
        case WM_CTLCOLOR:
            if(HIWORD(lParam)==CTLCOLOR_STATIC ||
               HIWORD(lParam)==CTLCOLOR_DLG) {
                SetBkColor(wParam,DARKBACKGROUND);
                SetTextColor(wParam,DARKTEXTCOLOUR);

                ClientToScreen(hwnd,&point);
                UnrealizeObject(hBrush);
                SetBrushOrg(wParam,point.x,point.y);

                return((DWORD)hBrush);

            }
            if(HIWORD(lParam)==CTLCOLOR_BTN) {
                SetBkColor(wParam,DARKBACKGROUND);
                SetTextColor(wParam,DARKBACKGROUND);

                ClientToScreen(hwnd,&point);
                UnrealizeObject(hBrush);
                SetBrushOrg(wParam,point.x,point.y);

                return((DWORD)hBrush);
            }
            break;
        case WM_COMMAND:
            switch(wParam) {
                case IDOK:
                    if(hBrush != NULL) DeleteObject(hBrush);
                    EndDialog(hwnd,wParam);
                    return(FALSE);
            }
            break;
    }

    return(FALSE);
}

DWORD FAR PASCAL AboutDlgProc(HWND hwnd,WORD message,WORD wParam,LONG lParam)
{
    static HBRUSH hBrush;
    POINT point;
    HWND dlgH;

    switch(message) {
        case WM_INITDIALOG:
            hBrush=CreateSolidBrush(DARKBACKGROUND);
            ItemName(MESSAGE_STRING,FetchString(MESSAGE_ABOUT));
            CentreWindow(hwnd);
            SetControlFont(hwnd,MESSAGE_STRING);
            SetControlFont(hwnd,IDOK);
            return(FALSE);
```

```
            case WM_CTLCOLOR:
                if(HIWORD(lParam)==CTLCOLOR_STATIC ||
                   HIWORD(lParam)==CTLCOLOR_DLG) {
                    SetBkColor(wParam,DARKBACKGROUND);
                    SetTextColor(wParam,DARKTEXTCOLOUR);

                    ClientToScreen(hwnd,&point);
                    UnrealizeObject(hBrush);
                    SetBrushOrg(wParam,point.x,point.y);

                    return((DWORD)hBrush);

                }
                if(HIWORD(lParam)==CTLCOLOR_BTN) {
                    SetBkColor(wParam,DARKBACKGROUND);
                    SetTextColor(wParam,DARKBACKGROUND);

                    ClientToScreen(hwnd,&point);
                    UnrealizeObject(hBrush);
                    SetBrushOrg(wParam,point.x,point.y);

                    return((DWORD)hBrush);
                }
                break;
            case WM_COMMAND:
                switch(wParam) {
                    case IDOK:
                        if(hBrush != NULL) DeleteObject(hBrush);
                        EndDialog(hwnd,wParam);
                        return(FALSE);
                }
                break;
        }

    return(FALSE);
}

void CentreWindow(HWND hwnd)
{
    RECT rect;
    unsigned int x,y;

    GetWindowRect(hwnd,&rect);
    x=(GetSystemMetrics(SM_CXSCREEN)-(rect.right-rect.left))/2;
    y=(GetSystemMetrics(SM_CYSCREEN)-(rect.bottom-rect.top))/2;
    SetWindowPos(hwnd,NULL,x,y,rect.right-rect.left,
        rect.bottom-rect.top,SWP_NOSIZE);
}

LPSTR FetchString(unsigned int n)
{
    static char b[257];
```

2-2 *Continued*

```
if(!LoadString(hInst,n,b,256))
        lstrcpy(b,"String table error - this application may be damaged");
    return(b);
}

int GetDeviceBits(HWND hwnd)
{
    HDC hdc;
    int i;

    hdc=GetDC(hwnd);
    i=(GetDeviceCaps(hdc,PLANES) * GetDeviceCaps(hdc,BITSPIXEL));
    ReleaseDC(hwnd,hdc);
    if(i > 8) i=24;
    return(i);
}

void DrawImage(HDC hdc,int x,int y,HBITMAP image)
{
    LPSTR p,pi;
    HDC hMemoryDC;
    HBITMAP hBitmap,hOldBitmap;
    LPBITMAPINFO bh;
    HANDLE hPal;
    LOGPALETTE *pLogPal;
    int i,n;

    if(image==NULL) return;

    if((p=LockResource(image))==NULL) return;

    bh=(LPBITMAPINFO)p;
    if(bh->bmiHeader.biBitCount > 8) n=256;
    else n=(1<<bh->bmiHeader.biBitCount);

    pi=p+sizeof(BITMAPINFOHEADER)+n*sizeof(RGBQUAD);

    if((pLogPal=(LOGPALETTE *)LocalAlloc(LMEM_FIXED,sizeof(LOGPALETTE)+
      256*sizeof(PALETTEENTRY))) != NULL) {
        pLogPal->palVersion=0x0300;
        pLogPal->palNumEntries=n;

        for(i=0;i<n;i++) {
            pLogPal->palPalEntry[i].peRed=bh->bmiColors[i].rgbRed;
            pLogPal->palPalEntry[i].peGreen=bh->bmiColors[i].rgbGreen;
            pLogPal->palPalEntry[i].peBlue=bh->bmiColors[i].rgbBlue;
            pLogPal->palPalEntry[i].peFlags=0;
        }

        hPal=CreatePalette(pLogPal);
```

```
            LocalFree((HANDLE)pLogPal);
            SelectPalette(hdc,hPal,0);
            RealizePalette(hdc);
    }

    if((hBitmap=CreateDIBitmap(hdc,(LPBITMAPINFOHEADER)p,CBM_INIT,pi,
        (LPBITMAPINFO)p,DIB_RGB_COLORS)) != NULL) {
        if((hMemoryDC=CreateCompatibleDC(hdc)) != NULL) {
            hOldBitmap=SelectObject(hMemoryDC,hBitmap);
            if(hOldBitmap) {
                BitBlt(hdc,x,y,(int)bh->bmiHeader.biWidth,
                    (int)bh->bmiHeader.biHeight,hMemoryDC,0,0,SRCCOPY);
                SelectObject(hMemoryDC,hOldBitmap);
            }
            DeleteDC(hMemoryDC);
        }
        DeleteObject(hBitmap);
    }

    UnlockResource(image);
}

int GetBitmapDimensions(LPSTR name,LPINT x,LPINT y,LPINT bits)
{
    HBITMAP hBitmap;
    LPBITMAPINFO bh;

    if((hBitmap=LoadResource(hInst,FindResource(hInst,name,RT_BITMAP))) != NULL) {
        if((bh=(LPBITMAPINFO)LockResource(hBitmap))!=NULL) {
            *x=(int)bh->bmiHeader.biWidth;
            *y=(int)bh->bmiHeader.biHeight;
            *bits=bh->bmiHeader.biBitCount;
            UnlockResource(hBitmap);
        } else return(FALSE);
        FreeResource(hBitmap);
    } else return(FALSE);
    return(TRUE);
}

void SetHelpSize(HWND hwnd)
{
    HELPWININFO helpinfo;
    char b[145];

    memset((char *)&helpinfo,0,sizeof(HELPWININFO));
    helpinfo.wStructSize=sizeof(HELPWININFO);
    helpinfo.x=10;
    helpinfo.y=10;
    helpinfo.dx=512;
    helpinfo.dy=1004;

    MakeHelpPathName(b);
    WinHelp(hwnd,b,HELP_SETWINPOS,(DWORD)&helpinfo);
```

2-2 *Continued*

```
}

void DoHelp(HWND hwnd,LPSTR keyword)
{
    char b[145];

    MakeHelpPathName(b);
    WinHelp(hwnd,b,HELP_KEY,(DWORD)keyword);
}

void MakeHelpPathName(LPSTR szFileName)
{
    LPSTR pcFileName;
    int nFileNameLen;

    nFileNameLen = GetModuleFileName(hInst,szFileName,144);
    pcFileName = szFileName+nFileNameLen;

    while(pcFileName > szFileName) {
      if(*pcFileName == '\\' || *pcFileName == ':') {
        *(++pcFileName) = '\0';
        break;
      }
     nFileNameLen--;
     pcFileName--;
     }

    if((nFileNameLen+13) < 144) lstrcat(szFileName,HELPFILE);
    else lstrcat(szFileName, "?");
}
```

Figure **2-3**   *The DEMO1.RC resource script.*

```
MainScreen DIALOG 69, 55, 260, 188
STYLE WS_POPUP | WS_CAPTION | WS_SYSMENU | WS_MINIMIZEBOX
CAPTION "Dialog Demo One"
MENU MainMenu
BEGIN
END


AboutBox DIALOG 72, 72, 220, 120
STYLE WS_POPUP | WS_CAPTION
CAPTION "About"
BEGIN
    CTEXT "", 101, 16, 20, 188, 72, WS_CHILD | WS_VISIBLE | WS_GROUP
    DEFPUSHBUTTON "OK", IDOK, 96, 100, 28, 12, WS_CHILD | WS_VISIBLE | WS_TABSTOP
END


ColourBox DIALOG 100, 100, 168, 72
STYLE DS_MODALFRAME | WS_POPUP | WS_CAPTION
```

```
CAPTION "Adjust Colour"
BEGIN
    SCROLLBAR 101, 44, 12, 93, 9, SBS_HORZ ¦ WS_CHILD ¦ WS_VISIBLE
    SCROLLBAR 102, 44, 24, 93, 9, SBS_HORZ ¦ WS_CHILD ¦ WS_VISIBLE
    SCROLLBAR 103, 44, 36, 93, 9, SBS_HORZ ¦ WS_CHILD ¦ WS_VISIBLE
    LTEXT "", 201, 140, 12, 20, 8, WS_CHILD ¦ WS_VISIBLE ¦ WS_GROUP
    LTEXT "", 202, 140, 24, 20, 8, WS_CHILD ¦ WS_VISIBLE ¦ WS_GROUP
    LTEXT "", 203, 140, 36, 20, 8, WS_CHILD ¦ WS_VISIBLE ¦ WS_GROUP
    RTEXT "Red  ", 301, 8, 12, 32, 8, SS_RIGHT ¦ WS_CHILD ¦ WS_VISIBLE ¦ WS_GROUP
    RTEXT "Green  ", 302, 8, 24, 32, 8, SS_RIGHT ¦ WS_CHILD ¦ WS_VISIBLE ¦ WS_GROUP
    RTEXT "Blue  ", 303, 8, 36, 32, 8, SS_RIGHT ¦ WS_CHILD ¦ WS_VISIBLE ¦ WS_GROUP
    DEFPUSHBUTTON "OK", IDOK, 132, 52, 28, 12, WS_CHILD ¦ WS_VISIBLE ¦ WS_TABSTOP
    CONTROL "", -1, "static", SS_BLACKFRAME ¦ WS_CHILD ¦ WS_VISIBLE, 8, 12, 32, 8
    CONTROL "", -1, "static", SS_BLACKFRAME ¦ WS_CHILD ¦ WS_VISIBLE, 8, 24, 32, 8
    CONTROL "", -1, "static", SS_BLACKFRAME ¦ WS_CHILD ¦ WS_VISIBLE, 8, 36, 32, 8
    CONTROL "", -1, "static", SS_BLACKFRAME ¦ WS_CHILD ¦ WS_VISIBLE, 140, 12, 20, 8
    CONTROL "", -1, "static", SS_BLACKFRAME ¦ WS_CHILD ¦ WS_VISIBLE, 140, 24, 20, 8
    CONTROL "", -1, "static", SS_BLACKFRAME ¦ WS_CHILD ¦ WS_VISIBLE, 140, 36, 20, 8
    PUSHBUTTON "Help", IDHELP, 96, 52, 28, 12, WS_CHILD ¦ WS_VISIBLE ¦ WS_TABSTOP
END

MainMenu MENU
BEGIN
    POPUP "File"
    BEGIN
        MENUITEM "&Buttons", 101
        MENUITEM "&Scroll Bars", 102
        MENUITEM "&Colours", 103
        MENUITEM "C&heck Boxes", 104
        MENUITEM "B&itmaps", 105
        MENUITEM "&List Boxes", 106
        MENUITEM "Co&mbo Boxes", 107
        MENUITEM SEPARATOR
        MENUITEM "E&xit", 199
    END

    POPUP "&Help"
    BEGIN
        MENUITEM "&Index", 901
        MENUITEM "&Using help", 905
        MENUITEM SEPARATOR
        MENUITEM "&About...", 999
    END

END

STRINGTABLE
BEGIN
    0,"Dialog Demo One\nCopyright \251 1993 Alchemy Mindworks Inc.\nFrom the
        book Windows Dialog Construction Set\rby Steven William Rimmer\r
        Published by Windcrest/McGraw Hill"
    1,"Help"
    201,"How can I insert disk number three when there's only room
```

2-3 *Continued*

```
      for two in the slot?"
   202,"Your Macintosh is about to explode.\rDo not panic... this is a
       popular feature of all Apple computers."
   203,"Yin and yang\rBlack and white\rMale and female\rHonesty and politics\n
       Toyota and automobiles"
   204,"Whatever this symbol means, avoid dropping anything so marked on your
       cat unless you're tired of its company."
   205,"When you see this symbol, Windows is working to rule."
   206,"When you see this symbol on your television, hit the mute button.\r
       It's a Sprint commercial."
   207,"Cassettes are a crutch for people who can't face reel to reel."
   208,"It's ten o'clock... do you know where your poodle is?"
   209,"Structural dialgram of the Canadian parlament."
END

DialogDemoOne ICON
BEGIN
   '00 00 01 00 01 00 20 20 10 00 00 00 00 00 E8 02'
   '00 00 16 00 00 00 28 00 00 00 20 00 00 00 40 00'
   '00 00 01 00 04 00 00 00 00 00 80 02 00 00 00 00'
   '00 00 00 00 00 00 00 00 00 00 00 00 00 00 00 00'
   '00 00 00 00 80 00 00 80 00 00 00 80 80 00 80 00'
   '00 00 80 00 80 00 80 80 00 00 80 80 80 00 C0 C0'
   'C0 00 00 00 FF 00 00 FF 00 00 00 FF FF 00 FF 00'
   '00 00 FF 00 FF 00 FF FF 00 00 FF FF FF 00 2A 2A'
   '2A 2A 2A 2A 2A 2A 2A 22 77 70 00 00 00 00 A2 A2'
   'A2 A2 A2 A2 A2 A2 A2 A2 22 70 00 00 00 00 2A 2A'
   '2A 2A 2A 2A 2A 2A AA AA A2 70 00 00 00 00 A2 A2'
   'A2 A2 AA AA AA AA B2 AA AA 77 77 77 77 00 2A 2A'
   'AA AA 2A 2A AA 2A AA A9 19 19 19 19 17 77 AA A2'
   'A2 AA AB AB AB AA 91 91 91 91 91 91 91 97 2A AA'
   'BA BA 2A AA A9 19 19 19 19 99 99 99 99 19 AB AB'
   'A2 AA AA 11 11 91 99 99 99 90 00 00 09 99 BA BA'
   'AA A1 01 11 19 19 19 19 90 00 00 00 00 09 AA A2'
   '00 10 10 11 11 91 91 00 00 00 00 70 00 00 2A 00'
   '00 00 01 01 11 17 77 00 00 00 09 70 00 00 A2 22'
   '22 22 22 22 22 22 27 77 77 70 09 70 00 00 2A 2A'
   '2A 2A AA AA AA AA 22 22 22 77 09 77 00 00 A2 AA'
   'AA AA A2 AA AA AA A2 A2 A2 27 79 17 70 00 2A AA'
   'AA 2A 22 22 2A 2A AA AA AA 2A 79 91 77 00 A2 A2'
   'A2 22 70 70 22 A2 A2 AB A2 A2 00 99 17 77 2A 2A'
   '22 87 07 07 02 2A 2A AA AA 27 00 09 91 91 A2 A2'
   'F8 88 77 70 72 A2 AB AB AB A0 00 00 99 99 2A 22'
   '8F 88 00 77 07 2A 2A AA AA 70 00 00 00 00 A2 28'
   'F8 F0 00 08 70 22 22 A2 A2 00 00 00 00 00 2A 2F'
   '8F 80 00 07 07 2A 2A AA A7 00 00 00 00 00 A7 28'
   'F8 FF 00 88 82 22 A2 A2 A0 00 00 00 00 00 22 7F'
   '8F FF FF 8F 82 2A 2A 2A 70 00 00 00 00 00 A7 0F'
   'FF FF F8 F8 F2 A2 A2 A2 00 00 00 00 00 00 A2 70'
   'FF FF 8F 8F 2A 2A 2A 20 00 00 00 00 00 00 A7 07'
   'FF FF F8 F8 22 A2 A2 A2 00 00 00 00 00 00 A2 70'
```

```
                '70 FF 8F 22 2A 2A 20 00 00 00 00 00 00 00 AA 07'
                '07 07 02 02 A2 A2 00 00 00 00 00 00 00 00 BA A0'
                '70 70 72 2A 2A 20 00 00 00 00 00 00 00 00 BB AA'
                'A7 A7 AA AA A0 00 00 00 00 00 00 00 00 00 AA BA'
                'AA AA AA 00 00 00 00 00 00 00 00 00 00 00 AA A0'
                '00 00 00 00 00 00 00 00 00 00 00 00 00 00 00 00'
                '01 FF 00 00 01 FF 00 00 01 FF 00 00 00 03 00 00'
                '00 00 00 00 00 00 00 00 00 00 00 00 00 01 F8 00 00'
                '07 FE 00 00 3F DF 00 00 3F 9F 00 00 01 9F 00 00'
                '00 8F 00 00 00 07 00 00 00 03 00 00 00 C0 00 00'
                '00 E0 00 00 01 F0 00 00 01 FF 00 00 03 FF 00 00'
                '03 FF 00 00 07 FF 00 00 07 FF 00 00 0F FF 00 00'
                '1F FF 00 00 3F FF 00 00 7F FF 00 00 FF FF 00 01'
                'FF FF 00 07 FF FF 00 3F FF FF 1F FF FF FF'
END
ButtonBox DIALOG 80, 72, 88, 112
STYLE DS_MODALFRAME | WS_POPUP | WS_CAPTION
CAPTION "Buttons"
BEGIN
    DEFPUSHBUTTON "OK", IDOK, 44, 92, 32, 12, WS_CHILD | WS_VISIBLE | WS_TABSTOP
    PUSHBUTTON "<", 201, 8, 12, 24, 24, WS_CHILD | WS_VISIBLE | WS_TABSTOP
    PUSHBUTTON "M", 202, 32, 12, 24, 24, WS_CHILD | WS_VISIBLE | WS_TABSTOP
    PUSHBUTTON "[", 203, 56, 12, 24, 24, WS_CHILD | WS_VISIBLE | WS_TABSTOP
    PUSHBUTTON "\\", 204, 8, 36, 24, 24, WS_CHILD | WS_VISIBLE | WS_TABSTOP
    PUSHBUTTON "6", 205, 32, 36, 24, 24, WS_CHILD | WS_VISIBLE | WS_TABSTOP
    PUSHBUTTON "(", 206, 56, 36, 24, 24, WS_CHILD | WS_VISIBLE | WS_TABSTOP
    PUSHBUTTON ">", 207, 8, 60, 24, 24, WS_CHILD | WS_VISIBLE | WS_TABSTOP
    PUSHBUTTON "\300", 208, 32, 60, 24, 24, WS_CHILD | WS_VISIBLE | WS_TABSTOP
    PUSHBUTTON "\314", 209, 56, 60, 24, 24, WS_CHILD | WS_VISIBLE | WS_TABSTOP
    PUSHBUTTON "Help", IDHELP, 12, 92, 28, 12, WS_CHILD | WS_VISIBLE | WS_TABSTOP
END


MessageBox DIALOG 72, 72, 220, 120
STYLE WS_POPUP | WS_CAPTION
CAPTION "Message"
BEGIN
    CTEXT "", 101, 16, 20, 188, 72, WS_CHILD | WS_VISIBLE | WS_GROUP
    DEFPUSHBUTTON "OK", IDOK, 96, 100, 28, 12, WS_CHILD | WS_VISIBLE | WS_TABSTOP
END


Bitmap16 BITMAP demo_16.bmp

Bitmap256 BITMAP demo_256.bmp

BitmapMenu BITMAP menu_bmp.bmp

ListText RCDATA listbox.txt

ListBitmap BITMAP list_bmp.bmp


BitmapBox DIALOG 72, 72, 72, 72
STYLE WS_POPUP | WS_CAPTION | WS_SYSMENU
CAPTION "Bitmap"
```

2-3 *Continued*

```
BEGIN
END
ScrollBox DIALOG 72, 72, 100, 100
STYLE WS_POPUP ¦ WS_CAPTION ¦ WS_VSCROLL ¦ WS_HSCROLL
CAPTION "Scroll Bars"
BEGIN
    DEFPUSHBUTTON "OK", IDOK, 56, 72, 28, 12, WS_CHILD ¦ WS_VISIBLE ¦ WS_TABSTOP
    RTEXT "Horizontal scroll", 101, 8, 12, 56, 8, SS_RIGHT ¦ WS_CHILD ¦
        WS_VISIBLE ¦ WS_GROUP
    LTEXT "", 201, 68, 12, 16, 8, WS_CHILD ¦ WS_VISIBLE ¦ WS_GROUP
    CONTROL "", -1, "static", SS_BLACKFRAME ¦ WS_CHILD ¦ WS_VISIBLE, 68, 12, 16, 8
    RTEXT "Vertical scroll", 102, 8, 24, 56, 8, SS_RIGHT ¦ WS_CHILD ¦
        WS_VISIBLE ¦ WS_GROUP
    LTEXT "", 202, 68, 24, 16, 8, WS_CHILD ¦ WS_VISIBLE ¦ WS_GROUP
    CONTROL "", -1, "static", SS_BLACKFRAME ¦ WS_CHILD ¦ WS_VISIBLE, 68, 24, 16, 8
    PUSHBUTTON "Help", IDHELP, 56, 56, 28, 12, WS_CHILD ¦ WS_VISIBLE ¦ WS_TABSTOP
END


CheckBox DIALOG 72, 72, 180, 84
STYLE DS_MODALFRAME ¦ WS_POPUP ¦ WS_CAPTION
CAPTION "Check Boxes and Radio Buttons"
BEGIN
    DEFPUSHBUTTON "OK", IDOK, 144, 64, 28, 12, WS_CHILD ¦ WS_VISIBLE ¦ WS_TABSTOP
    RADIOBUTTON "Normal", 101, 12, 16, 60, 8, WS_CHILD ¦ WS_VISIBLE ¦ WS_TABSTOP
    RADIOBUTTON "Invert", 102, 12, 28, 60, 8, WS_CHILD ¦ WS_VISIBLE ¦ WS_TABSTOP
    RADIOBUTTON "Hide", 103, 12, 40, 60, 8, WS_CHILD ¦ WS_VISIBLE ¦ WS_TABSTOP
    CHECKBOX "Horizontal lines", 201, 12, 56, 64, 8, WS_CHILD ¦
        WS_VISIBLE ¦ WS_TABSTOP
    CHECKBOX "Vertical lines", 202, 12, 68, 64, 8, WS_CHILD ¦ WS_VISIBLE ¦
        WS_TABSTOP
    CONTROL " Picture Effect ", 105, "button", BS_GROUPBOX ¦ WS_CHILD ¦
        WS_VISIBLE ¦ WS_GROUP, 8, 4, 68, 48
    PUSHBUTTON "Help", IDHELP, 108, 64, 28, 12, WS_CHILD ¦ WS_VISIBLE ¦ WS_TABSTOP
END


ListBox DIALOG 50, 20, 312, 224
STYLE DS_MODALFRAME ¦ WS_POPUP ¦ WS_CAPTION
CAPTION "List"
BEGIN
    DEFPUSHBUTTON "OK", IDOK, 276, 204, 28, 12, WS_CHILD ¦ WS_VISIBLE ¦ WS_TABSTOP
    LISTBOX 101, 8, 8, 152, 184, LBS_NOTIFY ¦ WS_CHILD ¦ WS_VISIBLE ¦
        WS_BORDER ¦ WS_VSCROLL
    LTEXT "Selected text:", 103, 8, 196, 152, 8, WS_CHILD ¦ WS_VISIBLE ¦ WS_GROUP
    EDITTEXT 102, 8, 204, 152, 12, ES_LEFT ¦ WS_CHILD ¦ WS_VISIBLE ¦
        WS_BORDER ¦ WS_TABSTOP
    PUSHBUTTON "Help", IDHELP, 240, 204, 28, 12, WS_CHILD ¦ WS_VISIBLE ¦ WS_TABSTOP
END


ComboBox DIALOG 50, 20, 312, 224
STYLE DS_MODALFRAME ¦ WS_POPUP ¦ WS_CAPTION
CAPTION "Combo Box"
```

```
BEGIN
    DEFPUSHBUTTON "OK", IDOK, 276, 204, 28, 12, WS_CHILD | WS_VISIBLE | WS_TABSTOP
    CONTROL "", 101, "COMBOBOX", CBS_DROPDOWNLIST | WS_CHILD | WS_VISIBLE |
        WS_TABSTOP, 8, 8, 152, 184
    LTEXT "Selected text:", 103, 8, 196, 152, 8, WS_CHILD | WS_VISIBLE | WS_GROUP
    EDITTEXT 102, 8, 204, 152, 12, ES_LEFT | WS_CHILD | WS_VISIBLE |
        WS_BORDER | WS_TABSTOP
    PUSHBUTTON "Help", IDHELP, 240, 204, 28, 12, WS_CHILD | WS_VISIBLE | WS_TABSTOP
END
```

 # Opening a few Windows

In creating a traditional Windows application, you would register a class for your application, call CreateWindow, and then set up a message loop to translate messages for the application window. The DialogBox function does all this for you. It also allows you to define what your window will look like and what controls and other objects it will contain through the use of dialog templates, as touched on in chapter 1. In effect, it lets you create a complex application window with something more reminiscent of Windows Paint or CorelDRAW, rather than a C compiler.

A dialog template specifies the parameters of a dialog window and its controls using a simple script language defined by Windows itself. Figure 2-3 is a protracted example of this language. In fact, while you'll frequently find it useful to fine- tune the RC files for your application with a text editor, in most cases you'll never have to bother with any of the obtuse flags and fields and such of the Windows dialog script language. There's software to do that for you.

The software in question is the Resource Workshop application that accompanies Borland C++ for Windows. Resource Workshop is like a C compiler for resource scripts. However, because dialogs are ultimately visual, it lets you manipulate windows and their controls as the visual objects they'll ultimately result in. Figure 2-4 illustrates what happens if you run Resource Workshop, open the DEMO1.RC file, and then select the MainScreen dialog.

This isn't a terribly interesting dialog—all it contains is a window and a menu bar. Mind you, its dialog script isn't all that complicated

Figure 2-4

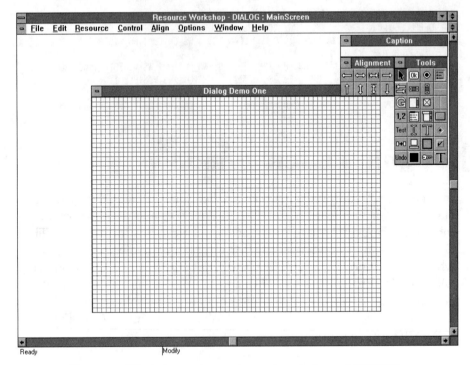

Resource Workshop editing the main window of DEMO1.

either, as shown back in Fig. 2-3. Figure 2-5 illustrates a better example of the Resource Workshop in action.

It's beyond the scope of this book to get into a detailed tutorial of how to make Resource Workshop do its tricks—Borland's documentation for it is characteristically replete. If you haven't used it until now, you should probably take an hour or so to familiarize yourself with its facilities.

You might want to look at a dialog template as a blueprint for a dialog. When you pass a template as the second argument to the DialogBox function, it creates the dialog for you and begins to direct messages to the message handler you specify. Message handlers were touched on in the previous chapter—you'll see one in action in a moment. The template name in this case is MainScreen.

Figure 2-5

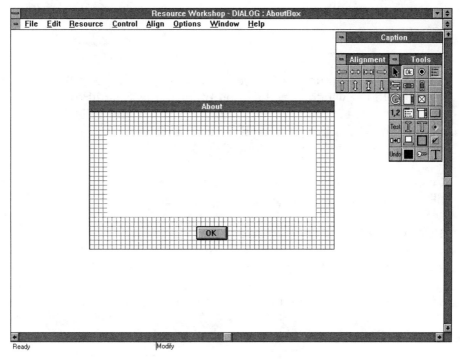

Resource Workshop editing a more complicated dialog.

In fact, a call to DialogBox involves three arguments. The first is an instance handle, which for the sake of this discussion can be thought of as a way to reference the physical EXE file that your application was launched from. This handle is necessary to allow functions like DialogBox to reference the resources in your application's EXE file. It's always provided to a Windows application when it first boots up. The second argument is the template discussed in the previous paragraph. The third object of import passed to DialogBox is a FARPROC. This is a pointer to a function that DialogBox can call to handle messages to the dialog about to be created.

That's about all there is to say about how DialogBox works—except for the minor details of how the function that handles messages works. Actually, *minor* might have been a poor choice of adjectives. One way or another, message handlers and the functions they in turn call comprise virtually all of a typical Windows application. Just about

61

everything under Windows happens as a result of responding to a message.

The message handler for the main window of DEMO1 is SelectProc, also to be found in the source code back in Fig. 2-2. It handles all the messages to the window, and among other things SelectProc calls other functions to create the dependent dialogs of the DEMO1 application. These in turn have their own message handlers, which might create still more dependent dialogs.

A windows message handler always has the same basic structure. It will always be passed four arguments. They are:

HWND hwnd A Window handle

WORD message The type of message to be processed

WORD wParam A 16-bit argument to the message

DWORD lParam A 32-bit argument to the message

Understanding what these objects really do is essential in understanding how a message handler works.

To begin with, HWND objects seem to float through Windows applications like oversized balloons at a concert. A window handle is a reference to the combination of a window's structure—in this case its dialog template—and its message handler. When you want to send a message to a particular window, you must tell the Windows kernel which window you're interested in by specifying an HWND.

Under Windows, every window is in effect a child of another window. Your main application window is a child of the Program Manager. When you create child windows, you'll typically specify the HWND of the parent window they're associated with. Keeping in mind that every control in a dialog is itself a window, specifying the handle of a dialog allows you to reference the controls therein. You'll see how controls are referenced presently.

The message argument of a message handler tells the function which message it's being asked to respond to. The message handler will be called once for each message sent to the window it's associated with. Messages are actually represented by numerical constants, which are defined in the WINDOWS.H header file. We'll deal with the specific messages that SelectProc knows how to respond to in a moment.

The wParam and lParam arguments to a message handler contain different sorts of information for different messages. Sometimes they're meaningless, and should be ignored. It's important to note that lParam is frequently used to hold a far pointer that references a more complex data structure.

The large switch function in SelectProc sorts out the stream of messages that are sent to the main window of DEMO1. The message handler for a window will typically be sent all sorts of messages it needn't respond to. Windows typically tells everyone about everything, in the hope that some of it will prove useful and messages that aren't relevant to an application can be ignored. Your applications will receive messages when the clipboard contents change, when the system palette is modified, when the clock in your computer is reset, and for hundreds of other occasions—none of which need be dealt with by your message handlers unless you're interested in what they have to say.

Some messages are rather more important. Here's a look at the messages that SelectProc actually responds to. We'll have a detailed look at what it does in responding to them in just a moment.

WM_INITDIALOG This message is sent to a window only once, when it's about to appear on your monitor. It allows a message handler to set itself up and initialize things.

WM_SYSCOMMAND This message means that someone has selected an item from the system menu of this window.

WM_PAINT This message appears whenever there's cause to repaint any of the client area—the useful part—of a window.

WM_COMMAND This message appears whenever someone clicks in a simple control or selects a menu item. It's where most of the work gets done.

WM_CTLCOLOR This message appears whenever Windows needs to know what color a window or one of its controls should be drawn in.

How you use these messages in a particular message handler will vary enormously with what your application is supposed to do. As an introduction to the actual functionality of DEMO1, however, let's begin with a look at what's really going on in SelectProc when these messages are responded to.

Handling the WM_INITDIALOG message

The WM_INITDIALOG message typically winds up as a catch-all for anything that needs to be done before a dialog is ready for polite company. You can use it to initialize controls, set up menu items, and so on. There are two very important things to keep in mind about it, however.

The first is that the WM_INITDIALOG message will be sent to your message handler just before its associated window is to be drawn on your screen. As such, you might use its appearance to move controls around, dim or activate them, and so on. One thing you can't use it for is to actually draw anything, because at the time when WM_INITDIALOG appears there's no window to draw in.

The second important aspect of WM_INITDIALOG concerns message handlers in general. The local variables you declare at the top of a message handler like SelectProc are allocated on the stack. This means that their contents will remain valid only for the period between the time your message handler is called and the time it returns from that call—that is, for the duration of one message.

If you require things to stick around for longer than this, you must declare them as static. Note that unlike stack variables, you can't explicitly initialize a static local variable. You can't say:

```
DWORD SelectProc(HWND hwnd,WORD message,WORD wParam,WORD lParam)
{

   static int i=10;
   . . .

}
```

If you want to initialize a static variable like this, you should do so when your message handler responds to the WM_INITDIALOG message.

The WM_INITDIALOG case in SelectProc begins by calling CreateSolidBrush, which creates a brush for use elsewhere in this function. I'll get to exactly what it does in a moment. It then calls SetHelpSize. This is a function, declared later in DEMO1.CPP, that defines how big the Windows Help application window will be if you happen to ask for help. As Windows Help is an integral part of any Windows application—even if almost no one actually uses it—we'll look at the details of creating and using Help files later on.

Notice that the SetHelpFile function has an argument—one of those ubiquitous window handles. The SetHelpFile function sets the size of the Help window for help called for from the parent window of DEMO1.CPP, rather than for all help calls.

The next function call, GetProfileString, is used to fetch items from WIN.INI. It's exceedingly convenient, as it allows you to query WIN.INI without getting involved in any of the string parsing and such otherwise required.

The applications discussed in this book all have a *control font*, that is, a font used to display the text in controls such as buttons and list boxes. This is wholly optional—if you don't define a control font, Windows will create your controls with the usual chunky Windows system font. We'll look at the control font issue in detail in just a moment. Right now, however, it's important to know the name of the control font.

The default font used in DEMO1 is Arial. This isn't a particularly interesting font, but it's one you can expect to be present in all Windows installations unless it has been explicitly removed. The adventurous might want to use a more evocative font for their controls. For this reason, rather than hard-wiring the Arial font into DEMO1, we'll check WIN.INI to see if a different font has been specified.

When you call GetProfileString it will look through WIN.INI for a section that begins with [DialogDemo], defined in DEMO1.CPP as the constant DIALOG_KEY. It if finds such a section, it will attempt to fetch an item along the lines of this one:

```
[DialogDemo]
ControlFont=Meath
```

If it finds an item named ControlFont, it will return whatever's to the right of its equal sign.

The Meath font is not part of Windows—it's a product of Cassady and Greene, and is unquestionably my favorite font. As can be seen in Fig. 2-6, however, it arguably doesn't represent the best choice for a font to draw control legends in. These are the actual arguments for GetProfileString:

```
GetProfileString(LPSTR section,LPSTR key,LPSTR defaultname,
 LPSTR buffer,int size);
```

The section argument defines the section of WIN.INI that GetProfileString is to search in. Section names are always enclosed in square brackets in WIN.INI, but not in the section argument to GetProfileString. In theory, the section name should be the name of your application or some derivative thereof. This will certainly be

Figure 2-6

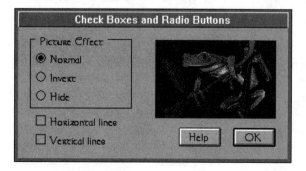

Controls using the Meath font—this is not calculated to make your applications well-liked.

helpful to users of your software if they have to sort out their WIN.INI files by hand. In reality it can be anything you like—all the demonstration programs in this book share a common WIN.INI section, called DialogDemo.

The key argument to GetProfileString is a pointer to the item to be searched for.

The defaultname argument to GetProfileString specifies what the call should return if the item specified by the key argument proves not to be in WIN.INI. In this application, the default font name is Arial—GetProfileString can return this if nothing better can be found.

The actual returned string found by GetProfileString will be stored in whatever is pointed to by the buffer argument. This string is assumed to be at least as long as the value passed for the size argument.

In DEMO1.CPP—as in all the programs to be discussed in this book—there's a constant defined as STRINGSIZE to take care of the sizes of small strings.

There are three macros defined in DEMO1.CPP that take care of the control font discussed a moment ago. You can find them up near the top of Fig. 2-2. They are:

CreateControlFont Attempts to create a font based on the font name in the global string ControlFontName. If it's successful, it will store handle to the new font in the global HFONT object controlfont.

SetControlFont Replaces the default Windows system font in a specific control with the font referenced by controlfont.

DestroyControlFont Destroys the font referenced by controlfont.

The CreateControlFont call should appear somewhere in the WM_INITDIALOG case for the main message handler of an application. The DestroyControlFont call should appear so that it will be invoked just before your application terminates. You'll get a more detailed look at SetControlFont shortly.

As an aside, the control font issue is one that you aren't compelled to agree with. In the applications to be discussed in this book, most of the dialog controls have had their fonts changed. This has been done as much to illustrate how to do it as because it's a good thing to implement in real-world software.

Allowing people to define the font for the controls in your applications is somewhat questionable. It allows the users of your software to customize it to their tastes, which Windows users in general seem to appreciate, but it also means that someone might choose a wildly inappropriate font. For example, if the control font were to be defined as a laterally expanded font, some controls with text in them might no longer be large enough to contain all the text you'd intended. Parts of important messages could vanish.

The call to LoadIcon takes care of one of the minor deficiencies inherent in creating a Windows application as a dialog, rather than through a direct call to CreateWindow. Doing so doesn't allow you to assign a Program Manager icon to your application implicitly; you must do so by loading your icon from the resource list of your application's EXE file and attaching it to your main window. The calls to LoadIcon and SetClassWord illustrate how this is done.

The CentreWindow function is defined later on in DEMO1.CPP, and represents another of those issues of Windows esthetics that you aren't compelled to agree with. By default, Program Manager spawns a new application window with its initial location based on the location of the parent window it's associated with. The CentreWindow function overrides this, and moves the window it references to the center of your screen. The argument to CentreWindow is the HWND that refers to the window you'd like to center.

The remaining code in the WM_INITDIALOG case of SelectProc takes care of matters amphibian—specifically, they put a tree frog in the system menu. The bug-eyed little creature can be seen in Fig. 2-7.

You might ask why there's a frog in the system menu of DEMO1. Perhaps the most philosophical answer to this would be that this is a demonstration, and it might as well demonstrate as much as possible. The techniques for including a frog in a menu can also be used to

Figure 2-7

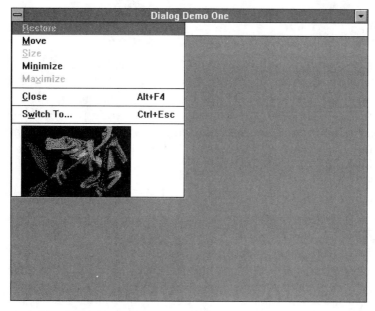

The DEMO1 system menu, including one tree frog.

install images of any other creatures you like, or for that matter, any other bitmap.

The call to GetSystemMenu will return a handle to the system menu, an HMENU object. The call to LoadBitmap will return a handle to a bitmap stored in the resource list of DEMO1.EXE. The bitmap is named BitmapMenu. You'll see the techniques for storing bitmaps in a resource script presently.

The two calls to AppendMenu add two additional menu items to the system menu for the main window of DEMO1. The first one adds a separator line. The second adds the bitmap referenced by hbitmap.

The first argument to AppendMenu is a handle to the menu to be modified. This need not be the system menu; the GetMenu call can be used to fetch a handle to the conventional menu of an application. The second argument is a flag to tell AppendMenu what sort of menu item to add. The third argument is the item number for the new item. This is defined by the constant SYS_BITMAP here. When you select the new item from the system menu, this is the value that

will be sent to SelectProc. You'll see how to respond to it later in this chapter.

The final argument to AppendMenu is the item to be added. This can take any of a number of forms, depending on the flags in the second argument. In this case we'll pass it a handle to a bitmap. The AppendMenu function can be used for less exotic purposes—you can, for example, append simple text items to a menu. You'll see how this is done when I explain the DoBitmap function of DEMO1 later in this chapter.

Handling the WM_COMMAND message

A WM_COMMAND message will be sent to the message handler of a window whenever one of the following events occurs:

> A menu item is selected. This doesn't include items in the system menu.

> A button is clicked.

> A check box is clicked.

> A radio button is clicked.

> An item is selected in a list box or combo box.

> An edit control is clicked.

For most applications, all the useful tasks of your software will be dispatched as a result of WM_COMMAND messages.

When a WM_COMMAND message appears at SelectProc, the wParam argument will hold the resource ID number of whatever was clicked, selected, or mildly frightened into sending it. The lParam argument will hold information about more complex controls, such as list and combo boxes. Ignore them for the moment.

It's useful to note that the WM_COMMAND message for a selected menu item and the one for a clicked button will look the same to a

Windows message handler. If you create a window that has buttons and menu items that do the same things, assigning them the same resource ID numbers will allow you to simplify the code that must respond to them.

As can be seen back in the DEMO1.CPP listing in Fig. 2-2, responding to a WM_COMMAND message typically involves another switch statement to sort out the resource IDs that might appear. Each of the case items is defined at the top of the DEMO1.CPP listing.

By convention, resource IDs for items created by an application should fall in the range of 100 through 900. In most cases, some of the IDs in the range of 900 through 999 are used for items in the Help menu, if there is one.

There are several predefined resource IDs for buttons. You should use these where you can—not only does it make sorting out the code to respond to WM_COMMAND messages much simpler, but it also makes trapping messages more realistic. We'll get into an example of this later on in dealing with attaching sounds to Windows events. The predefined constants are:

IDOK OK buttons

IDCANCEL Cancel buttons

IDYES Yes buttons

IDNO No buttons

IDABORT Abort buttons

IDRETRY Retry buttons

IDIGNORE Ignore buttons

In addition to these constants, Borland defines one more:

IDHELP Help buttons

It's important to note that you don't have to use these values. If you create a button with the text OK and the resource number 100, and you have the WM_COMMAND case in the message handler for its window respond appropriately to a WM_COMMAND message with a wParam value of 100, all will be well. The convention of predefined constants is a good one to follow, however.

As you'll see in the next chapter of this book, these constants will take on a more specific meaning in dealing with Borland's colorful BWCC custom control library.

More will be said about how these resource IDs come to be assigned to controls and menu items later in this chapter when we deal with creating the resource script for DEMO1.

Each of the cases in the wParam switch of the WM_COMMAND message section of SelectProc that handles an item of the File menu begins with FILE_—perhaps predictably. As you'll observe if you skip back to Fig. 2-2, these simply dispatch functions of DEMO1 by calling other functions. We'll deal with what these functions do later in this chapter.

The FILE_EXIT case takes care of some housekeeping, as it handles the termination of DEMO1. It calls WinHelp to dispose of any open Help windows associated with DEMO1. It deletes a number of static objects, such as the frog bitmap handle, calls DestroyControlFont to release the control font handle, and finally calls PostQuitMessage to wind everything down.

The three HELPM_ cases of this section of SelectProc deal with items from a more or less standard Help menu in DEMO1. In fact, when Resource Workshop creates a menu, it will optionally create a complete standard Windows Help menu for you. The one for DEMO1 was created this way, with a few items subsequently removed.

Windows Help is handled by spawning a child application called WINHELP.EXE from whatever application calls for help. There are hooks in Windows to make this pretty simple to do. There are two actual invocations of WINHELP.EXE in SelectProc. In the HELPM_INDEX case, the main index of the help file for DEMO1 will

be displayed, allowing you to click on dependent items in it. There is a dedicated help file called DEMO.HLP. A path to DEMO.HLP is created by the MakeHelpPathName function, which is declared further down in the DEMO1.CPP listing. Help is summoned through the WinHelp call—your application doesn't actually have to locate WINHELP.EXE and launch it explicitly.

The HELPM_USING case in SelectProc involves calling WinHelp in a somewhat peculiar way. This case doesn't load it with the help file for your application, but rather with a canned help file that Windows provides for help on using Help. Windows is a bit overprotective at times—users who observe that the help on Help function lacks a help on help on Help command are clearly witnessing an oversight, and one no doubt to be corrected in future releases of Windows.

The HELPM_ABOUT case has nothing to do with help—it will display the About dialog for DEMO1. It does exactly what was done when the main window for DEMO1 was created back in WinMain, save that it uses a different dialog template. Messages to the About dialog are handled by the AboutDlgProc, which is declared later in DEMO1.CPP.

As will turn up in looking at DEMO1, the message structure of a Windows application makes it very easy for one part of a message handler to communicate with another part. For example, one of the functions of DEMO1 will display a full color bitmap in a window—perhaps predictably, of another tree frog. This is usually activated by selecting the Bitmap item of the File menu. Doing so will send a WM_COMMAND message to SelectProc, calling for the frog. However, in order to justify the aforementioned frog in the System menu, selecting it will also call up the principal frog bitmap.

Clearly there are two ways to handle this. The SelectProc function could make two calls to the function that displays the frog in a window, in this case called DoBitmap. There would be one call to handle selecting Bitmap from the File menu and a second one to handle selecting the frog graphic from the system menu. This is a bit sloppy, however, as it means that if you change something in one case you must remember to do so for the other.

A much more elegant approach is to have only one case, to wit, the one for selecting Bitmap from the File menu. The code for dealing with selecting the frog graphic in the system menu can just send a WM_COMMAND message from electProc to SelectProc. This will make SelectProc think that the Bitmap item in the File menu has been selected.

Handling the WM_CTLCOLOR message

The principal window of DEMO1 is very easy to spot, even in a crowded Windows desktop, because it's bright green. This illustrates several useful things:

> ➤ It's possible to change the color of a window.

> ➤ It's very hard to miss a green window.

> ➤ Green is second only to purple as a color that almost nothing else looks good with.

Changing the color of a window isn't particularly easy—or perhaps it would be more correct to say that most of us would have a difficult time coming up with a more obtuse way of arranging for it to be done. You won't find any mention of a function in the Windows programming manuals along the lines of SetWindowBackground.

The mechanism for determining the color of a window is decidedly peculiar. Prior to actually drawing a window on your screen, and thereafter any time a window must be redrawn, Windows sends a number of WM_CTLCOLOR messages to the message handler for the window in question. What these messages are really saying is "tell me what color to use to draw this beast or I'll choose one for myself." Left to choose for itself, Windows will choose white.

To cause Windows to choose a different color, you must arrange for an HBRUSH object (a brush handle) to be returned by your message handler in response to a WM_CTLCOLOR message. In fact, you'll have to fiddle the brush handle a bit, as Windows is likely to dither colors that don't match exactly the colors in the currently selected

palette. The UnrealizeObject function adjusts a brush to keep its dither patterns aligned with those of the other objects in a window.

If you want to create a window with a gray background, you can obtain a brush handle by calling GetStockObject. The same is true for white and black windows. For windows of more adventurous shades, you'll have to create a brush using a call to CreateSolidBrush, or one of the other brush creation functions offered by Windows. The brush used to create the background of the main window of DEMO1 was created in its WM_INITDIALOG case.

Each of the applications in this book that uses brushes in this way defines four colors—BACKGROUND, DARKBACKGROUND, TEXTCOLOUR, and DARKTEXTCOLOUR—as can be seen back in Fig. 2-2. As a rule, BACKGROUND is the color for the main window and DARKBACKCOLOUR is the background for a subsidiary dialog window. TEXTCOLOUR and DARKTEXTCOLOUR are corresponding colors for text. In DEMO1, BACKGROUND is green and DARKBACKGROUND is mustard yellow.

You're free to change these colors, of course—the RGB macro used to define them near the top of DEMO1.CPP expects three arguments representing the amount of red, green, and blue light in the colors being defined. Each value can range from zero through 255. More will be said about Windows and its use of color later in this chapter.

There is something to be said for having a fairly limited range of colors in a Windows application, if you choose to use colored windows at all. Having colors that indicate the function of a dialog— such as a different color for dependent dialogs— is arguably useful. Having your application look like the aftermath of 200 belligerent male rhinoceroses destroying a paint factory, however, is both distracting and almost certain to prevent anyone from taking your software seriously, however inspired it might otherwise be.

Windows will send a WM_CTLCOLOR message to the message handler for a window once for each control in the window, as well as for the background of the window itself. You need not respond to all of these—any that don't provoke your message handler into returning

a brush handle will be treated by Windows as cause to use its default color scheme for the objects in question.

The high-order word of the lParam argument to a message handler responding to a WM_CTLCOLOR message will contain a constant defining what type of control the message pertains to. It can be one of the following:

CTLCOLOR_EDIT An edit control

CTLCOLOR_LISTBOX A list box

CTLCOLOR_MSGBOX A message box

CTLCOLOR_SCROLLBAR A scroll bar

CTLCOLOR_STATIC A static control

The low-order word of lParam contains the HWND of the control about to be drawn. You can fetch its resource ID like this:

```
id=GetWindowWord((LOWORD(lParam),GWW_ID);
```

You'll see how this can be useful later in this chapter. It's fair to note that in most applications the WM_CTLCOLOR message is useful only for cosmetic reasons. It's also worth noting that, in the next chapter, when we get into dealing with Microsoft's three-dimensional custom control library, responding to this message will turn out to have particularly nasty consequences.

It's not always obvious what setting the color for a Windows control will actually do. If you set the color of a scroll bar, for example, the new color will be reflected in the portion of the scroll bar where the thumb can travel. The rest of the scroll bar will be drawn normally. Setting the color for a button might appear to have no effect at all—in fact, it does, but only just. A standard Windows button has four pixels missing, one at each corner, to suggest that the corners of the button are rounded. Left to its own devices, Windows will make these pixels white, which would look peculiar against a colored background. You should return a brush handle for button controls that matches that of the background of the window they'll reside in.

Handling the WM_SYSCOMMAND message

A WM_SYSCOMMAND message is similar to a WM_COMMAND message, except that it's generated only if someone selects an item from the System menu of a window. There are two sorts of WM_SYSCOMMAND messages—those that result from selecting one of the default items of the System menu, and those that will appear if someone selects an item you've explicitly added to the System menu. These two sorts of messages are handled a bit differently.

In responding to a WM_SYSCOMMAND message, you should begin by seeing if the wParam argument AND 0FFF0H is equal to one of the constants that defines the default items in the system menu. The principal ones are:

SC_CLOSE Close the window

SC_HSCROLL Scroll the window horizontally

SC_MAXIMIZE Maximize the window

SC_MINIMIZE Minimize the window

SC_MOVE Move the window

SC_NEXTWINDOW Move to the next window

SC_PREVWINDOW Move to the previous window

SC_SIZE Resize the window

SC_VSCROLL Scroll the window vertically

In most applications the only one of these items you'll want to respond to explicitly is SC_CLOSE. If you look at DEMO1.CPP back in Fig. 2-2, you'll notice that if a WM_SYSCOMMAND message appears with SC_CLOSE as its wParam argument, a

WM_COMMAND message is sent by SelectProc to itself to simulate selecting Exit from the File menu. This allows DEMO1 to shut down in the same way whether the command originates from the File menu or the System menu.

If the wParam argument for a WM_SYSCOMMAND message doesn't turn out to contain one of the foregoing constants, you should next check to see if it represents one of the items you've added to the system menu. In the case of DEMO1, there's only one of these. It has the constant SYS_BITMAP. A WM_SYSCOMMAND message with its wParam message set to SYS_BITMAP will be sent to SelectProc if someone selects the frog graphic. The handler for this situation will send a WM_COMMAND message back to SelectProc to make it think that the Bitmap item of the File menu has actually been selected.

As an aside, in sending messages explicitly from SelectProc—in this case to itself—we've been using the SendMessage call. In fact, there's a second way to handle sending messages; you can use PostMessage. It's important to keep in mind the distinction between these two functions. In most cases you'll want to use SendMessage, but not always.

The SendMessage function sends a message directly to the window specified in its first argument. That is, it stops what your function is doing, sends the message, and doesn't return until the message has been responded to. By comparison, the PostMessage function will place a message in the Windows message queue and return immediately to wherever it was called from. The message will be responded to when it reaches the head of the queue.

Because the messages that PostMessage posts will not have been responded to by the time the function returns, you can't use PostMessage to deal with messages that result in a return value.

Use PostMessage rather than SendMessage in instances where you want whatever sends the message in question to complete its task before the message is responded to. For example, if you create a message handler that calls itself repeatedly from the same case using SendMessage, in effect becoming recursive, you might want to use PostMessage instead to avoid the possibility of overflowing your application's stack.

 Handling the WM_PAINT message

The SelectProc function does nothing useful with WM_PAINT messages sent to it. The WM_PAINT message is an occasion for drawing—or redrawing—those contents of a window that don't draw themselves. This includes everything but controls. As there are no drawn objects in the principal window of DEMO1, the WM_PAINT case of SelectProc has nothing to do.

A WM_PAINT message is sent to a message handler whenever all or part of its window requires redrawing. It's also sent when a window has just been created, so that its contents can be drawn initially.

The mechanism for generating WM_PAINT under Windows messages is a bit complex, but it's worth understanding. Whenever a rectangular area of a window requires redrawing, the coordinates of that area are added to the current update region—the region that defines those areas of a window that are no longer as they should be, and require updating. When it's time for a window to redraw itself—assuming its update region isn't empty—it will receive a WM_PAINT message. A window's message handler can respond to WM_PAINT in one of three ways:

> It can call GetUpdateRgn, work out which areas require updating, and redraw them.

> It can call GetUpdateRect and update a rectangular area that encloses the update region.

> It can just go ahead and repaint the entire window.

The approach you take to handling WM_PAINT messages in your application will be determined by the contents of your windows. For example, if a window contained a complex desktop publishing page that took twenty seconds to generate, you wouldn't want to redraw the whole works if only a small portion of it required updating. For simple windows, such as the ones in this book, it's adequate to repaint the entire window in response to a WM_PAINT message. The GetUpdateRgn and GetUpdateRect functions will not be mentioned again.

You can force a window to redraw itself by calling InvalidateRect. The InvalidateRect function allows you to explicitly add a rectangular area to the update region of a window. Here's how it's called:

```
RECT rect;
InvalidateRect(hwnd,&rect,TRUE);
```

The first argument to InvalidateRect is the HWND for the window to be updated. The second is a pointer to a RECT object that contains the coordinates of the area to be updated. If you make this argument NULL, the coordinates of the entire window will be added to the update region. The third argument is a flag to define whether the area to be updated should be erased or not.

Note that if you create a WM_PAINT handler that simply repaints the entire area of a window regardless of the contents of the update region, there's no real purpose in specifying a specific update rectangle in calls to InvalidateRect. You'll see more useful applications of the WM_PAINT message later in this chapter.

 # Secondary dialogs

The only real purpose of the main window of DEMO1 is to spawn a number of child windows—that, and to place a large green rectangle that's hard to miss in the center of your screen. The functions of the DEMO1 application, such as they are, are called through cases in the WM_COMMAND section of SelectProc. Each one is actually a dialog.

A *dialog* typically consists of a bit of code to set up and call DialogBox and a message handler to do all the work. These are analogous to what WinMain and SelectProc have been doing for the main window of DEMO1. Each of the message handlers will be a bit different and, in fact, this is where most of the interesting things take place.

 # A digression on string table resources

One of the functions that will turn up periodically in this section is FetchString. The FetchString function retrieves a numbered string from the string table resources of an application's EXE file. It's

declared in DEMO1.CPP, back in Fig. 2- 2. You can see an example of a string table resource in Fig. 2-3.

Most C programmers will be used to creating static text strings as local data, like this:

```
char mystring[]="Big, ugly frogs";
```

While easy to implement, creating strings this way has two consequences in a Windows environment. The first is that it makes changing the contents of strings fairly difficult. For example, to create a foreign language version of an application with hard-coded strings, you would pretty well have to recompile it once for every language you wanted to support. Finding and translating all the strings in an application can be particularly difficult if you've scattered strings all the way through its source code.

After a while you'll wind up with a lot of these things all over your program:

```
#if ENGLISH
char mystring[]="Big, ugly frogs";
#endif
#if GAELIC
char mystring[]="Losgann mor grannda";
#endif
```

By comparison, if you put all the strings for an application in string resources, they could be translated after the application was compiled using a resource editor, such as Resource Workshop.

The second reason for using string resources rather than static strings is that the former approach keeps your strings out of the data segment of your application. As was discussed in chapter 1 of this book, the common data segment of a Windows application must contain its stack, static data, and local heap. Reducing the amount of static data will leave more room for a local heap, frequently a worthwhile consideration.

It's considerably easier—and less likely to introduce subtle errors into your applications—if you create Windows software using string tables initially, rather than replacing all the strings in an existing application later on.

String table resources have a number for each string. It's important
to note that, while you can have multiple string table resources, you
shouldn't create two strings with the same number, even if they're in
different tables. The LoadString function will fetch a numbered
string from the resource list of your application's EXE file. Here's
how it works:

```
LoadString(hInst,number,buffer,STRINGSIZE);
```

The first argument to LoadString is the instance handle for your
application, as passed to WinMain. The second argument is the
number of the string you'd like to fetch. The third argument is a far
pointer to a buffer to put the string in. The fourth argument is the
size of buffer—if the string being fetched turns out to be longer than
this, it will be truncated.

The FetchString function in DEMO1 serves as a convenient interface
to LoadString. It accepts a string number as its argument and returns
a LPSTR pointer to the retrieved string. Note that the string it fetches
will be stored in a static buffer—you can use FetchString to fetch only
one string at a time.

As a final note about string table resources, Resource Workshop
includes a string table editor. However, as there are no inscrutable
flags or fields to worry about in a string table—each line consists of a
number, some text, and a semicolon to separate them—you can edit
string tables with the Borland C++ IDE editor, just as you would any
C language file. Open the RC file for your application and add
whatever strings you require.

Beware the bandersnatch, however—or rather, beware the two-
headed multitasking monster. If you like to keep Borland C++ and
Resource Workshop running concurrently, so that you can flip
between them, make sure you don't edit your RC file in Borland C++
and then change and save the RC file that was previously loaded into
Resource Workshop. Doing so will overwrite the changes made to it
in Borland C++.

⇨ The Buttons dialog

Figure 2-8 illustrates the dialog that appears if you select Buttons from the File menu of DEMO1. The two buttons at the bottom of the Buttons dialog should appear fairly commonplace, save that, like the other controls in DEMO1, they've had their fonts changed from the conventional Windows system font to the Arial font, as discussed earlier in this chapter. The matrix of nine buttons in the center of the dialog, however, is another matter.

Figure 2-8

The DEMO1 Buttons dialog.

In fact, there's nothing at all unusual happening in the center buttons—they're conventional Windows buttons with conventional text in them. Each button contains one character. The characters, however, are drawn from a nonalphabetic font, the WingDings ornament font that accompanies Windows.

The functions that display the Buttons dialog are DoButtons and its message handler ButtonDlgProc, both of which were declared back in Fig. 2-2. The DoButtons function fetches the ButtonBox dialog template, which is defined in Fig. 2-3.

There are two cases of interest in the ButtonDlgProc message handler. The WM_INITDIALOG case sets up the buttons in the dialog. Specifically, it uses the SetControlFont macro to change the

font in the OK and Help buttons. It also uses a direct call to CreateFont to set the font of each of the nine buttons. In this case, CreateFont creates 32-point WingDings.

In using nonalphabetic fonts such as WingDings, the Windows Character Map application is exceedingly useful for finding the symbols you're after.

The WM_COMMAND handler of ButtonDlgProc takes care of clicking on the various buttons in the Buttons dialog. The IDOK case deletes the static objects created in WM_INITDIALOG and terminates the dialog by calling EndDialog. It's worth noting that the second argument to EndDialog will be what the DialogBox function returns back in DoButton. This isn't relevant to this dialog, but it would be if you wanted your calling function to know which of several buttons had been clicked to terminate a dialog.

The IDHELP case handles cries for help. It calls the DoHelp function, which will be discussed in greater detail towards the end of this chapter.

The default case of the WM_COMMAND handler looks deceptively simple, but it actually works through a considerable degree of forethought and numerical trickery. The DoMessage function, as defined in DEMO1.CPP, will open a dialog and display your text of choice in it. You could use the Windows MessageBox function to do this—I created a dedicated dialog for this purpose, to keep its appearance consistent with the other dialogs in the application. The FetchString function, as was discussed in the previous section, returns a string loaded from the resource list of DEMO1.EXE.

The Buttons dialog will display some text in response to clicking on each of its nine center buttons. Each of the buttons has a resource ID, and each of the strings has a number. By making the resource ID numbers and the string numbers the same, the wParam argument of the WM_COMMAND message generated when one of the center buttons is clicked will be the string table number for the string it corresponds to. This saves a lot of code that would otherwise have been required to sort out the strings.

There's one very small catch to using nonalphabetic characters in a resource script, as I've done here. Character 255 seems to be particular to Resource Workshop. If it encounters this character in a string, the rest of the resource script will be ignored. While you could arguably use character 255 by placing it in a control from within your application, it's a very bad idea to store it in a string table resource.

Character 255 is the Microsoft flag logo in the WingDings font. Microsoft's development tools come with all manner of threats, innuendos, legal dogma, imbroglio, plague, and pestilence to be called down upon the brow of anyone who uses this symbol without three-part written permission and divine blessing. Hardly a particularly original or attractive character to begin with, you might well want to avoid the character 255 problem and perhaps several problems of litigation by passing on this one.

As a final note, if you look carefully at the ButtonBox resource script back in Fig. 2-3, you'll find the character constants that define the symbols that appear in the center buttons of the Buttons dialog. Some of these are simple ASCII characters, the codes of which correspond to symbols in the WingDings font. The latter two are written as \300 and \314 respectively—a bit suspect, perhaps, inasmuch as there are at most 256 characters in a font.

As with C, numeric character constants in a resource script are written in octal. These values work out to characters 192 and 204 respectively.

 # The Adjust Colour dialog

The Adjust Colour dialog is illustrated in Fig. 2-9. Like the Buttons dialog, it doesn't do anything particularly useful as it stands, although it illustrates things you might want to incorporate into your own applications. If you use the Graphic Workshop for Windows package included on the companion disk for this book, you'll find a similar dialog as a palette adjustment control in its View function.

The Adjust Colour dialog doesn't actually have all that much new to say about color per se—setting the color of a window was discussed

Figure 2-9

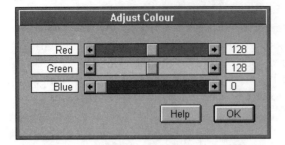

The DEMO1 Adjust Colour dialog.

earlier in this chapter. It does, however, illustrate how to work with independent scroll bar controls.

The three scroll bars in the dialog represent the amount of red, green, and blue light that's used to define the background color of the dialog. The background color will initially be set to the DARKBACKGROUND color defined at the top of DEMO1.CPP, and the scroll bar positions will reflect this. If you move the thumb of a scroll bar, the proportion of its corresponding color will change, and the dialog will be redrawn with a different color background.

As an aside, while this is a fairly simple way to choose colors, it's not a particularly intuitive one. We'll look at a much more elaborate dialog for color selection later in this book.

The Adjust Colour dialog is called forth by the DoColours function and its ColourDlgProc message handler, as defined back in Fig. 2-2. This is a fairly long message handler, with one new message case we haven't encountered previously—for the WM_HSCROLL message generated by the color scroll bars—and quite a lot happening in the cases that have turned up previously.

While it won't be apparent in Fig. 2-9, the three scroll bars that represent the amount of red, green, and blue light in the background of the dialog are themselves red, green, and blue. This is managed through a variation on the WM_CTLCOLOR message handler discussed earlier in this chapter. As was touched on then, it's possible to figure out the actual resource ID of each control the WM_CTLCOLOR message is sent to fetch a brush handle for. Having done this, the WM_CTLCOLOR

handler can return different brushes for different controls, and as such set their colors individually.

This, of course, requires that there be different brush handles to return. The WM_INITDIALOG case of ColourDlgProc creates four static brushes in the brush handle array hBrush. They're indexed through the use of some constants defined at the top of DEMO1.CPP:

RGB_RED   0
RGB_GREEN   1
RGB_BLUE   2
RGB_SIZE   3

In fact, these values are somewhat misapplied here. The first three actually represent the positions of the color values in a 24-bit color bitmap pixel or a palette entry in a non-Windows bitmap. The RGB_SIZE value defines the size of a 24-bit pixel or palette entry in bytes. They've been pressed into service here. The hBrush[RGB_SIZE] brush handle is used to define the background color brush.

Once the four colored brushes have been defined in WM_INITDIALOG, the three scroll bar controls are configured. The GetDlgItem returns the HWND of a control based on the HWND of the window it's a child of and its resource ID. The SetScrollRange function sets the minimum and maximum values of a scroll bar. In this case, you want the scroll bars to return values between zero and 255, the range of the bytes in an RGB color.

A WM_HSCROLL message will be sent to ColourDlgProc each time one of the scroll bar controls in the Adjust Colour dialog is changed. The WM_HSCROLL handler begins by fetching the resource ID of the scroll bar that has generated the message and then the current position of the scroll bar in question with the GetScrollPos function. It will then adjust the scroll bar's position based on the part of the scroll bar that was clicked. The wParam argument will contain a constant to define what was clicked. If the thumb was dragged, the low-order word of the lParam argument will contain the new position for the thumb.

Once the new position of the scroll bar has been determined, the appropriate scroll bar position text control must be updated and a

new brush must be created to define the background color of the Adjust Colour dialog. Calling InvalidateRect will cause the dialog to be redrawn.

It seems fair to observe that this is one of the few justifiable examples of multiple colors for controls—the colors actually reflect the functions of the scroll bars in the dialog. While you can define different colors for several classes of Windows controls, you should probably exercise some restraint in doing so, lest the previously mentioned belligerent male rhinoceroses come visit your software.

The Bitmap dialog

The Bitmap dialog is shown in Fig. 2-10. While this is another appearance of the frog that has turned up at various times throughout this book, you're free to use any picture you like for this function. I'll get into the details of replacing the frog with the amphibian of your choice in a moment.

Figure 2-10

The DEMO1 Bitmap dialog.

The Bitmap dialog has no controls at all—double click in the System menu icon to close it. Its sole purpose is to display that frog. However, there's quite a lot to displaying bitmaps in a useful and predictable way. Despite its graphical character, Windows doesn't get along all that well with graphics.

To understand why displaying bitmaps is so complicated, you should begin by understanding what Windows does with color. Many of the

graphics problems that Windows' users seem to experience are actually problems having to do with Windows idea of color and its hammerlock on the palette registers of your display card.

The simplest sort of Windows screen driver you're likely to encounter is a 16-color VGA card. This is what Windows will typically set itself up for when you first install it. In its 640 × 480 pixel graphics mode, a standard VGA card can display 16 colors drawn from a palette of about a quarter of a million.

In addition to being nice to look at, Windows is a multitasking operating system. In real terms, this means that you can have several applications visible on your screen at once, flipping between them as need be. This could be a bit of a problem in a multitasking operating system in which there was a finite number of available screen colors. You can imagine what might happen if each application could make off with the hardware screen palette for its own uses.

Windows might begin to display important system dialogs with white type on a white background, for example. This could be somewhat inconvenient.

Windows gets around this problem by prohibiting all applications from directly negotiating with the display hardware for screen colors. Rather, applications must ask Windows for colors and Windows, in turn, will provide them as best it can without mangling anything it considers fundamental to your continued perception of its display.

There's a set of twenty fixed colors that Windows will always have available. In fact, on a 16-color display, this means that there are 16 real colors and four additional dithered colors created from alternating dots of the first 16. Attempting to display colors other than the ones Windows provides for on a 16-color display will cause the colors in your graphic to be remapped to the nearest Windows fixed palette colors.

This can cause some fairly radical color shifts in 16-color images displayed on a 16-color system, and it will cause 256-color pictures, like the frog, to appear posterized and not all like their former selves.

Things will get noticeably better if you're running with a 256-color Windows screen driver in your system. In this case, Windows will still maintain its twenty reserved colors, but with 236 free palette entries to work with, it can usually juggle the palette of your graphic so that it will be subjected to no perceptible color shifts when it's displayed. For practical purposes you can display convincing photorealistic images with a 256-color Windows screen driver.

Imaging snobs will disagree vehemently with this, by the way, but they will typically have parted with some serious cash for their display adapters, and as such are pretty well obliged to.

If you're running Windows with a high-color or true-color display adapter—those supporting 32,768, 65,536 or 16,777,216 colors— all talk of palettes can be ignored. These cards behave as if they can display an infinite number of colors, and nothing need ever be remapped to be displayed on them.

A 256-color bitmap painted directly on a 16-color display looks rather dreadful. There is a way to improve on this process somewhat; you can dither the 256-color graphic down to 16 colors. While the results of doing so won't fool anyone into thinking he's looking at a photograph, it will look better than a simple remap.

The Graphic Workshop for Windows package on the companion disk for this book includes the facility of dithering an image to 16 colors, and making sure that the 16 colors it uses match the 16 reserved colors of the Windows palette. Figure 2-11 illustrates the result of dithering an image this way. The color dithering facilities are available through the Graphic Workshop Effects function.

If you want to display photorealistic bitmaps in a Windows application, you should store one 256-color version and one dithered 16-color version of each graphic and have your software choose one based on the display driver it finds itself running with. This can make the EXE file of your application fairly voluminous—especially if you use a lot of bitmaps, or ones with large dimensions—but it will offer the best possible image quality no matter what sort of system your software runs on.

Figure 2-11

Dithering an image with Graphic Workshop.

Later in this chapter we'll look at displaying monochrome bitmaps. The process is somewhat less complex, as it will work with bitmaps that are guaranteed to have no more than 16 colors.

The DoBitmap function in DEMO1.CPP creates the dialog for the Bitmap function and begins sending messages to its message handler, BitmapDlgProc. The dialog template for this function is a bit unusual, as it's impossible to know the dimensions of the bitmap to be displayed at compile time. At least, faking it so that one did would be fairly tedious. In this application, the window for the Bitmap dialog is set to an arbitrary size when it's created in the Resource Workshop and then resized by the WM_INITDIALOG case of BitmapDlgProc.

The WM_INITDIALOG case does a number of hitherto unencountered things. It begins by calling the GetDeviceBits function, which is declared in DEMO1.CPP. This will return the number of bits of color depth supported by the current screen driver. It figures this out by calling GetDeviceCaps, as can be seen in Fig. 2-2. This version of GetDeviceBits has been cooked somewhat, and will report a 24-bit device even if it's confronted with a 15- or 16-bit driver in your system. The reason for this is that while there are screen drivers with 15 and

16 bits of color depth, there's no such thing as a Windows bitmap structured this way. The next step up from 8 bits of color is 24 bits.

In displaying canned graphics in a dialog, the most reliable way to store the images themselves is as resource items in the resource list of your application's EXE file. The alternative is to store them as external BMP files—there are few good reasons for doing so, and a few notable ones for avoiding it. External files are much more prone to getting lost or modified, and they typically require more time to load.

You can include any graphic stored as a Windows BMP file in a program's resource list by installing a reference to it in your application's resource script. Here's how you'd do this for a file called FROG.BMP:

```
Frog256 BITMAP frog.bmp
```

This will create an object in the resource list of your application called Frog256, which can be fetched with the LoadResource or LoadBitmap calls.

Having determined the color depth of your display adapter, the WM_INITDIALOG case of BitmapDlgProc will call GetBitmapDimensions, another function declared in DEMO1.CPP. This function will fetch a named bitmap resource from the resource list of an application's EXE file and return its horizontal and vertical dimensions and the number of bits of color it requires. It does this by loading the bitmap and casting an LPBITMAPINFO pointer to it. The BITMAPINFO structure can be found at the beginning of all Windows bitmaps, and provides information about the image that follows it. With a few minor exceptions—such as the GetBitmapDimensions function in DEMO1.CPP—the applications of bitmaps in this book won't require that you get too deeply involved with Windows bitmap objects at this level.

Windows' implementation of bitmaps is mildly chaotic at the best of times, and being able to work with bitmapped images at a level that insulates you from most of the peculiarities of the craft will certainly make your life a lot less interesting— in much the same way that refusing a Federal Express shipment of live Peruvian pit-vipers will.

The final task of the WM_INITDIALOG handler of BitmapDlgProc is to append a text item to the System menu of the Bitmap dialog window. If you worked your way through the calls to AppendMenu that were used to put a frog in the System menu of the main window of DEMO1, you shouldn't have any difficulty in seeing what this code is up to. The second AppendMenu call installs a text string supplied by FetchString, rather than a bitmap.

As an aside, you might notice a size discrepancy between the frog in the Bitmap dialog and the one in the System menu of the main window of DEMO1. The two creatures were derived from the same source, but the latter was scaled down to half its original size and then dithered to 16 colors, both operations being handled by Graphic Workshop. While you're free to put any bitmap you like in a menu, ones of modest dimensions and color depth are less likely to make the menus they reside in unworkably slow.

The WM_PAINT handler of BitmapDlgProc actually draws the frog in its window. Keep in mind that the window area is initially invalid, and as such a WM_PAINT message will be sent to the window's message handler to draw its contents when the window has first been created.

The BeginPaint function returns a device context handle, an HDC, that references the display surface to be drawn on. In this case it's the surface of your monitor—later in this book we'll look at printing to an HDC object connected to a printer.

The GetDeviceBits function is again used to choose a bitmap to work with. The LoadResource call fetches the appropriate bitmap, the DrawImage function displays it, and the FreeResource call deletes it from memory when it's no longer required.

It would be awfully convenient if DrawImage were a Windows system call, but it's not. It's declared in DEMO1.CPP. It will paint a bitmap in a window. It has four arguments: a device context handle, the horizontal and vertical coordinates for the upper left corner of the bitmap relative to the upper left corner of the window's client area, and an HBITMAP handle to an image. In this application it will be used to paint the bitmap in the upper left corner of the window it resides in, so the coordinate arguments will both be zero.

The DrawImage function begins by locking the bitmap passed to it with a call to LockResource. The pointer returned by LockResource will be an LPBITMAPINFO object that defines the bitmap's characteristics and its palette.

The next bit of DrawImage creates a logical palette for the bitmap and "realizes" it, that is, lets Windows juggle its colors to maintain its 20 reserved palette entries. Finally, it uses the BitBlt call to display the bitmap, or perhaps more correctly, to allow it to be selected into the specified device context.

Despite its apparent complexity, the DrawImage function barely wets its feet in the trackless, shark-infested sea of bitmapped graphics and Windows. If you'd like to understand the subject in greater detail, you might want to have a look at my book Windows Bitmapped Graphics, published by Windcrest/McGraw Hill.

The Scroll Bars dialog

Scroll bars as controls have turned up previously in the Adjust Colour dialog. In addition to using them as discrete objects, Windows provides for every window it creates to have one vertical scroll bar along its right side and one horizontal scroll bar along its lower edge. This includes not only application windows and dialogs, but controls as well. You can, for example, create buttons with scroll bars. It's unclear why you'd want to do this, as the scroll bars in these cases don't actually do anything.

Figure 2-12 illustrates the Scroll Bars dialog. One of the least useful of the dialogs in the DEMO1 application, it will adjust the values in its two numeric text controls to correspond to the position of the thumbs of the horizontal and vertical scroll bars. The Scroll Bars dialog is created by the DoScrollbars function back in DEMO1.CPP. Its messages are handled by ScrollDlgProc.

The WM_INITDIALOG case of ScrollDlgProc sets up the scroll bars and their associated text controls. The SetScrollRange call sets the minimum and maximum values returned by a scroll bar at the extremes of its travel. The SetScrollPos call sets the initial thumb position—in this case each scroll bar is set to the middle of its travel.

Figure 2-12

The DEMO1 Scroll Bars dialog.

The second argument to each of these functions defines which scroll bar will be affected. If it's SB_HORZ or SB_VERT, the first argument is taken to be the HWND of the window the horizontal and vertical scroll bars are respectively attached to. If it's SB_CTL, the first argument is considered to be the HWND of a scroll bar control, such as those used in the Adjust Colour dialog.

A scroll bar that's attached to a window will send messages to its window's message handler when it's moved. These will be WM_VSCROLL for a vertical scroll bar and WM_HSCROLL for a horizontal scroll bar. You can cheat a bit in ScrollDlgProc, as a window can have only one vertical and one horizontal scroll bar attached to it, although it can have any number of scroll bar controls. As there are none of the latter in the Scroll Bars dialog, it will be pretty obvious which scroll bar has been changed if one of these messages shows up. The WM_HSCROLL and WM_VSCROLL handlers behave much as the scroll bar handler in the ColoursDlgProc message handler did.

In most cases you'd use scroll bars attached to a window to scroll through a document or a list.

The Check Boxes and Radio Buttons dialog

This dialog is shown in Fig. 2-13, and clearly represents another instance of an infestation of frogs. In this case the frog graphic can

Figure 2-13

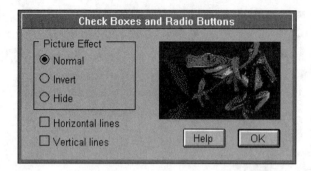

The DEMO1 Check
Boxes and Radio Buttons
dialog.

appear in several states, as defined by the check boxes in the dialog. This dialog also embodies a near relation of check boxes, these being radio buttons.

Check boxes and radio buttons are two-state controls. They can be either checked or unchecked. A check box is used to enable or disable a single option in a dialog. A set of radio buttons is used to select one of a number of mutually exclusive options. They're called *radio buttons* because they behave like the channel selector buttons on an old car radio. If you push one in, the previously selected button will pop out.

At least, they're supposed to. After a while most mechanical car radios develop spring failure and require the application of considerable violence to make them pop out. This is not a condition common to Windows' radio buttons.

The Check Boxes and Radio Buttons dialog is created by the perhaps fairly predictable DoCheck function, which sets up CheckDlgProc as its message handler.

The WM_INITDIALOG handler CheckDlgProc is singularly uncomplicated—it just sets the initial state of a few controls. It does, however, use one of a number of hitherto unmentioned macros from the top of the DEMO1.CPP listing, this being CheckOn. This macro sends the appropriate message to the control specified in its argument to make it appear that it has been selected.

Each of the dialog item macros assumes that there will be a declared local HWND variable called dlgH. They could have been created with

this object internal to them, but it's somewhat more efficient to handle things this way if there will be a lot of invocations of these macros. Not having to juggle the stack each time a macro expansion is encountered will save some processor time.

The interesting parts of CheckDlgProc are its WM_PAINT and WM_COMMAND cases. The WM_PAINT case displays the frog graphic with some special effects—the effects to be applied to it are determined by which of the check boxes and radio buttons in the dialog have been turned on. None of them are particularly difficult to understand.

➢ If the CHECK_HIDE button is on, the frog will be hidden by a gray rectangle.

➢ If the CHECK_INVERT button is on, the frog will be inverted black for white, managed by a white rectangle over it with the ROP2 mode set to R2_NOT.

➢ If the CHECK_HORZ button is on, the frog will be painted over with horizontal lines.

➢ If the CHECK_VERT button is on, the frog will be painted over with vertical lines.

The IsItemChecked function is actually another of those macros that's defined at the top of DEMO1.CPP. It will be true if a check box or radio button is checked, and false otherwise.

The WM_COMMAND case responds to WM_COMMAND messages sent to CheckDlgProc by the check boxes and radio buttons in question. Its response to them is to invalidate the area of the dialog window, which will cause a WM_PAINT message to be sent to CheckDlgProc as soon as Windows has a moment to spare. Since the WM_PAINT handler will redraw the graphic based on the state of the check boxes and radio buttons, changing the state of a button changes the graphic. It's convoluted, but it makes for a very elegant way to "connect" the dialog controls with the code that actually draws something.

 # The List dialog

The List dialog is illustrated in Fig. 2-14. For those who haven't sampled the reality of Victorian literature—but only seen Walt Disney's questionable interpretation of it—the poem therein is from *Alice Through the Looking Glass*. The graphic is by John Tenneil, who illustrated Lewis Carroll's original manuscript.

Figure 2-14

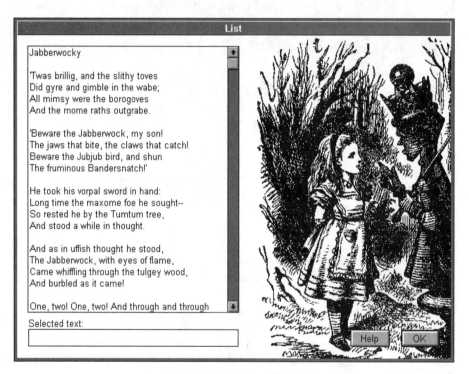

The DEMO1 List dialog.

I should note that the graphic in the List dialog is not appropriate for the poem "Jabberwocky," as it comes from a wholly different part of the story. The drawing that accompanies the poem itself didn't scan particularly well at the coarse resolution required to fit into a Windows dialog. Tenneil's illustrations have suffered enough over the years—it didn't seem conscionable to turn one of them into a blur of crunchy pixels and ill-defined lines.

The primary element of the List dialog is the large list box with Jabberwocky in it. List boxes are wonderfully handy controls, as they allow you to perform complex selection and display functions with breathtakingly small allotments of support code. Getting data into a list box control is easy, and the control itself will send a WM_COMMAND message to the parent window's message handler should someone click on an item in it. All the complexity in between is province of the list box itself, and you'll need never know what it involves.

The List dialog is created by the DoListbox function in DEMO1.CPP, which uses ListDlgProc as its message handler. The text for Jabberwocky and the bitmap of Alice and the Red Queen are stored as resource items. The text was entered in the Windows Notepad application, and is stored as an RCDATA object.

The WM_INITDIALOG case of ListDlgProc takes care of loading the list box with the text of Jabberwocky. This requires that it be loaded from the resource list of DEMO1.EXE, a procedure that works the same way as loading a bitmap would. The catch to this is that Windows doesn't really provide a way to know where the end of a resource's data occurred. There is a function called SizeResource, but it really returns a value that's constrained to be no smaller than the resource in question. It will usually be quite a bit larger, due to granulation. As such, the last line in the text of Jabberwocky is the word ENDMARKER. Once it has been loaded, the text will be parsed into lines until this final line is encountered. The end marker is defined by the constant LIST_END.

Adding a string to a list box is a bit tricky, as Windows doesn't provide a function to do it. Rather, you must send a message to the list box in question. The SendDlgItemMessage function can be used to send a message to a child control of a dialog. The message in this case is LB_INSERTSTRING. The wParam argument for the message should be −1, which tells the list box to add the string to the end of its list. The lParam argument should be a far pointer to the string to be added.

When you create list box controls in Resource Workshop, pay particular attention to the setting of the Sort flag. If it's on, a list box will sort its entries into ascending alphabetical order. This is ideal for directory entries, for example, but arguably less than ideal for poetry.

As an aside, in this example the contents of the list box being filled will all be in place prior to the dialog it's part of being drawn. If you have cause to add strings to a list box after it's visible, you might want to do this:

```
HWND dlgH;

dlgH=GetDlgItem(hwnd,LISTBOX);
SendMessage(dlgH,WM_SETREDRAW,FALSE,0L);

/* add to or modify the contents of the list box */

SendMessage(dlgH,WM_SETREDRAW,TRUE,0L);
```

The hwnd argument to GetDlgItem is the window handle of the dialog the list box in question resides in. The LISTBOX constant is the resource ID of the listbox.

Each time you change something in a list box, it will redraw itself by default. The first call to SendMessage turns the redrawing of the list box in question off, allowing you to make whatever changes you want behind its back. The second call turns it back on again. Aside from being cosmetically more attractive, this makes updating list boxes a great deal quicker.

The List dialog doesn't have a gray background, and as such ListDlgProc doesn't include a case to respond to WM_CTLCOLOR messages. This is largely for cosmetic reasons—the bitmap of Alice is black and white, and painting it on a gray background using DrawImage as it stands would leave a large white rectangle behind it. In the next chapter we'll look at a variation of DrawImage that gets around this problem.

The WM_COMMAND handler of ListDlgProc illustrates how to respond to a command message from a list box. The LIST_LIST constant is the resource ID of the list box, as defined at the top of DEMO1.CPP. The high-order word of the lParam argument will contain a constant to define what has happened to prompt the message in question. This will be LBN_DBLCLK if someone has double clicked on a list box item or LBN_SELCHANGE if someone has clicked once on an item.

In most dialogs, double clicking on a list box item should be treated as if an item had been selected and the OK button clicked. The WM_COMMAND handler takes care of this by sending a WM_COMMAND message to itself, simulating a click on the IDOK button.

If someone clicks once on an item in the list box, the LBN_SELCHANGE case of the LIST_LIST handler will find the currently selected item, fetch its text, and then place it in the LIST_SELECT text control. This involves three calls. As in many situations dealing with dialog controls, there are no defined Windows functions to perform the tasks involved. Rather, you must send messages to the list box you want to query using SendDlgItemMessage.

> The LB_GETCURSEL message will return the index of the currently selected list box item, or the constant LB_ERR if nothing is selected.

> The LB_GETTEXT message will fetch the text of an item from a list box. The wParam argument should be the index of the item to fetch and the lParam argument should be a pointer to a string large enough to receive it.

> The ItemName call is another macro from up at the top of DEMO1.CPP. It will set the text for any control that accepts simple text. It can be used with buttons, check boxes, and static text controls, for example.

List boxes are potentially among the most complex controls Windows offers, unless you want to consider the ones you actually create yourself. We'll be dealing with these later. We'll also be looking at variations on list boxes elsewhere in this book—you can warp them into being all sorts of things with a sufficient degree of cunning.

The Combo Box dialog

The Combo Box dialog is cosmetically similar to the List dialog, complete with Jabberwocky, Alice, the Red Queen, and things to select and click in. This combo box, however, embodies both a

scrollable list and a built-in text control to display the currently selected item. In fact, it behaves almost identically to the combination of the LIST_LIST and LIST_SELECT controls in the foregoing section, save that there's physically one less control to keep track of. Figure 2-15 illustrates the Combo Box dialog.

Figure 2-15

The DEMO1 Combo Box dialog.

The useful aspect of combo boxes as opposed to list boxes is that they remain closed most of the time, and as such take up relatively little space. Combo boxes come in three types, as illustrated in Fig. 2-16. Simple combo boxes are always open, and are really little more than a list box and a text control welded together. A drop-down combo box has a button to the right of its selection indicator, and will drop its list down when the button is clicked on. If you click in the selection field to the left of the button, you can edit the currently selected line. A drop-down list combo box is similar to a drop-down combo box, save that the selected element can't be edited. If you click in it, the list will drop down.

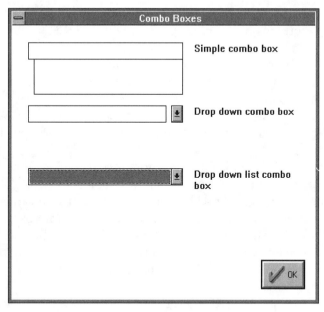

Figure 2-16

Three combo box styles.

The Combo Box dialog is created by the DoCombo function of DEMO1.CPP. Its messages are handled by ComboDlgProc. The ComboDlgProc function is effectively identical to the ListDlgProc, save that the list box messages have been replaced with combo box messages.

⇨ Creating help files

In one sense, it would be fairly easy to write a whole book about creating Windows help files. In another sense, you can master the important aspects of the craft in half an hour. The Windows Help facility is seethingly powerful, but rather like an E-type Jag in a traffic jam, much of its power is unnecessary for normal applications.

The DEMO1 application illustrates how to call the Windows Help facility. It, like all the applications in this book, expects help to be provided in the form of a help file called DEMO.HLP. Windows Help expects this file to be in the same directory as DEMO1.EXE, or

rather, DEMO1 tells it to do so. The MakeHelpPathName in DEMO1.CPP creates a complete path to DEMO.HLP.

Help under Windows is provided by spawning WINHELP.EXE and passing it the name of the help file you want to display help from. In fact, you don't even have to trouble yourself to locate WINHELP.EXE—just call the WinHelp function provided by Windows and all the grotty details will be handled for you behind your back.

Actually creating DEMO.HLP is a bit more involved. The system for doing so as provided by Microsoft, while workable, is convoluted and not at all well integrated. You'll need a copy of Microsoft Word for Windows, or any other word processor capable of working with Microsoft rich text format documents. These have the extension RTF. Word version 1.0 is preferable to version 2.0 if you have access to both. The Windows Write word processor won't suffice—it can't create RTF files.

You'll also need the HC.EXE help compiler, provided with Borland C++. Note that this is a DOS application. It must be run in a DOS session. The Help compiler translates an RTF file into an HLP file.

In most cases you'll want to edit a help file and switch to the DOS prompt from Word to compile it. If there are problems with your source document, you can switch back to Word, fix them, and then switch back to the DOS prompt to recompile them. The only catch to this is that if you have the SHARE command installed in your AUTOEXEC.BAT file, attempting to open your source file with HC.EXE when it's currently open in Word will provoke a sharing violation. It's a lot easier to create help files if you remove the SHARE command from your AUTOEXEC.BAT file.

In addition to a help source document—an RTF file set up to look like help to the Help compiler—you'll require a help project. This is a file that behaves much like a Borland C++ PRJ file. It tells the Help compiler where all the files that will make up your final HLP file reside. In this case there's only one source file, but the Help compiler wants a project file in any case. Help project files have the extension HPJ. Here's the DEMO.HPJ project file for DEMO.HLP:

```
[OPTIONS]
COMPRESS=true
```

```
WARNING=1
;
[FILES]
demo.rtf
```

The source rich text format file is called DEMO.RTF. The [OPTIONS] section of the DEMO.HPJ file has told the Help compiler that it can compress objects in the final help file. The WARNING=1 line suppresses some spurious warning messages.

Most of the work involved in creating DEMO.HLP was in writing the contents of DEMO.RTF. It seems fair to note that this is a very simple help file—it uses a fraction of the tricks that the Windows Help system can perform. I've left it thus both because it's intended to illustrate how to create a help file rather than how to confuse one, and because complex help sections with sounds and MIDI music and Windows AVI movies sprouting from every pore and bunion are arguably less than helpful. Most users, upon selecting Help, want to be helped rather than entertained.

For the sake of this discussion, then, a help file can contain the following elements:

> Text on the current page to tell you something

> Hot links to text on another page

> Index links

> Search items

The links between pages in a help document are handled in a way that only Martians who'd grown up on the wrong side of the planet could have thought of. The words that will eventually show up as a green hot-link item are entered as double underlined text. Immediately following that should be the name of the link to which the text refers, stored as hidden text.

You can set double underlines using one of the buttons in the button bar at the top of the Word for Windows workspace. You must set hidden text using the Character dialog of the Format menu.

If you open the Preferences item of the Word for Windows View menu, you'll come upon a dialog that lets you make hidden text visible. This feature should be enabled for creating help source documents so you can see what you're doing.

Figure 2-17 illustrates the first page of DEMO.HLP as seen in Word for Windows. The text with faint dashed underlines beneath it is hidden.

Figure 2-17

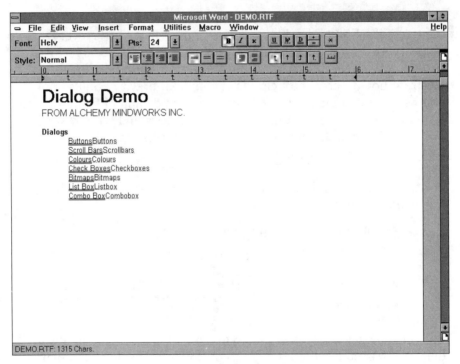

The first page of the DEMO.RTF help source file, as seen in Word for Windows.

The first page of a help source document typically consists of a list of hot-link items to pages throughout the rest of the document. Insert a page break at the end of each page.

Dependent pages of a help document consist of a heading, the text of the page, and the link items that reference the page in question. The text might contain further hot links—you can have pages call pages

that call other pages that call still other pages—and so on, until your users are wholly lost. Creating the link items is a serious nuisance—they're handled as special footnotes. To create a footnote in Word for Windows, select Footnote from the Insert menu. A dialog like the one in Fig. 2-18 will appear.

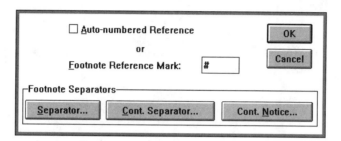

Figure 2-18

The Word for Windows footnote dialog.

Each footnote in a Word document has a symbol associated with it. There are three symbols that are particularly interesting to a basic help document, to wit:

$ This indicates that the footnote is the title of the topic page it's found on.

K This indicates that the footnote is a key word. It will appear in the key word search list if Search is selected in Windows Help.

This indicates that the footnote is a context string, that is, it's the target of a hot link. This text must match the hidden text on another page that refers to it.

Figure 2-19 illustrates a dependent page of DEMO.RTF. The three characters beside the heading are footnote markers. They won't appear in the final Help file.

To create the page in Fig. 2-19, enter the text for the heading and the body of the page. While you can choose any fonts you like for these, keep in mind that not all Windows systems have the same fonts on hand. The Arial and Times New Roman fonts are good

Figure 2-19

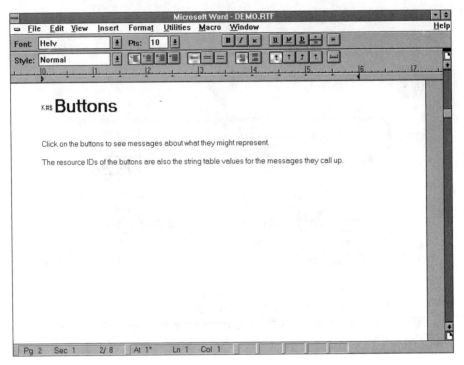

A dependent page of DEMO.RTF in Word for Windows.

choices to prevent font incompatibilities, as they're actually installed with Windows.

To create the links for this page, place your text cursor to the left of the heading. Select Footnote from the Word for Windows Insert menu and enter a $ character in the Footnote Reference Mark field. Click on OK. A new footnote will appear at the bottom of the current page with a text entry cursor beside it. Type in the text of the footnote you want to insert. In this case it would be Listbox. Repeat this procedure twice more to create footnotes using the # and K symbols.

When you've completed all the pages in your source RTF file, save it to disk. In Microsoft Word, you must do this by selecting Save As from the File menu, choosing Rich Text Format from the Options list, and then entering the file name you want to save your RTF file to—in this case, DEMO.RTF. Word for Windows is a bit proprietary about its files—it

doesn't think a file has really been saved unless it has been saved to a DOC Word document. As such, even if you've saved your RTF file, Word will prompt you to save it again when you exit. Click on No.

Now you're ready to try compiling your help file. You don't have to exit Word to do this, and you need not close your source document unless you still have SHARE installed. Switch to the DOS prompt, change directories to \BC\DIALOG—or wherever you have your RTF and HPJ files located—and type:

HC DEMO.HPJ

The Help compiler will print a line of dots to indicate it's busy thinking. If it encounters an error, it will abort the compile and print a message to the effect. The Help compiler's error messages are a bit cryptic.

Note that, like a C compiler, the Help compiler wants to resolve all the hot links in a source document. The hidden text links you create are analogous to function calls, and the footnote references to function declarations. As such, if you don't have # footnotes that match all the hidden text references in your source RTF file, the Help compiler will most certainly complain.

If things aren't quite in keeping with the Help compiler's liking, return to Word, fix your errors, save your source document again, and return to the DOS prompt for another shot at compiling it.

While the process of creating HLP files for the Windows Help system is less than elegant, you can become pretty fluent in its peculiar dialect of word processing without too much difficulty. It has only about half a dozen commands that you really have to keep track of. If you can master C, the Help system should be easy.

As an aside, there are numerous third-party products that offer to automate the creation of help files by allowing you to write them in a dedicated Help programming language, which the software in question will then turn into source RTF documents suitable for a trip through the Help compiler. While these packages might arguably make managing huge help projects somewhat easier—especially if you find that you've taken a profound dislike to the conventional

process of creating help files—they typically entail just as much of a learning curve as is required to create help files with Word.

If you have cause to use the Graphic Workshop for Windows shareware package included on the companion disk for this book, you might want to have a look at its Help system. While somewhat huge, it was created with nothing more than the tools and commands discussed in this section—that, and a great deal of typing.

Using control libraries

CHAPTER 3

"An ounce of image is worth a pound of performance."

The DEMO1 program in the previous chapter illustrated pretty much everything there is to say about using Windows' defined control types and writing the functions to support dialog boxes. The only potential drawback to writing Windows applications using nothing but the controls that turned up in chapter 2 is that they'd get a bit dull.

One of the less well-documented elements of the art form of creating Windows applications is finding a balance between using controls and other objects that are familiar enough to be easily recognized and worked with and those that are visually unique enough to be interesting. Windows software, in which every application has the potential to look like every other application, can get uninteresting fairly quickly.

If you've used commercial Windows applications to any extent, you'll probably appreciate that very few contemporary packages look like the windows and dialogs of DEMO1. The sterile, two-dimensional appearance of Windows as it first appeared in Windows 3.0 has gradually given way to three-dimensional objects, textured surfaces, and custom controls of all sorts.

Custom controls allow you to make your applications more visually interesting and more intuitive to use. In a commercial sense, they also make it look more refined. Software that looks like it belongs in the 1990s suggests that it's up to the challenges of the present. Cynical software authors might cite the quotation at the beginning of this chapter and describe all this "window dressing" as an ounce of image.

We looked at ways to improve on the general character of Windows slightly in the last chapter, such as using colored backgrounds for its dialogs. In this chapter we'll look at the application of two commercial custom control libraries. They'll avail you of a whole toolbox worth of facilities to make your applications stand out. Later in this book we'll explore custom controls you can create yourself.

Figures 3-1A through 3-1P illustrate two Windows applications, DEMO2 and DEMO3. They'll probably look at least passingly familiar, as they're derived from DEMO1 in the previous chapter.

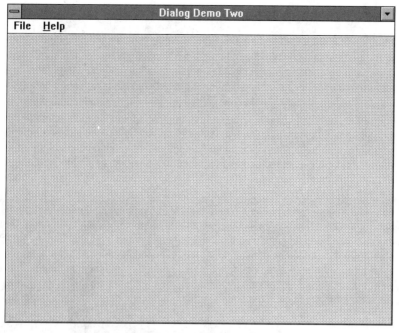

Figure 3-1A

The main dialog of the DEMO2 application.

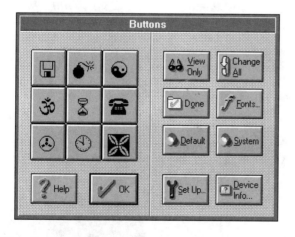

Figure 3-1B

The Buttons dialog of DEMO2.

They're cosmetically different, however, as they've been infested with custom controls.

The DEMO2 application illustrates the look and feel of the Borland Windows custom control library, usually called BWCC. The DEMO3

Figure 3-1C
Figure 3-1D

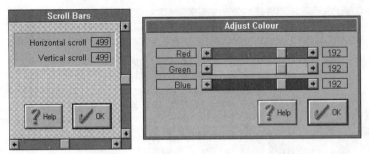

The Scroll Bars and Adjust Colour dialogs of DEMO2.

Figure 3-1E
Figure 3-1F

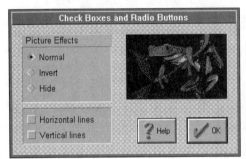

The Check Boxes and Radio Buttons dialog and Bitmap dialog of DEMO2.

Figure 3-1G

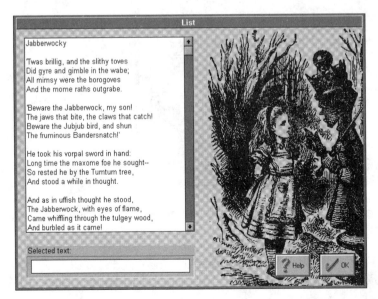

The List dialog of DEMO2.

Figure 3-1H

The Combo Box dialog of DEMO2.

Figure 3-1I

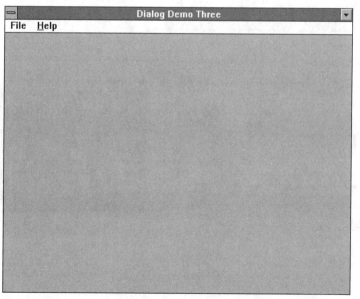

The principal dialog of the DEMO3 application.

Figure 3-1J
Figure 3-1K

*The Buttons dialog of
DEMO3.*

*The Scroll Bars dialog of
DEMO3.*

Figure 3-1L

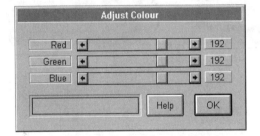

*The Adjust Colour dialog of
DEMO3.*

Figure 3-1M
Figure 3-1N

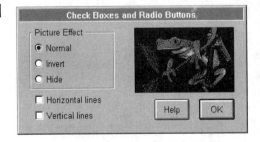

*The Check Boxes and Radio Buttons
dialog of DEMO3.*

The Bitmap dialog of DEMO3.

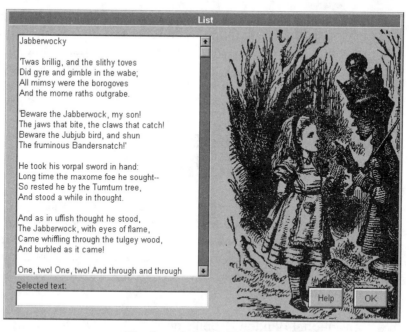

Figure 3-1O

The List dialog of DEMO3.

Figure 3-1P

The Combo Box dialog of DEMO3.

application uses Microsoft's CTL3D custom control library. These two sets of custom controls look a bit different, and offer slightly different sets of features and restrictions. Both are a little sneaky and unpredictable in places, and both are relatively poorly documented. We'll look at how to make them dance over the next few pages.

A brief digression about dynamic link libraries

Custom controls under Windows are handled as dynamic link libraries. You'll probably have noticed a number of these huddled in the shadows of most major Windows applications. They're stored in files with the extension DLL. It's important to understand a bit about how dynamic link libraries work to properly use the custom controls to be discussed in this chapter.

In a conventional Windows application, such as DEMO1.EXE, all the functions required to make the application go exist either within the application's code itself or as calls into the Windows API. In most cases, this works out well—Windows provides functions that many applications might need and your application's EXE file provides those additional functions that are pertinent only to its requirements.

The code that runs a custom control can be used by many applications. For example, consider the mechanism behind the green OK buttons that turn up in Borland C++ for Windows. If these buttons were managed by code hard-wired into Borland C++ and other applications that used similar buttons, there would be multiple copies of the same code in memory at once. This is the sort of thing that Windows considers to be very wasteful.

To this end, Windows allows for dynamic link libraries. You can create code as a dynamic link library and it will be available to any application that wants to call it. Dynamic link libraries are linked into Windows, and in effect look like normal API functions provided by Windows to your application.

In addition, dynamic link libraries offer a convenient way to make sections of your application easily upgradable. For example, one release of Borland's custom control library had a bug in it that caused buttons displayed on systems running Windows with a high-color driver to be partially chopped off. Repairing this problem required only the release of a new BWCC.DLL file, rather than the recompilation of all the applications written under Borland C++.

As an aside, if you're using the BWCC.DLL that came with Borland C++ for Windows 3.1, you might well have this slightly buggy version. The one included with Graphic Workshop for Windows on the companion disk for this book is the fixed one. Compare its date stamp with that of your copy of BWCC.DLL.

In order to write Windows applications that call functions stored in dynamic link libraries, you must have an import library for the DLL in question. An import library presents your application with callable C language functions, and routes calls to them to the code in the DLL it supports. Borland's custom controls are stored in BWCC.DLL. The import library is BWCC.LIB. In order to use the controls in BWCC.DLL, you must link BWCC.LIB into your application by including it in your Borland C++ project.

You'll see how an import library comes to pass when we look at how to create a custom DLL later in this book. Import libraries are provided with BWCC and CTL3D.

The only catch to using dynamic link libraries is that they must be accessible to Windows when an application that expects to find one calls for it. In order for Windows to find a DLL, it must reside in your \WINDOWS directory, your \WINDOWS\SYSTEM directory, your DOS path, or the same directory as the EXE files for your application.

In theory, all dynamic link libraries should be stored in your \WINDOWS\SYSTEM subdirectory so they'll be generally available to all applications that want to use them. In practice this often creates some logistical difficulties, such as DLL files with conflicting names or differing versions. There are, for example, differing versions of the Borland BWCC.DLL library, and applications written

for use with the current version might behave very strangely indeed if they find themselves confronted by an old copy.

There are, therefore, good arguments for keeping the DLL files that are specific to your application in a private directory.

An introduction to BWCC

Figure 3-2 illustrates the new controls that BWCC.DLL offers to a Windows application. Unlike the CTL3D library I'll discuss in the latter half of this chapter, Borland's library doesn't change the appearance of the existing Windows standard control objects. Rather, it adds a number of new controls that supplant the existing ones.

Figure 3-2

The custom controls offered by BWCC.DLL.

In creating a dialog, then, you could use either the standard Windows buttons or the Borland buttons illustrated back in Fig. 3-2. The same holds true for check boxes and radio buttons. Some of the standard Windows controls, such as list boxes, combo boxes, and scroll bars, don't have equivalents in the Borland custom control library. If you wanted to create a dialog with some of these objects in it, you'd have to use the standard Windows controls.

In addition to providing some custom controls, BWCC allows for a textured gray background for dialog windows. It also provides a very convenient way to create drop shadows and embossed lines.

You can create dialogs that include the Borland custom controls using the Resource Workshop application. Figure 3-3 illustrates the Resource Workshop toolbox items that pertain to custom controls.

Figure 3-3

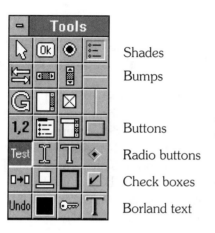

Shades

Bumps

Buttons

Radio buttons

Check boxes

Borland text

The Resource Workshop dialog editor tools that create Borland custom controls.

In most cases, Borland's controls behave just like the Windows controls they replace. There are a few extensions to the standard control classes, however—some of which can be a bit sneaky.

In creating a dialog to use Borland's custom controls, you should arrange to have the background of the dialog gray. Some of the Borland controls, such as check boxes and radio buttons, expect to be placed on a gray background. Their text objects are always drawn in black on gray.

There are two ways to create a gray background in a dialog with the BWCC library present. The first is to respond to the WM_CTLCOLOR message appropriately, as discussed in the previous chapter. The brush color you return should be RGB(192,192,192) to create a gray level that matches the backgrounds of Borland's custom controls.

The second way is to set the dialog class of each dialog window in your application to BorDlg. You can do this by double clicking on the frame

Figure 3-4

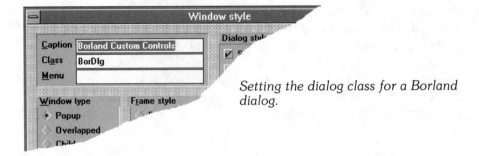

Setting the dialog class for a Borland dialog.

of a dialog being created in Resource Workshop to call up the Window Style dialog and setting the dialog class field, as illustrated in Fig. 3-4.

Dialogs of the BorDlg class have a textured gray surface. This has two important consequences for some of the techniques discussed in the previous chapter. The first is that brush handles returned by a message handler responding to WM_CTLCOLOR messages to define the background color of such a dialog will effectively be ignored. The second is that bitmaps painted in a dialog won't be visible. In a sense, the textured gray surface of a BorDlg dialog is painted over whatever is drawn directly on the window's surface.

There are few inherent advantages to using the BorDlg dialog class to create a textured gray background, save that doing so absolves the message handlers of your dialogs of the need to respond to WM_CTLCOLOR messages. If you anticipate wanting to change the colors of your dialog windows or painting bitmaps in them, it's arguably a good idea not to invoke this feature of BWCC.

Having said this, there's a somewhat undocumented approach to simulating the BorDlg background through WM_CTLCOLOR messages. This will allow you to create those dialogs that can't use the BorDlg class—because they contain bitmaps, for example— through a bit of cheating, and arrive at the same appearance as a genuine BorDlg dialog. We'll look at this facility later in this chapter.

⇨ Using Borland buttons

The Borland button controls have a number of notable properties. To begin with, as you'll have no doubt observed back in Fig. 3-2, they can include pictures. The graphic buttons in the Borland custom control libraries appear if you set the resource ID of a Borland button to one of a number of predefined constants, as illustrated in Fig. 3-5.

Figure 3-5

The standard Borland custom buttons.

If you use any other resource ID values, Borland's buttons will look more or less like conventional Windows buttons. They're slightly different, and as such it's preferable not to combine Borland buttons and standard Windows buttons in the same dialog. The actual values for the constants that define the Borland graphic buttons are as follows:

```
#define IDOK          1
#define IDCANCEL      2
#define IDABORT       3
#define IDRETRY       4
#define IDIGNORE      5
#define IDYES         6
#define IDNO          7
#define IDHELP      998
```

The first seven values are defined in WINDOWS.H, and are standard Windows constants. The last one, IDHELP, is native to Borland's

languages, and is defined in BWCC.H. You should avoid using these values as resource IDs for other controls.

If you double click on a Borland button control while you're creating a dialog in the Resource Workshop application, you'll see the Borland Button Style dialog, as illustrated in Fig. 3-6.

Figure 3-6

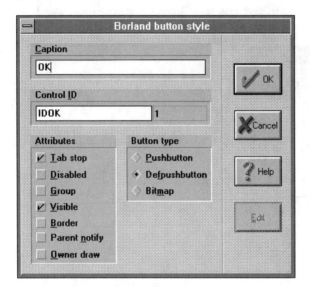

The Borland Button Style dialog.

There are three options in the Button Type control group. If you select Pushbutton, the button will appear normally. If you select Defpushbutton, the button will be the default button of your dialog, that is, it will have a thick black frame and hitting the Enter key on your keyboard will be considered the equivalent of clicking on this button.

If you select Bitmap, you'll have access to a rarely mentioned and only very infrequently useful feature of Borland's custom control library. It allows you to install static bitmaps in a dialog without having to resort to the DrawImage function discussed in the previous chapter. In fact, this would be a superb facility if it worked as well as it could.

It seems fair to observe that this arrangement will probably seem a bit flaky, and you might wonder why anyone would handle it thus. The reason is a bit obscure. Borland's custom graphic buttons, as discussed

a moment ago, are actually handled as bitmaps stored in BWCC.DLL. The code to display these buttons includes a function to paint bitmaps on your screen, probably very much like DrawImage from the previous chapter. When you define a button using the Bitmap option, you're really just telling BWCC to let you use its internal bitmap display calls.

While button controls can be used to display bitmaps, the bitmaps thus displayed don't behave like buttons. Clicking in one will have no effect.

Bitmaps for use with bitmap buttons must have resource numbers, rather than resource names. The numbers should be in the range 1,100 through 1,999. For this example, let's create a bitmap with the resource name 1,104. Figure 3-7 illustrates a resource list with this bitmap present.

Figure 3-7

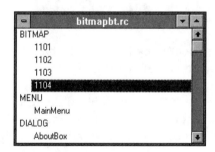

The resource list of an RC file with the bitmap to be used with a Borland bitmap control.

Now create or open the dialog in which you'd like the bitmap to appear. Create a Borland button object and double click on it to call up the Borland Button Style dialog. Select Bitmap in the Button Type control group. Click in the Control ID field and enter a number 1,000 less than the resource number of your bitmap. In this case, as the bitmap is number 1,104, the value in this field would be 104. When you click on OK to close the Borland Button Style dialog, your bitmap should appear.

If you see a small gray bitmap icon instead, there's something wrong in the numbering of your bitmap or of the Control ID value for the bitmap button you've created.

Bitmaps installed in a dialog this way can be used even if you have the class of the dialog set to BorDlg to get a textured gray background, something you can't do with DrawImage. There are some significant limitations to this facility as well, however:

➤ Monochrome bitmaps will be displayed black on white, rather than as black knocked out of the background, something you'll see later in this chapter.

➤ 256-color bitmaps will be displayed in wildly incorrect colors.

➤ 16-color bitmaps will be displayed correctly only if they use the Windows default palette.

The Borland bitmap button facility is something to keep in mind if you'd like to add some 16-color decorations to a dialog, but its limitations make it less than useful for working with complex graphics.

Making your own Borland buttons

The Buttons dialog for DEMO2, as shown back in Fig. 3-2, had rather more buttons in it than the Buttons dialog for DEMO1 from the previous chapter. If you've worked with the Borland language applications to some extent, some of these buttons will no doubt look familiar. In fact, they appear to have been shanghaied from Borland C++ for Windows and Resource Workshop—which, in fact, is exactly where they did come from.

There's a rather useful and largely undocumented facility of BWCC.DLL that allows you to create custom Borland bitmap buttons for your applications. In fact, Borland applications use it to display bitmapped buttons for functions like Fonts, Edit Icon, Device Info, and so on. Once you understand how it works it's very easy to use.

I've used buttons abstracted from other Borland applications in this example, but you're free to create original bitmap buttons if you like.

A bitmapped button, such as the green check mark OK button that turns up in pretty well all Borland's Windows applications, actually consists of three bitmaps. There's one for the default appearance of

the button, one for the button when it has been pressed, and a third one for the button if it has the focus of the dialog it's part of. This latter bitmap is usually the same as the default button bitmap save that there's a dashed gray line around the text.

When a Borland button is about to draw itself, it begins by looking through the resource list of your application for a set of three bitmaps to use. It then looks through the resource list of BWCC.DLL. If it finds no suitable bitmaps, it will draw itself using a text caption.

The bitmaps for a Borland button are identified using a somewhat complex resource numbering scheme. To begin with, the resource ID for the button itself must fall into the range of 1 through 999. In fact, resource IDs 1 through 7 are spoken for, as is resource ID 998. The former are the default Windows button constants—IDOK, IDABORT, and so on—and the latter is the Borland IDHELP value. Resource IDs 901 through 905 are also used by BWCC.

For this example, let's allow that the button in question has a resource ID of 401. In trolling around for bitmaps, BWCC.DLL will look for bitmaps 1401, 3401, and 5401. The bitmap numbered 1000 more than the resource ID of a button is taken as its default appearance. The bitmap numbered 3000 more than the resource ID is taken as its pressed appearance. The bitmap numbered 5000 more than the resource ID of a button is taken as its focused appearance.

These numbers assume that Windows is using a VGA or super VGA display of some sort. The BWCC.DLL library allows for special bitmaps to be used in the event an EGA display crawls out of the fetid swamps of time and rears its graying head. These bitmaps would be numbered 2401, 4401, and 6401 respectively. For the sake of completeness, you might want to have these bitmaps included in your applications if you create custom buttons. I've not done so in DEMO2.

Thus far, I've discussed resource objects as having names. They can also have numbers. For example, here's how you might include three bitmaps for the aforementioned button in the RC script of an application:

```
1401 BITMAP "VO-NORM.BMP"
3401 BITMAP "VO-PRES.BMP"
5401 BITMAP "VO-FOCS.BMP"
```

These are the actual resource script statements used to include the bitmaps for the View Only button, as it appeared back in Fig. 3-2.

With these bitmaps included in your application's RC file, button 401 will automatically be displayed with the bitmap images they contain, rather than with a text caption. It will also show up in Resource Workshop this way. The only thing to keep in mind about this feature is that every Borland button with the resource ID of 401 in your application will use this set of bitmaps. Make sure you plan accordingly.

You can create bitmaps for custom Borland buttons relatively easily using Resource Workshop's bitmap editor—you might want to start with some of the example button sets included on the companion disk for this book and modify them. The correct dimensions for a VGA Borland button are 69 × 39 pixels.

You might also be of a mind to steal a few of Borland's application buttons yourself, as I did for the DEMO2 program. Doing so is fairly easy. Use Resource Workshop to open the DLL and EXE files in the \BC\BIN directory where Borland C++ for Windows keeps its application files. Not all of the files include buttons—BCW.EXE and the WORKED3.DLL files are among the better sources. Actually, some of the EXE files are for DOS applications, and won't open at all.

The bitmaps for Borland's buttons are numbered just as I've described them here—they begin with resource ID 1000, and have corresponding ID values beginning with 3000 and 5000. There are also EGA bitmaps for each button, beginning with resource ID 2000.

When you find a button you like, use the Save Resource As item of the Resource Workshop Resource menu to write it out to a BMP file. Make sure you take all three bitmaps for any buttons you abstract.

There will be situations in which you can't use this facility as it's been described here—they occur, for example, when you need a button to change its appearance in different circumstances, or to have a resource ID value larger than 999. The BWCC.DLL library offers an undocumented way around this problem, too. You'll see it in action in the next chapter.

⇨ Check boxes, radio buttons, and groups

The other clickable things that Borland's custom control library offers your applications are more contemporary check boxes and radio buttons. These behave just like their Windows predecessors, except they're a bit smarter.

Note that the check boxes and radio buttons in BWCC are designed to be placed against a solid gray background, rather than against the textured background of the BorDlg dialog class. The interior of a drop shadow box will always be solid gray—to preserve the appearance of BorDlg class dialogs, these controls should appear only inside drop shadows.

You can define radio buttons to behave either as the conventional Windows radio buttons do, or as automatic radio buttons. In the former case, when a radio button is clicked, it will send a WM_COMMAND message to its parent window. The message handler for the parent window is responsible for setting its state. In the latter case, an automatic check box will change state automatically—it will still send a WM_COMMAND message to its parent window to indicate that something has happened, but the window's message handler need not manipulate the button state.

Check boxes can also be created this way—either to behave as default Windows-style check boxes would, in which the parent window of the control must set its state each time it's clicked, or to work automatically, in which it will keep track of its state by itself and notify its parent window only when it's clicked.

If you create several Borland automatic radio buttons in a dialog and surround them with a Borland drop shadow, the radio buttons will become an exclusive group. This means that clicking on one button in the group will automatically unselect all the others, without any intervention from the parent window's message handler.

Note that drop shadows can also be raised shadows, that is, the interior area can appear to be recessed or raised above the surface of a dialog window. You can define this by double clicking on the frame of a drop shadow object to call up the Borland Shade Style dialog. Select Group Shade in the Style Type control group for a drop shadow or Raised Shade for a relief shadow. Either type of shadow can be a group box for radio buttons.

One of the less than obvious things about drop shadows is that they can have captions. If you enter some text into the Caption field of the Borland Shade Style dialog, your drop shadow will have a caption above it, as illustrated in Fig. 3-8. Note that you can set the justification of the caption with the Alignment for Caption control group at the bottom of the Borland Shade Style dialog.

Figure 3-8

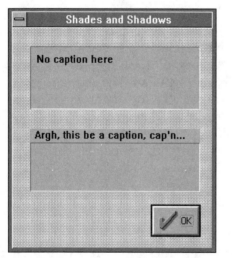

A Borland drop shadow with a caption.

In addition to the drop shadow objects offered by BWCC, there are two line types: embossed horizontal and vertical lines. The tools for these are located immediately under the drop shadow tool in the Resource Workshop dialog editor. These objects have no functional effect on a dialog—they're wholly cosmetic. They're useful to separate areas of drop shadow boxes, for example.

There are a few other things worth mentioning about Resource Workshop. You might want to keep these in mind as you develop dialogs for your applications:

> The Windows gray frames and gray rectangle objects are actually drawn in the same color used for your Windows desktop background, which need not be gray. In my case it's green.

> Clicking on the Test button when you're working with an icon in the current version of Resource Workshop will hang Windows, as of this writing.

> The Windows Text object tool and the Borland Text object tool—the latter being a black T in the lower right corner of the dialog editor toolbox—produce different objects that behave effectively the same, save that Borland's text objects have a gray background by default.

> If your dialog has a button with the IDOK constant as its resource ID, clicking on it will exit the dialog editor's test mode.

> Resizing a Borland bitmap button won't make it any larger.

> Some versions of BWCC.DLL produce mangled bitmap buttons if your Windows screen driver supports more than 256 colors.

> Calling up the Borland Shade Style dialog to change the characteristics of a drop shadow might cause Resource Workshop to generate some spurious warnings. The most common of these is "Resource Workshop 164, Compile Error, Incomplete Expression." Ignore them.

It's probably worth noting that while Borland's custom controls appear different from the standard Windows controls they replace and they result in different resource objects, they behave just like standard Windows objects. Borland's buttons, radio buttons, and check boxes return WM_COMMAND messages to the message handlers of their parent windows with the resource ID of the control in question in the wParam message.

→ Using Borland's custom controls

In order to incorporate Borland's buttons, drop shadows, and other custom control types in the dialogs of your applications, you must do the following:

➢ Add the line #include <bwcc.h> to the other #include directives for your application's C language source files. It should appear after #include <windows.h>.

➢ Call BWCCGetVersion in WinMain before you do anything else. This isn't absolutely necessary, but it's a good check to make sure BWCC.DLL is available.

➢ Add BWCC.LIB to the project file for your application. This library can be found in the \BC\LIB or BORLANDC\LIB directory of your hard drive.

In addition, of course, you must use the Borland control objects rather than the standard Windows control objects in Resource Workshop when you create your application dialogs.

If you want to paint bitmaps in a dialog using something like the DrawImage function discussed in the previous chapter, you will have to refrain from using the BorDlg dialog class for the reasons discussed earlier in this chapter. You might not want your application's dialogs to have varying appearances, however—flat gray for dialogs with bitmaps and textured gray for everything else. There's a way around this. Rather than having WM_CTLCOLOR messages return a handle to a flat gray brush for dialogs with bitmaps in them, they can return a handle to the brush used to paint the window backgrounds for BorDlg class dialogs.

The BWCCGetPattern function returns an HBRUSH brush handle that, when used to paint an area of a window, will result in the same textured gray pattern that appears in BorDlg class dialogs. However, because this is really just a brush applied to the background of a window, you can draw and paint over it.

Here's a WM_CTLCOLOR handler to implement this. It assumes that
there's a POINT object called point and an HBRUSH object called
hbrush.

```
case WM_CTLCOLOR:
 if(HIWORD(lParam)==CTLCOLOR_STATIC ||
    HIWORD(lParam)==CTLCOLOR_DLG) {
      SetBkColor(wParam,RGB(192,192,192));
      SetTextColor(wParam,RGB(0,0,0));
      hbrush=BWCCGetPattern();
      ClientToScreen(hwnd,&point);
      UnrealizeObject(hbrush);
      SetBrushOrg(wParam,point.x,point.y);
      return((DWORD)hbrush);
  }

 if(HIWORD(lParam)==CTLCOLOR_BTN) {
      SetBkColor(wParam,RGB(192,192,192));
      SetTextColor(wParam,RGB(0,0,0));
      hbrush=BWCCGetPattern();
      ClientToScreen(hwnd,&point);
      UnrealizeObject(hbrush);
      SetBrushOrg(wParam,point.x,point.y);
      return((DWORD)hbrush);
  }

  break;
```

Rather than creating a brush or calling GetStockObject to fetch one,
this variation of the WM_CTLCOLOR handler calls BWCCGetPattern
to fetch the brush that BWCC.DLL uses. Note that this is effectively a
stock object—you should not call DeleteObject to destroy it or the
entire fabric of the universe will become twisted and time as we know
it will cease to be.

Actually, this isn't entirely true. Deleting this brush and then
replacing it with another brush will cause all subsequent dialogs
drawn with this brush to be drawn with a new background. This will
affect not only your application, but any other application that makes
calls to BWCC as well. There are good arguments for avoiding this.

The last bit of BWCC lore of note is the function BWCCMessageBox.
Windows defines a function called MessageBox that will open a
dialog, display some text in a window, and wait for some response. It
allows for a variety of icons and button combinations. In the DEMO1
application, the DoMessage function performed much the same

task—the MessageBox call wasn't used because its old-style white dialogs would look peculiar when everything else was gray.

The BWCCMessageBox function accepts the same arguments as the API MessageBox function, except it displays dialogs in keeping with the appearance of other Borland objects. Figure 3-9 illustrates the result of calling BWCCMessageBox. The DoMessage function in the DEMO2 application is really a call to BWCCMessageBox.

Figure 3-9

The BWCCMessageBox function at work.

⇨ Borland's custom controls in real life—DEMO2.CPP

The DEMO2 application works pretty much like DEMO1 from the previous chapter, save that it uses Borland's custom controls and dialog class. It also illustrates how to sneak around most of the limitations of BWCC.DLL. The complete source code for DEMO2.CPP is listed in Fig. 3-10. In addition to DEMO2.CPP, you'll need DEMO2.RC, as shown in Fig. 3-11. Suitable DEF and project files for DEMO2 are included with the source code on the companion disk for this book.

Figure 3-10   *The DEMO2.CPP source code.*

```
/*
    Dialog Demo 2
    Copyright (c) 1993 Alchemy Mindworks Inc.
*/

#include <windows.h>
```

```
#include <bwcc.h>
#include <stdio.h>
#include <stdlib.h>
#include <ctype.h>
#include <alloc.h>
#include <string.h>
#include <dos.h>
#include <time.h>

#define say(s)      MessageBox(NULL,s,"Yo...",MB_OK | MB_ICONSTOP);
#define saynumber(f,s)    {char b[128]; sprintf((LPSTR)b,(LPSTR)f,s); \
    MessageBox(NULL,b,"Debug Message",MB_OK | MB_ICONSTOP); }

#define STRINGSIZE          129         /* how big is a string? */

#ifndef IDHELP
#define IDHELP              998
#endif

#define MESSAGE_STRING      101         /* message box object */

#define FILE_BUTTONS        101
#define FILE_SCROLLBARS     102
#define FILE_COLOURS        103
#define FILE_CHECKBOXES     104
#define FILE_BITMAP         105
#define FILE_LISTBOX        106
#define FILE_COMBOBOX       107
#define FILE_EXIT           199

#define HELPM_INDEX         901
#define HELPM_USING         905
#define HELPM_ABOUT         999

#define COLOUR_REDSET       101
#define COLOUR_GREENSET     102
#define COLOUR_BLUESET      103
#define COLOUR_REDVAL       201
#define COLOUR_GREENVAL     202
#define COLOUR_BLUEVAL      203
#define COLOUR_REDTEXT      301
#define COLOUR_GREENTEXT    302
#define COLOUR_BLUETEXT     303

#define BUTTON_BASE         201
#define BUTTON_BASECOUNT    9

#define BITMAP16            "Bitmap16"
#define BITMAP256           "Bitmap256"

#define SCROLL_HORZTEXT     101
#define SCROLL_VERTTEXT     102
#define SCROLL_HORZVAL      201
```

3-10 *Continued*

```
#define SCROLL_VERTVAL       202
#define SCROLL_MAX           999

#define CHECK_NORMAL         101
#define CHECK_INVERT         102
#define CHECK_HIDE           103
#define CHECK_TITLE          105
#define CHECK_HORZ           201
#define CHECK_VERT           202

#define CHECK_LEFT           184
#define CHECK_TOP            16
#define CHECK_BITMAP         MENUBITMAP

#define LIST_LIST            101
#define LIST_TEXT            "ListText"
#define LIST_END             "ENDMARKER"
#define LIST_SELECT          102
#define LIST_TSELECT         103
#define LIST_BITMAP          "ListBitmap"

#define COMBO_COMBO          101
#define COMBO_TEXT           "ListText"
#define COMBO_SELECT         102
#define COMBO_TSELECT        103
#define COMBO_BITMAP         "ListBitmap"

#define HELPFILE             "DEMO.HLP"

#define DIALOG_KEY           "DialogDemo"

#define DINGBATS             "WingDings"

#define MENUBITMAP           "BitmapMenu"
#define SYS_BITMAP           300

#define MESSAGE_ABOUT        0
#define MESSAGE_HELP         1

#define LIGHTGREY            RGB(192,192,192)

#define RGB_RED              0
#define RGB_GREEN            1
#define RGB_BLUE             2
#define RGB_SIZE             3

#define CreateControlFont()     if(ControlFontName[0]) \
                controlfont=CreateFont(16,0,0,0,0,0,0,0,\
                ANSI_CHARSET,OUT_DEFAULT_PRECIS,CLIP_DEFAULT_PRECIS,\
                DEFAULT_QUALITY,DEFAULT_PITCH | FF_DONTCARE,\
                ControlFontName)
```

```c
#define SetControlFont(hwnd,id) {HWND dlgH;\
                if(controlfont != NULL) {\
                    dlgH=GetDlgItem(hwnd,id);\
                    SendMessage(dlgH,WM_SETFONT,(WORD)controlfont,FALSE);\
                }\
                }

#define DestroyControlFont()    if(controlfont != NULL) \
        DeleteObject(controlfont)

#define DoMessage(hwnd,string)       BWCCMessageBox(hwnd,string, \
        "Message",MB_OK | MB_ICONINFORMATION)

#define CheckOn(item)       SendDlgItemMessage(hwnd,item,BM_SETCHECK,1,0L);
#define CheckOff(item)      SendDlgItemMessage(hwnd,item,BM_SETCHECK,0,0L);
#define ItemOn(item)        { dlgH=GetDlgItem(hwnd,item); EnableWindow(dlgH,TRUE); }
#define ItemOff(item)       { dlgH=GetDlgItem(hwnd,item); EnableWindow(dlgH,FALSE); }
#define IsItemChecked(item)     SendDlgItemMessage(hwnd,item,BM_GETCHECK,0,0L)
#define ItemName(item,string)   { dlgH=GetDlgItem(hwnd,item); \
        SetWindowText(dlgH,(LPSTR)string); }
#define GetItemName(item,string) { dlgH=GetDlgItem(hwnd,item); \
        GetWindowText(dlgH,(LPSTR)string,BIGSTRINGSIZE); }

#ifndef max
#define max(a,b)                (((a)>(b))?(a):(b))
#endif
#ifndef min
#define min(a,b)                (((a)<(b))?(a):(b))
#endif

/* prototypes */
DWORD FAR PASCAL SelectProc(HWND hwnd,WORD message,WORD wParam,LONG lParam);
DWORD FAR PASCAL AboutDlgProc(HWND hwnd,WORD message,WORD wParam,LONG lParam);
DWORD FAR PASCAL ColourDlgProc(HWND hwnd,WORD message,WORD wParam,LONG lParam);
DWORD FAR PASCAL ButtonDlgProc(HWND hwnd,WORD message,WORD wParam,LONG lParam);
DWORD FAR PASCAL MessageDlgProc(HWND hwnd,WORD message,WORD wParam,LONG lParam);
DWORD FAR PASCAL BitmapDlgProc(HWND hwnd,WORD message,WORD wParam,LONG lParam);
DWORD FAR PASCAL ScrollDlgProc(HWND hwnd,WORD message,WORD wParam,LONG lParam);
DWORD FAR PASCAL CheckDlgProc(HWND hwnd,WORD message,WORD wParam,LONG lParam);
DWORD FAR PASCAL ListDlgProc(HWND hwnd,WORD message,WORD wParam,LONG lParam);
DWORD FAR PASCAL ComboDlgProc(HWND hwnd,WORD message,WORD wParam,LONG lParam);

void DrawImage(HDC hdc,int x,int y,HBITMAP image,DWORD op);
void DoColours(HWND hwnd);
void DoButtons(HWND hwnd);
void DoBitmap(HWND hwnd);
void DoScrollbars(HWND hwnd);
void DoCheck(HWND hwnd);
void DoListbox(HWND hwnd);
void DoCombo(HWND hwnd);
void SetHelpSize(HWND hwnd);
void DoHelp(HWND hwnd,LPSTR keyword);
void MakeHelpPathName(LPSTR szFileName);
```

3-10 *Continued*

```
void CentreWindow(HWND hwnd);

int GetDeviceBits(HWND hwnd);
int GetBitmapDimensions(LPSTR name,LPINT x,LPINT y,LPINT bits);

LPSTR FetchString(unsigned int n);

/* globals*/
char szAppName[]="DialogDemoTwo";
char ControlFontName[STRINGSIZE+1]="Arial";

LPSTR messagehook;
HANDLE hInst;
HFONT controlfont=NULL;

#pragma warn -par
int PASCAL WinMain(HANDLE hInstance,HANDLE hPrevInstance,
    LPSTR lpszCmdParam,int nCmdShow)
{
    FARPROC dlgProc;
    int r=0;

    BWCCGetVersion();
    hInst=hInstance;

    dlgProc=MakeProcInstance((FARPROC)SelectProc,hInst);
    r=DialogBox(hInst,"MainScreen",NULL,dlgProc);

    FreeProcInstance(dlgProc);

    return(r);
}

DWORD FAR PASCAL SelectProc(HWND hwnd,WORD message,WORD wParam,LONG lParam)
{
    HMENU hmenu;
    FARPROC lpfnDlgProc;
    PAINTSTRUCT ps;
    static HICON hIcon;
    static HBITMAP hBitmap;
    char b[129];

    switch(message) {
        case WM_SYSCOMMAND:
            switch(wParam & 0xfff0) {
                case SC_CLOSE:
                    SendMessage(hwnd,WM_COMMAND,FILE_EXIT,0L);
                    break;
            }
            switch(wParam) {
                case SYS_BITMAP:
```

```
                    SendMessage(hwnd,WM_COMMAND,FILE_BITMAP,0L);
                    break;
            }
            break;
        case WM_INITDIALOG:
            SetHelpSize(hwnd);

            GetProfileString(DIALOG_KEY,"ControlFont",
              ControlFontName,b,STRINGSIZE);
            if(lstrlen(b)) lstrcpy(ControlFontName,b);
            CreateControlFont();

            hIcon=LoadIcon(hInst,szAppName);
            SetClassWord(hwnd,GCW_HICON,(WORD)hIcon);
            CentreWindow(hwnd);

            hmenu=GetSystemMenu(hwnd,FALSE);
            hBitmap=LoadBitmap(hInst,MENUBITMAP);
            AppendMenu(hmenu,MF_SEPARATOR,NULL,NULL);
            AppendMenu(hmenu,MF_BITMAP,SYS_BITMAP,(LPSTR)(LONG)hBitmap);
            break;
        case WM_PAINT:
            BeginPaint(hwnd,&ps);
            EndPaint(hwnd,&ps);
            break;
        case WM_COMMAND:
            switch(wParam) {
                case HELPM_INDEX:
                    MakeHelpPathName(b);
                    WinHelp(hwnd,b,HELP_INDEX,NULL);
                    break;
                case HELPM_USING:
                    WinHelp(hwnd,"",HELP_HELPONHELP,NULL);
                    break;
                case HELPM_ABOUT:
                    if((lpfnDlgProc=MakeProcInstance
                      ((FARPROC)AboutDlgProc,hInst)) != NULL) {
                        DialogBox(hInst,"AboutBox",hwnd,lpfnDlgProc);
                        FreeProcInstance(lpfnDlgProc);
                    }
                    break;
                case FILE_BUTTONS:
                    DoButtons(hwnd);
                    break;
                case FILE_COLOURS:
                    DoColours(hwnd);
                    break;
                case FILE_BITMAP:
                    DoBitmap(hwnd);
                    break;
                case FILE_SCROLLBARS:
                    DoScrollbars(hwnd);
                    break;
                case FILE_CHECKBOXES:
```

139

3-10 *Continued*

```
                DoCheck(hwnd);
                break;
            case FILE_LISTBOX:
                DoListbox(hwnd);
                break;
            case FILE_COMBOBOX:
                DoCombo(hwnd);
                break;
            case FILE_EXIT:
                MakeHelpPathName(b);
                WinHelp(hwnd,b,HELP_QUIT,NULL);

                DeleteObject(hBitmap);
                FreeResource(hIcon);
                DestroyControlFont();
                PostQuitMessage(0);
                break;
        }
        break;

    }

    return(FALSE);
}

void DoCombo(HWND hwnd)
{
    FARPROC lpfnDlgProc;

    if((lpfnDlgProc=MakeProcInstance((FARPROC)ComboDlgProc,hInst)) != NULL) {
        DialogBox(hInst,"ComboBox",hwnd,lpfnDlgProc);
        FreeProcInstance(lpfnDlgProc);
    }
}

DWORD FAR PASCAL ComboDlgProc(HWND hwnd,WORD message,WORD wParam,LONG lParam)
{
    PAINTSTRUCT ps;
    HWND dlgH;
    HDC hdc;
    HANDLE handle;
    HBITMAP hBitmap;
    RECT rect;
    POINT point;
    HBRUSH hbrush;
    LPSTR p;
    long l;
    char b[129];
    int i,x,y;

    switch(message) {
```

```
case WM_INITDIALOG:
    if((handle=LoadResource(hInst,
       FindResource(hInst,COMBO_TEXT,RT_RCDATA))) != NULL) {

        if((p=(LPSTR)LockResource(handle))!=NULL) {
            for(b[0]=0;;) {
                for(i=0;p[i] >= 32 && i < 129;++i) b[i]=p[i];
                b[i++]=0;
                if(!lstrcmp(b,LIST_END)) break;
                p+=i;
                while(*p==10) ++p;
                SendDlgItemMessage(hwnd,COMBO_COMBO,
                    CB_INSERTSTRING,-1,(LONG)b);
            }

            UnlockResource(handle);
        }
        FreeResource(handle);
    }

    SendDlgItemMessage(hwnd,COMBO_COMBO,CB_SETCURSEL,0,0L);

    SetControlFont(hwnd,COMBO_COMBO);
    SetControlFont(hwnd,COMBO_SELECT);
    SetControlFont(hwnd,COMBO_TSELECT);

    CentreWindow(hwnd);

    break;
case WM_CTLCOLOR:
    if(HIWORD(lParam)==CTLCOLOR_STATIC ||
       HIWORD(lParam)==CTLCOLOR_DLG) {
        SetBkColor(wParam,RGB(192,192,192));
        SetTextColor(wParam,RGB(0,0,0));

        hbrush=BWCCGetPattern();
        ClientToScreen(hwnd,&point);

        UnrealizeObject(hbrush);
        SetBrushOrg(wParam,point.x,point.y);

        return((DWORD)hbrush);

    }
    if(HIWORD(lParam)==CTLCOLOR_BTN) {
        SetBkColor(wParam,RGB(192,192,192));
        SetTextColor(wParam,RGB(0,0,0));

        hbrush=BWCCGetPattern();
        ClientToScreen(hwnd,&point);
        UnrealizeObject(hbrush);
        SetBrushOrg(wParam,point.x,point.y);
```

3-10 *Continued*

```
                return((DWORD)hbrush);
            }
            break;
        case WM_PAINT:
            hdc=BeginPaint(hwnd,&ps);

            if(GetBitmapDimensions(COMBO_BITMAP,&x,&y,&i)) {
                GetClientRect(hwnd,&rect);
                if((hBitmap=LoadResource(hInst,FindResource(hInst,
                  COMBO_BITMAP,RT_BITMAP))) != NULL) {
                    DrawImage(hdc,rect.right-rect.left-x,0,hBitmap,SRCAND);
                    FreeResource(hBitmap);
                }
            }

            EndPaint(hwnd,&ps);
            break;
        case WM_COMMAND:
            switch(wParam) {
                case IDHELP:
                    DoHelp(hwnd,(LPSTR)"Combobox");
                    break;
                case COMBO_COMBO:
                    switch(HIWORD(lParam)) {
                        case CBN_DBLCLK:
                            SendMessage(hwnd,WM_COMMAND,IDOK,0L);
                            break;
                        case CBN_SELCHANGE:
                            if((l=SendDlgItemMessage(hwnd,
                              COMBO_COMBO,CB_GETCURSEL,0,0L)) != LB_ERR) {
                                SendDlgItemMessage(hwnd,COMBO_COMBO,
                                CB_GETLBTEXT,(unsigned int)l,(LONG)(LPSTR)b);
                                ItemName(COMBO_SELECT,b);
                            }
                            break;
                    }
                    break;
                case IDOK:
                    EndDialog(hwnd,wParam);
                    break;
            }
            break;
    }

    return(FALSE);
}

void DoListbox(HWND hwnd)
{
    FARPROC lpfnDlgProc;
```

```
            if((lpfnDlgProc=MakeProcInstance((FARPROC)ListDlgProc,hInst)) != NULL) {
                DialogBox(hInst,"ListBox",hwnd,lpfnDlgProc);
                FreeProcInstance(lpfnDlgProc);
            }
        }

DWORD FAR PASCAL ListDlgProc(HWND hwnd,WORD message,WORD wParam,LONG lParam)
{
        PAINTSTRUCT ps;
        HWND dlgH;
        HDC hdc;
        HANDLE handle;
        HBITMAP hBitmap;
        RECT rect;
        LPSTR p;
        POINT point;
        HBRUSH hbrush;
        long l;
        char b[129];
        int i,x,y;

        switch(message) {
            case WM_INITDIALOG:
                if((handle=LoadResource(hInst,FindResource(hInst,
                  LIST_TEXT,RT_RCDATA))) != NULL) {

                    if((p=(LPSTR)LockResource(handle))!=NULL) {
                        for(b[0]=0;;) {
                            for(i=0;p[i] >= 32 && i < 129;++i) b[i]=p[i];
                            b[i++]=0;
                            if(!lstrcmp(b,LIST_END)) break;
                            p+=i;
                            while(*p==10) ++p;
                            SendDlgItemMessage(hwnd,LIST_LIST,LB_INSERTSTRING,
                                -1,(LONG)b);
                        }

                    UnlockResource(handle);
                    }
                    FreeResource(handle);
                }

            SetControlFont(hwnd,LIST_LIST);
            SetControlFont(hwnd,LIST_SELECT);
            SetControlFont(hwnd,LIST_TSELECT);

            CentreWindow(hwnd);

            break;
            case WM_CTLCOLOR:
                if(HIWORD(lParam)==CTLCOLOR_STATIC ||
                    HIWORD(lParam)==CTLCOLOR_DLG) {
                  SetBkColor(wParam,RGB(192,192,192));
```

143

3-10 *Continued*

```
                SetTextColor(wParam,RGB(0,0,0));

                hbrush=BWCCGetPattern();
                ClientToScreen(hwnd,&point);

                UnrealizeObject(hbrush);
                SetBrushOrg(wParam,point.x,point.y);

                return((DWORD)hbrush);

            }
        if(HIWORD(lParam)==CTLCOLOR_BTN) {
            SetBkColor(wParam,RGB(192,192,192));
            SetTextColor(wParam,RGB(0,0,0));

            hbrush=BWCCGetPattern();
            ClientToScreen(hwnd,&point);
            UnrealizeObject(hbrush);
            SetBrushOrg(wParam,point.x,point.y);

            return((DWORD)hbrush);
        }
        break;
    case WM_PAINT:
        hdc=BeginPaint(hwnd,&ps);

        if(GetBitmapDimensions(LIST_BITMAP,&x,&y,&i)) {
            GetClientRect(hwnd,&rect);
            if((hBitmap=LoadResource(hInst,FindResource(hInst,
                LIST_BITMAP,RT_BITMAP))) != NULL) {
                DrawImage(hdc,rect.right-rect.left-x,0,hBitmap,SRCAND);
                FreeResource(hBitmap);
            }
        }

        EndPaint(hwnd,&ps);
        break;
    case WM_COMMAND:
        switch(wParam) {
            case IDHELP:
                DoHelp(hwnd,(LPSTR)"Listbox");
                break;
            case LIST_LIST:
                switch(HIWORD(lParam)) {
                    case LBN_DBLCLK:
                        SendMessage(hwnd,WM_COMMAND,IDOK,0L);
                        break;
                    case LBN_SELCHANGE:
                        if((l=SendDlgItemMessage(hwnd,LIST_LIST,
                            LB_GETCURSEL,0,0L)) != LB_ERR) {
                            SendDlgItemMessage(hwnd,LIST_LIST,
```

```
                                      LB_GETTEXT,(unsigned int)l,(LONG)(LPSTR)b);
                              ItemName(LIST_SELECT,b);
                          }
                          break;
                  }
                  break;
              case IDOK:
                  EndDialog(hwnd,wParam);
                  break;
          }
          break;
      }

      return(FALSE);
}

void DoCheck(HWND hwnd)
{
      FARPROC lpfnDlgProc;

      if((lpfnDlgProc=MakeProcInstance((FARPROC)CheckDlgProc,hInst)) != NULL) {
          DialogBox(hInst,"CheckBox",hwnd,lpfnDlgProc);
          FreeProcInstance(lpfnDlgProc);
      }
}

DWORD FAR PASCAL CheckDlgProc(HWND hwnd,WORD message,WORD wParam,LONG lParam)
{
      PAINTSTRUCT ps;
      HBITMAP hBitmap;
      HPEN hPen;
      POINT point;
      HDC hdc;
      HBRUSH hbrush;
      int i,x,y;

      switch(message) {
          case WM_INITDIALOG:
              SetControlFont(hwnd,CHECK_NORMAL);
              SetControlFont(hwnd,CHECK_INVERT);
              SetControlFont(hwnd,CHECK_HIDE);
              SetControlFont(hwnd,CHECK_HORZ);
              SetControlFont(hwnd,CHECK_VERT);
              SetControlFont(hwnd,CHECK_TITLE);

              CheckOn(CHECK_NORMAL);

              CentreWindow(hwnd);

              break;
          case WM_CTLCOLOR:
              if(HIWORD(lParam)==CTLCOLOR_STATIC ||
                 HIWORD(lParam)==CTLCOLOR_DLG) {
```

3-10 *Continued*

```
        SetBkColor(wParam,RGB(192,192,192));
        SetTextColor(wParam,RGB(0,0,0));

        hbrush=BWCCGetPattern();
        ClientToScreen(hwnd,&point);

        UnrealizeObject(hbrush);
        SetBrushOrg(wParam,point.x,point.y);

        return((DWORD)hbrush);

    }
    if(HIWORD(lParam)==CTLCOLOR_BTN) {
        SetBkColor(wParam,RGB(192,192,192));
        SetTextColor(wParam,RGB(0,0,0));

        hbrush=BWCCGetPattern();
        ClientToScreen(hwnd,&point);
        UnrealizeObject(hbrush);
        SetBrushOrg(wParam,point.x,point.y);

        return((DWORD)hbrush);
    }
    break;
case WM_PAINT:
    hdc=BeginPaint(hwnd,&ps);

        if(GetBitmapDimensions(CHECK_BITMAP,&x,&y,&i)) {

            if((hBitmap=LoadResource(hInst,FindResource(hInst,
              CHECK_BITMAP,RT_BITMAP))) != NULL) {

            DrawImage(hdc,CHECK_LEFT,CHECK_TOP,hBitmap,SRCCOPY);
            FreeResource(hBitmap);

            if(IsItemChecked(CHECK_HIDE)) {
                SelectObject(hdc,GetStockObject(LTGRAY_BRUSH));
                SelectObject(hdc,GetStockObject(NULL_PEN));
                Rectangle(hdc,CHECK_LEFT,CHECK_TOP,
                        CHECK_LEFT+x+1,
                        CHECK_TOP+y+1);
                SelectObject(hdc,GetStockObject(NULL_BRUSH));
            }
            if(IsItemChecked(CHECK_INVERT)) {
                SelectObject(hdc,GetStockObject(WHITE_BRUSH));
                SelectObject(hdc,GetStockObject(NULL_PEN));
                SetROP2(hdc,R2_NOT);
                Rectangle(hdc,CHECK_LEFT,CHECK_TOP,
                        CHECK_LEFT+x+1,
                        CHECK_TOP+y+1);
            }
```

```
                        if(IsItemChecked(CHECK_HORZ)) {
                            hPen=CreatePen(PS_SOLID,2,LIGHTGREY);
                            SelectObject(hdc,hPen);
                            for(i=0;i<=y;i+=4) {
                                MoveTo(hdc,CHECK_LEFT,CHECK_TOP+i);
                                LineTo(hdc,CHECK_LEFT+x,CHECK_TOP+i);
                            }
                            DeleteObject(hPen);
                        }
                        if(IsItemChecked(CHECK_VERT)) {
                            hPen=CreatePen(PS_SOLID,2,LIGHTGREY);
                            SelectObject(hdc,hPen);
                            for(i=0;i<=x;i+=4) {
                                MoveTo(hdc,CHECK_LEFT+i,CHECK_TOP);
                                LineTo(hdc,CHECK_LEFT+i,CHECK_TOP+y);
                            }
                            DeleteObject(hPen);
                        }
                    }
                }

            EndPaint(hwnd,&ps);
            break;
        case WM_COMMAND:
            switch(wParam) {
                case IDHELP:
                    DoHelp(hwnd,(LPSTR)"Checkboxes");
                    break;
                case CHECK_NORMAL:
                case CHECK_HIDE:
                case CHECK_INVERT:
                case CHECK_HORZ:
                case CHECK_VERT:
                    InvalidateRect(hwnd,NULL,FALSE);
                    break;
                case IDOK:
                    EndDialog(hwnd,wParam);
                    break;
            }
            break;
    }

    return(FALSE);
}

void DoScrollbars(HWND hwnd)
{
    FARPROC lpfnDlgProc;

    if((lpfnDlgProc=MakeProcInstance((FARPROC)ScrollDlgProc,hInst)) != NULL) {
        DialogBox(hInst,"ScrollBox",hwnd,lpfnDlgProc);
        FreeProcInstance(lpfnDlgProc);
    }
```

3-10 *Continued*

```
}

DWORD FAR PASCAL ScrollDlgProc(HWND hwnd,WORD message,WORD wParam,LONG lParam)
{
    PAINTSTRUCT ps;
    HWND dlgH;
    char b[33];
    int n,jump,pos;

    switch(message) {
        case WM_INITDIALOG:
            SetScrollRange(hwnd,SB_HORZ,0,SCROLL_MAX,TRUE);
            SetScrollPos(hwnd,SB_HORZ,SCROLL_MAX/2,TRUE);
            n=GetScrollPos(hwnd,SB_HORZ);

            dlgH=GetDlgItem(hwnd,SCROLL_HORZVAL);
            sprintf(b," %d",n);
            SetWindowText(dlgH,b);
            EnableWindow(dlgH,TRUE);

            SetScrollRange(hwnd,SB_VERT,0,SCROLL_MAX,TRUE);
            SetScrollPos(hwnd,SB_VERT,SCROLL_MAX/2,TRUE);
            n=GetScrollPos(hwnd,SB_VERT);

            dlgH=GetDlgItem(hwnd,SCROLL_VERTVAL);
            sprintf(b," %d",n);
            SetWindowText(dlgH,b);
            EnableWindow(dlgH,TRUE);

            SetControlFont(hwnd,SCROLL_HORZVAL);
            SetControlFont(hwnd,SCROLL_VERTVAL);
            SetControlFont(hwnd,SCROLL_HORZTEXT);
            SetControlFont(hwnd,SCROLL_VERTTEXT);

            CentreWindow(hwnd);
            break;
        case WM_VSCROLL:
            pos=GetScrollPos(hwnd,SB_VERT);
            jump=SCROLL_MAX/10;
            switch(wParam) {
                case SB_LINEUP:
                    pos-=1;
                    break;
                case SB_LINEDOWN:
                    pos+=1;
                    break;
                case SB_PAGEUP:
                    pos-=jump;
                    break;
                case SB_PAGEDOWN:
                    pos+=jump;
```

```
                break;
            case SB_THUMBPOSITION:
                pos=LOWORD(lParam);
                break;
        }

        if(pos < 0 ) pos=0;
        else if(pos >= SCROLL_MAX) pos=SCROLL_MAX;

        if(pos != GetScrollPos(hwnd,SB_VERT)) {
            SetScrollPos(hwnd,SB_VERT,pos,TRUE);
            sprintf(b," %d",pos);
            ItemName(SCROLL_VERTVAL,b);
            InvalidateRect(hwnd,NULL,FALSE);
        }
        break;
    case WM_HSCROLL:
        pos=GetScrollPos(hwnd,SB_HORZ);
        jump=SCROLL_MAX/10;
        switch(wParam) {
            case SB_LINEUP:
                pos-=1;
                break;
            case SB_LINEDOWN:
                pos+=1;
                break;
            case SB_PAGEUP:
                pos-=jump;
                break;
            case SB_PAGEDOWN:
                pos+=jump;
                break;
            case SB_THUMBPOSITION:
                pos=LOWORD(lParam);
                break;
        }

        if(pos < 0 ) pos=0;
        else if(pos >= SCROLL_MAX) pos=SCROLL_MAX;

        if(pos != GetScrollPos(hwnd,SB_HORZ)) {
            SetScrollPos(hwnd,SB_HORZ,pos,TRUE);
            sprintf(b," %d",pos);
            ItemName(SCROLL_HORZVAL,b);
            InvalidateRect(hwnd,NULL,FALSE);
        }
        break;
    case WM_PAINT:
        BeginPaint(hwnd,&ps);
        EndPaint(hwnd,&ps);
        break;
    case WM_COMMAND:
        switch(wParam) {
```

3-10 *Continued*

```
                case IDHELP:
                    DoHelp(hwnd,(LPSTR)"Scrollbars");
                    break;
                case IDOK:
                    EndDialog(hwnd,wParam);
                    break;
            }
            break;
    }

    return(FALSE);
}

void DoBitmap(HWND hwnd)
{
    FARPROC lpfnDlgProc;

    if((lpfnDlgProc=MakeProcInstance((FARPROC)BitmapDlgProc,hInst)) != NULL) {
        DialogBox(hInst,"BitmapBox",hwnd,lpfnDlgProc);
        FreeProcInstance(lpfnDlgProc);
    }
}

DWORD FAR PASCAL BitmapDlgProc(HWND hwnd,WORD message,WORD wParam,LONG lParam)
{
    PAINTSTRUCT ps;
    HBITMAP hBitmap;
    HMENU hmenu;
    HDC hdc;
    LPSTR p;
    POINT point;
    HBRUSH hbrush;
    static char *bitsize[2]={ BITMAP16,BITMAP256 };
    int i,j,x,y;

    switch(message) {
        case WM_INITDIALOG:
            if(GetDeviceBits(hwnd) <= 4) p=bitsize[0];
            else p=bitsize[1];

            if(GetBitmapDimensions(p,&x,&y,&i)) {
                i=(GetSystemMetrics(SM_CXSCREEN)-x)/2;
                j=(GetSystemMetrics(SM_CYSCREEN)-y)/2;
                SetWindowPos(hwnd,NULL,i,j,
                    x,y+GetSystemMetrics(SM_CYCAPTION),SWP_NOZORDER);
            }
            hmenu=GetSystemMenu(hwnd,FALSE);
            AppendMenu(hmenu,MF_SEPARATOR,NULL,NULL);
            AppendMenu(hmenu,MF_STRING,IDHELP,FetchString(MESSAGE_HELP));
            break;
        case WM_CTLCOLOR:
```

```
        if(HIWORD(lParam)==CTLCOLOR_STATIC ||
          HIWORD(lParam)==CTLCOLOR_DLG) {
          SetBkColor(wParam,RGB(192,192,192));
          SetTextColor(wParam,RGB(0,0,0));

          hbrush=BWCCGetPattern();
          ClientToScreen(hwnd,&point);

          UnrealizeObject(hbrush);
          SetBrushOrg(wParam,point.x,point.y);

          return((DWORD)hbrush);

        }
        if(HIWORD(lParam)==CTLCOLOR_BTN) {
          SetBkColor(wParam,RGB(192,192,192));
          SetTextColor(wParam,RGB(0,0,0));

          hbrush=BWCCGetPattern();
          ClientToScreen(hwnd,&point);
          UnrealizeObject(hbrush);
          SetBrushOrg(wParam,point.x,point.y);

          return((DWORD)hbrush);
        }
        break;

    case WM_PAINT:
        hdc=BeginPaint(hwnd,&ps);
        if(GetDeviceBits(hwnd) <= 4) p=bitsize[0];
        else p=bitsize[1];

        if((hBitmap=LoadResource(hInst,FindResource(hInst,p,RT_BITMAP))) != NULL) {
            DrawImage(hdc,0,0,hBitmap,SRCCOPY);
            FreeResource(hBitmap);
        }

        EndPaint(hwnd,&ps);
        break;
    case WM_SYSCOMMAND:
        switch(wParam & 0xfff0) {
            case SC_CLOSE:
                SendMessage(hwnd,WM_COMMAND,IDOK,0L);
                break;
        }
        switch(wParam) {
            case IDHELP:
                SendMessage(hwnd,WM_COMMAND,IDHELP,0L);
                break;
        }
        break;
    case WM_COMMAND:
        switch(wParam) {
```

151

3-10 *Continued*

```
                case IDHELP:
                    DoHelp(hwnd,(LPSTR)"Bitmaps");
                    break;
                case IDOK:
                    EndDialog(hwnd,wParam);
                    break;
            }
            break;
    }

    return(FALSE);
}

void DoButtons(HWND hwnd)
{
    FARPROC lpfnDlgProc;

    if((lpfnDlgProc=MakeProcInstance((FARPROC)ButtonDlgProc,hInst)) != NULL) {
        DialogBox(hInst,"ButtonBox",hwnd,lpfnDlgProc);
        FreeProcInstance(lpfnDlgProc);
    }
}

DWORD FAR PASCAL ButtonDlgProc(HWND hwnd,WORD message,WORD wParam,LONG lParam)
{
    static HFONT hFont;
    PAINTSTRUCT ps;
    HWND dlgH;
    int i;

    switch(message) {
        case WM_INITDIALOG:
            if((hFont=CreateFont(32,0,0,0,0,0,0,0,
                SYMBOL_CHARSET,OUT_DEFAULT_PRECIS,CLIP_DEFAULT_PRECIS,
                DEFAULT_QUALITY,DEFAULT_PITCH | FF_DONTCARE,
                DINGBATS)) != NULL) {
                for(i=0;i<BUTTON_BASECOUNT;++i) {
                    dlgH=GetDlgItem(hwnd,BUTTON_BASE+i);
                    SendMessage(dlgH,WM_SETFONT,(WORD)hFont,FALSE);
                }
            }

            CentreWindow(hwnd);

            break;
        case WM_PAINT:
            BeginPaint(hwnd,&ps);
            EndPaint(hwnd,&ps);
            break;
        case WM_COMMAND:
            switch(wParam) {
```

```
                    case IDHELP:
                        DoHelp(hwnd,(LPSTR)"Buttons");
                        break;
                    case IDOK:
                        if(hFont != NULL) DeleteObject(hFont);
                        EndDialog(hwnd,wParam);
                        break;
                    default:
                        DoMessage(hwnd,FetchString(wParam));
                        break;
                }
                break;
        }

        return(FALSE);
}

void DoColours(HWND hwnd)
{
        FARPROC lpfnDlgProc;

        if((lpfnDlgProc=MakeProcInstance((FARPROC)ColourDlgProc,hInst)) != NULL) {
            DialogBox(hInst,"ColourBox",hwnd,lpfnDlgProc);
            FreeProcInstance(lpfnDlgProc);
        }
}

DWORD FAR PASCAL ColourDlgProc(HWND hwnd,WORD message,WORD wParam,LONG lParam)
{
        static HBRUSH hBrush[RGB_SIZE+1];
        static COLORREF colour=LIGHTGREY;
        PAINTSTRUCT ps;
        POINT point;
        HWND dlgH;
        HDC hdc;
        char b[33];
        int n,w;

        switch(message) {
            case WM_INITDIALOG:
                hBrush[RGB_RED]=CreateSolidBrush(RGB(255,0,0));
                hBrush[RGB_GREEN]=CreateSolidBrush(RGB(0,255,0));
                hBrush[RGB_BLUE]=CreateSolidBrush(RGB(0,0,255));
                hBrush[RGB_SIZE]=CreateSolidBrush(colour);

                dlgH=GetDlgItem(hwnd,COLOUR_REDSET);
                SetScrollRange(dlgH,SB_CTL,0,255,TRUE);
                SetScrollPos(dlgH,SB_CTL,GetRValue(colour),TRUE);
                n=GetScrollPos(dlgH,SB_CTL);

                dlgH=GetDlgItem(hwnd,COLOUR_REDVAL);
                sprintf(b,"  %d",n);
                SetWindowText(dlgH,b);
```

3-10 *Continued*

```
            EnableWindow(dlgH,TRUE);

            dlgH=GetDlgItem(hwnd,COLOUR_GREENSET);
            SetScrollRange(dlgH,SB_CTL,0,255,TRUE);
            SetScrollPos(dlgH,SB_CTL,GetGValue(colour),TRUE);
            n=GetScrollPos(dlgH,SB_CTL);

            dlgH=GetDlgItem(hwnd,COLOUR_GREENVAL);
            sprintf(b,"  %d",n);
            SetWindowText(dlgH,b);
            EnableWindow(dlgH,TRUE);

            dlgH=GetDlgItem(hwnd,COLOUR_BLUESET);
            SetScrollRange(dlgH,SB_CTL,0,255,TRUE);
            SetScrollPos(dlgH,SB_CTL,GetBValue(colour),TRUE);
            n=GetScrollPos(dlgH,SB_CTL);

            dlgH=GetDlgItem(hwnd,COLOUR_BLUEVAL);
            sprintf(b,"  %d",n);
            SetWindowText(dlgH,b);
            EnableWindow(dlgH,TRUE);

            SetControlFont(hwnd,COLOUR_REDTEXT);
            SetControlFont(hwnd,COLOUR_GREENTEXT);
            SetControlFont(hwnd,COLOUR_BLUETEXT);

            SetControlFont(hwnd,COLOUR_REDVAL);
            SetControlFont(hwnd,COLOUR_GREENVAL);
            SetControlFont(hwnd,COLOUR_BLUEVAL);

            CentreWindow(hwnd);

            break;
        case WM_CTLCOLOR:
            if(HIWORD(lParam)==CTLCOLOR_SCROLLBAR) {
                SetBkColor(wParam,GetSysColor(COLOR_CAPTIONTEXT));
                SetTextColor(wParam,GetSysColor(COLOR_WINDOWFRAME));
                w=GetWindowWord(LOWORD(lParam),GWW_ID);
                switch(w) {
                    case COLOUR_REDSET:
                        ClientToScreen(hwnd,&point);
                        UnrealizeObject(hBrush[RGB_RED]);
                        SetBrushOrg(wParam,point.x,point.y);
                        return((DWORD)hBrush[RGB_RED]);
                    case COLOUR_GREENSET:
                        ClientToScreen(hwnd,&point);
                        UnrealizeObject(hBrush[RGB_GREEN]);
                        SetBrushOrg(wParam,point.x,point.y);
                        return((DWORD)hBrush[RGB_GREEN]);
                    case COLOUR_BLUESET:
                        ClientToScreen(hwnd,&point);
```

```
                    UnrealizeObject(hBrush[RGB_BLUE]);
                    SetBrushOrg(wParam,point.x,point.y);
                    return((DWORD)hBrush[RGB_BLUE]);
            }
        }
        else if(HIWORD(lParam)==CTLCOLOR_DLG) {
            SetBkColor(wParam,LIGHTGREY);
            SetTextColor(wParam,RGB(0,0,0));

            ClientToScreen(hwnd,&point);
            UnrealizeObject(hBrush[RGB_SIZE]);
            SetBrushOrg(wParam,point.x,point.y);

            return((DWORD)hBrush[RGB_SIZE]);
        }
        break;
    case WM_HSCROLL:
        w=GetWindowWord(HIWORD(lParam),GWW_ID);

        dlgH=GetDlgItem(hwnd,w);
        n=GetScrollPos(dlgH,SB_CTL);
        switch(wParam) {
            case SB_LINEUP:
                n-=1;
                break;
            case SB_LINEDOWN:
                n+=1;
                break;
            case SB_PAGEUP:
                n-=10;
                break;
            case SB_PAGEDOWN:
                n+=10;
                break;
            case SB_THUMBPOSITION:
                n=LOWORD(lParam);
                break;
        }

        if(n < 0) n=0;
        else if(n > 255) n=255;

        if(n != GetScrollPos(dlgH,SB_CTL)) {
            SetScrollPos(dlgH,SB_CTL,n,TRUE);
            switch(w) {
                case COLOUR_REDSET:
                    dlgH=GetDlgItem(hwnd,COLOUR_REDVAL);
                    sprintf(b,"  %d",n);
                    SetWindowText(dlgH,b);
                    colour=RGB(n,GetGValue(colour),GetBValue(colour));
                    break;
                case COLOUR_GREENSET:
                    dlgH=GetDlgItem(hwnd,COLOUR_GREENVAL);
```

3-10 *Continued*

```
                        sprintf(b," %d",n);
                        SetWindowText(dlgH,b);
                        colour=RGB(GetRValue(colour),n,GetBValue(colour));
                        break;
                    case COLOUR_BLUESET:
                        dlgH=GetDlgItem(hwnd,COLOUR_BLUEVAL);
                        sprintf(b," %d",n);
                        SetWindowText(dlgH,b);
                        colour=RGB(GetRValue(colour),GetGValue(colour),n);
                        break;
                }
                DeleteObject(hBrush[RGB_SIZE]);
                hdc=GetDC(hwnd);
                hBrush[RGB_SIZE]=CreateSolidBrush(colour);

                ReleaseDC(hwnd,hdc);

                InvalidateRect(hwnd,NULL,TRUE);
            }
            return(FALSE);
        case WM_PAINT:
            BeginPaint(hwnd,&ps);
            EndPaint(hwnd,&ps);
            break;
        case WM_COMMAND:
            switch(wParam) {
                case IDHELP:
                    DoHelp(hwnd,(LPSTR)"Colours");
                    break;
                case IDOK:
                    if(hBrush[RGB_RED] != NULL)
                        DeleteObject(hBrush[RGB_RED]);
                    if(hBrush[RGB_GREEN] != NULL)
                        DeleteObject(hBrush[RGB_GREEN]);
                    if(hBrush[RGB_BLUE] != NULL)
                        DeleteObject(hBrush[RGB_BLUE]);
                        if(hBrush[RGB_SIZE] != NULL)
                        DeleteObject(hBrush[RGB_SIZE]);
                    EndDialog(hwnd,wParam);
                    break;
            }
            break;
    }

    return(FALSE);
}

DWORD FAR PASCAL AboutDlgProc(HWND hwnd,WORD message,WORD wParam,LONG lParam)
{
    HWND dlgH;
```

```
        switch(message) {
            case WM_INITDIALOG:
                ItemName(MESSAGE_STRING,FetchString(MESSAGE_ABOUT));
                CentreWindow(hwnd);
                SetControlFont(hwnd,MESSAGE_STRING);
                return(FALSE);
            case WM_COMMAND:
                switch(wParam) {
                    case IDOK:
                        EndDialog(hwnd,wParam);
                        return(FALSE);
                }
                break;
        }

        return(FALSE);
}

void CentreWindow(HWND hwnd)
{
    RECT rect;
    unsigned int x,y;

    GetWindowRect(hwnd,&rect);
    x=(GetSystemMetrics(SM_CXSCREEN)-(rect.right-rect.left))/2;
    y=(GetSystemMetrics(SM_CYSCREEN)-(rect.bottom-rect.top))/2;
    SetWindowPos(hwnd,NULL,x,y,rect.right-rect.left,rect.bottom-rect.top,
      SWP_NOSIZE);
}

LPSTR FetchString(unsigned int n)
{
    static char b[257];

    if(!LoadString(hInst,n,b,256))
        lstrcpy(b,"String table error - this application may be damaged");
    return(b);
}

int GetDeviceBits(HWND hwnd)
{
    HDC hdc;
    int i;

    hdc=GetDC(hwnd);
    i=(GetDeviceCaps(hdc,PLANES) * GetDeviceCaps(hdc,BITSPIXEL));
    ReleaseDC(hwnd,hdc);
    if(i > 8) i=24;
    return(i);
}

void DrawImage(HDC hdc,int x,int y,HBITMAP image,DWORD op)
{
```

3-10 *Continued*

```
LPSTR p,pi;
HDC hMemoryDC;
HBITMAP hBitmap,hOldBitmap;
LPBITMAPINFO bh;
HANDLE hPal;
LOGPALETTE *pLogPal;
int i,n;

if(image==NULL) return;

if((p=LockResource(image))==NULL) return;

bh=(LPBITMAPINFO)p;
if(bh->bmiHeader.biBitCount > 8) n=256;
else n=(1<<bh->bmiHeader.biBitCount);

pi=p+sizeof(BITMAPINFOHEADER)+n*sizeof(RGBQUAD);

if((pLogPal=(LOGPALETTE *)LocalAlloc(LMEM_FIXED,
  sizeof(LOGPALETTE)+256*sizeof(PALETTEENTRY))) != NULL) {
    pLogPal->palVersion=0x0300;
    pLogPal->palNumEntries=n;

    for(i=0;i<n;i++) {
        pLogPal->palPalEntry[i].peRed=bh->bmiColors[i].rgbRed;
        pLogPal->palPalEntry[i].peGreen=bh->bmiColors[i].rgbGreen;
        pLogPal->palPalEntry[i].peBlue=bh->bmiColors[i].rgbBlue;
        pLogPal->palPalEntry[i].peFlags=0;
    }

    hPal=CreatePalette(pLogPal);
    LocalFree((HANDLE)pLogPal);

    SelectPalette(hdc,hPal,0);
    RealizePalette(hdc);
}

if((hBitmap=CreateDIBitmap(hdc,(LPBITMAPINFOHEADER)p,CBM_INIT,pi,
    (LPBITMAPINFO)p,DIB_RGB_COLORS)) != NULL) {
    if((hMemoryDC=CreateCompatibleDC(hdc)) != NULL) {
        hOldBitmap=SelectObject(hMemoryDC,hBitmap);
        if(hOldBitmap) {
            BitBlt(hdc,x,y,(int)bh->bmiHeader.biWidth,
              (int)bh->bmiHeader.biHeight,hMemoryDC,0,0,op);
            SelectObject(hMemoryDC,hOldBitmap);
        }
        DeleteDC(hMemoryDC);
    }
    DeleteObject(hBitmap);
}
```

```
            UnlockResource(image);
    }

    int GetBitmapDimensions(LPSTR name,LPINT x,LPINT y,LPINT bits)
    {
        HBITMAP hBitmap;
        LPBITMAPINFO bh;

        if((hBitmap=LoadResource(hInst,FindResource(hInst,name,RT_BITMAP))) != NULL) {
            if((bh=(LPBITMAPINFO)LockResource(hBitmap))!=NULL) {
                *x=(int)bh->bmiHeader.biWidth;
                *y=(int)bh->bmiHeader.biHeight;
                *bits=bh->bmiHeader.biBitCount;
                UnlockResource(hBitmap);
            } else return(FALSE);
            FreeResource(hBitmap);
        } else return(FALSE);
        return(TRUE);
    }

    void SetHelpSize(HWND hwnd)
    {
        HELPWININFO helpinfo;
        char b[145];

        memset((char *)&helpinfo,0,sizeof(HELPWININFO));
        helpinfo.wStructSize=sizeof(HELPWININFO);
        helpinfo.x=10;
        helpinfo.y=10;
        helpinfo.dx=512;
        helpinfo.dy=1004;

        MakeHelpPathName(b);
        WinHelp(hwnd,b,HELP_SETWINPOS,(DWORD)&helpinfo);
    }

    void DoHelp(HWND hwnd,LPSTR keyword)
    {
        char b[145];

        MakeHelpPathName(b);
        WinHelp(hwnd,b,HELP_KEY,(DWORD)keyword);
    }

    void MakeHelpPathName(LPSTR szFileName)
    {
        LPSTR pcFileName;
        int nFileNameLen;

        nFileNameLen = GetModuleFileName(hInst,szFileName,144);
        pcFileName = szFileName+nFileNameLen;

        while(pcFileName > szFileName) {
```

3-10 *Continued*

```
    if(*pcFileName == '\\' || *pcFileName == ':') {
      *(++pcFileName) = '\0';
      break;
    }
    nFileNameLen--;
    pcFileName--;
  }

  if((nFileNameLen+13) < 144) lstrcat(szFileName,HELPFILE);
  else lstrcat(szFileName, "?");
}
```

Figure 3-11 *The DEMO2.RC resource script.*

```
MainScreen DIALOG 69, 55, 260, 188
STYLE WS_POPUP | WS_CAPTION | WS_SYSMENU | WS_MINIMIZEBOX
CLASS "BorDlg"
CAPTION "Dialog Demo Two"
MENU MainMenu
BEGIN
END


AboutBox DIALOG 72, 72, 220, 124
STYLE WS_POPUP | WS_CAPTION
CLASS "BorDlg"
CAPTION "About"
BEGIN
    CONTROL "OK", IDOK, "BorBtn", BS_DEFPUSHBUTTON | WS_CHILD | WS_VISIBLE |
      WS_TABSTOP, 94, 96, 32, 20
    CONTROL "", 102, "BorShade", 32769 | WS_CHILD | WS_VISIBLE, 8, 8, 204, 80
    CONTROL "", 101, "BorStatic", SS_CENTER | WS_CHILD | WS_VISIBLE,
      16, 16, 188, 64
END


ColourBox DIALOG 100, 100, 168, 80
STYLE DS_MODALFRAME | WS_POPUP | WS_CAPTION
CAPTION "Adjust Colour"
BEGIN
    SCROLLBAR 101, 44, 12, 93, 9, SBS_HORZ | WS_CHILD | WS_VISIBLE
    SCROLLBAR 102, 44, 24, 93, 9, SBS_HORZ | WS_CHILD | WS_VISIBLE
    SCROLLBAR 103, 44, 36, 93, 9, SBS_HORZ | WS_CHILD | WS_VISIBLE
    CONTROL "OK", IDOK, "BorBtn", BS_DEFPUSHBUTTON | WS_CHILD | WS_VISIBLE |
      WS_TABSTOP, 128, 52, 32, 20
    CONTROL "Help", IDHELP, "BorBtn", BS_PUSHBUTTON | WS_CHILD | WS_VISIBLE |
      WS_TABSTOP, 88, 52, 32, 20
    CONTROL "Red  ", 301, "BorStatic", SS_RIGHT | WS_CHILD | WS_VISIBLE |
      WS_BORDER, 8, 12, 32, 8
    CONTROL "Green  ", 302, "BorStatic", SS_RIGHT | WS_CHILD | WS_VISIBLE |
      WS_BORDER, 8, 24, 32, 8
    CONTROL "Blue  ", 303, "BorStatic", SS_RIGHT | WS_CHILD | WS_VISIBLE |
```

```
        WS_BORDER, 8, 36, 32, 8
        CONTROL "", 201, "BorStatic", SS_LEFT | WS_CHILD | WS_VISIBLE |
        WS_BORDER, 140, 12, 20, 8
        CONTROL "", 202, "BorStatic", SS_LEFT | WS_CHILD | WS_VISIBLE |
        WS_BORDER, 140, 24, 20, 8
        CONTROL "", 203, "BorStatic", SS_LEFT | WS_CHILD | WS_VISIBLE |
        WS_BORDER, 140, 36, 20, 8
END

MainMenu MENU
BEGIN
    POPUP "File"
    BEGIN
        MENUITEM "&Buttons", 101
        MENUITEM "&Scroll Bars", 102
        MENUITEM "&Colours", 103
        MENUITEM "C&heck Boxes", 104
        MENUITEM "B&itmaps", 105
        MENUITEM "&List Boxes", 106
        MENUITEM "Co&mbo Boxes", 107
        MENUITEM SEPARATOR
        MENUITEM "E&xit", 199
    END

    POPUP "&Help"
    BEGIN
        MENUITEM "&Index", 901
        MENUITEM "&Using help", 905
        MENUITEM SEPARATOR
        MENUITEM "&About...", 999
    END

END

STRINGTABLE
BEGIN
    0,"Dialog Demo Two\nCopyright \251 1993 Alchemy Mindworks Inc.\nFrom the book
      Windows Dialog Construction Set\rby Steven William Rimmer\r
      Published by Windcrest/McGraw Hill"
    1,"Help"
    201,"How can I insert disk number three when there's only room for
      two in the slot?"
    202,"Your Macintosh is about to explode.\rDo not panic... this is a popular
      feature of all Apple computers."
    203,"Yin and yang\rBlack and white\rMale and female\rHonesty and politics\n
      Toyota and automobiles"
    204,"Whatever this symbol means, avoid dropping anything so marked on your cat
      unless you're tired of its company."
    205,"When you see this symbol, Windows is working to rule."
    206,"When you see this symbol on your television, hit the mute button.\r
      It's a Sprint commercial."
    207,"Cassettes are a crutch for people who can't face reel to reel."
    208,"It's ten o'clock... do you know where your poodle is?"
```

161

3-11 *Continued*

```
    209,"Structural dialgram of the Canadian parlament."
    401,"View Only\n\nThe paint won't be dry 'til tomorrow."
    402,"Change All\n\nHow to find the bad plug in a small imported car."
    403,"Done\n\nRemove cat from oven, garnish with parsley and serve."
    404,"Fonts\n\nClick here to fill four megabytes of your hard drive."
    405,"Default\n\nOnly works properly during months with an R in them."
    406,"System\n\nWarrantee expires upon opening package."
    407,"Setup\n\nInsert disk number one in drive C. Hit any key."
    408,"Device Info\n\nIt's broken... come back later."
END

DialogDemoTwo ICON
BEGIN
    '00 00 01 00 01 00 20 20 10 00 00 00 00 00 E8 02'
    '00 00 16 00 00 00 28 00 00 00 20 00 00 00 40 00'
    '00 00 01 00 04 00 00 00 00 00 80 02 00 00 00 00'
    '00 00 00 00 00 00 00 00 00 00 00 00 00 00 00 00'
    '00 00 00 00 80 00 00 80 00 00 00 80 80 00 80 00'
    '00 00 80 00 80 00 80 80 00 00 80 80 80 00 C0 C0'
    'C0 00 00 00 FF 00 00 FF 00 00 00 FF FF 00 FF 00'
    '00 00 FF 00 FF 00 FF FF 00 00 FF FF FF 00 2A 2A'
    '2A 2A 2A 2A 2A 2A 2A 22 77 70 00 00 00 00 A2 A2'
    'A2 A2 A2 A2 A2 A2 A2 A2 22 70 00 00 00 00 2A 2A'
    '2A 2A 2A 2A 2A 2A AA AA A2 70 00 00 00 00 A2 A2'
    'A2 A2 AA AA AA AA B2 AA AA 77 77 77 77 00 2A 2A'
    'AA AA 2A 2A AA 2A AA A9 19 19 19 19 17 77 AA A2'
    'A2 AA AB AB AB AA 91 91 91 91 91 91 91 97 2A AA'
    'BA BA 2A AA A9 19 19 19 19 99 99 99 99 19 AB AB'
    'A2 AA AA 11 11 91 99 99 99 90 00 00 09 99 BA BA'
    'AA A1 01 11 19 19 19 19 90 00 00 00 00 09 AA A2'
    '00 10 10 11 11 91 91 00 00 00 00 70 00 00 7A 00'
    'UU 00 01 01 11 17 77 00 00 00 09 70 00 00 A2 22'
    '22 22 22 22 22 22 27 77 77 70 09 70 00 00 2A 2A'
    '2A 2A AA AA AA AA 22 22 22 77 09 77 00 00 A2 AA'
    'AA AA A2 AA AA AA A2 A2 A2 27 79 17 70 00 2A AA'
    'AA 2A 22 22 2A AA AA AA 2A 79 91 77 00 A2 A2'
    'A2 22 70 70 22 A2 A2 AB A2 A2 00 99 17 77 2A 2A'
    '22 87 07 07 02 2A 2A AA AA 27 00 09 91 91 A2 A2'
    'F8 88 77 70 72 A2 AB AB AB A0 00 00 99 99 2A 22'
    '8F 88 00 77 07 2A 2A AA AA 70 00 00 00 00 A2 28'
    'F8 F0 00 08 70 22 22 A2 A2 00 00 00 00 00 2A 2F'
    '8F 80 00 07 07 2A 2A AA A7 00 00 00 00 00 A7 28'
    'F8 FF 00 88 82 22 A2 A2 A0 00 00 00 00 00 22 7F'
    '8F FF FF 8F 82 2A 2A 2A 70 00 00 00 00 00 A7 0F'
    'FF FF F8 F8 F2 A2 A2 A2 00 00 00 00 00 00 A2 70'
    'FF FF 8F 8F 2A 2A 2A 20 00 00 00 00 00 00 A7 07'
    'FF FF F8 F8 22 A2 A2 00 00 00 00 00 00 00 A2 70'
    '70 FF 8F 22 2A 2A 20 00 00 00 00 00 00 00 AA 07'
    '07 07 02 02 A2 A2 00 00 00 00 00 00 00 00 BA A0'
    '70 70 72 2A 2A 20 00 00 00 00 00 00 00 00 BB AA'
    'A7 A7 AA AA A0 00 00 00 00 00 00 00 00 00 AA BA'
```

```
                'AA AA AA 00 00 00 00 00 00 00 00 00 00 00 AA A0'
                '00 00 00 00 00 00 00 00 00 00 00 00 00 00 00 00'
                '01 FF 00 00 01 FF 00 00 01 FF 00 00 00 03 00 00'
                '00 00 00 00 00 00 00 00 00 00 00 00 01 F8 00 00'
                '07 FE 00 00 3F DF 00 00 3F 9F 00 00 01 9F 00 00'
                '00 8F 00 00 00 07 00 00 00 03 00 00 00 C0 00 00'
                '00 E0 00 00 01 F0 00 00 01 FF 00 00 03 FF 00 00'
                '03 FF 00 00 07 FF 00 00 07 FF 00 00 0F FF 00 00'
                '1F FF 00 00 3F FF 00 00 7F FF 00 00 FF FF 00 01'
                'FF FF 00 07 FF FF 00 3F FF FF 1F FF FF FF'
        END

        ButtonBox DIALOG 80, 72, 172, 120
        STYLE DS_MODALFRAME ¦ WS_POPUP ¦ WS_CAPTION
        CLASS "BorDlg"
        CAPTION "Buttons"
        BEGIN
            PUSHBUTTON "<", 201, 8, 12, 24, 24, WS_CHILD ¦ WS_VISIBLE ¦ WS_TABSTOP
            PUSHBUTTON "M", 202, 32, 12, 24, 24, WS_CHILD ¦ WS_VISIBLE ¦ WS_TABSTOP
            PUSHBUTTON "[", 203, 56, 12, 24, 24, WS_CHILD ¦ WS_VISIBLE ¦ WS_TABSTOP
            PUSHBUTTON "\\", 204, 8, 36, 24, 24, WS_CHILD ¦ WS_VISIBLE ¦ WS_TABSTOP
            PUSHBUTTON "6", 205, 32, 36, 24, 24, WS_CHILD ¦ WS_VISIBLE ¦ WS_TABSTOP
            PUSHBUTTON "(", 206, 56, 36, 24, 24, WS_CHILD ¦ WS_VISIBLE ¦ WS_TABSTOP
            PUSHBUTTON ">", 207, 8, 60, 24, 24, WS_CHILD ¦ WS_VISIBLE ¦ WS_TABSTOP
            PUSHBUTTON "\300", 208, 32, 60, 24, 24, WS_CHILD ¦ WS_VISIBLE ¦ WS_TABSTOP
            PUSHBUTTON "\314", 209, 56, 60, 24, 24, WS_CHILD ¦ WS_VISIBLE ¦ WS_TABSTOP
            CONTROL "OK", IDOK, "BorBtn", BS_DEFPUSHBUTTON ¦ WS_CHILD ¦ WS_VISIBLE ¦
                WS_TABSTOP, 48, 92, 32, 20
            CONTROL "Help", IDHELP, "BorBtn", BS_PUSHBUTTON ¦ WS_CHILD ¦ WS_VISIBLE ¦
                WS_TABSTOP, 8, 92, 32, 20
            CONTROL "", 401, "BorBtn", BS_PUSHBUTTON ¦ WS_CHILD ¦ WS_VISIBLE ¦
                WS_TABSTOP, 96, 12, 32, 20
            CONTROL "", 210, "BorShade", 3 ¦ WS_CHILD ¦ WS_VISIBLE, 88, 0, 2, 120
            CONTROL "", 402, "BorBtn", BS_PUSHBUTTON ¦ WS_CHILD ¦ WS_VISIBLE ¦
                WS_TABSTOP, 132, 12, 32, 20
            CONTROL "", 403, "BorBtn", BS_PUSHBUTTON ¦ WS_CHILD ¦ WS_VISIBLE ¦
                WS_TABSTOP, 96, 36, 32, 20
            CONTROL "", 404, "BorBtn", BS_PUSHBUTTON ¦ WS_CHILD ¦ WS_VISIBLE ¦
                WS_TABSTOP, 132, 36, 32, 20
            CONTROL "", 405, "BorBtn", BS_PUSHBUTTON ¦ WS_CHILD ¦ WS_VISIBLE ¦
                WS_TABSTOP, 96, 60, 32, 20
            CONTROL "", 407, "BorBtn", BS_PUSHBUTTON ¦ WS_CHILD ¦ WS_VISIBLE ¦
                WS_TABSTOP, 96, 92, 32, 20
            CONTROL "", 408, "BorBtn", BS_PUSHBUTTON ¦ WS_CHILD ¦ WS_VISIBLE ¦
                WS_TABSTOP, 132, 92, 32, 20
            CONTROL "", 406, "BorBtn", BS_PUSHBUTTON ¦ WS_CHILD ¦ WS_VISIBLE ¦
                WS_TABSTOP, 132, 60, 32, 20
        END

        BitmapBox DIALOG 72, 72, 72, 72
        STYLE WS_POPUP ¦ WS_CAPTION ¦ WS_SYSMENU
        CAPTION "Bitmap"
        BEGIN
```

3-11 *Continued*

```
END

ScrollBox DIALOG 72, 72, 100, 100
STYLE WS_POPUP | WS_CAPTION | WS_VSCROLL | WS_HSCROLL
CLASS "BorDlg"
CAPTION "Scroll Bars"
BEGIN
    LTEXT "", 201, 68, 12, 16, 8, WS_CHILD | WS_VISIBLE | WS_GROUP
    CONTROL "", -1, "static", SS_BLACKFRAME | WS_CHILD | WS_VISIBLE, 68, 12, 16, 8
    LTEXT "", 202, 68, 24, 16, 8, WS_CHILD | WS_VISIBLE | WS_GROUP
    CONTROL "", -1, "static", SS_BLACKFRAME | WS_CHILD | WS_VISIBLE, 68, 24, 16, 8
    CONTROL "OK", IDOK, "BorBtn", BS_DEFPUSHBUTTON | WS_CHILD | WS_VISIBLE |
        WS_TABSTOP, 52, 64, 32, 20
    CONTROL "Help", IDHELP, "BorBtn", BS_PUSHBUTTON | WS_CHILD | WS_VISIBLE |
        WS_TABSTOP, 12, 64, 32, 20
    CONTROL "Horizontal scroll", 101, "BorStatic", SS_RIGHT | WS_CHILD |
        WS_VISIBLE, 8, 12, 56, 8
    CONTROL "Vertical scroll", 102, "BorStatic", SS_RIGHT | WS_CHILD |
        WS_VISIBLE, 8, 24, 56, 8
    CONTROL "", 103, "BorShade", 32769 | WS_CHILD | WS_VISIBLE, 4, 8, 84, 28
END

CheckBox DIALOG 72, 72, 180, 100
STYLE DS_MODALFRAME | WS_POPUP | WS_CAPTION
CAPTION "Check Boxes and Radio Buttons"
BEGIN
    CONTROL "OK", IDOK, "BorBtn", BS_DEFPUSHBUTTON | WS_CHILD | WS_VISIBLE |
        WS_TABSTOP, 140, 72, 32, 20
    CONTROL "Help", IDHELP, "BorBtn", BS_PUSHBUTTON | WS_CHILD | WS_VISIBLE |
        WS_TABSTOP, 100, 72, 32, 20
    CONTROL " Picture Effects", 105, "BorShade", 32769 | WS_CHILD |
        WS_VISIBLE, 8, 8, 72, 52
    CONTROL "Normal", 101, "BorRadio", BS_AUTORADIOBUTTON | WS_CHILD |
        WS_VISIBLE, 12, 20, 60, 10
    CONTROL "Invert", 102, "BorRadio", BS_AUTORADIOBUTTON | WS_CHILD |
        WS_VISIBLE, 12, 32, 60, 10
    CONTROL "Hide", 103, "BorRadio", BS_AUTORADIOBUTTON | WS_CHILD |
        WS_VISIBLE, 12, 44, 60, 10
    CONTROL "Horizontal lines", 201, "BorCheck", BS_AUTOCHECKBOX |
        WS_CHILD | WS_VISIBLE | WS_TABSTOP, 12, 68, 64, 10
    CONTROL "Vertical lines", 202, "BorCheck", BS_AUTOCHECKBOX |
        WS_CHILD | WS_VISIBLE | WS_TABSTOP, 12, 80, 64, 10
    CONTROL "", 106, "BorShade", 32769 | WS_CHILD | WS_VISIBLE, 8, 64, 72, 28
END

ListBox DIALOG 50, 20, 312, 224
STYLE DS_MODALFRAME | WS_POPUP | WS_CAPTION
CAPTION "List"
BEGIN
    LISTBOX 101, 8, 8, 152, 172, LBS_NOTIFY | WS_CHILD |
        WS_VISIBLE | WS_BORDER | WS_VSCROLL
```

```
    EDITTEXT 102, 12, 200, 144, 12, ES_LEFT | WS_CHILD |
      WS_VISIBLE | WS_BORDER | WS_TABSTOP
    CONTROL "OK", IDOK, "BorBtn", BS_DEFPUSHBUTTON |
      WS_CHILD | WS_VISIBLE | WS_TABSTOP, 272, 196, 32, 20
    CONTROL "Help", IDHELP, "BorBtn", BS_PUSHBUTTON |
      WS_CHILD | WS_VISIBLE | WS_TABSTOP, 232, 196, 32, 20
    CONTROL "Selected text:", 103, "BorShade", 32769 |
      WS_CHILD | WS_VISIBLE, 8, 188, 152, 28
END

ComboBox DIALOG 50, 20, 312, 224
STYLE DS_MODALFRAME | WS_POPUP | WS_CAPTION
CAPTION "Combo Box"
BEGIN
    CONTROL "", 101, "COMBOBOX", CBS_DROPDOWNLIST |
      WS_CHILD | WS_VISIBLE | WS_TABSTOP, 8, 8, 152, 172
    EDITTEXT 102, 12, 200, 144, 12, ES_LEFT | WS_CHILD |
      WS_VISIBLE | WS_BORDER | WS_TABSTOP
    CONTROL "OK", IDOK, "BorBtn", BS_DEFPUSHBUTTON |
      WS_CHILD | WS_VISIBLE | WS_TABSTOP, 272, 196, 32, 20
    CONTROL "Help", IDHELP, "BorBtn", BS_PUSHBUTTON |
      WS_CHILD | WS_VISIBLE | WS_TABSTOP, 236, 196, 32, 20
    CONTROL "Selected text:", 103, "BorShade", 32769 |
      WS_CHILD | WS_VISIBLE, 8, 188, 152, 29
END

Bitmap16 BITMAP demo_16.bmp

Bitmap256 BITMAP demo_256.bmp

BitmapMenu BITMAP menu_bmp.bmp

ListText RCDATA listbox.txt

ListBitmap BITMAP list_bmp.bmp

1401 BITMAP "VO-NORM.BMP"
3401 BITMAP "VO-PRES.BMP"
5401 BITMAP "VO-FOCS.BMP"

1402 BITMAP "CA-NORM.BMP"
3402 BITMAP "CA-PRES.BMP"
5402 BITMAP "CA-FOCS.BMP"

1403 BITMAP "DN-NORM.BMP"
3403 BITMAP "DN-PRES.BMP"
5403 BITMAP "DN-FOCS.BMP"

1404 BITMAP "FT-NORM.BMP"
3404 BITMAP "FT-PRES.BMP"
5404 BITMAP "FT-FOCS.BMP"

1405 BITMAP "DF-NORM.BMP"
```

3-11 *Continued*

```
3405 BITMAP "DF-PRES.BMP"
5405 BITMAP "DF-FOCS.BMP"

1406 BITMAP "SY-NORM.BMP"
3406 BITMAP "SY-PRES.BMP"
5406 BITMAP "SY-FOCS.BMP"

1407 BITMAP "SB-NORM.BMP"
3407 BITMAP "SB-PRES.BMP"
5407 BITMAP "SB-FOCS.BMP"

1408 BITMAP "DI-NORM.BMP"
3408 BITMAP "DI-PRES.BMP"
5408 BITMAP "DI-FOCS.BMP"
```

Most of DEMO2.CPP will look familiar, as it's identical to the DEMO1.CPP program discussed extensively in chapter 2. The differences between them has to do with how you should work with Borland's custom controls and dialog class.

The first thing to note is the addition of the BWCCGetVersion call in WinMain. In fact, the version of the BWCC.DLL library usually doesn't matter. This call just forces your application to make sure the BWCC.DLL library is loaded, or it forces Windows to attempt to load it if it's not. If BWCC.DLL isn't available, Windows will protest and terminate your application.

It's preferable for any problems with the availability of a DLL to happen when your application first boots up, rather than, for example, when someone goes to save a file that he or she has just spent the last half hour working on.

The SelectProc function in DEMO2 lacks a WM_CTLCOLOR case, as the background is defined by the class of the MainScreen dialog template in DEMO2.RC.

The DoCombo and DoListbox functions and their corresponding message handlers, ComboDlgProc and ListDlgProc respectively, illustrate one of the major differences of DEMO2 as it pertains to working with bitmaps in dialogs. In DEMO1, the DrawImage function always painted bitmaps, overwriting whatever was beneath them. For

this reason the backgrounds of the Combo Box and List dialogs were left white, so the black and white bitmap of Alice and the Red Queen wouldn't appear to be inset in an odd size white rectangle in an otherwise gray window. In this version of these dialogs, the window backgrounds are gray, as can be seen in Fig. 3-12.

Figure 3-12

A gray looking-glass—the List dialog of DEMO2.

Creating the gray background of a BorDlg class dialog without actually using the BorDlg class was discussed a moment ago. The tricky part is painting a bitmap over the background so that the black portions of the bitmap appear black and the white portions appear transparent, allowing the textured gray surface to show through.

The DrawImage function in DEMO2.CPP allows for one more argument than it did in DEMO1. The op argument is the drawing operation code to be used when painting a bitmap. If you pass SCRCOPY for this argument, the bitmap in question will be painted

normally. If you pass SRCAND, it will be ANDed with the existing background. If the bitmap is monochrome, this will result in painting the black parts and leaving the white parts transparent. Using SRCAND with color bitmaps will produce some very unusual graphics.

As an aside, there's no reason why this version of DrawImage can't be used with the solid dialog backgrounds used in the DEMO1 application, should you want to go back and retrofit it.

The DoCheck function of DEMO2 and its message handler CheckDlgProc illustrate how to use the brush handle returned by BWCCGetPattern as a dialog background. The CheckBox dialog template can't use the BorDlg class, as this dialog contains a bitmap. As such, its background must be created synthetically, as was discussed earlier in this chapter.

Note that the sections of the WM_COMMAND handler in CheckDlgProc that respond to clicks in the radio buttons and check boxes of the Check Boxes and Radio Buttons dialog are somewhat simpler, as these're automatic buttons. It's not necessary for CheckDlgProc to manage their appearances—all it's responsible for is redrawing the frog when one of them is clicked.

The DoBitmap function and its BitmapDlgProc message handler haven't changed from DEMO1, save that the background of the window is painted with the BWCCGetPattern brush. This might seem a bit suspect, as the entire window will be full of frog, its size having been defined as the dimensions of the bitmap it's to contain. In fact, this matters only in the second or two between the appearance of the window and the appearance of the bitmap—it takes a noticeable amount of time for the bitmap to be fetched from the resource list of DEMO1.EXE and then displayed.

The DoButton function of DEMO2.CPP and its message handler ButtonDlgProc are also unchanged from DEMO1.CPP, save that there's no WM_CTLCOLOR message handler involved and the calls to DoMessage provoked by those sarcastic little symbol buttons are now really calling BWCCMessageBox. Note that if you don't like the electric blue i icon that DoMessage currently displays, you can change it by modifying the DoMessage macro up at the top of

DEMO2.CPP. The arguments for BWCCMessageBox, including the flags for various icons and buttons that can appear in the message dialog, are identical to those of the standard Windows MessageBox call.

The DoColours function in DEMO2.CPP and the ColourDlgProc message handler that supports it are unchanged from DEMO1.CPP, a situation that makes the Adjust Colour dialog look decidedly odd. Because it uses the dialog background to illustrate the color being defined by its sliders, the dialog background can't be painted using the BWCCGetPattern brush. When I discuss DEMO3.CPP in a moment—under conditions in which returning brush handles in response to a WM_CTRCOLOR message will immediately drop Windows into a black hole—you'll see a slightly different arrangement for this dialog.

Introducing the Microsoft CTL3D library

There are some limitations to the Borland custom controls. For one thing, they require that you use control objects other than the ones Windows would ordinarily define. This could make adding a three-dimensional appearance to an existing application—perhaps one with all manner of dialogs already created—a fairly daunting task.

In addition, there are those who will argue that the colorful Borland buttons don't look very corporate, sophisticated, or "'90s." I'm inclined to ignore this argument myself, on the grounds that people who think that gray is a color probably also feel that art is a product and dialog is a verb. Hopefully the '90s is a passing phase.

The Microsoft CTL3D custom control library is a worthwhile alternative to BWCC, and despite its origins will get along just fine with applications written in Borland's languages. It's fundamentally different from Borland's custom control library, however, in that it adds no new control objects or window classes to your applications. Rather, it changes the appearance of the existing ones.

In theory you can change a flat Windows application, such as DEMO1 from the previous chapter, into a three-dimensional one by simply applying CTL3D to it. This involves adding a library to the project file for your application and making three calls in its WinMain function. In practice, however, implementing CTL3D usually isn't quite this easy. There are cosmetic niceties to be observed—things that look acceptable in a flat dialog but don't work under CTL3D—and a few programming techniques that will offend CTL3D to the point of causing a general protection fault.

The most notable of these is the practice of responding to WM_CTLCOLOR messages, as has been used in the previous two programs. If you return brush handles this way for an application that uses CTL3D, it will crash very colorfully indeed. In fact, there's no reason to do so, as CTL3D causes all windows to be drawn with a gray background in any case.

You should respond to WM_CTLCOLOR messages in an application that uses CTL3D, but only like this:

```
case WM_CTLCOLOR:
 return(Ctl3dCtlColorEx(message,wParam,lParam));
```

As you might expect, this limitation will have a few effects on the demonstration program you've seen thus far.

Whereas Borland's BWCC package is part of its language products, Microsoft appears to have released CTL3D for popular consumption by anyone who wants to implement it. It can be found on most bulletin boards and on CompuServe, free for downloading. The current version, as of this writing, is included on the companion disk for this book. You'll need CTL3D.DLL, CTL3D.LIB, CTL3D.H, and DRAW3D.H to compile the DEMO3 program to be discussed in this section.

The "predator" beta of Borland C++ for Windows 4.0, as mentioned in the first chapter of this book, came with CTL3D as well as BWCC.

The complete source code for DEMO3.CPP is listed in Fig. 3-13. In addition to DEMO3.CPP, you'll need DEMO3.RC, as shown in Fig. 3-14. Suitable DEF and project files for DEMO3 are included with the source code on the companion disk for this book.

The DEMO3.CPP source code.

Figure 3-13

```c
/*
    Dialog Demo 3
    Copyright (c) 1993 Alchemy Mindworks Inc.
*/

#include <windows.h>
#include <stdio.h>
#include <stdlib.h>
#include <ctype.h>
#include <alloc.h>
#include <string.h>
#include <dos.h>
#include <time.h>
#include "ctl3d.h"
#include "draw3d.h"

#define say(s)      MessageBox(NULL,s,"Yo...",MB_OK | MB_ICONSTOP);
#define saynumber(f,s)    {char b[128]; sprintf((LPSTR)b,(LPSTR)f,s); \
    MessageBox(NULL,b,"Debug Message",MB_OK | MB_ICONSTOP); }

#define STRINGSIZE          129         /* how big is a string? */

#ifndef IDHELP
#define IDHELP              998
#endif

#define MESSAGE_STRING      101         /* message box object */

#define FILE_BUTTONS        101
#define FILE_SCROLLBARS     102
#define FILE_COLOURS        103
#define FILE_CHECKBOXES     104
#define FILE_BITMAP         105
#define FILE_LISTBOX        106
#define FILE_COMBOBOX       107
#define FILE_EXIT           199

#define HELPM_INDEX         901
#define HELPM_USING         905
#define HELPM_ABOUT         999

#define COLOUR_REDSET       101
#define COLOUR_GREENSET     102
#define COLOUR_BLUESET      103
#define COLOUR_REDVAL       201
#define COLOUR_GREENVAL     202
#define COLOUR_BLUEVAL      203
#define COLOUR_REDTEXT      301
#define COLOUR_GREENTEXT    302
#define COLOUR_BLUETEXT     303
```

3-13 *Continued*

```
#define BUTTON_BASE          201
#define BUTTON_BASECOUNT     9

#define BITMAP16             "Bitmap16"
#define BITMAP256            "Bitmap256"

#define SCROLL_HORZTEXT      101
#define SCROLL_VERTTEXT      102
#define SCROLL_HORZVAL       201
#define SCROLL_VERTVAL       202
#define SCROLL_MAX           999

#define CHECK_NORMAL         101
#define CHECK_INVERT         102
#define CHECK_HIDE           103
#define CHECK_TITLE          105
#define CHECK_HORZ           201
#define CHECK_VERT           202

#define CHECK_LEFT           184
#define CHECK_TOP            10
#define CHECK_BITMAP         MENUBITMAP

#define CHECK_SWLEFT         20
#define CHECK_SWTOP          108
#define CHECK_SWRIGHT        180
#define CHECK_SWBOTTOM       132

#define LIST_LIST            101
#define LIST_TEXT            "ListText"
#define LIST_END             "ENDMARKER"
#define LIST_SELECT          102
#define LIST_TSELECT         103
#define LIST_BITMAP          "ListBitmap"

#define COMBO_COMBO          101
#define COMBO_TEXT           "ListText"
#define COMBO_SELECT         102
#define COMBO_TSELECT        103
#define COMBO_BITMAP         "ListBitmap"

#define HELPFILE             "DEMO.HLP"

#define DIALOG_KEY           "DialogDemo"

#define DINGBATS             "WingDings"

#define MENUBITMAP           "BitmapMenu"
#define SYS_BITMAP           300

#define MESSAGE_ABOUT        0
```

```
#define MESSAGE_HELP          1

#define LIGHTGREY             RGB(192,192,192)

#define RGB_RED               0
#define RGB_GREEN             1
#define RGB_BLUE              2
#define RGB_SIZE              3

#define CreateControlFont()     if(ControlFontName[0]) \
            controlfont=CreateFont(16,0,0,0,0,0,0,0, \
            ANSI_CHARSET,OUT_DEFAULT_PRECIS,CLIP_DEFAULT_PRECIS, \
            DEFAULT_QUALITY,DEFAULT_PITCH | FF_DONTCARE, \
            ControlFontName)

#define SetControlFont(hwnd,id) {HWND dlgH; \
            if(controlfont != NULL) { \
                dlgH=GetDlgItem(hwnd,id); \
                SendMessage(dlgH,WM_SETFONT,(WORD)controlfont,FALSE); \
            } \
            }

#define DestroyControlFont()    if(controlfont != NULL) \
      DeleteObject(controlfont)

#define CheckOn(item)      SendDlgItemMessage(hwnd,item,BM_SETCHECK,1,0L);
#define CheckOff(item)     SendDlgItemMessage(hwnd,item,BM_SETCHECK,0,0L);
#define ItemOn(item)     { dlgH=GetDlgItem(hwnd,item); EnableWindow(dlgH,TRUE); }
#define ItemOff(item)    { dlgH=GetDlgItem(hwnd,item); EnableWindow(dlgH,FALSE); }
#define IsItemChecked(item)      SendDlgItemMessage(hwnd,item,BM_GETCHECK,0,0L)
#define ItemName(item,string)    { dlgH=GetDlgItem(hwnd,item); \
      SetWindowText(dlgH,(LPSTR)string); }
#define GetItemName(item,string) { dlgH=GetDlgItem(hwnd,item); \
      GetWindowText(dlgH,(LPSTR)string,BIGSTRINGSIZE); }

#define DoMessage(hwnd,string)    MessageBox(hwnd,string, \
      "Message",MB_OK | MB_ICONINFORMATION)

#ifndef max
#define max(a,b)              (((a)>(b)))?(a):(b))
#endif
#ifndef min
#define min(a,b)              (((a)<(b)))?(a):(b))
#endif

/* prototypes */
DWORD FAR PASCAL SelectProc(HWND hwnd,WORD message,WORD wParam,LONG lParam);
DWORD FAR PASCAL AboutDlgProc(HWND hwnd,WORD message,WORD wParam,LONG lParam);
DWORD FAR PASCAL ColourDlgProc(HWND hwnd,WORD message,WORD wParam,LONG lParam);
DWORD FAR PASCAL ButtonDlgProc(HWND hwnd,WORD message,WORD wParam,LONG lParam);
DWORD FAR PASCAL MessageDlgProc(HWND hwnd,WORD message,WORD wParam,LONG lParam);
DWORD FAR PASCAL BitmapDlgProc(HWND hwnd,WORD message,WORD wParam,LONG lParam);
DWORD FAR PASCAL ScrollDlgProc(HWND hwnd,WORD message,WORD wParam,LONG lParam);
```

3-13 *Continued*

```
DWORD FAR PASCAL CheckDlgProc(HWND hwnd,WORD message,WORD wParam,LONG lParam);
DWORD FAR PASCAL ListDlgProc(HWND hwnd,WORD message,WORD wParam,LONG lParam);
DWORD FAR PASCAL ComboDlgProc(HWND hwnd,WORD message,WORD wParam,LONG lParam);

void DrawImage(HDC hdc,int x,int y,HBITMAP image,DWORD op);
void DoColours(HWND hwnd);
void DoButtons(HWND hwnd);
void DoBitmap(HWND hwnd);
void DoScrollbars(HWND hwnd);
void DoCheck(HWND hwnd);
void DoListbox(HWND hwnd);
void DoCombo(HWND hwnd);
void SetHelpSize(HWND hwnd);
void DoHelp(HWND hwnd,LPSTR keyword);
void MakeHelpPathName(LPSTR szFileName);
void CentreWindow(HWND hwnd);

int GetDeviceBits(HWND hwnd);
int GetBitmapDimensions(LPSTR name,LPINT x,LPINT y,LPINT bits);

LPSTR FetchString(unsigned int n);

/* globals*/
char szAppName[]="DialogDemoThree";
char ControlFontName[STRINGSIZE+1]="Arial";

LPSTR messagehook;
HANDLE hInst;
HFONT controlfont=NULL;

#pragma warn -par
int PASCAL WinMain(HANDLE hInstance,HANDLE hPrevInstance,
     LPSTR lpszCmdParam,int nCmdShow)
{
    FARPROC dlgProc;
    int r=0;

    hInst=hInstance;

    Ctl3dRegister(hInstance);
    Ctl3dAutoSubclass(hInstance);

    dlgProc=MakeProcInstance((FARPROC)SelectProc,hInst);
    r=DialogBox(hInst,"MainScreen",NULL,dlgProc);

    FreeProcInstance(dlgProc);

    Ctl3dUnregister(hInstance);

    return(r);
}
```

```
DWORD FAR PASCAL SelectProc(HWND hwnd,WORD message,WORD wParam,LONG lParam)
{
    HMENU hmenu;
    FARPROC lpfnDlgProc;
    PAINTSTRUCT ps;
    static HICON hIcon;
    static HBITMAP hBitmap;
    char b[129];

    switch(message) {
        case WM_CTLCOLOR:
            return(Ctl3dCtlColorEx(message,wParam,lParam));
        case WM_SYSCOLORCHANGE:
            Ctl3dColorChange();
            break;
        case WM_SYSCOMMAND:
            switch(wParam & 0xfff0) {
                case SC_CLOSE:
                    SendMessage(hwnd,WM_COMMAND,FILE_EXIT,0L);
                    break;
            }
            switch(wParam) {
                case SYS_BITMAP:
                    SendMessage(hwnd,WM_COMMAND,FILE_BITMAP,0L);
                    break;
            }
            break;
        case WM_INITDIALOG:
            SetHelpSize(hwnd);

            GetProfileString(DIALOG_KEY,"ControlFont",
                ControlFontName,b,STRINGSIZE);
            if(lstrlen(b)) lstrcpy(ControlFontName,b);
            CreateControlFont();

            hIcon=LoadIcon(hInst,szAppName);
            SetClassWord(hwnd,GCW_HICON,(WORD)hIcon);
            CentreWindow(hwnd);

            hmenu=GetSystemMenu(hwnd,FALSE);
            hBitmap=LoadBitmap(hInst,MENUBITMAP);
            AppendMenu(hmenu,MF_SEPARATOR,NULL,NULL);
            AppendMenu(hmenu,MF_BITMAP,SYS_BITMAP,(LPSTR)(LONG)hBitmap);
            break;
        case WM_PAINT:
            BeginPaint(hwnd,&ps);
            EndPaint(hwnd,&ps);
            break;
        case WM_COMMAND:
            switch(wParam) {
                case HELPM_INDEX:
                    MakeHelpPathName(b);
                    WinHelp(hwnd,b,HELP_INDEX,NULL);
```

3-13 *Continued*

```
                break;
            case HELPM_USING:
                WinHelp(hwnd,"",HELP_HELPONHELP,NULL);
                break;
            case HELPM_ABOUT:
                if((lpfnDlgProc=MakeProcInstance
                   ((FARPROC)AboutDlgProc,hInst)) != NULL) {
                    DialogBox(hInst,"AboutBox",hwnd,lpfnDlgProc);
                    FreeProcInstance(lpfnDlgProc);
                }
                break;
            case FILE_BUTTONS:
                DoButtons(hwnd);
                break;
            case FILE_COLOURS:
                DoColours(hwnd);
                break;
            case FILE_BITMAP:
                DoBitmap(hwnd);
                break;
            case FILE_SCROLLBARS:
                DoScrollbars(hwnd);
                break;
            case FILE_CHECKBOXES:
                DoCheck(hwnd);
                break;
            case FILE_LISTBOX:
                DoListbox(hwnd);
                break;
            case FILE_COMBOBOX:
                DoCombo(hwnd);
                break;
            case FILE_EXIT:
                MakeHelpPathName(b);
                WinHelp(hwnd,b,HELP_QUIT,NULL);

                DeleteObject(hBitmap);
                FreeResource(hIcon);
                DestroyControlFont();
                PostQuitMessage(0);
                break;
        }
        break;

    }

    return(FALSE);
}

void DoCombo(HWND hwnd)
{
```

```
        FARPROC lpfnDlgProc;

        if((lpfnDlgProc=MakeProcInstance((FARPROC)ComboDlgProc,hInst)) != NULL) {
            DialogBox(hInst,"ComboBox",hwnd,lpfnDlgProc);
            FreeProcInstance(lpfnDlgProc);
        }
    }

    DWORD FAR PASCAL ComboDlgProc(HWND hwnd,WORD message,WORD wParam,LONG lParam)
    {
        PAINTSTRUCT ps;
        HWND dlgH;
        HDC hdc;
        HANDLE handle;
        HBITMAP hBitmap;
        RECT rect;
        LPSTR p;
        long l;
        char b[129];
        int i,x,y;

        switch(message) {
            case WM_INITDIALOG:
                if((handle=LoadResource(hInst,FindResource(hInst,
                    COMBO_TEXT,RT_RCDATA))) != NULL) {

                    if((p=(LPSTR)LockResource(handle))!=NULL) {
                        for(b[0]=0;;) {
                            for(i=0;p[i] >= 32 && i < 129;++i) b[i]=p[i];
                            b[i++]=0;
                            if(!lstrcmp(b,LIST_END)) break;
                            p+=i;
                            while(*p==10) ++p;
                            SendDlgItemMessage(hwnd,
                                COMBO_COMBO,CB_INSERTSTRING,-1,(LONG)b);
                        }

                        UnlockResource(handle);
                    }
                    FreeResource(handle);
                }

                SendDlgItemMessage(hwnd,COMBO_COMBO,CB_SETCURSEL,0,0L);

                SetControlFont(hwnd,IDOK);
                SetControlFont(hwnd,IDHELP);
                SetControlFont(hwnd,COMBO_COMBO);
                SetControlFont(hwnd,COMBO_SELECT);
                SetControlFont(hwnd,COMBO_TSELECT);

                CentreWindow(hwnd);

                break;
```

3-13 *Continued*

```
        case WM_CTLCOLOR:
            return(Ctl3dCtlColorEx(message,wParam,lParam));
        case WM_PAINT:
            hdc=BeginPaint(hwnd,&ps);

            if(GetBitmapDimensions(COMBO_BITMAP,&x,&y,&i)) {
                GetClientRect(hwnd,&rect);
                if((hBitmap=LoadResource(hInst,FindResource(hInst,COMBO_BITMAP,RT_BITMAP))) != NULL) {
                    DrawImage(hdc,rect.right-rect.left-x,0,hBitmap,SRCAND);
                    FreeResource(hBitmap);
                }
            }

            EndPaint(hwnd,&ps);
            break;
        case WM_COMMAND:
            switch(wParam) {
                case IDHELP:
                    DoHelp(hwnd,(LPSTR)"Combobox");
                    break;
                case COMBO_COMBO:
                    switch(HIWORD(lParam)) {
                        case CBN_DBLCLK:
                            SendMessage(hwnd,WM_COMMAND,IDOK,0L);
                            break;
                        case CBN_SELCHANGE:
                            if((l=SendDlgItemMessage(hwnd,COMBO_COMBO,
                              CB_GETCURSEL,0,0L)) != LB_ERR) {
                                SendDlgItemMessage(hwnd,COMBO_COMBO,
                                    CB_GETLBTEXT,(unsigned int)l,(LONG)(LPSTR)b);
                                ItemName(COMBO_SELECT,b);
                            }
                            break;
                    }
                    break;
                case IDOK:
                    EndDialog(hwnd,wParam);
                    break;
            }
            break;
        }

    return(FALSE);
}

void DoListbox(HWND hwnd)
{
    FARPROC lpfnDlgProc;
```

```
        if((lpfnDlgProc=MakeProcInstance((FARPROC)ListDlgProc,hInst)) != NULL) {
            DialogBox(hInst,"ListBox",hwnd,lpfnDlgProc);
            FreeProcInstance(lpfnDlgProc);
        }
}

DWORD FAR PASCAL ListDlgProc(HWND hwnd,WORD message,WORD wParam,LONG lParam)
{
    PAINTSTRUCT ps;
    HWND dlgH;
    HDC hdc;
    HANDLE handle;
    HBITMAP hBitmap;
    RECT rect;
    LPSTR p;
    long l;
    char b[129];
    int i,x,y;

    switch(message) {
        case WM_INITDIALOG:
            if((handle=LoadResource(hInst,FindResource(hInst,LIST_TEXT,
                RT_RCDATA))) != NULL) {

                if((p=(LPSTR)LockResource(handle))!=NULL) {
                    for(b[0]=0;;) {
                        for(i=0;p[i] >= 32 && i < 129;++i) b[i]=p[i];
                        b[i++]=0;
                        if(!lstrcmp(b,LIST_END)) break;
                        p+=i;
                        while(*p==10) ++p;
                        SendDlgItemMessage(hwnd,
                            LIST_LIST,LB_INSERTSTRING,-1,(LONG)b);
                    }

                    UnlockResource(handle);
                }
                FreeResource(handle);
            }

            SetControlFont(hwnd,IDOK);
            SetControlFont(hwnd,IDHELP);
            SetControlFont(hwnd,LIST_LIST);
            SetControlFont(hwnd,LIST_SELECT);
            SetControlFont(hwnd,LIST_TSELECT);

            CentreWindow(hwnd);

            break;
        case WM_CTLCOLOR:
            return(Ctl3dCtlColorEx(message,wParam,lParam));
        case WM_PAINT:
            hdc=BeginPaint(hwnd,&ps);
```

3-13 *Continued*

```
            if(GetBitmapDimensions(LIST_BITMAP,&x,&y,&i)) {
                GetClientRect(hwnd,&rect);
                if((hBitmap=LoadResource(hInst,FindResource
                    (hInst,LIST_BITMAP,RT_BITMAP))) != NULL) {
                    DrawImage(hdc,rect.right-rect.left-x,0,hBitmap,SRCAND);
                    FreeResource(hBitmap);
                }
            }

            EndPaint(hwnd,&ps);
            break;
        case WM_COMMAND:
            switch(wParam) {
                case IDHELP:
                    DoHelp(hwnd,(LPSTR)"Listbox");
                    break;
                case LIST_LIST:
                    switch(HIWORD(lParam)) {
                        case LBN_DBLCLK:
                            SendMessage(hwnd,WM_COMMAND,IDOK,0L);
                            break;
                        case LBN_SELCHANGE:
                            if((l=SendDlgItemMessage(hwnd,LIST_LIST,
                                LB_GETCURSEL,0,0L)) != LB_ERR) {
                                SendDlgItemMessage(hwnd,LIST_LIST,
                                    LB_GETTEXT,(unsigned int)l,(LONG)(LPSTR)b);
                                ItemName(LIST_SELECT,b);
                            }
                            break;
                    }
                    break;
                case IDOK:
                    EndDialog(hwnd,wParam);
                    break;
            }
            break;
    }

    return(FALSE);
}

void DoCheck(HWND hwnd)
{
    FARPROC lpfnDlgProc;

    if((lpfnDlgProc=MakeProcInstance((FARPROC)CheckDlgProc,hInst)) != NULL) {
        DialogBox(hInst,"CheckBox",hwnd,lpfnDlgProc);
        FreeProcInstance(lpfnDlgProc);
    }
}
```

```
DWORD FAR PASCAL CheckDlgProc(HWND hwnd,WORD message,WORD wParam,LONG lParam)
{
    PAINTSTRUCT ps;
    HBITMAP hBitmap;
    HPEN hPen;
    HDC hdc;
    int i,x,y;

    switch(message) {
        case WM_INITDIALOG:

            SetControlFont(hwnd,CHECK_NORMAL);
            SetControlFont(hwnd,CHECK_INVERT);
            SetControlFont(hwnd,CHECK_HIDE);
            SetControlFont(hwnd,CHECK_HORZ);
            SetControlFont(hwnd,CHECK_VERT);
            SetControlFont(hwnd,CHECK_TITLE);
            SetControlFont(hwnd,IDOK);
            SetControlFont(hwnd,IDHELP);

            CheckOn(CHECK_NORMAL);

            CentreWindow(hwnd);

            break;
        case WM_CTLCOLOR:
            return(Ctl3dCtlColorEx(message,wParam,lParam));
        case WM_PAINT:
            hdc=BeginPaint(hwnd,&ps);

            if(GetBitmapDimensions(CHECK_BITMAP,&x,&y,&i)) {

                if((hBitmap=LoadResource(hInst,FindResource(hInst,
                   CHECK_BITMAP,RT_BITMAP))) != NULL) {

                    DrawImage(hdc,CHECK_LEFT,CHECK_TOP,hBitmap,SRCCOPY);
                    FreeResource(hBitmap);

                    if(IsItemChecked(CHECK_HIDE)) {
                        SelectObject(hdc,GetStockObject(LTGRAY_BRUSH));
                        SelectObject(hdc,GetStockObject(NULL_PEN));
                        Rectangle(hdc,CHECK_LEFT,CHECK_TOP,
                                  CHECK_LEFT+x+1,
                                  CHECK_TOP+y+1);
                        SelectObject(hdc,GetStockObject(NULL_BRUSH));
                    }
                    if(IsItemChecked(CHECK_INVERT)) {
                        SelectObject(hdc,GetStockObject(WHITE_BRUSH));
                        SelectObject(hdc,GetStockObject(NULL_PEN));
                        SetROP2(hdc,R2_NOT);
                        Rectangle(hdc,CHECK_LEFT,CHECK_TOP,
                                  CHECK_LEFT+x+1,
                                  CHECK_TOP+y+1);
```

3-13 *Continued*

```
            }
            if(IsItemChecked(CHECK_HORZ)) {
                hPen=CreatePen(PS_SOLID,2,LIGHTGREY);
                SelectObject(hdc,hPen);
                for(i=0;i<=y;i+=4) {
                    MoveTo(hdc,CHECK_LEFT,CHECK_TOP+i);
                    LineTo(hdc,CHECK_LEFT+x,CHECK_TOP+i);
                }
                DeleteObject(hPen);
            }
            if(IsItemChecked(CHECK_VERT)) {
                hPen=CreatePen(PS_SOLID,2,LIGHTGREY);
                SelectObject(hdc,hPen);
                for(i=0;i<=x;i+=4) {
                    MoveTo(hdc,CHECK_LEFT+i,CHECK_TOP);
                    LineTo(hdc,CHECK_LEFT+i,CHECK_TOP+y);
                }
                DeleteObject(hPen);
            }
        }
    }

    EndPaint(hwnd,&ps);
    break;
case WM_COMMAND:
    switch(wParam) {
        case IDHELP:
            DoHelp(hwnd,(LPSTR)"Checkboxes");
            break;
        case CHECK_NORMAL:
            CheckOn(CHECK_NORMAL);
            CheckOff(CHECK_INVERT);
            CheckOff(CHECK_HIDE);
            InvalidateRect(hwnd,NULL,FALSE);
            break;
        case CHECK_HIDE:
            CheckOff(CHECK_NORMAL);
            CheckOff(CHECK_INVERT);
            CheckOn(CHECK_HIDE);
            InvalidateRect(hwnd,NULL,FALSE);
            break;
        case CHECK_INVERT:
            CheckOff(CHECK_NORMAL);
            CheckOn(CHECK_INVERT);
            CheckOff(CHECK_HIDE);
            InvalidateRect(hwnd,NULL,FALSE);
            break;
        case CHECK_HORZ:
            case CHECK_VERT:
            if(IsItemChecked(wParam)) {
                CheckOff(wParam);
```

```
                }
                else {
                    CheckOn(wParam);
                }
                InvalidateRect(hwnd,NULL,FALSE);
                break;
            case IDOK:
                EndDialog(hwnd,wParam);
                break;
        }
        break;
    }

    return(FALSE);
}

void DoScrollbars(HWND hwnd)
{
    FARPROC lpfnDlgProc;

    if((lpfnDlgProc=MakeProcInstance((FARPROC)ScrollDlgProc,hInst)) != NULL) {
        DialogBox(hInst,"ScrollBox",hwnd,lpfnDlgProc);
        FreeProcInstance(lpfnDlgProc);
    }
}

DWORD FAR PASCAL ScrollDlgProc(HWND hwnd,WORD message,WORD wParam,LONG lParam)
{
    PAINTSTRUCT ps;
    HWND dlgH;
    char b[33];
    int n,jump,pos;

    switch(message) {
        case WM_INITDIALOG:
            SetScrollRange(hwnd,SB_HORZ,0,SCROLL_MAX,TRUE);
            SetScrollPos(hwnd,SB_HORZ,SCROLL_MAX/2,TRUE);
            n=GetScrollPos(hwnd,SB_HORZ);

            dlgH=GetDlgItem(hwnd,SCROLL_HORZVAL);
            sprintf(b," %d",n);
            SetWindowText(dlgH,b);
            EnableWindow(dlgH,TRUE);

            SetScrollRange(hwnd,SB_VERT,0,SCROLL_MAX,TRUE);
            SetScrollPos(hwnd,SB_VERT,SCROLL_MAX/2,TRUE);
            n=GetScrollPos(hwnd,SB_VERT);

            dlgH=GetDlgItem(hwnd,SCROLL_VERTVAL);
            sprintf(b," %d",n);
            SetWindowText(dlgH,b);
            EnableWindow(dlgH,TRUE);
```

3-13 *Continued*

```
            SetControlFont(hwnd,SCROLL_HORZVAL);
            SetControlFont(hwnd,SCROLL_VERTVAL);
            SetControlFont(hwnd,SCROLL_HORZTEXT);
            SetControlFont(hwnd,SCROLL_VERTTEXT);
            SetControlFont(hwnd,IDHELP);
            SetControlFont(hwnd,IDOK);

            CentreWindow(hwnd);
            break;
        case WM_VSCROLL:
            pos=GetScrollPos(hwnd,SB_VERT);
            jump=SCROLL_MAX/10;
            switch(wParam) {
                case SB_LINEUP:
                    pos-=1;
                    break;
                case SB_LINEDOWN:
                    pos+=1;
                    break;
                case SB_PAGEUP:
                    pos-=jump;
                    break;
                case SB_PAGEDOWN:
                    pos+=jump;
                    break;
                case SB_THUMBPOSITION:
                    pos=LOWORD(lParam);
                    break;
            }

            if(pos < 0 ) pos=0;
            else if(pos >= SCROLL_MAX) pos=SCROLL_MAX;

            if(pos != GetScrollPos(hwnd,SB_VERT)) {
                SetScrollPos(hwnd,SB_VERT,pos,TRUE);
                sprintf(b," %d",pos);
                ItemName(SCROLL_VERTVAL,b);
                InvalidateRect(hwnd,NULL,FALSE);
            }
            break;
        case WM_HSCROLL:
            pos=GetScrollPos(hwnd,SB_HORZ);
            jump=SCROLL_MAX/10;
            switch(wParam) {
                case SB_LINEUP:
                    pos-=1;
                    break;
                case SB_LINEDOWN:
                    pos+=1;
                    break;
                case SB_PAGEUP:
```

```
                    pos-=jump;
                    break;
                case SB_PAGEDOWN:
                    pos+=jump;
                    break;
                case SB_THUMBPOSITION:
                    pos=LOWORD(lParam);
                    break;
            }

            if(pos < 0 ) pos=0;
            else if(pos >= SCROLL_MAX) pos=SCROLL_MAX;

            if(pos != GetScrollPos(hwnd,SB_HORZ)) {
                SetScrollPos(hwnd,SB_HORZ,pos,TRUE);
                sprintf(b," %d",pos);
                ItemName(SCROLL_HORZVAL,b);
                InvalidateRect(hwnd,NULL,FALSE);
            }
            break;
        case WM_CTLCOLOR:
            return(Ctl3dCtlColorEx(message,wParam,lParam));
        case WM_PAINT:
            BeginPaint(hwnd,&ps);
            EndPaint(hwnd,&ps);
            break;
        case WM_COMMAND:
            switch(wParam) {
                case IDHELP:
                    DoHelp(hwnd,(LPSTR)"Scrollbars");
                    break;
                case IDOK:
                    EndDialog(hwnd,wParam);
                    break;
            }
            break;
    }

    return(FALSE);
}

void DoBitmap(HWND hwnd)
{
    FARPROC lpfnDlgProc;

    if((lpfnDlgProc=MakeProcInstance((FARPROC)BitmapDlgProc,hInst)) != NULL) {
        DialogBox(hInst,"BitmapBox",hwnd,lpfnDlgProc);
        FreeProcInstance(lpfnDlgProc);
    }
}

DWORD FAR PASCAL BitmapDlgProc(HWND hwnd,WORD message,WORD wParam,LONG lParam)
{
```

3-13 *Continued*

```
PAINTSTRUCT ps;
HBITMAP hBitmap;
HMENU hmenu;
HDC hdc;
LPSTR p;
static char *bitsize[2]={ BITMAP16,BITMAP256 };
int i,j,x,y;

switch(message) {
    case WM_INITDIALOG:
        if(GetDeviceBits(hwnd) <= 4) p=bitsize[0];
        else p=bitsize[1];

        if(GetBitmapDimensions(p,&x,&y,&i)) {
            i=(GetSystemMetrics(SM_CXSCREEN)-x)/2;
            j=(GetSystemMetrics(SM_CYSCREEN)-y)/2;
            SetWindowPos(hwnd,NULL,i,j,
                x,y+GetSystemMetrics(SM_CYCAPTION),SWP_NOZORDER);
        }
        hmenu=GetSystemMenu(hwnd,FALSE);
        AppendMenu(hmenu,MF_SEPARATOR,NULL,NULL);
        AppendMenu(hmenu,MF_STRING,IDHELP,FetchString(MESSAGE_HELP));
        break;
    case WM_CTLCOLOR:
        return(Ctl3dCtlColorEx(message,wParam,lParam));
    case WM_PAINT:
        hdc=BeginPaint(hwnd,&ps);
        if(GetDeviceBits(hwnd) <= 4) p=bitsize[0];
        else p=bitsize[1];

        if((hBitmap=LoadResource(hInst,
          FindResource(hInst,p,RT_BITMAP))) != NULL) {
            DrawImage(hdc,0,0,hBitmap,SRCCOPY);
            FreeResource(hBitmap);
        }

        EndPaint(hwnd,&ps);
        break;
    case WM_SYSCOMMAND:
        switch(wParam & 0xfff0) {
            case SC_CLOSE:
                SendMessage(hwnd,WM_COMMAND,IDOK,0L);
                break;
        }
        switch(wParam) {
            case IDHELP:
                SendMessage(hwnd,WM_COMMAND,IDHELP,0L);
                break;
        }
        break;
    case WM_COMMAND:
```

```
            switch(wParam) {
                case IDHELP:
                    DoHelp(hwnd,(LPSTR)"Bitmaps");
                    break;
                case IDOK:
                    EndDialog(hwnd,wParam);
                    break;
            }
            break;
    }

    return(FALSE);
}

void DoButtons(HWND hwnd)
{
    FARPROC lpfnDlgProc;

    if((lpfnDlgProc=MakeProcInstance((FARPROC)ButtonDlgProc,hInst)) != NULL) {
        DialogBox(hInst,"ButtonBox",hwnd,lpfnDlgProc);
        FreeProcInstance(lpfnDlgProc);
    }
}

DWORD FAR PASCAL ButtonDlgProc(HWND hwnd,WORD message,WORD wParam,LONG lParam)
{
    static HFONT hFont;
        PAINTSTRUCT ps;
    HWND dlgH;
    int i;

    switch(message) {
        case WM_INITDIALOG:
            if((hFont=CreateFont(32,0,0,0,0,0,0,0,
                SYMBOL_CHARSET,OUT_DEFAULT_PRECIS,CLIP_DEFAULT_PRECIS,
                DEFAULT_QUALITY,DEFAULT_PITCH | FF_DONTCARE,
                DINGBATS)) != NULL) {
                for(i=0;i<BUTTON_BASECOUNT;++i) {
                    dlgH=GetDlgItem(hwnd,BUTTON_BASE+i);
                    SendMessage(dlgH,WM_SETFONT,(WORD)hFont,FALSE);
                }
            }

            SetControlFont(hwnd,IDHELP);
            SetControlFont(hwnd,IDOK);

            CentreWindow(hwnd);

            break;
        case WM_CTLCOLOR:
            return(Ctl3dCtlColorEx(message,wParam,lParam));
        case WM_PAINT:
            BeginPaint(hwnd,&ps);
```

3-13 *Continued*

```
                EndPaint(hwnd,&ps);
                break;
        case WM_COMMAND:
            switch(wParam) {
                case IDHELP:
                    DoHelp(hwnd,(LPSTR)"Buttons");
                    break;
                case IDOK:
                    if(hFont != NULL) DeleteObject(hFont);
                    EndDialog(hwnd,wParam);
                    break;
                default:
                    DoMessage(hwnd,FetchString(wParam));
                    break;
            }
            break;
    }

    return(FALSE);
}

void DoColours(HWND hwnd)
{
    FARPROC lpfnDlgProc;

    if((lpfnDlgProc=MakeProcInstance((FARPROC)ColourDlgProc,hInst)) != NULL) {
        DialogBox(hInst,"ColourBox",hwnd,lpfnDlgProc);
        FreeProcInstance(lpfnDlgProc);
    }
}

DWORD FAR PASCAL ColourDlgProc(HWND hwnd,WORD message,WORD wParam,LONG lParam)
{
    static HBRUSH hBrush;
    static COLORREF colour=LIGHTGREY;
    PAINTSTRUCT ps;
    HWND dlgH;
    HDC hdc;
    char b[33];
    int n,w;

    switch(message) {
        case WM_INITDIALOG:
            hBrush=CreateSolidBrush(colour);

            dlgH=GetDlgItem(hwnd,COLOUR_REDSET);
            SetScrollRange(dlgH,SB_CTL,0,255,TRUE);
            SetScrollPos(dlgH,SB_CTL,GetRValue(colour),TRUE);
            n=GetScrollPos(dlgH,SB_CTL);

            dlgH=GetDlgItem(hwnd,COLOUR_REDVAL);
```

```
sprintf(b," %d",n);
SetWindowText(dlgH,b);
EnableWindow(dlgH,TRUE);

dlgH=GetDlgItem(hwnd,COLOUR_GREENSET);
SetScrollRange(dlgH,SB_CTL,0,255,TRUE);
SetScrollPos(dlgH,SB_CTL,GetGValue(colour),TRUE);
n=GetScrollPos(dlgH,SB_CTL);

dlgH=GetDlgItem(hwnd,COLOUR_GREENVAL);
sprintf(b," %d",n);
SetWindowText(dlgH,b);
EnableWindow(dlgH,TRUE);

dlgH=GetDlgItem(hwnd,COLOUR_BLUESET);
SetScrollRange(dlgH,SB_CTL,0,255,TRUE);
SetScrollPos(dlgH,SB_CTL,GetBValue(colour),TRUE);
n=GetScrollPos(dlgH,SB_CTL);

dlgH=GetDlgItem(hwnd,COLOUR_BLUEVAL);
sprintf(b," %d",n);
SetWindowText(dlgH,b);
EnableWindow(dlgH,TRUE);

SetControlFont(hwnd,COLOUR_REDTEXT);
SetControlFont(hwnd,COLOUR_GREENTEXT);
SetControlFont(hwnd,COLOUR_BLUETEXT);

SetControlFont(hwnd,COLOUR_REDVAL);
SetControlFont(hwnd,COLOUR_GREENVAL);
SetControlFont(hwnd,COLOUR_BLUEVAL);
SetControlFont(hwnd,IDHELP);
SetControlFont(hwnd,IDOK);

CentreWindow(hwnd);

break;
case WM_HSCROLL:
    w=GetWindowWord(HIWORD(lParam),GWW_ID);

    dlgH=GetDlgItem(hwnd,w);
    n=GetScrollPos(dlgH,SB_CTL);
    switch(wParam) {
        case SB_LINEUP:
            n-=1;
            break;
        case SB_LINEDOWN:
            n+=1;
            break;
        case SB_PAGEUP:
            n-=10;
            break;
        case SB_PAGEDOWN:
```

3-13 *Continued*

```
                n+=10;
                break;
        case SB_THUMBPOSITION:
                n=LOWORD(lParam);
                break;
    }

    if(n < 0) n=0;
    else if(n > 255) n=255;

    if(n != GetScrollPos(dlgH,SB_CTL)) {
        SetScrollPos(dlgH,SB_CTL,n,TRUE);
        switch(w) {
            case COLOUR_REDSET:
                dlgH=GetDlgItem(hwnd,COLOUR_REDVAL);
                sprintf(b," %d",n);
                SetWindowText(dlgH,b);
                colour=RGB(n,GetGValue(colour),GetBValue(colour));
                break;
            case COLOUR_GREENSET:
                dlgH=GetDlgItem(hwnd,COLOUR_GREENVAL);
                sprintf(b," %d",n);
                SetWindowText(dlgH,b);
                colour=RGB(GetRValue(colour),n,GetBValue(colour));
                break;
            case COLOUR_BLUESET:
                dlgH=GetDlgItem(hwnd,COLOUR_BLUEVAL);
                sprintf(b," %d",n);
                SetWindowText(dlgH,b);
                colour=RGB(GetRValue(colour),GetGValue(colour),n);
                break;
        }
        DeleteObject(hBrush);
        hdc=GetDC(hwnd);
        hBrush=CreateSolidBrush(colour);

        ReleaseDC(hwnd,hdc);

        InvalidateRect(hwnd,NULL,TRUE);
    }
    return(FALSE);
case WM_CTLCOLOR:
    return(Ctl3dCtlColorEx(message,wParam,lParam));
case WM_PAINT:
    hdc=BeginPaint(hwnd,&ps);
    SelectObject(hdc,GetStockObject(BLACK_PEN));
    SelectObject(hdc,hBrush);
    Rectangle(hdc,CHECK_SWLEFT,CHECK_SWTOP,CHECK_SWRIGHT,CHECK_SWBOTTOM);
    SelectObject(hdc,GetStockObject(NULL_BRUSH));
    EndPaint(hwnd,&ps);
    break;
```

```
            case WM_COMMAND:
                switch(wParam) {
                    case IDHELP:
                        DoHelp(hwnd,(LPSTR)"Colours");
                        break;
                    case IDOK:
                        if(hBrush != NULL) DeleteObject(hBrush);
                        EndDialog(hwnd,wParam);
                        break;
                }
                break;
    }

    return(FALSE);
}

DWORD FAR PASCAL AboutDlgProc(HWND hwnd,WORD message,WORD wParam,LONG lParam)
{
    HWND dlgH;

    switch(message) {
        case WM_INITDIALOG:
            ItemName(MESSAGE_STRING,FetchString(MESSAGE_ABOUT));
            CentreWindow(hwnd);
            SetControlFont(hwnd,MESSAGE_STRING);
            SetControlFont(hwnd,IDOK);
            return(FALSE);
        case WM_CTLCOLOR:
            return(Ctl3dCtlColorEx(message,wParam,lParam));
        case WM_COMMAND:
            switch(wParam) {
                case IDOK:
                    EndDialog(hwnd,wParam);
                    return(FALSE);
            }
            break;
    }

    return(FALSE);
}

void CentreWindow(HWND hwnd)
{
    RECT rect;
    unsigned int x,y;

    GetWindowRect(hwnd,&rect);
    x=(GetSystemMetrics(SM_CXSCREEN)-(rect.right-rect.left))/2;
    y=(GetSystemMetrics(SM_CYSCREEN)-(rect.bottom-rect.top))/2;
    SetWindowPos(hwnd,NULL,x,y,rect.right-rect.left,rect.bottom-rect.top,
      SWP_NOSIZE);
}
```

191

3-13 *Continued*

```
LPSTR FetchString(unsigned int n)
{
    static char b[257];

    if(!LoadString(hInst,n,b,256))
        lstrcpy(b,"String table error - this application may be damaged");
    return(b);
}

int GetDeviceBits(HWND hwnd)
{
    HDC hdc;
    int i;

    hdc=GetDC(hwnd);
    i=(GetDeviceCaps(hdc,PLANES) * GetDeviceCaps(hdc,BITSPIXEL));
    ReleaseDC(hwnd,hdc);
    if(i > 8) i=24;
    return(i);
}

void DrawImage(HDC hdc,int x,int y,HBITMAP image,DWORD op)
{
    LPSTR p,pi;
    HDC hMemoryDC;
    HBITMAP hBitmap,hOldBitmap;
    LPBITMAPINFO bh;
    HANDLE hPal;
    LOGPALETTE *pLogPal;
    int i,n;

    if(image==NULL) return;

    if((p=LockResource(image))==NULL) return;

    bh=(LPBITMAPINFO)p;
    if(bh->bmiHeader.biBitCount > 8) n=256;
    else n=(1<<bh->bmiHeader.biBitCount);

    pi=p+sizeof(BITMAPINFOHEADER)+n*sizeof(RGBQUAD);

    if((pLogPal=(LOGPALETTE *)LocalAlloc(LMEM_FIXED,sizeof(LOGPALETTE)+
      256*sizeof(PALETTEENTRY))) != NULL) {
        pLogPal->palVersion=0x0300;
        pLogPal->palNumEntries=n;

        for(i=0;i<n;i++) {
            pLogPal->palPalEntry[i].peRed=bh->bmiColors[i].rgbRed;
            pLogPal->palPalEntry[i].peGreen=bh->bmiColors[i].rgbGreen;
            pLogPal->palPalEntry[i].peBlue=bh->bmiColors[i].rgbBlue;
            pLogPal->palPalEntry[i].peFlags=0;
```

```
        }

        hPal=CreatePalette(pLogPal);
        LocalFree((HANDLE)pLogPal);

        SelectPalette(hdc,hPal,0);
        RealizePalette(hdc);
    }

    if((hBitmap=CreateDIBitmap(hdc,(LPBITMAPINFOHEADER)p,CBM_INIT,pi,
        (LPBITMAPINFO)p,DIB_RGB_COLORS)) != NULL) {
        if((hMemoryDC=CreateCompatibleDC(hdc)) != NULL) {
            hOldBitmap=SelectObject(hMemoryDC,hBitmap);
            if(hOldBitmap) {
                BitBlt(hdc,x,y,(int)bh->bmiHeader.biWidth,
                    (int)bh->bmiHeader.biHeight,hMemoryDC,0,0,op);
                SelectObject(hMemoryDC,hOldBitmap);
            }
            DeleteDC(hMemoryDC);
        }
        DeleteObject(hBitmap);
    }

    UnlockResource(image);
}

int GetBitmapDimensions(LPSTR name,LPINT x,LPINT y,LPINT bits)
{
    HBITMAP hBitmap;
    LPBITMAPINFO bh;

    if((hBitmap=LoadResource(hInst,FindResource(hInst,name,RT_BITMAP))) != NULL) {
        if((bh=(LPBITMAPINFO)LockResource(hBitmap))!=NULL) {
            *x=(int)bh->bmiHeader.biWidth;
            *y=(int)bh->bmiHeader.biHeight;
            *bits=bh->bmiHeader.biBitCount;
            UnlockResource(hBitmap);
        } else return(FALSE);
        FreeResource(hBitmap);
    } else return(FALSE);
    return(TRUE);
}

void SetHelpSize(HWND hwnd)
{
    HELPWININFO helpinfo;
    char b[145];

    memset((char *)&helpinfo,0,sizeof(HELPWININFO));
    helpinfo.wStructSize=sizeof(HELPWININFO);
    helpinfo.x=10;
    helpinfo.y=10;
    helpinfo.dx=512;
```

3-13 *Continued*

```
    helpinfo.dy=1004;

    MakeHelpPathName(b);
    WinHelp(hwnd,b,HELP_SETWINPOS,(DWORD)&helpinfo);
}

void DoHelp(HWND hwnd,LPSTR keyword)
{
    char b[145];

    MakeHelpPathName(b);
    WinHelp(hwnd,b,HELP_KEY,(DWORD)keyword);
}

void MakeHelpPathName(LPSTR szFileName)
{
    LPSTR pcFileName;
    int nFileNameLen;

    nFileNameLen = GetModuleFileName(hInst,szFileName,144);
    pcFileName = szFileName+nFileNameLen;

    while(pcFileName > szFileName) {
        if(*pcFileName == '\\' || *pcFileName == ':') {
            *(++pcFileName) = '\0';
            break;
        }
        nFileNameLen--;
        pcFileName--;
    }

    if((nFileNameLen+13) < 144) lstrcat(szFileName,HELPFILE);
    else lstrcat(szFileName, "?");
}
```

Figure 3-14 *The DEMO3.RC resource script.*

```
MainScreen DIALOG 69, 55, 260, 188
STYLE WS_POPUP | WS_CAPTION | WS_SYSMENU | WS_MINIMIZEBOX
CAPTION "Dialog Demo Three"
MENU MainMenu
BEGIN
END

AboutBox DIALOG 72, 72, 220, 128
STYLE WS_POPUP | WS_CAPTION
CAPTION "About"
BEGIN
    CTEXT "", 101, 16, 16, 188, 72, WS_CHILD | WS_VISIBLE | WS_GROUP
    DEFPUSHBUTTON "OK", IDOK, 96, 104, 28, 16, WS_CHILD | WS_VISIBLE | WS_TABSTOP
```

```
        CONTROL "", -1, "static", SS_BLACKFRAME | WS_CHILD | WS_VISIBLE, 8, 8, 204, 88
END


ColourBox DIALOG 100, 100, 168, 76
STYLE DS_MODALFRAME | WS_POPUP | WS_CAPTION
CAPTION "Adjust Colour"
BEGIN
    SCROLLBAR 101, 44, 12, 93, 9, SBS_HORZ | WS_CHILD | WS_VISIBLE
    SCROLLBAR 102, 44, 24, 93, 9, SBS_HORZ | WS_CHILD | WS_VISIBLE
    SCROLLBAR 103, 44, 36, 93, 9, SBS_HORZ | WS_CHILD | WS_VISIBLE
    LTEXT "", 201, 140, 12, 20, 8, WS_CHILD | WS_VISIBLE | WS_GROUP
    LTEXT "", 202, 140, 24, 20, 8, WS_CHILD | WS_VISIBLE | WS_GROUP
    LTEXT "", 203, 140, 36, 20, 8, WS_CHILD | WS_VISIBLE | WS_GROUP
    RTEXT "Red  ", 301, 8, 12, 32, 8, SS_RIGHT | WS_CHILD |
      WS_VISIBLE | WS_GROUP
    RTEXT "Green  ", 302, 8, 24, 32, 8, SS_RIGHT | WS_CHILD |
      WS_VISIBLE | WS_GROUP
    RTEXT "Blue  ", 303, 8, 36, 32, 8, SS_RIGHT | WS_CHILD |
      WS_VISIBLE | WS_GROUP
    CONTROL "", -1, "static", SS_GRAYFRAME | WS_CHILD |
      WS_VISIBLE, 8, 12, 32, 8
    CONTROL "", -1, "static", SS_GRAYFRAME | WS_CHILD |
      WS_VISIBLE, 8, 24, 32, 8
    CONTROL "", -1, "static", SS_GRAYFRAME | WS_CHILD |
      WS_VISIBLE, 8, 36, 32, 8
    CONTROL "", -1, "static", SS_WHITEFRAME | WS_CHILD |
      WS_VISIBLE, 140, 12, 20, 8
    CONTROL "", -1, "static", SS_WHITEFRAME | WS_CHILD |
      WS_VISIBLE, 140, 24, 20, 8
    CONTROL "", -1, "static", SS_WHITEFRAME | WS_CHILD |
      WS_VISIBLE, 140, 36, 20, 8
    DEFPUSHBUTTON "OK", IDOK, 132, 52, 28, 16, WS_CHILD |
      WS_VISIBLE | WS_TABSTOP
    PUSHBUTTON "Help", IDHELP, 96, 52, 28, 16, WS_CHILD |
      WS_VISIBLE | WS_TABSTOP
    CONTROL "", -1, "static", SS_BLACKFRAME | WS_CHILD |
      WS_VISIBLE, 8, 52, 84, 16
END


MainMenu MENU
BEGIN
    POPUP "File"
    BEGIN
        MENUITEM "&Buttons", 101
        MENUITEM "&Scroll Bars", 102
        MENUITEM "&Colours", 103
        MENUITEM "C&heck Boxes", 104
        MENUITEM "B&itmaps", 105
        MENUITEM "&List Boxes", 106
        MENUITEM "Co&mbo Boxes", 107
        MENUITEM SEPARATOR
        MENUITEM "E&xit", 199
    END
```

3-14 *Continued*

```
POPUP "&Help"
BEGIN
    MENUITEM "&Index", 901
    MENUITEM "&Using help", 905
    MENUITEM SEPARATOR
    MENUITEM "&About...", 999
END

END

STRINGTABLE
BEGIN
    0,"Dialog Demo Three\nCopyright \251 1993 Alchemy Mindworks Inc.\n
      From the book Windows Dialog Construction Set\rby Steven William Rimmer\r
      Published by Windcrest/McGraw Hill"
    1,"Help"
    201,"How can I insert disk number three when there's only room for
      two in the slot?"
    202,"Your Macintosh is about to explode.\rDo not panic... this is a popular
      feature of all Apple computers."
    203,"Yin and yang\rBlack and white\rMale and female\rHonesty and politics\n
      Toyota and automobiles"
    204,"Whatever this symbol means, avoid dropping anything so marked on your
      cat unless you're tired of its company."
    205,"When you see this symbol, Windows is working to rule."
    206,"When you see this symbol on your television, hit the mute button.\r
      It's a Sprint commercial."
    207,"Cassettes are a crutch for people who can't face reel to reel."
    208,"It's ten o'clock... do you know where your poodle is?"
    209,"Structural dialgram of the Canadian parlament."
END

DialogDemoThree ICON
BEGIN
    '00 00 01 00 01 00 20 20 10 00 00 00 00 00 E8 02'
    '00 00 16 00 00 00 28 00 00 00 20 00 00 00 40 00'
    '00 00 01 00 04 00 00 00 00 00 80 02 00 00 00 00'
    '00 00 00 00 00 00 00 00 00 00 00 00 00 00 00 00'
    '00 00 00 00 80 00 00 80 00 00 00 80 80 00 80 00'
    '00 00 80 00 80 00 80 80 00 00 80 80 80 00 C0 C0'
    'C0 00 00 00 FF 00 00 FF 00 00 00 FF FF 00 FF 00'
    '00 00 FF 00 FF 00 FF FF 00 00 FF FF FF 00 2A 2A'
    '2A 2A 2A 2A 2A 2A 2A 22 77 70 00 00 00 00 A2 A2'
    'A2 A2 A2 A2 A2 A2 A2 A2 22 70 00 00 00 00 2A 2A'
    '2A 2A 2A 2A 2A AA AA A2 70 00 00 00 00 A2 2A'
    'A2 A2 AA AA AA AA B2 AA AA 77 77 77 77 00 2A 2A'
    'AA AA 2A 2A AA 2A AA A9 19 19 19 19 17 77 AA A2'
    'A2 AA AB AB AB AA 91 91 91 91 91 91 91 97 2A AA'
    'BA BA 2A AA A9 19 19 19 19 99 99 99 99 19 AB AB'
    'A2 AA AA 11 11 91 99 99 99 90 00 00 09 99 BA BA'
    'AA A1 01 11 19 19 19 19 90 00 00 00 00 09 AA A2'
```

```
        '00 10 10 11 11 91 91 00 00 00 00 70 00 00 2A 00'
        '00 00 01 01 11 17 77 00 00 00 09 70 00 00 A2 22'
        '22 22 22 22 22 22 27 77 77 70 09 70 00 00 2A 2A'
        '2A 2A AA AA AA AA 22 22 22 77 09 77 00 00 A2 AA'
        'AA AA A2 AA AA AA A2 A2 A2 27 79 17 70 00 2A AA'
        'AA 2A 22 22 2A 2A AA AA AA 2A 79 91 77 00 A2 A2'
        'A2 22 70 70 22 A2 A2 AB A2 A2 00 99 17 77 2A 2A'
        '22 87 07 07 02 2A 2A AA AA 27 00 09 91 91 A2 A2'
        'F8 88 77 70 72 A2 AB AB AB A0 00 00 99 99 2A 22'
        '8F 88 00 77 07 2A 2A AA AA 70 00 00 00 00 A2 28'
        'F8 F0 00 08 70 22 22 A2 A2 00 00 00 00 00 2A 2F'
        '8F 80 00 07 07 2A 2A AA A7 00 00 00 00 00 A7 28'
        'F8 FF 00 88 82 22 A2 A2 A0 00 00 00 00 00 22 7F'
        '8F FF FF 8F 82 2A 2A 2A 70 00 00 00 00 00 A7 0F'
        'FF FF F8 F8 F2 A2 A2 A2 00 00 00 00 00 00 A2 70'
        'FF FF 8F 8F 2A 2A 2A 20 00 00 00 00 00 00 A7 07'
        'FF FF F8 F8 22 A2 A2 00 00 00 00 00 00 00 A2 70'
        '70 FF 8F 22 2A 2A 20 00 00 00 00 00 00 00 AA 07'
        '07 07 02 02 A2 A2 00 00 00 00 00 00 00 00 BA A0'
        '70 70 72 2A 2A 20 00 00 00 00 00 00 00 00 BB AA'
        'A7 A7 AA AA A0 00 00 00 00 00 00 00 00 00 AA BA'
        'AA AA AA 00 00 00 00 00 00 00 00 00 00 00 AA A0'
        '00 00 00 00 00 00 00 00 00 00 00 00 00 00 00 00'
        '01 FF 00 00 01 FF 00 00 01 FF 00 00 03 00 00 00'
        '00 00 00 00 00 00 00 00 00 00 00 00 01 F8 00 00'
        '07 FE 00 00 3F DF 00 00 3F 9F 00 00 01 9F 00 00'
        '00 8F 00 00 00 07 00 00 03 00 00 00 C0 00 00 00'
        '00 E0 00 00 01 F0 00 00 01 FF 00 00 03 FF 00 00'
        '03 FF 00 00 07 FF 00 00 07 FF 00 00 0F FF 00 00'
        '1F FF 00 00 3F FF 00 00 7F FF 00 00 FF FF 00 01'
        'FF FF 00 07 FF FF 00 3F FF FF 1F FF FF FF'
END
ButtonBox DIALOG 80, 72, 88, 112
STYLE DS_MODALFRAME ¦ WS_POPUP ¦ WS_CAPTION
CAPTION "Buttons"
BEGIN
        PUSHBUTTON "<", 201, 8, 12, 24, 24, WS_CHILD ¦ WS_VISIBLE ¦ WS_TABSTOP
        PUSHBUTTON "M", 202, 32, 12, 24, 24, WS_CHILD ¦ WS_VISIBLE ¦ WS_TABSTOP
        PUSHBUTTON "[", 203, 56, 12, 24, 24, WS_CHILD ¦ WS_VISIBLE ¦ WS_TABSTOP
        PUSHBUTTON "\\", 204, 8, 36, 24, 24, WS_CHILD ¦ WS_VISIBLE ¦ WS_TABSTOP
        PUSHBUTTON "6", 205, 32, 36, 24, 24, WS_CHILD ¦ WS_VISIBLE ¦ WS_TABSTOP
        PUSHBUTTON "(", 206, 56, 36, 24, 24, WS_CHILD ¦ WS_VISIBLE ¦ WS_TABSTOP
        PUSHBUTTON ">", 207, 8, 60, 24, 24, WS_CHILD ¦ WS_VISIBLE ¦ WS_TABSTOP
        PUSHBUTTON "\300", 208, 32, 60, 24, 24, WS_CHILD ¦ WS_VISIBLE ¦ WS_TABSTOP
        PUSHBUTTON "\314", 209, 56, 60, 24, 24, WS_CHILD ¦ WS_VISIBLE ¦ WS_TABSTOP
        DEFPUSHBUTTON "OK", IDOK, 48, 92, 28, 16, WS_CHILD ¦ WS_VISIBLE ¦ WS_TABSTOP
        PUSHBUTTON "Help", IDHELP, 12, 92, 28, 16, WS_CHILD ¦ WS_VISIBLE ¦ WS_TABSTOP
END

MessageBox DIALOG 72, 72, 220, 128
STYLE WS_POPUP ¦ WS_CAPTION
CAPTION "Message"
BEGIN
```

3-14 *Continued*

```
    CTEXT "", 101, 16, 16, 188, 72, WS_CHILD | WS_VISIBLE | WS_GROUP
    DEFPUSHBUTTON "OK", IDOK, 96, 104, 28, 16, WS_CHILD | WS_VISIBLE | WS_TABSTOP
    CONTROL "", -1, "static", SS_BLACKFRAME | WS_CHILD | WS_VISIBLE, 8, 8, 204, 88
END

Bitmap16 BITMAP demo_16.bmp

Bitmap256 BITMAP demo_256.bmp

BitmapMenu BITMAP menu_bmp.bmp

ListText RCDATA listbox.txt

ListBitmap BITMAP list_bmp.bmp

BitmapBox DIALOG 72, 72, 72, 72
STYLE WS_POPUP | WS_CAPTION | WS_SYSMENU
CAPTION "Bitmap"
BEGIN
END

ScrollBox DIALOG 72, 72, 100, 100
STYLE WS_POPUP | WS_CAPTION | WS_VSCROLL | WS_HSCROLL
CAPTION "Scroll Bars"
BEGIN
    RTEXT "Horizontal scroll", 101, 8, 12, 56, 8, SS_RIGHT |
      WS_CHILD | WS_VISIBLE | WS_GROUP
    LTEXT "", 201, 68, 12, 16, 8, WS_CHILD | WS_VISIBLE | WS_GROUP
    CONTROL "", -1, "static", SS_BLACKFRAME | WS_CHILD |
      WS_VISIBLE, 68, 12, 16, 8
    RTEXT "Vertical scroll", 102, 8, 24, 56, 8, SS_RIGHT |
      WS_CHILD | WS_VISIBLE | WS_GROUP
    LTEXT "", 202, 68, 24, 16, 8, WS_CHILD | WS_VISIBLE | WS_GROUP
    CONTROL "", -1, "static", SS_BLACKFRAME | WS_CHILD |
      WS_VISIBLE, 68, 24, 16, 8
    DEFPUSHBUTTON "OK", IDOK, 56, 68, 28, 16, WS_CHILD |
      WS_VISIBLE | WS_TABSTOP
    PUSHBUTTON "Help", IDHELP, 20, 68, 28, 16, WS_CHILD |
      WS_VISIBLE | WS_TABSTOP
END

CheckBox DIALOG 72, 72, 180, 84
STYLE DS_MODALFRAME | WS_POPUP | WS_CAPTION
CAPTION "Check Boxes and Radio Buttons"
BEGIN
    RADIOBUTTON "Normal", 101, 12, 16, 60, 8, WS_CHILD | WS_VISIBLE | WS_TABSTOP
    RADIOBUTTON "Invert", 102, 12, 28, 60, 8, WS_CHILD | WS_VISIBLE | WS_TABSTOP
    RADIOBUTTON "Hide", 103, 12, 40, 60, 8, WS_CHILD | WS_VISIBLE | WS_TABSTOP
    CHECKBOX "Horizontal lines", 201, 12, 56, 64, 8, WS_CHILD |
      WS_VISIBLE | WS_TABSTOP
    CHECKBOX "Vertical lines", 202, 12, 68, 64, 8, WS_CHILD | WS_VISIBLE | WS_TABSTOP
```

```
        CONTROL " Picture Effect ", 105, "button", BS_GROUPBOX | WS_CHILD |
            WS_VISIBLE | WS_GROUP, 8, 4, 68, 48
        DEFPUSHBUTTON "OK", IDOK, 144, 60, 28, 16, WS_CHILD | WS_VISIBLE | WS_TABSTOP
        PUSHBUTTON "Help", IDHELP, 108, 60, 28, 16, WS_CHILD | WS_VISIBLE | WS_TABSTOP
END


ListBox DIALOG 50, 20, 312, 224
STYLE DS_MODALFRAME | WS_POPUP | WS_CAPTION
CAPTION "List"
BEGIN
    LISTBOX 101, 8, 8, 152, 184, LBS_NOTIFY | WS_CHILD | WS_VISIBLE |
        WS_BORDER | WS_VSCROLL
    LTEXT "Selected text:", 103, 8, 196, 152, 8, WS_CHILD | WS_VISIBLE | WS_GROUP
    EDITTEXT 102, 8, 204, 152, 12, ES_LEFT | WS_CHILD | WS_VISIBLE |
        WS_BORDER | WS_TABSTOP
    DEFPUSHBUTTON "OK", IDOK, 276, 200, 28, 16, WS_CHILD |
        WS_VISIBLE | WS_TABSTOP
    PUSHBUTTON "Help", IDHELP, 240, 200, 28, 16, WS_CHILD |
        WS_VISIBLE | WS_TABSTOP
END


ComboBox DIALOG 50, 20, 312, 224
STYLE DS_MODALFRAME | WS_POPUP | WS_CAPTION
CAPTION "Combo Box"
BEGIN
    CONTROL "", 101, "COMBOBOX", CBS_DROPDOWNLIST | WS_CHILD |
        WS_VISIBLE | WS_TABSTOP, 8, 8, 152, 184
    LTEXT "Selected text:", 103, 8, 196, 152, 8, WS_CHILD |
        WS_VISIBLE | WS_GROUP
    EDITTEXT 102, 8, 204, 152, 12, ES_LEFT | WS_CHILD |
        WS_VISIBLE | WS_BORDER | WS_TABSTOP
    DEFPUSHBUTTON "OK", IDOK, 276, 200, 28, 16, WS_CHILD |
        WS_VISIBLE | WS_TABSTOP
    PUSHBUTTON "Help", IDHELP, 240, 200, 28, 16, WS_CHILD |
        WS_VISIBLE | WS_TABSTOP
END
```

Once again, the DEMO3 program doesn't do too much differently from its predecessors, and as its predecessors did nothing useful to speak of you probably won't want to spend a lot of time working with the application itself. However, seeing how it works—and specifically, how it works with CTL3D—might be considerably more worthwhile.

The first important change in DEMO3.CPP can be found in its WinMain function. The Ctl3dRegister and Ctl3dAutoSubclass functions set up the CTL3D library and link it into the window-creation functions for your application. Unlike BWCC, CTL3D will automatically apply its three-dimensional look and feel to all the

windows in an application without being told explicitly to do so. This will prove especially useful when you look at the Windows common dialogs later in this book, as they're wont to unexpectedly sprout dialogs that you can't control from within an application.

The Ctl3dUnregister function, called at the end of WinMain, unhooks CTL3D when your application terminates.

Automatic subclassing, as handled by Ctl3dAutoSubclass, is the easiest way to apply CTL3D to all the windows in your application, but there are two reasons why you might not want to do this. The first is that it doesn't work all that well for applications written to be backwards compatible with Windows 3.0. Fortunately, not many users of Windows still use version 3.0, so this might be regarded as a moot point.

The other reason for not applying CTL3D to every pore and crevice of your application is that you might want a few dialogs that aren't subject to the restrictions of the CTL3D library, most notably that of insisting that the dialog background color always be gray. If this is the case, you can omit the call to Ctl3dAutoSubclass in WinMain and call Ctl3dSubclass in the WM_INITDIALOG handler for each dialog you'd like to have CTL3D applied to. Here's what the call would look like:

```
case WM_INITDIALOG:
  Ctl3dSubclass(hwnd,CTL3D_ALL);
  break;
```

The first argument to Ctl3dSubclass is the HWND for the window the call applies to. The second is a flag defined in CTL3D.H. The DEMO3 application will use automatic subclassing.

The SelectProc function of DEMO3.CPP looks pretty much like that of the previous two applications, except for the handlers for the WM_CTLCOLOR and WM_SYSCOLORCHANGE messages. The former was touched on a moment ago. The latter hasn't appeared previously—you should call Ctl3dColorChange in response to it to allow CTL3D to update its controls if someone thoughtlessly changes the system palette.

For the most part, the dialogs of DEMO3 haven't changed structurally from the previous implementations of this program, and this will

usually be true for applying CTL3D to existing Windows programs. There are a few things to watch out for, however, should you do so:

> The three-dimensional appearance of controls created by CTL3D usually involves making them slightly larger. If you have dialogs with controls very densely arranged, you might have to move them around a bit.

> The BS_LEFTTEXT option isn't supported for check boxes and radio buttons.

> Conventional static frames are transformed into three-dimensional shadows by CTL3D. Specifically, black frames and rectangles will become drop shadows, gray frames and rectangles will become raised areas, and white frames and rectangles will become bumps. These are all slightly larger than conventional frames.

Microsoft also notes that if you use the debugging version of Windows, terminating an application that uses CTL3D will cause Windows to warn you of a brush and a bitmap not having been freed. This is spurious, and can be ignored.

Finally, the current version of CTL3D, as of this writing, intimates that it will not function under Windows 4.0. If this is the case, Microsoft will release an update for the library for the new Windows.

Working with CTL3D

A quick look through the DEMO3.CPP source code will suggest that little has changed from DEMO1.CPP in the previous chapter. One of the attractive features of CTL3D is that it does its work with very little disruption of the applications it's applied to. All the WM_CTLCOLOR handlers in the dependent dialogs of DEMO3 have been modified, of course. The most radical changes appear in the ColourDlgProc function.

In the original DEMO1 program, the Adjust Colour dialog changed its window background color in response to the settings of three scroll bars that define its color content. For reasons discussed earlier in this

section, this won't work with CTL3D. This version of the Adjust Colour dialog draws a colored tile to represent the color defined by its scroll bars. The scroll bars are all gray—setting them up to have red, green, and blue backgrounds also requires that ColourDlgProc return brush handles. Note that unlike the gray backgrounds created by BWCC, you can draw and paint on the windows created by CTL3D.

Using Resource Workshop to create dialogs for use with CTL3D requires a bit of imagination. The Resource Workshop package allows you to add other control libraries to it, but they must conform to its own standard for DLL structures. As CTL3D does not, attempting to use it as a control library attached to Resource Workshop will come to naught. Mostly, it will just crash Resource Workshop. In fact, Resource Workshop will pop up a dialog telling you so just before it plummets into oblivion.

To create dialogs that use CTL3D effects, then, you must use Resource Workshop to design flat dialogs and keep in mind what will change when your application loads up CTL3D. This basically applies to the minutely larger controls that CTL3D draws and the way it handles static frames and rectangles.

While less than wholly state of the art, this approach is useful in that it allows you to see what your dialogs will look like should CTL3D choose not to function.

A CTL3D function directory

As of this writing, the CTL3D library provides the following functions:

BOOL Ctl3dRegister(HANDLE hInst) The Ctl3dRegister function registers your application as a client of CTL3D. It will return TRUE if three-dimensional controls can be used with your application, and FALSE otherwise. Specifically, it will return FALSE if the system it finds itself running on has something other than a VGA card, or if you're running an unsuitable version of Windows.

BOOL Ctl3dUnRegister(HANDLE hInst) The Ctl3dUnRegister function unhooks CTL3D from your application. It returns TRUE if no controls in your application are using CTL3D, and FALSE otherwise.

PUBLIC BOOL FAR PASCAL Ctl3dAutoSubclass(HANDLE hInst) The Ctl3dAutoSubclass function automatically adds CTL3D effects to all the dialogs in your application. It will return TRUE if this operation is successful, and FALSE if you're running Windows 3.0, if there isn't enough memory for its internal buffers, or if it can't install its internal hooks.

WORD Ctl3dGetVer(void) The Ctl3dGetVer function returns the version of the copy of CTL3D that's in use. The high-order byte is the major version number and the low-order byte is the minor version number.

BOOL Ctl3dEnabled(void) The Ctl3dEnabled will return TRUE if CTL3D can function in your current Windows environment, and FALSE if it can't.

BOOL Ctl3dSubclassCtl(HWND hwnd) The Ctl3dSubclassCtl function will add CTL3D's effects to a single control. The window handle passed to it should be the handle for the control in question, usually fetched by a call to GetDlgItem. You would use Ctl3dSubclassCtl to subclass controls that don't appear in dialog boxes. It returns TRUE if the subclass function has been successful, and FALSE if it has not.

PUBLIC BOOL FAR PASCAL Ctl3dSubclassDlg(HWND hwnd, WORD grbit) The Ctl3dSubclassDlg function subclasses all the controls in a dialog box. The grbit argument is a set of flags that indicates which control types in the dialog should be subclassed. The flags are:

CTL3D_BUTTONS	Subclass buttons
CTL3D_LISTBOXES	Subclass list boxes
CTL3D_EDITS	Subclass edit controls
CTL3D_COMBOS	Subclass combo boxes
CTL3D_STATICTEXTS	Subclass static text controls

CTL3D_STATICFRAMES   Subclass static frames
CTL3D_ALL   Subclass all controls

HBRUSH Ctl3dCtlColorEx(UINT message, WPARAM wParam, LPARAM lParam) The Ctl3dCtlColorEx function handles WM_CTLCOLOR messages correctly for CTL3D. It will return a brush handle, or NULL if an error occurred. If Ctl3dCtlColorEx is called from a Window message handler, rather than a dialog message handler, it should be invoked like this:

```
case WM_CTLCOLOR:
 if((hBrush=Ctl3dCtlColorEx(wm,wParam,lParam)) != NULL)
  return(hBrush);
 else
  return(DefWindowProc(hwnd,message,wParam,lParam));
```

BOOL Ctl3dColorChange(VOID) The Ctl3dColorChange function handles changes in the system palette. It should be called in response to a WM_SYSCOLORCHANGE message. It returns TRUE if the palette change was handled successfully and FALSE if there was an error.

Using common dialogs

CHAPTER 4

"I've hit the control key—why am I not in control?"

One of the justifications for a massive graphical user interface like Windows, which ties up half your hard drive and requires more memory to run a word processor than a DOS application would require to manage the sum of all human knowledge, is that Windows applications should be intuitive and easy to use. The thing that's intended to make them thus is the commonality of user interface objects—menus, for example, work the same way in all Windows applications, and if you know how to work them in one package you're a long way toward learning the craft for a number of others. At least, that's the way it's supposed to be.

Under Windows 3.0, menus and buttons and such all looked the same, but it might well be argued that most new computer users don't experience difficulties with things like menus and buttons no matter what they look like. Operations such as opening a file, by comparison, can really fox people if the dialog for doing so isn't intuitive and well thought-out. Under Windows 3.0, every application that opened files was required to set up a hand-made dialog to do so. Perhaps not surprisingly, every application set up one that was just a bit different.

Windows 3.1 includes a facility to provide common dialogs for a number of the things most Windows applications are called upon to do, such as opening and saving files, printing, selecting fonts and screen colors, and so on. For reasons discussed at length in the previous chapter, this set of common dialogs is stored as a dynamic link library, COMMDLG.DLL. For practical purposes, you can treat these functions as if they were native to Windows.

The Windows common dialogs have the advantages of both standardizing the user interface of several common elements of Windows applications—a laudable undertaking—as well as absolving software authors of a great deal of work that would otherwise be involved in creating these dialogs—a still more laudable undertaking. In addition, while the Windows common dialogs can be dull and predictable and about as exciting as watching politicians lying, they can also be wild and adventurous and highly personalized. Figures 4-1A through 4-1F illustrate this.

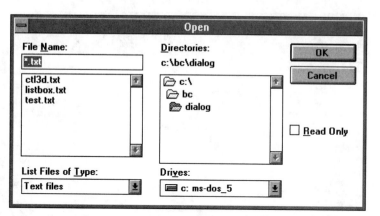

Figure 4-1A

The conventional Windows Open dialog.

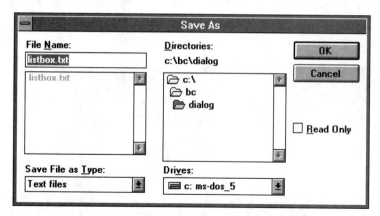

Figure 4-1B

The conventional Windows Save As dialog.

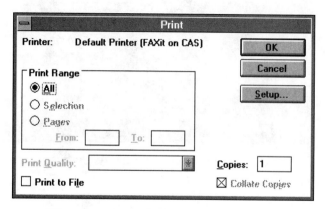

Figure 4-1C

The conventional Windows Print dialog.

Figure 4-1D

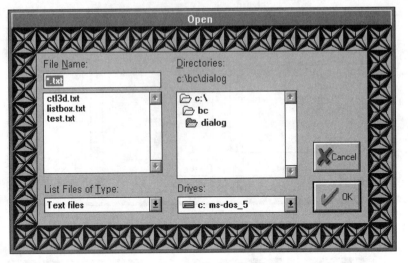

A customized Open dialog.

Figure 4-1E

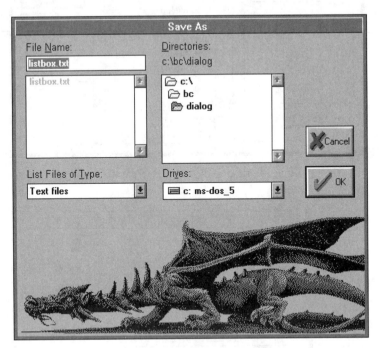

A customized Save As dialog.

Figure 4-1F

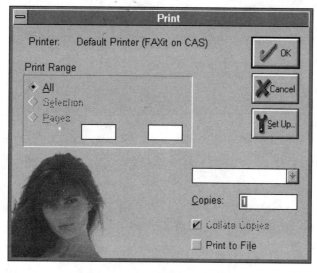

A customized Print dialog.

The Windows common dialog mechanism allows you to customize common dialogs for your own applications to an unprecedented degree. You can change the colors and locations of controls, add bitmaps, respond to controls in unconventional ways—there's a lot you can do with them, in fact, once you understand how they work.

There's one small catch, however. All the customized dialogs back in Fig. 4-1 are wholly impossible to create. While a nuisance, this too can be overcome, as you'll see later in this chapter.

⇨ An introduction to common dialogs

The COMMDLG.DLL library offers dialogs to do the following:

➢ Choose colors

➢ Select fonts

➢ Fetch a filename to open

➢ Fetch a filename to save to

➤ Set up the parameters required to print

➤ Select a printer to print to

➤ Fetch text to search for

➤ Fetch text to search for and replace it with when it's found

We'll deal with all but the last two functions in this chapter. The procedure for working with each of these functions in its simplest sense is agreeably uncomplicated. They all look like conventional Windows calls—you need not even explicitly add an import library to your application's project file to use COMMDLG.DLL. Just make sure you include the COMMDLG.H file along with the other headers you use. This is how you would get a filename to open:

```
int GetFileName(HWND hwnd,LPSTR path)
{
OPENFILENAME ofn;
char szFile[256];
char szFileTitle[256],szFilter[768],*p;
int r;

lstrcpy(szFile,{"*.TXT");

p=szFilter;
lstrcpy(p,"Text files");
p+=lstrlen(p)+1;
lstrcpy(p,szFile);
p+=lstrlen(p)+1;

lstrcpy(p,"All files");
p+=lstrlen(p)+1;
lstrcpy(p,"*.*");
p+=lstrlen(p)+1;
*p=0;
memset((char *)&ofn,0,sizeof(OPENFILENAME));

szFileTitle[0]=0;

ofn.lStructSize=sizeof(OPENFILENAME);
ofn.hwndOwner=hwnd;
ofn.hInstance=hInst;
ofn.lpstrFilter=szFilter;
ofn.nFilterIndex=1;
ofn.lpstrFile=szFile;
ofn.nMaxFile=sizeof(szFile);
ofn.lpstrFileTitle=szFileTitle;
ofn.nMaxFileTitle=sizeof(szFileTitle);
ofn.Flags=OFN_PATHMUSTEXIST | OFN_FILEMUSTEXIST;
ofn.lpstrTitle="Open";
```

```
r=GetOpenFileName(&ofn);

lstrcpy(path,ofn.lpstrFile);

return(r);
}
```

The GetOpenFileName call will display the File Open dialog, set up a file type filter, and wait for some mouse action. When it's done, the lpstrFile element of the OPENFILENAME object passed to it will contain the selected filename. The GetOpenFileName function will return a true value if the OK button in the File Open dialog was clicked, and a false value otherwise.

In order to work with the GetOpenFileName call, you'll require some understanding of the mysteries of the OPENFILENAME object and its members. In fact, inasmuch as all the common dialogs use similar objects and a similar interface approach, once you have this dragon on the ropes, the rest of the common dialogs should prove to be little more than lizards with bad breath.

Here's a look at those members of OPENFILENAME you'll probably want to joust with. This list isn't as venomous as it might appear, as many of its elements can be ignored for simple applications of GetOpenFileName. Note that prior to setting up anything in an OPENFILENAME object, the whole structure should be overwritten with zero bytes. As such, any elements you ignore can be considered set to NULL or zero.

DWORD lStructSize This is the size of the structure in bytes. Reason denies the possibility that any data structure's size will require a long integer to store it, but let's ignore this for the moment. This should always be set to sizeof(OPENFILENAME).

HWND hwndOwner This is the HWND of the parent window for the Open File dialog.

HINSTANCE hInstance This is the instance handle for your application, as initially passed to WinMain. It's not actually needed for simple applications of GetOpenFileName—I'll discuss how it's used later in this chapter.

LPCSTR lpstrFilter This is a list of file type filters that will appear in the File Type combo box. Each filter should consist of a text name for the file type involved, such as Text Files, followed by a zero byte, followed by a wildcard to match the files, followed by another zero byte. A final additional zero byte indicates the end of the list.

DWORD nFilterIndex This is a number representing which of the filters pointed to by lpstrFilter should be the default filter for the Open File dialog. The first filter is referenced by an index value of one.

LPSTR lpstrFile This element points to a string that will initially appear in the File Name edit control of the Open File dialog. This buffer is also where the name returned by GetOpenFileName will be stored.

DWORD nMaxFile This element defines how big the buffer at lpstrFile is.

LPCSTR lpstrInitialDir This element defines the initial directory for the file dialog. If it's NULL, the current directory will be used.

LPCSTR lpstrTitle This element points to a string to be used as the title of the Open File dialog. Leaving it NULL will cause the default title of Open to be used.

LPCSTR lpstrDefExt This element points to the default extension for the files to be opened. If a filename is entered without an extension, this one will be glued onto it. If this element is left NULL, no default extension will be used.

LPARAM lCustData This can be 32 bits of anything you like. It will be passed to a custom secondary message handler for the Open File dialog as the lParam argument for the WM_INITDIALOG message. We'll be looking at custom secondary message handlers extensively later in this chapter, as this is the mechanism for modifying the common dialogs.

UINT (CALLBACK *lpfnHook) This is a FARPROC to a custom message handler for the File Open dialog.

LPCSTR lpTemplateName This is the name of a custom dialog template for the File Open dialog.

DWORD Flags This is a set of flags that define how the File Open dialog is to be handled.

The lCustData, lpfnHook, and lpTemplateName elements won't turn up in real life until later in this chapter—their application is a bit exotic. The Flags element of an OPENFILENAME object can contain any combination of the following flags:

OFN_READONLY This flag causes the Read Only check box to be initially checked in the File Open dialog. If the Read Only check box is selected when GetOpenFileName returns, this flag will be set in the Flags element of the OPENFILENAME object it returns.

OFN_OVERWRITEPROMPT This flag applies only to saving files. It will cause a prompt to appear if the filename selected currently exists.

OFN_HIDEREADONLY This flag will cause the Read Only check box to be hidden.

OFN_NOCHANGEDIR This flag will return to the current directory as it was when GetOpenFileName was called once a filename has been selected.

OFN_SHOWHELP This flag will enable the Help button in an Open File dialog.

OFN_ENABLEHOOK This flag will cause messages to be sent to the message handler specified by the lpfnHook element of an OPENFILENAME object.

OFN_ENABLETEMPLAT This flag will cause a dialog template to be loaded from the resource list of your application, rather than from COMMDLG.DLL.

OFN_ENABLETEMPLATEHANDLE This flag indicates that the hInstance element of an OPENFILENAME object is the instance of preloaded dialog template.

OFN_NOVALIDATE This flag turns off the filter that checks for illegal characters in an entered filename.

OFN_ALLOWMULTISELECT This flag allows multiple selections from the filename selection list box in the File Open dialog.

OFN_EXTENSIONDIFFERENT This flag will be set by GetOpenFileName if the extension of the returned filename differs from that specified by the lpstrDefExt element of an OPENFILENAME object.

OFN_PATHMUSTEXIST This flag requires that only valid paths be entered into the Open File dialog.

OFN_FILEMUSTEXIST This flag requires that only filenames that reflect extant files be entered into the Open File dialog.

OFN_CREATEPROMPT This flag applies to saving files. It will cause a prompt to appear if a user enters a nonexistent filename, asking if it's to be created.

OFN_SHAREAWARE If this flag is set when GetOpenFileName returns, the call has failed because of a network sharing violation.

OFN_NOREADONLYRETURN This flag specifies that filenames returned from the File Open dialog will not be read-only or be on a write-protected volume or directory.

OFN_NOTESTFILECREATE This flag is for saving files. It specifies that the selected file should not be created before the Save As dialog is closed.

There are two fairly important things to keep in mind about all this. The first is that you can use a function like the GetFileName code without having to understand everything it's up to. The second is that even if you want to really get into working with these objects in detail, you'll very likely never have to worry about well over half of these flags and structure elements. Clearly, the authors of the common dialogs decided to allow for every eventuality, no matter how obscure it might be.

The calls to open and save files use the same data structure and flags, and are handled almost identically. The other common dialog calls to be discussed in this chapter also work in fairly similar ways, and if you understand what GetOpenFileName is up to you'll probably have no difficulty in working with the other common dialog calls.

Exercising the common dialogs

Figure 4-2 illustrates the DEMO4 application and its dependent dialogs. These are all generated by calls to COMMDLG.DLL. The DEMO4 application actually does something useful—it's a simple text editor, along the lines of Windows Notepad. It also serves to illustrate the extremes to which a Windows text edit control can be stretched.

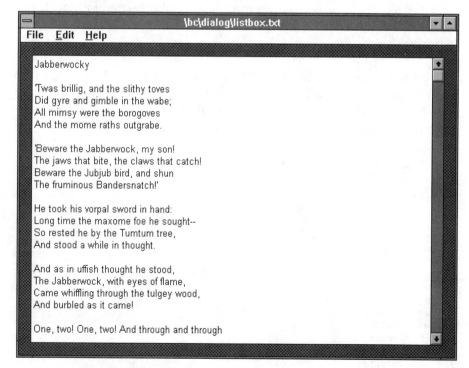

Figure 4-2

The DEMO4 application. Jabberwocks abound.

A few of the functions of DEMO4 are slightly contrived to make use of as many of the common dialogs as possible. For example, the Adjust Colour dialog sets the color of the border around the text editing window. This is hardly an essential element of an application like this one.

If you look carefully at Fig. 4-2, you'll notice that DEMO4 uses a resizable window. While there's no reason why a dialog window can't be resizable, this suggests a bit of a problem for its contents. In this case, the big text edit control in the center of the window must resize along with the application window, something that Windows doesn't explicitly allow for. In working through DEMO4.CPP, you'll see how one window can size its dependent controls and windows.

Finally, the DEMO4 application will illustrate how to turn a simple text edit control into a pretty sophisticated word processor. While operations such as merging text and graphics, assigning multiple fonts in a document, and working with files larger than 64 kilobytes long are all functions not within the purview of a text edit control, the amount of simple text manipulation one of these things can perform is pretty remarkable.

The complete source code for DEMO4.CPP is listed in Fig. 4-3. In addition to DEMO4.CPP, you'll need DEMO4.RC, as shown in Fig. 4-4. Suitable DEF and project files for DEMO4 are included with the source code on the companion disk for this book.

Figure 4-3   *The DEMO4.CPP source code.*

```
/*
    Dialog Demo 4
    Copyright (c) 1993 Alchemy Mindworks Inc.
*/

#include <windows.h>
#include <stdio.h>
#include <stdlib.h>
#include <ctype.h>
#include <alloc.h>
#include <string.h>
#include <dos.h>
#include <time.h>
#include <dir.h>
#include <commdlg.h>
```

```
#define say(s)       MessageBox(NULL,s,"Yo...",MB_OK ¦ MB_ICONSTOP);
#define saynumber(f,s)    {char b[128]; sprintf((LPSTR)b,(LPSTR)f,s); \
      MessageBox(NULL,b,"Debug Message",MB_OK ¦ MB_ICONSTOP); }

#define STRINGSIZE        129         /* how big is a string? */

#ifndef IDHELP
#define IDHELP            998
#endif

#define MESSAGE_STRING    101         /* message box object */

#define MAIN_EDIT         401

#define FILE_OPEN         101
#define FILE_SAVE         102
#define FILE_SAVEAS       103
#define FILE_FONT         104
#define FILE_PRINT        105
#define FILE_COLOUR       106
#define FILE_EXIT         199

#define EDIT_UNDO         201
#define EDIT_CUT          202
#define EDIT_COPY         203
#define EDIT_PASTE        204

#define HELPM_INDEX       901
#define HELPM_USING       905
#define HELPM_ABOUT       999

#define HELPFILE          "DEMO.HLP"

#define DIALOG_KEY        "DialogDemo"

#define MESSAGE_ABOUT     0
#define MESSAGE_HELP      1
#define MESSAGE_TEXTFILES 2
#define MESSAGE_ALLFILES  3
#define MESSAGE_BADREAD   4
#define MESSAGE_BADWRITE  5
#define MESSAGE_BADPRINT  6

#define BACKGROUND        RGB(0,64,0)
#define DARKBACKGROUND    RGB(128,128,0)

#define TEXTCOLOUR        RGB(255,255,0)
#define DARKTEXTCOLOUR    RGB(0,0,0)

#define CreateControlFont()    if(ControlFontName[0]) \
              controlfont=CreateFont(16,0,0,0,0,0,0,0, \
              ANSI_CHARSET,OUT_DEFAULT_PRECIS,CLIP_DEFAULT_PRECIS, \
              DEFAULT_QUALITY,DEFAULT_PITCH ¦ FF_DONTCARE, \
```

4-3 *Continued*

```
                ControlFontName)

#define SetControlFont(hwnd,id) {HWND dlgH;\
                if(controlfont != NULL) {\
                    dlgH=GetDlgItem(hwnd,id);\
                    SendMessage(dlgH,WM_SETFONT,(WORD)controlfont,FALSE);\
                }\
                }

#define DestroyControlFont()    if(controlfont != NULL) \
        DeleteObject(controlfont)

#define CheckOn(item)      SendDlgItemMessage(hwnd,item,BM_SETCHECK,1,0L);
#define CheckOff(item)     SendDlgItemMessage(hwnd,item,BM_SETCHECK,0,0L);
#define ItemOn(item)      { dlgH=GetDlgItem(hwnd,item); EnableWindow(dlgH,TRUE); }
#define ItemOff(item)     { dlgH=GetDlgItem(hwnd,item); EnableWindow(dlgH,FALSE); }
#define IsItemChecked(item)      SendDlgItemMessage(hwnd,item,BM_GETCHECK,0,0L)
#define ItemName(item,string)    { dlgH=GetDlgItem(hwnd,item); \
        SetWindowText(dlgH,(LPSTR)string); }
#define GetItemName(item,string) { dlgH=GetDlgItem(hwnd,item); \
        GetWindowText(dlgH,(LPSTR)string,BIGSTRINGSIZE); }

/* bad memory management techniques... conveniently packaged */
#define FixedGlobalAlloc(n)     MAKELONG(0,GlobalAlloc(GPTR,(DWORD)n))
#define FixedGlobalFree(p)      GlobalFree((GLOBALHANDLE)HIWORD((LONG)p));

#ifndef max
#define max(a,b)                (((a)>(b))?(a):(b))
#endif
#ifndef min
#define min(a,b)                (((a)<(b))?(a):(b))
#endif

/* prototypes */
DWORD FAR PASCAL SelectProc(HWND hwnd,WORD message,WORD wParam,LONG lParam);
DWORD FAR PASCAL AboutDlgProc(HWND hwnd,WORD message,WORD wParam,LONG lParam);
DWORD FAR PASCAL MessageDlgProc(HWND hwnd,WORD message,WORD wParam,LONG lParam);

void DoMessage(HWND hwnd,LPSTR message);
void SetHelpSize(HWND hwnd);
void DoHelp(HWND hwnd,LPSTR keyword);
void MakeHelpPathName(LPSTR szFileName);
void CentreWindow(HWND hwnd);
void SetFileOpen(HWND hwnd);

int GetFileName(HWND hwnd,LPSTR path);
int GetNewFileName(HWND hwnd,LPSTR path);
int LoadFile(HWND hwnd,int listbox,char *path);
int SaveFile(HWND hwnd,int listbox,char *path);
int SelectFont(HWND hwnd,HFONT FAR *hfont);
int SelectColour(HWND hwnd,COLORREF FAR *clr);
```

```
    int SelectFind(HWND hwnd,LPSTR text);
    int DoPrint(HWND hwnd,int listbox);
    int DoPaste(HWND hwnd,int listbox);
    int DoCopy(HWND hwnd,int listbox);
    int DoCut(HWND hwnd,int listbox);
    int DoUndo(HWND hwnd,int listbox);

    LPSTR FetchString(unsigned int n);

    /* globals*/
    char szAppName[]="DialogDemoFour";
    char ControlFontName[STRINGSIZE+1]="Arial";

    LPSTR messagehook=NULL;
    HANDLE hInst;
    HFONT controlfont=NULL;

    #pragma warn -par
    int PASCAL WinMain(HANDLE hInstance,HANDLE hPrevInstance,\
        LPSTR lpszCmdParam,int nCmdShow)
    {
        FARPROC dlgProc;
        int r=0;

        hInst=hInstance;

        if(lstrlen(lpszCmdParam)) messagehook=lpszCmdParam;
        else messagehook=NULL;

        dlgProc=MakeProcInstance((FARPROC)SelectProc,hInst);
        r=DialogBox(hInst,"MainScreen",NULL,dlgProc);

        FreeProcInstance(dlgProc);

        return(r);
    }

    DWORD FAR PASCAL SelectProc(HWND hwnd,WORD message,WORD wParam,LONG lParam)
    {
        static HBRUSH hBrush;
        static HFONT hFont;
        static COLORREF colour;
        HFONT oldFont;
        FARPROC lpfnDlgProc;
        PAINTSTRUCT ps;
        RECT mainrect;
        static HICON hIcon;
        char b[STRINGSIZE+1],name[16],ext[8];
        HWND dlgH;
        POINT point;

        switch(message) {
            case WM_SYSCOMMAND:
```

219

4-3 *Continued*

```
        switch(wParam & 0xfff0) {
            case SC_CLOSE:
                SendMessage(hwnd,WM_COMMAND,FILE_EXIT,0L);
                break;
        }
        break;
    case WM_INITDIALOG:
        colour=BACKGROUND;
        hBrush=CreateSolidBrush(colour);
        hFont=CreateFont(16,0,0,0,0,0,0,0,ANSI_CHARSET,
            OUT_DEFAULT_PRECIS,CLIP_DEFAULT_PRECIS,
            DEFAULT_QUALITY,DEFAULT_PITCH | FF_DONTCARE,\
            ControlFontName);

        SetHelpSize(hwnd);

        GetProfileString(DIALOG_KEY,"ControlFont",
            ControlFontName,b,STRINGSIZE);
        if(lstrlen(b)) lstrcpy(ControlFontName,b);
        CreateControlFont();

        hIcon=LoadIcon(hInst,szAppName);
        SetClassWord(hwnd,GCW_HICON,(WORD)hIcon);
        CentreWindow(hwnd);
        SetControlFont(hwnd,MAIN_EDIT);

        if(messagehook != NULL) {
            lstrcpy(b,messagehook);
            if(!LoadFile(hwnd,MAIN_EDIT,b))
                DoMessage(hwnd,FetchString(MESSAGE_BADREAD));
            else {
                SetWindowText(hwnd,strlwr(b));
                SetFileOpen(hwnd);
            }
        }
    case WM_SIZE:
        GetClientRect(hwnd,&mainrect);

        dlgH=GetDlgItem(hwnd,MAIN_EDIT);
        MoveWindow(dlgH,mainrect.left+16,mainrect.top+16,mainrect.right-
            mainrect.left-32,mainrect.bottom-mainrect.top-32,TRUE);

        break;
    case WM_CTLCOLOR:
        if(HIWORD(lParam)==CTLCOLOR_STATIC ||
            HIWORD(lParam)==CTLCOLOR_DLG) {
            SetBkColor(wParam,DARKBACKGROUND);
            SetTextColor(wParam,TEXTCOLOUR);

            ClientToScreen(hwnd,&point);
            UnrealizeObject(hBrush);
```

```
            SetBrushOrg(wParam,point.x,point.y);

            return((DWORD)hBrush);

        }
        if(HIWORD(lParam)==CTLCOLOR_BTN) {
            SetBkColor(wParam,DARKBACKGROUND);
            SetTextColor(wParam,TEXTCOLOUR);

            ClientToScreen(hwnd,&point);
            UnrealizeObject(hBrush);
            SetBrushOrg(wParam,point.x,point.y);

            return((DWORD)hBrush);
        }
        break;
case WM_PAINT:
    BeginPaint(hwnd,&ps);
    EndPaint(hwnd,&ps);
    break;
case WM_COMMAND:
    switch(wParam) {
        case HELPM_INDEX:
            MakeHelpPathName(b);
            WinHelp(hwnd,b,HELP_INDEX,NULL);
            break;
        case HELPM_USING:
            WinHelp(hwnd,"",HELP_HELPONHELP,NULL);
            break;
        case HELPM_ABOUT:
            if((lpfnDlgProc=MakeProcInstance
              ((FARPROC)AboutDlgProc,hInst)) != NULL) {
                DialogBox(hInst,"AboutBox",hwnd,lpfnDlgProc);
                FreeProcInstance(lpfnDlgProc);
            }
            break;
        case EDIT_UNDO:
            DoUndo(hwnd,MAIN_EDIT);
            break;
        case EDIT_CUT:
            DoCut(hwnd,MAIN_EDIT);
            break;
        case EDIT_COPY:
            DoCopy(hwnd,MAIN_EDIT);
            break;
        case EDIT_PASTE:
            DoPaste(hwnd,MAIN_EDIT);
            break;
        case FILE_COLOUR:
            if(SelectColour(hwnd,&colour)) {
                DeleteObject(hBrush);
                hBrush=CreateSolidBrush(colour);
                InvalidateRect(hwnd,NULL,TRUE);
```

4-3 *Continued*

```
            }
        break;
    case FILE_FONT:
        oldFont=hFont;
        if(SelectFont(hwnd,&hFont)) {
            if(oldFont != NULL) DeleteObject(oldFont);
            dlgH=GetDlgItem(hwnd,MAIN_EDIT);
            SendMessage(dlgH,WM_SETFONT,(WORD)hFont,TRUE);
        }
        break;
    case FILE_OPEN:
        if(GetFileName(hwnd,b)) {
            if(!LoadFile(hwnd,MAIN_EDIT,b))
                DoMessage(hwnd,FetchString(MESSAGE_BADREAD));
            else {
                SetWindowText(hwnd,strlwr(b));
                SetFileOpen(hwnd);
            }
        }
        break;
    case FILE_PRINT:
        if(!DoPrint(hwnd,MAIN_EDIT))
            DoMessage(hwnd,FetchString(MESSAGE_BADPRINT));
        break;
    case FILE_SAVE:
        fnsplit(b,NULL,NULL,name,ext);
        lstrcat(name,ext);
        lstrcpy(b,name);
        if(!SaveFile(hwnd,MAIN_EDIT,b))
            DoMessage(hwnd,FetchString(MESSAGE_BADWRITE));
        break;
    case FILE_SAVEAS:
        GetWindowText(hwnd,b,128);
        fnsplit(b,NULL,NULL,name,ext);
        lstrcat(name,ext);
        lstrcpy(b,name);
        if(GetNewFileName(hwnd,b)) {
            if(!SaveFile(hwnd,MAIN_EDIT,b))
                DoMessage(hwnd,FetchString(MESSAGE_BADWRITE));
        }
        break;
    case FILE_EXIT:
        if(hBrush != NULL) DeleteObject(hBrush);
        if(hFont != NULL) DeleteObject(hFont);
        MakeHelpPathName(b);
        WinHelp(hwnd,b,HELP_QUIT,NULL);

        FreeResource(hIcon);
        DestroyControlFont();
        PostQuitMessage(0);
        break;
```

```
            }
        break;

    }

    return(FALSE);
}

int SaveFile(HWND hwnd,int listbox,char *path)
{
    HCURSOR hSaveCursor,hHourGlass;
    LPSTR p;
    HWND dlgH;
    unsigned int size;
    int fh;

    hHourGlass=LoadCursor(NULL,IDC_WAIT);
    hSaveCursor=SetCursor(hHourGlass);

    if((fh=_lcreat(path,0))==-1) {
        SetCursor(hSaveCursor);
        return(FALSE);
    }

    dlgH=GetDlgItem(hwnd,listbox);
    size=GetWindowTextLength(dlgH);

    if((p=(LPSTR)FixedGlobalAlloc(size+1))==NULL) {
        SetCursor(hSaveCursor);
        _lclose(fh);
        return(FALSE);
    }

    GetWindowText(dlgH,p,size);

    --size;
    if(_lwrite(fh,p,size) != size) {
        SetCursor(hSaveCursor);
        FixedGlobalFree(p)
        _lclose(fh);
        return(FALSE);
    }

    FixedGlobalFree(p);

    _lclose(fh);
    SetCursor(hSaveCursor);
    return(TRUE);
}

int LoadFile(HWND hwnd,int listbox,char *path)
{
    HCURSOR hSaveCursor,hHourGlass;
```

4-3 *Continued*

```
LPSTR p;
HWND dlgH;
long l;
int fh;

hHourGlass=LoadCursor(NULL,IDC_WAIT);
hSaveCursor=SetCursor(hHourGlass);

if((fh=_lopen(path,OF_READ))==-1) {
    SetCursor(hSaveCursor);
    return(FALSE);
}

l=_llseek(fh,0L,SEEK_END);
_llseek(fh,0L,SEEK_SET);

if(l > 0xfff0L) {
    _lclose(fh);
    SetCursor(hSaveCursor);
    return(FALSE);
}

if((p=(LPSTR)FixedGlobalAlloc(l))==NULL) {
    _lclose(fh);
    SetCursor(hSaveCursor);
    return(FALSE);
}

if(_lread(fh,p,(unsigned int)l) != (unsigned int)l) {
    FixedGlobalFree(p);
    _lclose(fh);
    SetCursor(hSaveCursor);
    return(FALSE);
}

ItemName(listbox,p);

FixedGlobalFree(p);

_lclose(fh);

SetCursor(hSaveCursor);

return(TRUE);
}

void DoMessage(HWND hwnd,LPSTR message)
{
    FARPROC lpfnDlgProc;

    messagehook=message;
```

```
    if((lpfnDlgProc=MakeProcInstance((FARPROC)MessageDlgProc,hInst)) != NULL) {
        DialogBox(hInst,"MessageBox",hwnd,lpfnDlgProc);
        FreeProcInstance(lpfnDlgProc);
    }
}

DWORD FAR PASCAL MessageDlgProc(HWND hwnd,WORD message,WORD wParam,LONG lParam)
{
    static HBRUSH hBrush;
    POINT point;
    HWND dlgH;

    switch(message) {
        case WM_INITDIALOG:
            hBrush=CreateSolidBrush(DARKBACKGROUND);
            ItemName(MESSAGE_STRING,messagehook);
            CentreWindow(hwnd);
            SetControlFont(hwnd,MESSAGE_STRING);
            SetControlFont(hwnd,IDOK);
            return(FALSE);
        case WM_CTLCOLOR:
            if(HIWORD(lParam)==CTLCOLOR_STATIC ||
               HIWORD(lParam)==CTLCOLOR_DLG) {
                SetBkColor(wParam,DARKBACKGROUND);
                SetTextColor(wParam,DARKTEXTCOLOUR);

                ClientToScreen(hwnd,&point);
                UnrealizeObject(hBrush);
                SetBrushOrg(wParam,point.x,point.y);

                return((DWORD)hBrush);

            }
            if(HIWORD(lParam)==CTLCOLOR_BTN) {
                SetBkColor(wParam,DARKBACKGROUND);
                SetTextColor(wParam,DARKTEXTCOLOUR);

                ClientToScreen(hwnd,&point);
                UnrealizeObject(hBrush);
                SetBrushOrg(wParam,point.x,point.y);

                return((DWORD)hBrush);
            }
            break;
        case WM_COMMAND:
            switch(wParam) {
                case IDOK:
                    if(hBrush != NULL) DeleteObject(hBrush);
                    EndDialog(hwnd,wParam);
                    return(FALSE);
            }
            break;
    }
```

4-3 *Continued*

```
    return(FALSE);
}

DWORD FAR PASCAL AboutDlgProc(HWND hwnd,WORD message,WORD wParam,LONG lParam)
{
    static HBRUSH hBrush;
    POINT point;
    HWND dlgH;

    switch(message) {
        case WM_INITDIALOG:
            hBrush=CreateSolidBrush(DARKBACKGROUND);
            ItemName(MESSAGE_STRING,FetchString(MESSAGE_ABOUT));
            CentreWindow(hwnd);
            SetControlFont(hwnd,MESSAGE_STRING);
            SetControlFont(hwnd,IDOK);
            return(FALSE);
        case WM_CTLCOLOR:
            if(HIWORD(lParam)==CTLCOLOR_STATIC ||
               HIWORD(lParam)==CTLCOLOR_DLG) {
                SetBkColor(wParam,DARKBACKGROUND);
                SetTextColor(wParam,DARKTEXTCOLOUR);

                ClientToScreen(hwnd,&point);
                UnrealizeObject(hBrush);
                SetBrushOrg(wParam,point.x,point.y);

                return((DWORD)hBrush);
            }
            if(HIWORD(lParam)==CTLCOLOR_BTN) {
                SetBkColor(wParam,DARKBACKGROUND),
                SetTextColor(wParam,DARKTEXTCOLOUR);

                ClientToScreen(hwnd,&point);
                UnrealizeObject(hBrush);
                SetBrushOrg(wParam,point.x,point.y);

                return((DWORD)hBrush);
            }
            break;
        case WM_COMMAND:
            switch(wParam) {
                case IDOK:
                    if(hBrush != NULL) DeleteObject(hBrush);
                    EndDialog(hwnd,wParam);
                    return(FALSE);
            }
            break;
    }

    return(FALSE);
```

```
    }

void CentreWindow(HWND hwnd)
{
    RECT rect;
    unsigned int x,y;

    GetWindowRect(hwnd,&rect);
    x=(GetSystemMetrics(SM_CXSCREEN)-(rect.right-rect.left))/2;
    y=(GetSystemMetrics(SM_CYSCREEN)-(rect.bottom-rect.top))/2;
    SetWindowPos(hwnd,NULL,x,y,rect.right-rect.left,rect.bottom-rect.top,
      SWP_NOSIZE);
}

LPSTR FetchString(unsigned int n)
{
    static char b[257];

    if(!LoadString(hInst,n,b,256))
        lstrcpy(b,"String table error - this application may be damaged");
    return(b);
}

void SetHelpSize(HWND hwnd)
{
    HELPWININFO helpinfo;
    char b[145];

    memset((char *)&helpinfo,0,sizeof(HELPWININFO));
    helpinfo.wStructSize=sizeof(HELPWININFO);
    helpinfo.x=10;
    helpinfo.y=10;
    helpinfo.dx=512;
    helpinfo.dy=1004;

    MakeHelpPathName(b);
    WinHelp(hwnd,b,HELP_SETWINPOS,(DWORD)&helpinfo);
}

void DoHelp(HWND hwnd,LPSTR keyword)
{
    char b[145];

    MakeHelpPathName(b);
    WinHelp(hwnd,b,HELP_KEY,(DWORD)keyword);
}

void MakeHelpPathName(LPSTR szFileName)
{
    LPSTR pcFileName;
    int nFileNameLen;

    nFileNameLen = GetModuleFileName(hInst,szFileName,144);
```

4-3 *Continued*

```
    pcFileName = szFileName+nFileNameLen;

    while(pcFileName > szFileName) {
        if(*pcFileName == '\\' || *pcFileName == ':') {
            *(++pcFileName) = '\0';
            break;
        }
        nFileNameLen--;
        pcFileName--;
    }

    if((nFileNameLen+13) < 144) lstrcat(szFileName,HELPFILE);
    else lstrcat(szFileName, "?");
}

int GetFileName(HWND hwnd,LPSTR path)
{
    OPENFILENAME ofn;
    char szDirName[257],szFile[256],szFileTitle[256],szFilter[768],*p;
    int r;

    getcwd(szDirName,256);
    if(szDirName[lstrlen(szDirName)-1] != '\\') lstrcat(szDirName,"\\");

    lstrcpy(szFile,"*.TXT");

    p=szFilter;
    lstrcpy(p,FetchString(MESSAGE_ALLFILES));
    p+=lstrlen(p)+1;
    lstrcpy(p,szFile);
    p+=lstrlen(p)+1;

    lstrcpy(p,FetchString(MESSAGE_TEXTFILES));
    p+=lstrlen(p)+1;
    lstrcpy(p,"*.*");
    p+=lstrlen(p)+1;
    *p=0;

    memset((char *)&ofn,0,sizeof(OPENFILENAME));

    szFileTitle[0]=0;

    ofn.lStructSize=sizeof(OPENFILENAME);
    ofn.hwndOwner=hwnd;
    ofn.hInstance=hInst;
    ofn.lpstrFilter=szFilter;
    ofn.nFilterIndex=0;
    ofn.lpstrFile=szFile;
    ofn.nMaxFile=sizeof(szFile);
    ofn.lpstrFileTitle=szFileTitle;
    ofn.nMaxFileTitle=sizeof(szFileTitle);
```

```
    ofn.lpstrInitialDir=szDirName;
    ofn.Flags=OFN_PATHMUSTEXIST | OFN_FILEMUSTEXIST;
    ofn.lpstrTitle="Open";
    ofn.nFileExtension=0;
    ofn.lpstrDefExt=NULL;
    r=GetOpenFileName(&ofn);

    lstrcpy(path,ofn.lpstrFile);

    return(r);
}

int GetNewFileName(HWND hwnd,LPSTR path)
{
    OPENFILENAME ofn;
    char szDirName[257],szFile[256],szFileTitle[256],szFilter[768],*p;
    int r;

    getcwd(szDirName,256);
    if(szDirName[lstrlen(szDirName)-1] != '\\') lstrcat(szDirName,"\\");

    lstrcpy(szFile,path);

    p=szFilter;
    lstrcpy(p,FetchString(MESSAGE_ALLFILES));
    p+=lstrlen(p)+1;
    lstrcpy(p,szFile);
    p+=lstrlen(p)+1;

    lstrcpy(p,FetchString(MESSAGE_TEXTFILES));
    p+=lstrlen(p)+1;
    lstrcpy(p,"*.*");
    p+=lstrlen(p)+1;
    *p=0;

    memset((char *)&ofn,0,sizeof(OPENFILENAME));

    szFileTitle[0]=0;

    ofn.lStructSize=sizeof(OPENFILENAME);
    ofn.hwndOwner=hwnd;
    ofn.hInstance=hInst;
    ofn.lpstrFilter=szFilter;
    ofn.nFilterIndex=0;
    ofn.lpstrFile=szFile;
    ofn.nMaxFile=sizeof(szFile);
    ofn.lpstrFileTitle=szFileTitle;
    ofn.nMaxFileTitle=sizeof(szFileTitle);
    ofn.lpstrInitialDir=szDirName;
    ofn.Flags=OFN_PATHMUSTEXIST | OFN_OVERWRITEPROMPT;
    ofn.lpstrTitle="Save As";
    ofn.nFileExtension=0;
    ofn.lpstrDefExt=NULL;
```

4-3 *Continued*

```
    r=GetSaveFileName(&ofn);

    lstrcpy(path,ofn.lpstrFile);

    return(r);
}

int SelectFont(HWND hwnd,HFONT FAR *hfont)
{
    LOGFONT lf;
    CHOOSEFONT cf;
    int r;

    memset((char *)&cf,0,sizeof(CHOOSEFONT));

    GetObject((HFONT)*hfont,sizeof(LOGFONT),(LPSTR)&lf);

    cf.lStructSize=sizeof(CHOOSEFONT);
    cf.hwndOwner=hwnd;
    cf.hInstance=hInst;
    cf.lpLogFont=&lf;
    cf.Flags=CF_TTONLY : CF_SCREENFONTS : CF_INITTOLOGFONTSTRUCT : CF_ANSIONLY;
    cf.rgbColors=BACKGROUND;
    cf.nFontType=REGULAR_FONTTYPE;
    if((r=ChooseFont(&cf)) != FALSE)
  *hfont=CreateFontIndirect(cf.lpLogFont);

    return(r);
}

int SelectColour(IWND hwnd,COLORREF FAR *clr)
{
    CHOOSECOLOR cc;
    COLORREF pclr[16];
    int i,r;

    for(i=0;i<16;++i) pclr[i]=RGB(i<<4,i<<4,i<<4);

    memset((char *)&cc,0,sizeof(CHOOSECOLOR));

    cc.lStructSize=sizeof(CHOOSECOLOR);
    cc.hwndOwner=hwnd;
    cc.hInstance=hInst;
    cc.rgbResult=*clr;
    cc.lpCustColors=pclr;
    cc.Flags=CC_FULLOPEN : CC_RGBINIT;

    r=ChooseColor(&cc);

    *clr=cc.rgbResult;
```

```
        return(r);
}

int DoPrint(HWND hwnd,int listbox)
{

    HCURSOR hSaveCursor,hHourGlass;
    TEXTMETRIC tm;
    HWND dlgH;
    PRINTDLG pd;
    LPSTR p,pr;
    unsigned int i,size,length,pagesize,textdeep,top;
    char b[STRINGSIZE+1];

    memset((char *)&pd,0,sizeof(PRINTDLG));
    GetWindowText(hwnd,b,STRINGSIZE);

    pd.lStructSize=sizeof(PRINTDLG);
    pd.hwndOwner=hwnd;
    pd.hInstance=hInst;
    pd.Flags=PD_RETURNDC ¦ PD_NOPAGENUMS ¦ PD_NOSELECTION;

    if(!PrintDlg(&pd)) return(FALSE);

    hHourGlass=LoadCursor(NULL,IDC_WAIT);
    hSaveCursor=SetCursor(hHourGlass);

    dlgH=GetDlgItem(hwnd,listbox);
    size=GetWindowTextLength(dlgH);

    if((p=(LPSTR)FixedGlobalAlloc(size+1))==NULL) {
        SetCursor(hSaveCursor);
        return(FALSE);
    }

    GetWindowText(dlgH,p,size);

    --size;

    GetTextMetrics(pd.hDC,&tm);
    textdeep=tm.tmHeight+tm.tmExternalLeading;
    pagesize=GetDeviceCaps(pd.hDC,VERTRES)/textdeep;

    Escape(pd.hDC,STARTDOC,strlen(b),b,NULL);

    pr=p;
    top=i=0;
        do {
        while(*pr < 32 && size) {
            if(*pr==13) {
                top+=textdeep;
                ++i;
            }
            ++pr;
```

4-3 *Continued*

```
        --size;
    }

    if(++i >= pagesize) {
        Escape(pd.hDC,NEWFRAME,0,NULL,NULL);
        top=i=0;
    }

    if(size) {
        for(length=0;pr[length]>=32;++length);
        TextOut(pd.hDC,0,top,pr,length);
        pr+=length;
        size-=length;
    }

} while(size);

Escape(pd.hDC,NEWFRAME,0,NULL,NULL);

Escape(pd.hDC,ENDDOC,0,NULL,NULL);

DeleteDC(pd.hDC);

FixedGlobalFree(p);
SetCursor(hSaveCursor);
return(TRUE);
}

int DoPaste(HWND hwnd,int listbox)
{
    GLOBALHANDLE gh;
    LPSTR p;

    if(!IsClipboardFormatAvailable(CF_TEXT)) return(FALSE);

    OpenClipboard(hwnd);

    gh=GetClipboardData(CF_TEXT);

    if((p=GlobalLock(gh)) != NULL) {
        SendDlgItemMessage(hwnd,listbox,EM_REPLACESEL,0,(DWORD)p);
        GlobalUnlock(gh);
    }

    CloseClipboard();
    return(TRUE);
}

int DoCopy(HWND hwnd,int listbox)
{
    GLOBALHANDLE gh;
```

```
        LPSTR p,pr;
        HWND dlgH;
        unsigned long l;
        unsigned int i,start,end,size;

        l=SendDlgItemMessage(hwnd,listbox,EM_GETSEL,0,0L);
        start=LOWORD(l);
        end=HIWORD(l);

        dlgH=GetDlgItem(hwnd,listbox);
        size=GetWindowTextLength(dlgH);

        if((p=(LPSTR)FixedGlobalAlloc(size+1))==NULL) return(FALSE);

        GetWindowText(dlgH,p,size);

        size=end-start;

        if((gh=GlobalAlloc(GHND,size+1)) != NULL) {
            if((pr=GlobalLock(gh)) != NULL) {
                for(i=0;i<size;++i) pr[i]=p[start+i];
                pr[i]=0;
                GlobalUnlock(gh);

                OpenClipboard(hwnd);
                EmptyClipboard();
                SetClipboardData(CF_TEXT,gh);
                CloseClipboard();
            }
        }

        FixedGlobalFree(p);

        return(TRUE);
}

int DoCut(HWND hwnd,int listbox)
{
    DoCopy(hwnd,listbox);
    SendDlgItemMessage(hwnd,listbox,EM_REPLACESEL,0,(DWORD)"");
}

int DoUndo(HWND hwnd,int listbox)
{
    SendDlgItemMessage(hwnd,listbox,EM_UNDO,0,0L);
}

void SetFileOpen(HWND hwnd)
{
    HMENU hmenu;

    hmenu=GetMenu(hwnd);
    EnableMenuItem(hmenu,FILE_SAVE,MF_BYCOMMAND | MF_ENABLED);
```

4-3 *Continued*

```
EnableMenuItem(hmenu,FILE_SAVEAS,MF_BYCOMMAND | MF_ENABLED);
EnableMenuItem(hmenu,FILE_FONT,MF_BYCOMMAND | MF_ENABLED);
EnableMenuItem(hmenu,FILE_PRINT,MF_BYCOMMAND | MF_ENABLED);
EnableMenuItem(hmenu,EDIT_UNDO,MF_BYCOMMAND | MF_ENABLED);
EnableMenuItem(hmenu,EDIT_CUT,MF_BYCOMMAND | MF_ENABLED);
EnableMenuItem(hmenu,EDIT_COPY,MF_BYCOMMAND | MF_ENABLED);
EnableMenuItem(hmenu,EDIT_PASTE,MF_BYCOMMAND | MF_ENABLED);
}
```

Figure 4-4   *The DEMO4.RC resource script.*

```
MainScreen DIALOG 29, 28, 300, 208
STYLE WS_POPUP | WS_CAPTION | WS_SYSMENU | WS_THICKFRAME |
    WS_MINIMIZEBOX | WS_MAXIMIZEBOX
CAPTION "Dialog Demo Four"
MENU MainMenu
BEGIN
    CONTROL "", 401, "EDIT", ES_LEFT | ES_MULTILINE |
        ES_AUTOVSCROLL | ES_WANTRETURN | WS_CHILD | WS_VISIBLE |
        WS_BORDER | WS_VSCROLL | WS_TABSTOP, 8, 8, 284, 192
END

AboutBox DIALOG 72, 72, 220, 128
STYLE WS_POPUP | WS_CAPTION
CAPTION "About"
BEGIN
    CTEXT "", 101, 16, 16, 188, 72, WS_CHILD | WS_VISIBLE | WS_GROUP
    DEFPUSHBUTTON "OK", IDOK, 96, 104, 28, 16, WS_CHILD | WS_VISIBLE | WS_TABSTOP
    CONTROL "", -1, "static", SS_BLACKFRAME | WS_CHILD | WS_VISIBLE, 8, 8, 204, 88
END

MainMenu MENU
BEGIN
    POPUP "File"
    BEGIN
        MENUITEM "&Open..", 101
        MENUITEM "&Save", 102, GRAYED
        MENUITEM "Save &as..", 103, GRAYED
        MENUITEM SEPARATOR
        MENUITEM "&Font", 104, GRAYED
        MENUITEM "&Print", 105, GRAYED
        MENUITEM "&Colour", 106
        MENUITEM SEPARATOR
        MENUITEM "E&xit", 199
    END

    POPUP "&Edit"
    BEGIN
        MENUITEM "&Undo", 201, GRAYED
        MENUITEM "&Cut\tShift+Del", 202, GRAYED
```

```
        MENUITEM "&Copy\tCtrl+Ins", 203, GRAYED
        MENUITEM "&Paste\tShift+Ins", 204, GRAYED
    END

    POPUP "&Help"
    BEGIN
        MENUITEM "&Index", 901
        MENUITEM "&Using help", 905
        MENUITEM SEPARATOR
        MENUITEM "&About...", 999
    END

END


STRINGTABLE
BEGIN
    0,"Dialog Demo Four\nCopyright \251 1993 Alchemy Mindworks Inc.\n
       From the book Windows Dialog Construction Set\rby Steven William Rimmer\r
       Published by Windcrest/McGraw Hill"
    1,"Help"
    2,"All files "
    3,"Text files "
    4,"There has been an error loading your file.\n\n\nKick your computer."
    5,"There has been an error saving your file.\n\n\n
       Must be elevator music at work."
    6,"There has been an error printing your file.\n\n\nWindows is haunted."
END

DialogDemoFour ICON
BEGIN
    '00 00 01 00 01 00 20 20 10 00 00 00 00 00 E8 02'
    '00 00 16 00 00 00 28 00 00 00 20 00 00 00 40 00'
    '00 00 01 00 04 00 00 00 00 00 80 02 00 00 00 00'
    '00 00 00 00 00 00 00 00 00 00 00 00 00 00 00 00'
    '00 00 00 00 80 00 00 80 00 00 00 80 80 00 80 00'
    '00 00 80 00 80 00 80 80 00 00 80 80 80 00 C0 C0'
    'C0 00 00 00 FF 00 00 FF 00 00 00 FF FF 00 FF 00'
    '00 00 FF 00 FF 00 FF FF 00 00 FF FF FF 00 2A 2A'
    '2A 2A 2A 2A 2A 2A 22 77 70 00 00 00 00 A2 2A'
    'A2 A2 A2 A2 A2 A2 A2 A2 22 70 00 00 00 00 2A 2A'
    '2A 2A 2A 2A 2A 2A AA AA A2 70 00 00 00 00 A2 2A'
    'A2 A2 AA AA AA AA B2 AA AA 77 77 77 77 00 2A 2A'
    'AA AA 2A 2A AA 2A AA A9 19 19 19 19 17 77 AA A2'
    'A2 AA AB AB AB AA 91 91 91 91 91 91 91 97 2A AA'
    'BA BA 2A AA A9 19 19 19 19 99 99 99 99 19 AB AB'
    'A2 AA AA 11 11 91 99 99 99 90 00 00 09 99 BA BA'
    'AA A1 01 11 19 19 19 19 90 00 00 00 00 09 AA A2'
    '00 10 10 11 11 91 91 00 00 00 00 70 00 00 2A 00'
    '00 00 01 01 11 17 77 00 00 00 09 70 00 00 A2 22'
    '22 22 22 22 22 22 27 77 77 70 09 70 00 00 2A 2A'
    '2A 2A AA AA AA AA 22 22 22 77 09 77 00 00 A2 AA'
    'AA AA A2 AA AA AA A2 A2 A2 27 79 17 70 00 2A AA'
    'AA 2A 22 22 2A 2A AA AA AA 2A 79 91 77 00 A2 A2'
```

4-4 *Continued*

```
'A2 22 70 70 22 A2 A2 AB A2 A2 00 99 17 77 2A 2A'
'22 87 07 07 02 2A 2A AA AA 27 00 09 91 91 A2 A2'
'F8 88 77 70 72 A2 AB AB AB A0 00 00 99 99 2A 22'
'8F 88 00 77 07 2A 2A AA AA 70 00 00 00 00 A2 28'
'F8 F0 00 08 70 22 22 A2 A2 00 00 00 00 00 2A 2F'
'8F 80 00 07 07 2A 2A AA A7 00 00 00 00 00 A7 28'
'F8 FF 00 88 82 22 A2 A2 A0 00 00 00 00 00 22 7F'
'8F FF FF 8F 82 2A 2A 2A 70 00 00 00 00 00 A7 0F'
'FF FF F8 F8 F2 A2 A2 A2 00 00 00 00 00 00 A2 70'
'FF FF 8F 8F 2A 2A 2A 20 00 00 00 00 00 00 A7 07'
'FF FF F8 F8 22 A2 A2 00 00 00 00 00 00 00 A2 70'
'70 FF 8F 22 2A 2A 20 00 00 00 00 00 00 00 AA 07'
'07 07 02 02 A2 A2 00 00 00 00 00 00 00 00 BA A0'
'70 70 72 2A 2A 20 00 00 00 00 00 00 00 00 BB AA'
'A7 A7 AA AA A0 00 00 00 00 00 00 00 00 00 AA BA'
'AA AA AA 00 00 00 00 00 00 00 00 00 00 00 AA A0'
'00 00 00 00 00 00 00 00 00 00 00 00 00 00 00 00'
'01 FF 00 00 01 FF 00 00 01 FF 00 00 03 00 00 00'
'00 00 00 00 00 00 00 00 00 00 00 00 01 F8 00 00'
'07 FE 00 00 3F DF 00 00 3F 9F 00 00 01 9F 00 00'
'00 8F 00 00 00 07 00 00 00 03 00 00 00 C0 00 00'
'00 E0 00 00 01 F0 00 00 01 FF 00 00 03 FF 00 00'
'03 FF 00 00 07 FF 00 00 07 FF 00 00 0F FF 00 00'
'1F FF 00 00 3F FF 00 00 7F FF 00 00 FF FF 00 01'
'FF FF 00 07 FF FF 00 3F FF FF 1F FF FF FF'
END

MessageBox DIALOG 72, 72, 220, 128
STYLE WS_POPUP | WS_CAPTION
CAPTION "Message"
BEGIN
    CTEXT "", 101, 16, 16, 188, 72, WS_CHILD | WS_VISIBLE | WS_GROUP
    DEFPUSHBUTTON "OK", IDOK, 96, 104, 28, 16, WS_CHILD | WS_VISIBLE | WS_TABSTOP
    CONTROL "", -1, "static", SS_BLACKFRAME | WS_CHILD | WS_VISIBLE, 8, 8, 204, 88
END
```

The basic structure of DEMO4 is similar to the earlier applications that have appeared in this book. It consists of a principal message handler for its MainScreen dialog, which in turn launches dependent dialogs. Many of the elements in SelectProc will look as they did in the earlier applications.

There's one important difference in WinMain. It checks the lpszCmdParm argument. This is a pointer to a string that contains the command-line arguments to DEMO4, if there are any. Command-line arguments might seem a bit unusual in an environment that

doesn't support a command line directly, but there are actually two common ways to arrive at them. The first is by adding arguments to the command line in the Properties dialog for an application, as found in the Windows Program Manager. The second is to add arguments to the Arguments dialog in Borland C++ for Windows.

In the WinMain function for DEMO4, if there's a command-line argument passed to the DEMO4.EXE application it will be pointed to by messagehook. If no argument is present, as indicated by lpszCmdParm having no length, messagehook will be NULL. This will allow SelectProc to know if there's a command-line argument to be dealt with.

Should DEMO4 be run with a command-line argument, it will interpret it as the path to a text filename and attempt to load it without waiting for someone to select Open from the File menu. Among other things, this is very handy for debugging an application like DEMO4, as it means it can open with a file all loaded up and ready to work with.

The first important element of SelectProc is its WM_INITDIALOG message handler case. This sets up a number of defaults required to make DEMO4 behave. It begins by defining the border color in the color object and a brush to paint it with in hbrush. It then creates a default font in hfont. When the application opens, this will be the same as the control font, mostly because it has to start somewhere. You can't actually use the control font itself, as the font for the main text edit control might change. If the control font were to be changed from, for example, 16-point Arial to 36-point Arnold Boecklin, the controls in DEMO4 would become singularly difficult to read.

The last thing of import in the WM_INITDIALOG handler of SelectProc is the code that tests messagehook and calls LoadFile if it isn't NULL. We'll look at the workings of LoadFile a bit later in this chapter. For the moment, it's sufficient to note that it will attempt to load the file passed as its third argument into the text edit control whose resource ID is passed as its second argument in the window whose handle is passed as its first argument.

Admittedly, a fair bit of code is required to make all this happen. One of the things that makes C programming a bit easier to conceptualize

is that it can be very top-down; you need not worry about how a function like LoadFile really works 'til after lunch. If you have someone you can delegate programming tasks to, you might never need to worry about such things at all.

There's no break statement at the end of the WM_INITDIALOG case of SelectProc, and this isn't an accidental omission. When it's done initializing the principal dialog of DEMO4, it falls through to the WM_SIZE case. This case will also be invoked if a genuine WM_SIZE message is sent to the main window of DEMO4. Such a message will appear when the window is resized.

The code in the WM_SIZE handler resizes all the controls in the main window of DEMO4 if the window itself is resized. Fortunately, there's only one control present, and as such the code is fairly simple. If you have a look at the Graphic Workshop for Windows package on the companion disk for this book, you'll note that its principal window has quite a few controls. It uses the same approach as DEMO4 does, but its WM_SIZE handler is seethingly complex.

The call to GetClientRect in the WM_SIZE handler fetches the new dimensions of the client area of the principal dialog of DEMO4 after it has been resized. The MoveWindow call resizes the text edit control based on the window size.

In theory it shouldn't be necessary to invoke the WM_SIZE case when DEMO4 first opens. This is a bit of a nod toward convenience, actually. It would be difficult to fiddle the size of the main text edit control in Resource Workshop so that it appeared initially with the same border size it would after WM_SIZE had adjusted it. By letting the WM_SIZE handler have a shot at it first, even though no WM_SIZE message has actually appeared, it can be fudged to fit right from the start.

Most of the rest of the SelectProc function deals with handling WM_COMMAND messages generated by the menus of DEMO4. Some of its cases, such as the ones dealing with Help, will also be familiar, as they appeared in an earlier application. The remaining ones call functions that use the Windows common dialogs, which is the really interesting part of DEMO4.

⇨ Opening and saving a file

The FILE_OPEN case of the WM_COMMAND handler loads a text file and stores it in the MAIN_EDIT text editing control of DEMO4. The LoadFile function does the actual work involved. If the LoadFile returns a true value, indicating that the whole affair went off as it was intended to, the name of the loaded file will be used to replace the title of the main window of DEMO4 and a number of menu items will be adjusted through the SetFileOpen function. This latter call handles things like enabling the Save and Save As item, as well as a number of other functions that should be active only if a file has been loaded.

Getting a filename to open is handled by the GetFileName function, as declared in DEMO4.CPP. This function essentially contains the call to GetOpenFileName, which was discussed at length earlier in this chapter. The only new elements added to it are two calls to FetchString to replace two hard-wired text strings.

The LoadFile function is deceptively simple. In fact, it's simple because a text edit control can do all the difficult work of parsing strings and such. It begins by setting up the hourglass cursor to indicate that things might take a while. It then opens the file to be loaded with a call to _lopen. It works out how large the file is by seeking to the end of it, reading the file position, and then seeking back to the beginning. It checks to make sure it's not being asked to load a file that's larger than will fit in a text edit control.

Knowing how big the file to be loaded is, it allocates a buffer for it using the FixedGlobalAlloc macro. We'll get to what this really is in a moment. It calls _lread to load the file contents and uses the ItemName macro to store the text file contents in the MAIN_EDIT control. The FixedGlobalFree macro deallocates the buffer.

If you have a look up at the top of the DEMO4.CPP listing, you'll find a declaration for ItemName. It uses a call to SetWindowText to load text into the text edit control. The SetWindowText function is a versatile little troll. If it's passed the handle to a genuine window it will set the title text. If it's passed the handle to a static text or text edit control it will replace the editing text in the control with new

text. If it's passed the handle to a button, check box, or radio button it will change the title text.

Perhaps not surprisingly, saving a file works pretty much like opening a file, but in reverse. It's handled by the SaveFile function. The _lcreat function is used to create a file to write the text in question to. If the file exists it will be deleted and recreated. The GetWindowTextLength function is used to figure out how long the current contents of the MAIN_EDIT control are. As with SetWindowText, this function will behave appropriately for both windows and controls. The FixedGlobalAlloc function is used to allocate a buffer to store the text in, and GetWindowText fetches it from the MAIN_EDIT control. The _lwrite function is used to write the text to disk.

The function to get a filename to save to is called GetNewFileName, as declared in DEMO4.CPP. It uses a call to GetSaveFileName. The OPENFILENAME object passed to this function is identical to the one passed to GetOpenFileName, as discussed earlier in this chapter, save that a few of the flags are different. You'll probably want to use the OFN_PATHMUSTEXIST and OFN_OVERWRITEPROMP flags to save a file, and the OFN_PATHMUSTEXIST and OFN_FILEMUSTEXIT flags to open a file.

As an aside, most text editors and word processors would modify the approach used by DEMO4 for saving a file somewhat. Rather than immediately sending the existing contents of a file to be saved into a cosmic black hole, you might want to consider renaming the existing file, if one exists, to one with the extension BAK. This means that if something goes wrong in saving your file, the penultimate version will still be around as a BAK file.

The drawback to this, of course—as most users of Borland C++ will observe sooner or later—is that BAK files tend to accumulate. Unless you habitually drop to DOS and disperse the milling throngs of BAK files on your hard drive every so often, their numbers can swell into the megabytes, eventually forming their own political party and demanding special national holidays.

 Bad memory management— a brief digression

The FixedGlobalAlloc and FixedGlobalFree macros, as declared at the top of DEMO4.CPP, are exactly what they purport to be—bad memory-management techniques, conveniently packaged. At least, they can be. The degree of badness involved in their application will be determined by how they're applied.

To understand how these calls should be used, you'll have to understand a bit about how Windows manages its memory. This will prove very important later in this chapter, as well, although for very different reasons. Casual memory management under Windows is a lot like cordless bungee jumping, only more likely to get you into trouble.

A Windows application regards the memory in your computer as being of two types. There's *local memory* and *global memory*. Local memory is memory that resides in the local data segment of an application. This segment contains all the static data allocated by your application, your application's stack, and its local heap. The local heap is where memory allocated by the malloc and LocalAlloc functions comes from.

The advantage of the local heap is that it can be referenced by near pointers. Near and far pointers were discussed at length in chapter 1. Things referenced by near pointers can be accessed more efficiently, and the code that does so can be tighter, faster, and smaller.

The only catch in using the common data segment and allocating memory from the local heap is that both are relatively small objects. A single segment can encompass no more than 64 kilobytes of memory. Having allocated some of this for your application's stack and another chunk for its static data, your application will be able to allocate local memory only from what's left—say 30 or 40 kilobytes tops for a moderately sized application.

It would be unwise to count on there being local memory available for a large buffer, such as the one used to load a text file into in the LoadFile function discussed in the previous section. This approach

would be fairly reliable for small text files, such as the poem that has turned up as example text in the applications in this book, but it would surely fail if you attempted to load a text file approaching the limits of what a text edit control can store.

The alternative to local memory is, perhaps not surprisingly, global memory. Global memory is regarded by Windows as being everything that isn't in your local data segment and isn't already spoken for by other applications. The global memory pool is available to all the applications running on your system, as well as to Windows itself. It's very craftily managed to make it almost impossible to run out of memory.

When you ask for memory from the global memory pool, typically through a call to GlobalAlloc, Windows will check the available memory to see if it can honor your request. If it can, it will pass you a handle to the buffer you've asked for. If there isn't sufficient contiguous free memory available, it will attempt to do some "garbage collection," that is, it will juggle the allocated buffers in memory to free up any space trapped between them and see if this has generated a large enough block of memory to honor your request.

If there still isn't enough memory to provide you with the buffer you've asked for, Windows will start considering extreme measures. Its final resort will be to find some presently allocated buffers in memory and "spill" them, that is, write their contents to temporary disk files and free the memory they're occupying to allow your buffer to be allocated.

Note that I mentioned that Windows passes you a memory handle when you call GlobalAlloc. This isn't the same as a memory pointer. A *memory handle* is a number that tells Windows which previously allocated buffer you're interested in, but it doesn't actually define where the memory is. It's something of a claim check for memory. To derive a pointer to global memory referenced by a handle, you must call GlobalLock. The GlobalLock call gives Windows sufficient warning of your intentions. It allows Windows to find your allocated buffer in memory and prevent any future garbage collections from moving it until it's unlocked again. If your buffer has been previously spilled to disk, calling GlobalLock will cause Windows to load it back

into real memory so you can work with it, possibly spilling other buffers to disk in the process.

The use of memory handles rather than global memory pointers allows buffers to be locked in memory for as short a time as possible. This, in turn, allows Windows the greatest degree of freedom in juggling allocated buffers to make the best use of its available memory.

The handle-based memory management that Windows uses for global memory allocation is very powerful, and is the central element in Windows' effective use of memory. The catch to using it is that it's inconvenient—allocating a buffer, even if it will be allocated, locked, used, unlocked, and freed very quickly, involves managing both a GLOBALHANDLE and an LPSTR object.

The FixedGlobalAlloc macro uses a little-documented function of GlobalAlloc, which allows it to return a locked pointer to an allocated global buffer rather than a handle. The FixedGlobalFree function deallocates such a pointer. Using the FixedGlobalAlloc macro rather than calling GlobalAlloc followed by GlobalLock will create a global buffer that Windows can't juggle, which will thus impede Windows memory management for as long as it's in existence.

There's no real penalty in using FixedGlobalAlloc if you want to allocate and immediately lock a global buffer in the conventional way. The FixedGlobalAlloc macro is a good approach to allocating temporary buffers that will be in existence for a very short time, such as the one that appeared in the LoadFile function in the foregoing section.

It's a very bad idea to use FixedGlobalAlloc to allocate buffers that will stick around for the life of your application, or any reasonable portion thereof. Doing so will seriously cripple Windows' memory management, and cause the Microsoft thought-police to break down your door and seize your mouse. No foolin'.

Selecting fonts

While it's impossible to change the fonts used to display selected portions of the text in a text edit control, you can assign any font you

like to the entire contents of a text edit control. The mechanism for doing so has already been discussed in conjunction with creating a control font for the various buttons and such of the applications in this book. Figures 4-5A through 4-5D illustrate some applications of this in DEMO4. It seems fair to observe that none of the fonts in these screens come with Windows. They're all third-party fonts. Windows itself is a bit conservative in the fonts it provides when it first comes out of the box.

Figure 4-5

An alternate font in use with DEMO4. (The figures that follow show DEMO4 with three other fonts.)

The FILE_FONT case of the WM_COMMAND handler in SelectProc deletes the existing font handle in hfont and creates a new one by calling the SelectFont function. If SelectFont returns a true value, it will send a WM_SETFONT message to the MAIN_EDIT control, passing it the new font.

The SelectFont function, defined later in DEMO4.CPP, illustrates how to use the ChooseFont common dialog call. This bit of code is similar in structure to the GetOpenFileName call discussed earlier in this chapter. Its data object is CHOOSEFONT, and the whole works is

somewhat simpler. Here are the important objects of a CHOOSEFONT structure:

DWORD lStructSize This element is the size of the structure in bytes. This should always be set to sizeof(CHOOSEFONT).

HWND hwndOwner This element is the HWND of the parent window for the Font dialog.

HINSTANCE hInstance This element is the instance handle for your application, as initially passed to WinMain.

HDC hDC This element identifies the printer device context for which printer fonts are to be selected. This assumes that you'll be selecting printer fonts, of course, as specified by the CF_PRINTERFONTS flag. If you're using ChooseFont to select display fonts, this element is ignored.

LPLOGFONT lpLogFont This element points to a LOGFONT. If you initialize this font before calling ChooseFont, the font dialog will be set up to initially select the font you've specified, or the closest passable match. The selected font will be returned in this structure.

WORD iPointSize This element will return the size of the selected font in tenths of a point.

LPARAM lCustData This element can hold 32 bits of anything you like. It will be passed to a custom message handler for the Fonts dialog as the lParam argument for the WM_INITDIALOG message.

UINT (CALLBACK *lpfnHook) This element is a FARPROC to a custom message handler for the Fonts dialog.

LPCSTR lpTemplateName This element is the name of a custom dialog template for the Fonts dialog.

DWORD rgbColors This element contains a COLORREF value used to define the text color if the CF_EFFECTS flag is set.

WORD nSizeMin, nSizeMax These elements define the minimum and maximum point size that can be selected with the font dialog if the CF_LIMITSIZE flag is set.

DWORD Flags This element is a set of flags that define how the Fonts dialog is to be handled.

The following are the flags that can appear in the Flags element of a CHOOSEFONT structure.

CF_SCREENFONTS Enables the listing of screen fonts.

CF_PRINTERFONTS Enables the listing of printer fonts supported by the printer referenced by the hDC element of the CHOOSEFONT object in question.

CF_BOTH Enables both screen and printer fonts.

CF_SHOWHELP Causes a Help button to be displayed in the Fonts dialog.

CF_ENABLEHOOK Directs messages to the Fonts dialog to be processed by the function whose FARPROC is stored in the lpfnHook element of the CHOOSEFONT object in question.

CF_ENABLETEMPLATE Causes the Fonts dialog to be created using a specific dialog template from the resource list of your application, rather than the default dialog template in COMMDLG.DLL.

CF_ENABLETEMPLATEHANDLE This flag indicates that the hInstance element of a CHOOSEFONT object is the instance of a preloaded dialog template.

CF_INITTOLOGFONTSTRUCT This flag indicates that the ChooseFont function should initialize its dialog based on the LOGFONT passed to it in the lpLogFont element of its CHOOSEFONT object.

CF_EFFECTS This flag indicates that the Fonts dialog should enable its strikeout and underline options.

CF_APPLY This flag causes the Font dialog to display an Apply button.

CF_ANSIONLY This flag causes only alphabetic fonts to appear in the Font dialog's font selector list.

CF_NOVECTORFONTS This flag causes vector fonts to be excluded from the Font dialog's selector list.

CF_NOOEMFONTS This flag has the same effect as CF_NOVECTORFONTS.

CF_NOSIMULATIONS This flag prohibits the Font dialog from displaying GDI font simulations.

CF_LIMITSIZE This flag causes the Font dialog to limit the size of the selectable fonts to a range specified by the nSizeMin and nSizeMax elements of the CHOOSEFONT object in question.

CF_FIXEDPITCHONLY This flag allows only monospaced fonts to be displayed in the Font dialog's font selector list.

CF_WYSIWYG This flag specifies that only fonts available both as screen and printer fonts are to be displayed in the Font dialog's font selector list. The CF_BOTH and CF_SCALABLEONLY flags should also be set if this flag is used.

CF_FORCEFONTEXIST This flag will cause the Font dialog to complain if a nonexistent font is selected.

CF_SCALABLEONLY This flag prohibits the Font dialog box from displaying nonscalable fonts, that is, bitmap fonts.

CF_TTONLY This flag enables the listing of TrueType fonts.

CF_NOFACESEL This flag disables the Face Name control of a Font dialog.

CF_NOSTYLESEL This flag disables the Font Style control of a Font dialog.

CF_NOSIZESEL This flag disables the Size control of a Font dialog.

A pointer to the current HFONT in use by the MAIN_EDIT control is passed to SelectFont. The LOGFONT referenced by this HFONT is fetched into a local LOGFONT object, If, by a call to GetObject. The ChooseFont call can use this LOGFONT to initialize the Font dialog so that its initial contents represent the existing font characteristics. When ChooseFont returns, the HFONT pointed to by hfont argument of SelectFont will be filled in with the new HFONT select through the Font dialog.

The GetObject call is extremely useful—it will fetch the contents of any Windows object referenced by a handle and store it in a data structure.

It's worth noting the flags that have been used in this call to ChooseFont. The CF_TTONLY flag specifies that we're interested in only TrueType fonts. The CF_SCREENFONTS flags tells the Font dialog that we're interested in selecting only fonts for displaying on a monitor, rather than for printing. The CF_INITTOLOGFONTSTRUCT flag tells the ChooseFont function that it should initialize itself based on the LOGFONT passed to it. Finally, the CF_ANSIONLY flag specifies that only alphabetic fonts are to be available, excluding symbol fonts from the Font dialog's font list.

As with the GetOpenFileName call discussed earlier in this chapter, the ChooseFont function embodies a lot of features you probably won't want to get involved with. We'll implement a few more of them later in this chapter, but a number of the flags and elements of a CHOOSEFONT structure defy practical applications.

⇨ Selecting colors

As has been touched on earlier in this book, color is a touchy subject for Windows. While it allows you to specify any color you like, drawn from a theoretical palette of about 16 million colors, attempting to display a color it doesn't support in its currently available palette might produce unexpected results. Confronted with the prospect of creating a color not available to it on a system with a palette-driven Windows screen driver, Windows will dither.

Dithered colors approach the colors they're supposed to represent, but they do so using a pattern of alternating colored dots. As such, painting with a dithered color will cause ostensibly flat surfaces to appear to be textured.

There are all sorts of applications for selecting colors. You might, for example, want to allow your users to select the colors of various dialogs and other objects in your application. Windows offers a common dialog to handle selecting a color. It has the advantage of being fairly flexible and easy to work with, and the disadvantage of not being particularly intuitive to use. Color selectors have appeared in several high-end applications, such as Corel Draw, which arguably make more sense the first time you come upon one. They, however, are not available in the Windows common dialog library.

Figures 4-6A and B illustrate two variations on the Windows Color dialog. You can have the dialog configure itself differently, depending on the flags you set when you call for it.

Figure 4-6A

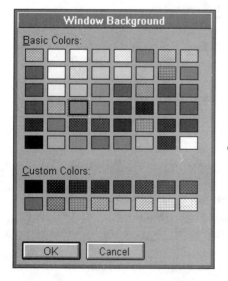

Variation #1 of the Windows Color dialog.

The DEMO4 application handles selecting a color for its window mat by calling the SelectColour function. This, in turn, sets up a CHOOSECOLOR object and passes it to the common dialog call ChooseColor. This works much like the other common dialog calls

249

Figure 4-6B

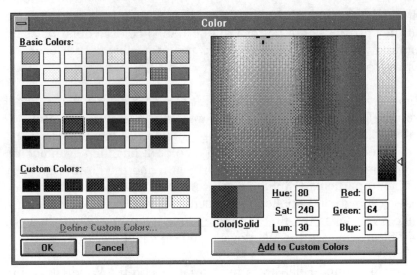

Variation #2 of the Windows Color dialog.

you've seen thus far, save that it's quite a lot simpler. A CHOOSECOLOR object has the following elements:

DWORD lStructSize This element is the size of the structure in bytes. This should always be set to sizeof(CHOOSECOLOR).

HWND hwndOwner This element is the HWND of the parent window for the Color dialog.

HINSTANCE hInstance This element is the instance handle for your application, as initially passed to WinMain.

LPARAM lCustData This element can be 32 bits of anything you like. It will be passed to a custom message handler for the Color dialog as the lParam argument for the WM_INITDIALOG message.

UINT (CALLBACK *lpfnHook) This element is a FARPROC to a custom message handler for the Color dialog.

LPCSTR lpTemplateName This element is the name of a custom dialog template for the Color dialog.

COLORREF rgbResult This element is a COLORREF object to hold the selected color, as filled in by ChooseColor.

COLORREF FAR* lpCustColors This element is a far pointer to an array of COLORREF objects that define the custom colors for the ChooseColor dialog.

DWORD Flags This element is a set of flags that define how the Color dialog is to be handled.

With the exception of the two COLORREF items, all of these elements have turned up before.

The custom colors provided by the Colors dialog allow your application to offer a selection of predefined colors in addition to its default color tiles. It supports 16 custom colors. In this application they've been defined as 16 shades of gray, but you're free to set them to anything you like. Depending on how you implement the Colors dialog, users of your application might be able to change them, defining their own custom colors.

The for loop in SelectColour illustrates how to initialize the array of COLORREF objects passed to ChooseColor. The Flags element of a CHOOSECOLOR object can contain a combination of the following flags:

CC_RGBINIT This flag indicates that the rgbResult element in the CHOOSECOLOR object in question has been initialized with an RGB color prior to calling ChooseColor, and that this should be used as the initial color value in the Color dialog.

CC_FULLOPEN This flag causes the entire Colors dialog box to appear when it initially opens, including the custom color selector.

CC_PREVENTFULLOPEN This flag disables the Define Custom Colors button, effectively preventing the right half of the full Colors dialog from appearing.

CC_SHOWHELP This flag causes a Help button to be displayed in the Colors dialog.

CC_ENABLEHOOK This flag directs messages to the Fonts dialog to be processed by the function whose FARPROC is stored in the lpfnHook element of the CHOOSECOLOR object in question.

CC_ENABLETEMPLATE This flag causes the Colors dialog to be created using a specific dialog template from the resource list of your application, rather than the default dialog template in COMMDLG.DLL.

CC_ENABLETEMPLATEHANDLE This flag indicates that the hInstance element of a CHOOSECOLOR object is the instance of a preloaded dialog template.

Implementing the Colors dialog using ChooseColor is one of the least involved of the Windows common dialogs. You should give a bit of thought to how many of its features you want enabled, however. A fairly complex dialog in its fully opened state, Colors arguably provides more color selection options than many applications need— or can realistically handle. In many cases you might find that just using the small version of Colors, with its array of colored tiles and little else, is all that's really called for.

⇨ Printing

The subject of printing under Windows is a somewhat immense one. It requires a thorough understanding of several diverse disciplines and various areas of Windows programming, and a perverse enjoyment of things that don't work properly during months with an R in them. Really mastering Windows printing is a lot easier if you happen to be God. (Demigods and lesser mortals will do well to approach this subject with caution.)

Not even flirting briefly with apotheosis, this section will touch only very lightly upon the topic of printing from within a Windows application. In principle it's fairly easy to understand, even if no real-world application of it can be handled at this level.

When an application writes text to a window, what really happens is that Windows provides the application in question with a device context handle, an HDC, and the text is written to that. Printing

under Windows works the same way—Windows provides your application with a device context handle that represents your printer's display surface, rather than that of your monitor, and you can print to that just as you would to a window.

This sort of device-independent approach to output is convenient as far as it goes, as it allows you to use the same text functions to print with that you're probably familiar with for manipulating text in a Window. It begins to fall apart, however, when you observe the conceptual differences between a printer and a monitor. Among the important ones are:

> A monitor can't run out of light, while a printer can run out of paper.

> Having finished printing to a page, you must cause the printer to eject its page. Monitors can eject things only after their warranties have expired.

> Some printers, such as dot-matrix printers, can print in only one direction, to wit, down the page.

> Printers are millions of times slower to output things to than monitors—or, at least, they are when you're in a hurry.

Dealing with printers as display surfaces requires that a Windows application be able to dispatch commands in addition to the GDI calls it uses to actually print things. These additional commands do things like ejecting a page or aborting a print job. They're called *escapes*, and are handled by the Escape function.

As an aside, they're called *escapes* because back in the late Middle Ages, when printers were a lot simpler and windows occurred only as openings in walls, printers were controlled by sending them the special Esc character followed by some data. Most dot-matrix printers are still controlled thus, as are some laser printers. But Windows insulates you from knowing this—you don't have to know exactly how to eject the page from a printer, for example, to print from a Windows application. All you need do is call the Escape function and pass it the NEWFRAME escape command. Windows will translate this into whichever incantations are applicable for ejecting a page from your printer.

All that remains of those barbaric times is the Esc key on PC keyboards. It's no longer particularly fashionable to require its use in applications, as if it were a reminder of an ugly past.

Printing in DEMO4 is very simple. Assuming that you've loaded a document into the MAIN_EDIT control, calling the DoPrint function will cause it to be printed. This actually does two things—it calls PrintDlg to display the standard Windows Print dialog, and ultimately to fetch an HDC to the printer you'd like to drive, and it then handles the GDI and Escape calls to actually print something.

To keep the DEMO4 application's source code down to a manageable level of enormity, the DoPrint function does very elementary printing. It outputs text in 12-point Courier type, no matter which font is selected to display text in the MAIN_EDIT control.

The PrintDlg function of the Windows common dialog library works pretty much like the other common dialog functions. It expects to be passed a pointer to a PRINTDLG object. A PRINTDLG object contains the following:

DWORD lStructSize This element is the size of the structure in bytes, and should always be set to sizeof(PRINTDLG).

HWND hwndOwner This element is the HWND of the parent window for the Print dialog.

HINSTANCE hInstance This element is the instance handle for your application, as initially passed to WinMain.

LPARAM lCustData This element can be 32 bits of anything you like. It will be passed to a custom message handler for the Print dialog as the lParam argument for the WM_INITDIALOG message.

UINT (CALLBACK *lpfnPrintHook) This element is a FARPROC to a custom message handler for the Print dialog.

UINT (CALLBACK *lpfnSetupHook) This element is a FARPROC to a custom message handler for the Print Setup dialog.

LPCSTR lpPrintTemplateName This element is the name of a custom dialog template for the Print dialog.

LPCSTR lpSetupTemplateName This element is the name of a custom dialog template for the Setup dialog.

DWORD Flags This element is a set of flags that define how the Print dialog is to be handled.

HGLOBAL hDevMode This element is a handle to a block of memory that contains a DEVMODE object, which can be used to initialize the dialog controls. We won't be dealing with this.

HGLOBAL hDevNames This element is a handle to a block of memory that contains a DEVNAMES object, a structure that contains names for the printer driver, the printer, and the output port. We won't be dealing with this object either—in most applications, the PrintDlg function is called to acquire this information.

HDC hDC This element is filled by PrintDlg with the HDC of the selected printer.

UINT nFromPage This value specifies the initial first page when PrintDlg is called, and is filled in with the user-selected first page when it returns. The PD_PAGENUMS flag must be set.

UINT nToPage This value specifies the initial final page when PrintDlg is called, and is filled in with the user-selected final page when it returns. The PD_PAGENUMS flag must be set.

UINT nMinPage This value can be set to the minimum number of pages to be printed before calling PrintDlg.

UINT nMaxPage This value can be set to the maximum number of pages to be printed before calling PrintDlg.

UINT nCopies This value can be filled with the default number of copies to be printed before calling PrintDlg. When PrintDlg returns, it will contain the selected number of copies. This value is used if hDevMode is NULL.

HGLOBAL hPrintTemplate This element is a global memory handle for a block of memory that contains a preloaded dialog template for the Print dialog. We won't be using it here.

HGLOBAL hSetupTemplate This element is a global memory handle for a block of memory that contains a preloaded dialog template for the Print Setup dialog. We won't be using this one, either.

The following are the flags that can appear in the Flags element of a PRINTDLG structure.

PD_ALLPAGES This flag is set when PrintDlg returns to indicate that the All option was selected in the Print dialog.

PD_SELECTION This flag causes the Selection option to be initially selected.

PD_PAGENUMS This flag causes the Pages option to be initially selected.

PD_NOSELECTION This flag disables the Selection option.

PD_NOPAGENUMS This flag disables the Pages option.

PD_COLLATE This flag causes the Collate option to be initially selected.

PD_PRINTTOFILE This flag causes the Print To File option to be initially selected.

PD_PRINTSETUP This flag causes the Print Setup dialog to be displayed, rather than the Print dialog.

PD_NOWARNING This flag prevents a warning from appearing if there's no default printer.

PD_RETURNDC This causes a printer device context handle to be returned in the hDC element of the PRINTDLG object in question.

PD_RETURNIC This causes an information context handle to be returned in the hDC element of the PRINTDLG object in question.

PD_RETURNDEFAULT This causes the PrintDlg function to return DEVMODE and DEVNAMES structures in the hDevMode and hDevNames elements of the PRINTDLG object in question. These fields should initially be NULL.

PD_SHOWHELP This flag causes Print dialog to display a Help button.

PD_ENABLEPRINTHOOK This flag directs messages to the Print dialog to be processed by the function whose FARPROC is stored in the lpfnPrintHook element of the PRINTDLG object in question.

PD_ENABLESETUPHOOK This flag directs messages to the Print Setup dialog to be processed by the function whose FARPROC is stored in the lpfnSetupHook element of the PRINTDLG object in question.

PD_ENABLEPRINTTEMPLATE This flag causes the Print dialog to be created using a specific dialog template from the resource list of your application, rather than the default dialog template in COMMDLG.DLL.

PD_ENABLESETUPTEMPLATE This flag causes the Print Setup dialog to be created using a specific dialog template from the resource list of your application, rather than the default dialog template in COMMDLG.DLL.

PD_ENABLEPRINTTEMPLATEHANDLE This flag indicates that the hInstance element of the PRINTDLG object is the instance of preloaded Print dialog template.

PD_ENABLESETUPTEMPLATEHANDLE This flag indicates that the hInstance element of the PRINTDLG object is the instance of preloaded Print Setup dialog template.

PD_DISABLEPRINTTOFILE This flag disables the Print To File option.

PD_HIDEPRINTTOFILE This flag hides the Print To File option.

Once the PrintDlg call is complete, pd.hDC should contain the device context handle for your printer. A call to the somewhat reprehensible FixedGlobalAlloc macro will allocate a buffer to hold the text to be printed, and GetWindowText will fetch it from the MAIN_EDIT control.

The GetTextMetrics call fetches information about the font currently selected into an HDC. The default font for printing is 12-point Courier, which is what we'll be using in this case. The GetDeviceCaps function can be used to calculate the number of lines that will fit on a page by fetching the page size and dividing it by the size of each line.

The STARTDOC printer escape tells the printer to expect something to be printed.

The large do loop in DoPrint handles the actual printing. It fetches lines from the text to be printed and paints them on the printer's display surface with TextOut. When enough lines have been printed to fill the current page, it sends the NEWFRAME escape and begins a new page. The ENDDOC escape tells your printer than no more printing can be expected to occur for a while, and that it can nip out back for a beer.

As was mentioned earlier in this section, the DoPrint function implements very simple printing. It exists primarily to illustrate the use of the PrintDlg function. You can certainly enhance it if you want to.

⇨ Undo, Cut, Copy, and Paste

The as yet undiscussed element of DEMO4 is its Edit menu—it supports the common Windows functions of Undo, Cut, Copy, and Paste. In fact, these tasks are particularly easy to implement in a text edit control, as there are messages to the control that makes them work. The only moderately tricky aspect of them is that they require a brush with that most ineffable of Windows phenomena, the clipboard.

The Windows clipboard is a pretty uncomplicated soul in theory, made somewhat less so only because nothing ever works as it's supposed to in theory. The clipboard can hold one object at a time, and it always remembers what sort of object it has under its hat. As

such, if you store a text object on the clipboard and tell the clipboard that's what it's been fed, subsequent applications that attempt to paste from the clipboard will know they're looking at text rather than, for example, the data of a bitmap.

Applications that support pasting from the clipboard are typically aware of the clipboard data formats they can make sense of. For example, the Windows Notepad application will allow you to paste text into one of its documents, but if the clipboard contains a bitmap it will disable the Paste item of its Edit menu, as it can't handle pictures.

The DoPaste function of DEMO4 illustrates how to paste from the clipboard into a text edit control. It begins by inquiring whether the clipboard does indeed contain text at the moment by calling IsClipboardFormatAvailable. Perhaps predictably, the CF_TEXT constant is the Windows clipboard format flag for simple text objects.

The OpenClipboard function tells Windows that you'll be wanting to access the clipboard contents presently. The GetClipboardData function returns a global memory handle to the current clipboard object. It's given a clipboard format argument because there might be situations in which the clipboard contains multiple types for the same basic object. This happens primarily with more complex clipboard formats, such as bitmaps.

The memory handle returned by GetClipboardData is a conventional Windows global handle. However, there are some restrictions as to how you should use it. Specifically, you can lock and unlock it to access its contents. It's not a good idea to modify its contents directly, and it would be very, very nasty indeed were you to attempt to clear the clipboard by freeing this handle.

Once the clipboard data has been locked, pasting it into an edit control is pretty effortless. The EM_REPLACESEL message will replace the currently selected text in a text edit control with the text pointed to by its lParam argument. If no text is currently selected, it will paste the specified text at the current cursor location.

Once the clipboard's contents are no longer required, the clipboard should be closed with a call to CloseClipboard.

259

Copying text to the clipboard is a bit more involved than pasting from it. To begin with, you must fetch the currently selected text from the text edit control in question. The EM_GETSEL message returns a DWORD that contains the start location of the selected text in its low-order word and the end location in its high-order word. The text in the text edit control can be fetched into a buffer just as it was in the DoPrint function discussed earlier in this chapter.

To paste data onto the clipboard, you must begin by storing it in a conventional global memory block. The clipboard must be opened and cleared with calls to OpenClipboard and EmptyClipboard respectively. The SetClipboardData call tells the clipboard what type of data is being passed to it and passes it the global memory handle of the data block. The CloseClipboard function tells the clipboard it can go back to sleep.

Note that once you've assigned a global memory handle to the clipboard, your application has effectively lost ownership of it. It must not subsequently free or otherwise modify its contents.

The Cut function of DEMO4 is very easy to implement, as it doesn't involve any negotiations with the clipboard. It merely uses the EM_REPLACESEL message to replace the currently selected text in a text edit control with an empty string.

The Undo function is equally uninvolved. Sending an EM_UNDO message to a text edit control will cause its most recent change to be reversed, with no additional action required from your software. In fact, this option is qualified to some extent—it assumes that the text edit control in question has been able to allocate an undo buffer and such. You can actually query a text edit control to see if it can undo a previous action by sending it an EM_CANUNDO message. The value returned by this message will be TRUE if the control in question can correctly respond to an EM_UNDO message, and FALSE otherwise.

Text edit controls have a wealth of infrequently used features, only some of which have been discussed in this section. You might want to consult the Microsoft Software Development Kit documentation—or Borland's equivalent—for a complete list of the messages that can be sent to a text edit control.

Customizing common dialogs

The potential limitation to using the Windows common dialogs as they appear in DEMO4 is the same as that of using the standard Windows controls and dialog windows as they appeared earlier in this book. While they work well enough, they're about as exciting as watching the shopping channel with an unloaded gun.

Furthermore, if you've chosen to apply some of the techniques from the previous chapter to make your Windows applications a bit more interesting, you probably won't want all the textured, three-dimensional surfaces of your dialogs to be interspersed with the flat, white sterility of the common dialogs whenever you go to open a file or print something. This is the sort of thing that makes software look decidedly unprofessional—or worse, written with a code-generation package.

As I touched on earlier in this chapter, the common dialog library does include a mechanism to allow you to refine the function and appearance of common dialogs. This comes in two parts, and you're free to inflict either or both on any of the common dialogs you choose to implement. Specifically, each of the common dialog data structures includes a string pointer to specify the name of an alternate dialog template, and a FARPROC to specify a secondary message handler. The former option lets you change the appearance of a dialog and the latter allows you to create a message handler to get a shot at the dialog messages in question before the dialog itself does.

Customizing common dialogs like this has several potential catches. We'll deal with most of them in this chapter. There are some things you can do to the common dialogs with impunity, and others that seem harmless enough but will typically crash COMMDLG.DLL pretty effectively. There are one or two things that, as discussed earlier in this chapter, do seem to be wholly impossible. Finally, there are areas of taste and decorum involved in customizing the common dialogs that are between you and your sensibilities.

Microsoft's documentation for common dialogs speaks obliquely to the issue of appropriate and inappropriate customizations. It seems a

safe bet that most of what will be discussed in this section would leave the authors of this document smoking profusely at the ears.

⇨ The impossible bits

Figure 4-7 illustrates a modified Print dialog. The notable elements of it are that some of its controls have been relocated slightly and that it includes a picture. In fact, this is arguably not a very well-chosen picture in practical terms, as it's a 256-color graphic. Displaying this dialog on a system with a 16-color Windows screen driver would make the picture look like it had been painted in a high wind.

Figure 4-7

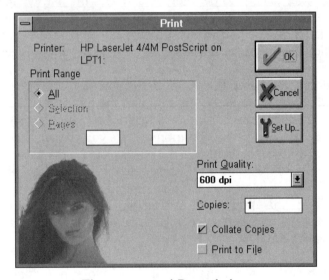

The customized Print dialog.

One day 16-color Windows screen drivers will be something people regard as barbaric historical curiosities, and these sorts of problems will no longer arise. In the meantime, an application should properly handle a bitmap like this one using two graphics—one for 16-color displays and one for everything else—as was done in chapter 2. In the interest of simplicity, I've not done so here.

In looking at Fig. 4-7, you'll probably say something like "But that's hardly impossible" and proceed to apply the techniques of the

foregoing chapters to implement it. Inasmuch as common dialogs can have user-defined message handlers—the previous section said so—all that should be involved is a call to DrawImage.

As might be expected, this won't work quite as it should. In fact, it won't work at all. The reason for this disappointing failure has to do with Windows' rather macabre sense of segments.

When the frog in chapter 2 appeared in a window, things like the hInstance value passed to FindResource and the text string that held the name of the resource to be found were stored as static objects in the local data segment of the application. Specifically, the hInstance value was stored as a global variable and the resource name as a simple string. In passing such values to FindResource—or in using them in any other way in a message handler—they're referenced explicitly through the local data segment.

In more technical terms, this means that the DS register of your system's processor holds the value of the local data segment of your application while all this argument passing and such is taking place. Confident in knowing this, Windows can address static objects using near pointers.

When the secondary message handler for a common dialog is called, it's not called by your application even through it resides in your application's code. It's called by COMMDLG.DLL. This means that the DS register points to the local data segment of COMMDLG.DLL, not of your application. Windows doesn't know this, however, and if you attempt to access static data from within a secondary message handler for a common dialog, Windows will think the data segment is correct. It will fetch things with the offsets of the objects in your application's local data segment but from the data segment of COMMDLG.DLL.

Nothing good will come of this. Not being able to access global variables and static data from within the secondary message handler of a common dialog will severely limit what you could do to customize it.

Clearly, the problem inherent in all this is in finding a way to tell your common dialog secondary message handler what the data segment of your application is. You can't simply store it in a global variable,

because by definition global variables can't be accessed in this
situation. One potential solution would seem to be passing it to your
message handler in the lCustData element of the common dialog data
structure in question, as this value will turn up in the lParam argument
of the WM_INITDIALOG message sent to your message handler.

This latter approach will work, but only very briefly. The
WM_INITDIALOG case would indeed know the correct data segment
for the local data segment of your application, but in order for the
other cases of your message handler to be able to use it—the
WM_PAINT case, for example, which is responsible for painting
bitmaps in a window—it would have to be stored in a static variable.
However, without knowing the data segment value, subsequent cases
would be unable to fetch the data segment value.

This is the sort of thing that might well have toppled ancient
civilizations on other worlds, and as such accounts for the generally
uninteresting programs to be found with a radio telescope. The
solution to this somewhat insurmountable problem lies in a bit of
insight into the geography of segments under Windows. It involves
some cheating, but it works admirably.

A dynamic link library is distinct from a Windows application in a
number of ways, one of which is that while it has a local data
segment of its own, it lacks a distinct stack segment. It doesn't need
one, of course, as the functions in a dynamic link library are always
called from a Windows application, and Windows applications do
have stack segments. The functions in a dynamic link library will use
the stack space of whatever dares call them.

This means that while the data segment value of a secondary message
handler for a common dialog will not be that of your application, the
stack segment value will be.

As was touched on earlier, the local data segment of a Windows
application contains three distinct objects: the static data, the local heap,
and the application's stack. This means that—at least for small- and
medium-model applications—the data segment and the stack segment
are actually the same segment. When Windows allocates memory in the
local heap, it does so with an eye toward not overwriting the stack.

In a secondary message handler for a common dialog, the data segment is a mystery but the stack segment is known. Since the data segment should be the same as the stack segment to access data in the local data segment of an application, the problem should be soluble by simply assigning the data segment the value of the stack segment.

Under Borland's languages, there are "pseudovariables" for all the machine registers. These are generally a bit dangerous under Windows, but this is one instance in which you can do a bit of juggling with them. Here's how to assign the data segment correctly in the secondary message handler of a common dialog:

```
_DS=_SS;
```

That's it—put this line of code before any references to static data and it will magically become accessible. Keep in mind, however, that this incantation is decidedly short-lived. It sticks around for the duration of only one message, and as such must be installed at the start of the code for every case in which you'll be dealing with static data. This is an easy thing to forget, and can be the cause of some very peculiar bugs.

If the language you're working in doesn't allow for direct access to the processor registers you might have to resort to a bit of in-line assembly language, like this:

```
asm push SS
asm pop DS
```

This effectively makes DS equal to SS by pushing SS onto the stack and then popping it off into the DS register.

Creating common dialog templates

To create a customized common dialog that has a physically different window size or placement of its controls, you must supply a new template for it in the resource list of your Windows application's EXE file. Its resource name should be passed in the lpTemplateName element of the common dialog data structure that pertains to your

dialog. The appropriate flag should be ORed with the Flags element of the data structure to indicate that a template name has been provided.

In practice, you'd probably never want to create a common dialog template from scratch. It's decidedly fiddly, and not at all necessary. While it might not be obvious, Microsoft has provided you with a complete set of dialog templates for the common dialogs. They're stored in COMMDLG.DLL.

One of the many talents of Borland's Resource Workshop is its ability to disassemble EXE and DLL files. While it won't provide you with source code for the executable bits of these files, it will unpack their resource lists into a form that can be treated just like the resources in an RC file.

To unpack COMMDLG.DLL into its component resources, use the Open function of the Resource Workshop File menu. Set the file type to DLL and navigate to your \WINDOWS\SYSTEM directory. Select COMMDLG.DLL. After a moment's thought, Resource Workshop will present you with a resource list similar to what you'd see upon opening an RC file. If you scroll down to the list of dialogs, you'll see something like Fig. 4-8.

Figure 4-8

The dialog templates available in COMMDLG.DLL, as found through Resource Workshop.

For the most part, resources are numbered rather than named in COMMDLG.DLL. Here's what the dialog templates correspond to:

CHOOSECOLOR	The Colors dialog
1536	The Open dialog
1537	The Open dialog for multiple files
1538	The Print dialog
1539	The Print Setup dialog

1540	The Find dialog
1541	The Replace dialog
1542	The Font dialog

Figure 4-9 illustrates a fairly simple modification to the Save dialog. The window size has expanded a bit and a dragon has appeared therein. To create this dialog, you would begin by opening COMMDLG.DLL with Resource Workshop. The template for the Save dialog is the same of that for the Open dialog, dialog 1536. Select this item from the resource list and select Copy from the Resource Workshop Edit menu. This will copy the complete dialog template for this dialog to the Windows clipboard.

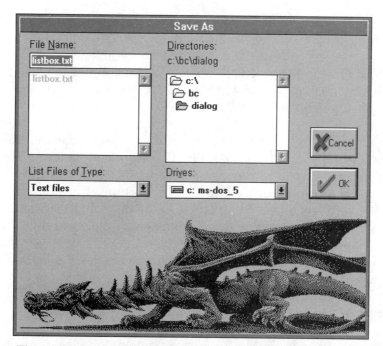

Figure 4-9

The Windows Save dialog infested with dragons. Nonflammable dialog controls are recommended in this application.

Switch to the program manager and start a second copy of Resource Workshop. Open the RC file for the application that will have the custom Save dialog in it. Select Paste from the Resource Workshop Edit menu and dialog 1536 will appear in its resource list. I prefer

named dialog templates—I renamed this entry to FileSave, but you're free to refer to it as you please. Now double click on the new entry to open the Resource Workshop dialog editor and modify the contents of the Open dialog.

Note that because you've moved a copy of the Open dialog template to the resource script of your own application, any changes you make to it will affect only the dialog as it appears in your software, and then only when you specifically tell the GetSaveFileName dialog to use your modified template. You need not worry about mangling COMMDLG.DLL, nor about having unwarranted dragons popping up in dialogs all over Windows.

If you plan to do a lot of this sort of thing—if your applications will make frequent use of customized common dialogs—you might want to consider copying each of the common dialog templates from COMMDLG.DLL into an RC file of its own so you needn't wait for Resource Workshop to disassemble COMMDLG.DLL every time you need a dialog template.

There are some things that are fairly safe to do in a common dialog template when you're customizing it. There are quite a few other things that are certain to provoke protected-mode faults and other Windows catastrophes of truly cosmic proportions. For example, there are very few of the controls in a common dialog that can be safely deleted—the only one that's genuinely dispensable is the Help button, should you decide you don't require it. You can, however, move controls around as you see fit. You can replace the conventional Windows buttons with Borland buttons, as was done back in Fig. 4-6. You can add controls and other objects, as long as you're careful not to duplicate any of the resource ID numbers of the existing controls.

You can also change the control class of a common dialog template—for example, you could change the background from white to textured gray by setting the dialog class to BorDlg. In most cases doing so will require considerable readjustment of the dialog, however, as there will turn out to be numerous objects that aren't particularly well located for a textured background.

There's a good argument for not moving everything around in a common dialog just because you can. The layout of the default common dialogs might not be as well thought-out as you'd like, but it's what everyone is used to. Having the landscaping of your custom common dialogs laid out more or less like the default Windows common dialogs will avoid forcing the users of your software to learn to work a whole new set of dialogs. This, after all, is why there are common dialogs to begin with.

Creating secondary message handlers

A secondary message handler for a common dialog works pretty much like a conventional dialog message handler, save that there are a few things it shouldn't do. This is a message handler for the Open dialog:

```
DWORD CALLBACK FileOpenHookProc(HWND hwnd,unsigned int message,
 unsigned int wParam,unsigned long lParam)
{
 RECT rect;
 PAINTSTRUCT ps;
 POINT point;
 HDC hdc;
 HBITMAP hBitmap;
 int x,y,i;

 switch(message) {
    case WM_INITDIALOG:
       CentreWindow(hwnd);
       _DS=_SS;
       SetControlFont(hwnd,1088); //path
       SetControlFont(hwnd,1089); //List files of type
       SetControlFont(hwnd,1090); //File name
       SetControlFont(hwnd,1091); //Drives
       SetControlFont(hwnd,2001); //Directories
       return(FALSE);
    case WM_CTLCOLOR:
       if(HIWORD(lParam)==CTLCOLOR_STATIC ||
          HIWORD(lParam)==CTLCOLOR_DLG) {
          SetBkColor(wParam,LIGHTGRAY);
          SetTextColor(wParam,BLACK);

          ClientToScreen(hwnd,&point);
          UnrealizeObject(GetStockObject(LTGRAY_BRUSH));
```

```
        SetBrushOrg(wParam,point.x,point.y);

        return((DWORD)GetStockObject(LTGRAY_BRUSH));
    }
    if(HIWORD(lParam)==CTLCOLOR_BTN) {
        SetBkColor(wParam,LIGHTGRAY);
        SetTextColor(wParam,BLACK);

        ClientToScreen(hwnd,&point);
        UnrealizeObject(GetStockObject(BLACK_BRUSH));
        SetBrushOrg(wParam,point.x,point.y);

        return((DWORD)GetStockObject(BLACK_BRUSH));
    }
    break;
case WM_PAINT:
    hdc=BeginPaint(hwnd,&ps);

    _DS=_SS;
    if(GetBitmapDimensions(FILEOPEN_BITMAP,&x,&y,&i)) {
        GetClientRect(hwnd,&rect);
        if((hBitmap=LoadResource(hInst,
        FindResource(hInst,FILEOPEN_BITMAP,
        RT_BITMAP))) != NULL) {
            DrawImage(hdc,0,0,hBitmap,SRCAND);
            FreeResource(hBitmap);
        }
    }
    EndPaint(hwnd,&ps);
    break;
    }
    return(FALSE);
}
```

The WM_INITDIALOG of FileOpenHookProc sets the control font for
the text controls in the Open dialog. The resource ID values for these
objects aren't defined anywhere convenient—if you want to work with
one of the controls or other objects in a common dialog template,
you'll pretty well have to open the template in Resource Workshop,
select the control in question, and read its resource ID value.

The IDOK and IDCANCEL buttons don't have the control font
applied to them as they're actually Borland bitmap buttons in this
particular dialog. Note that the data segment has been adjusted in the
WM_INITDIALOG case of FileOpenHookProc. This is necessary
because the SetControlFont macro actually refers to the controlfont
HFONT object, which is stored as a global variable.

The WM_CTLCOLOR case of FileOpenHookProc sets up a gray background for the dialog, as was discussed earlier in this book. The Open dialog is one of those that would require considerable fine-tuning were it used with the textured Borland background. It takes to a flat, gray background much more readily. There are no static or global objects involved in this, so there's no need to meddle with the data segment. If you were to use custom brushes to define the background color of the dialog, rather than stock ones, this would not be the case, and you'd need the _DS=_SS assignment.

The WM_PAINT case of FileOpenHookProc deals with painting a bitmap in the Open dialog. It works pretty much as the bitmap calls have worked earlier in this book. It paints using the SRCAND mode, which causes the bitmap to appear as black against whatever the color of the dialog happens to be, rather than black against white.

One of the things that doesn't appear in the dialogs in this chapter are Help buttons. While you're certainly free to include the Help function in common dialogs, it's arguably stretching the issue of help a bit far. If you do have a Help button in a dialog, you can respond to it by looking for the appropriate WM_COMMAND message in your secondary message handler.

There's one minor catch to including a Help button in a common dialog that you intend to modify. The resource ID for the Help button in an unmodified common dialog is 1038. The resource ID for the Borland Help button—the bitmap of the blue question mark—is IDHELP, or 998. A Borland Help button must have this ID, as this is what causes BWCC.DLL to draw it as a bitmap rather than a conventional button.

If you'll be responding to a Help button from within the message handler of a common dialog, make sure you respond to the correct value for WM_COMMAND—1038 for the conventional Windows button and IDHELP for a Borland Help button. If you're not certain what to use, respond to both. Also, note that the flags that affect the display of the Help buttons in common dialogs assume they'll have the conventional Windows resource IDs. They won't work if you've exchanged the normal Windows Help button for a Borland Help button.

You might also want to have a look at how the Setup button is handled in the Print dialog later in this chapter for another approach to having a Borland Help button in a common dialog.

The other approach to responding to requests for help from within a common dialog is to register the HELPMSGSTRING constant with a call to RegisterWindowMessage. This call will return a value that the parent window that spawns a common dialog can watch for. If the message argument to the message handler of the parent window contains this value, the common dialog in question has asked for help. The parent window should call WinHelp accordingly.

This is rather more complicated than it needs to be, and if you'll be creating a message handler for a common dialog you can safely ignore it, assuming you don't feel comfortable with the prospect of ignoring Help for common dialogs entirely.

A secondary message handler for a common dialog receives the WM_INITDIALOG message after the default message handler in COMMDLG.DLL, and all other messages before the default message handler. The WM_INITDIALOG handler in a secondary message handler must return FALSE if the primary message handler in COMMDLG.DLL for the dialog should process the WM_INITDIALOG message as well, and TRUE if it should not.

A secondary message handler must never call EndDialog to terminate a common dialog. In most cases it will never need to, as the primary message handler in COMMDLG.DLL will do so when you click on the OK or Cancel button of the dialog in question. If you'd like to terminate a common dialog early, you should do this:

```
PostMessage(hwnd,WM_COMMAND,IDABORT,0L);
```

Note that if you abort a common dialog this way, the return value of the function you called to generate the dialog in the first place—GetOpenFileName, for example—will be whatever is in the low word of the lParam argument to PostMessage.

Borland buttons and common dialogs

Figure 4-10 illustrates the principal window and the dependent dialogs of the DEMO5 application. While this will look superficially like the DEMO4 program discussed earlier in this chapter, it embodies most of the ideas we've dealt with herein for customizing common dialogs. The DEMO5 application arguably customizes some of the common dialogs a bit excessively.

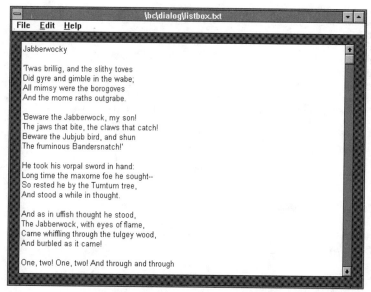

The DEMO5 application.

Figure 4-10

There's little about DEMO5 that qualifies as being genuinely new. In a sense, it fuses the DEMO4 source code with the Borland custom controls dealt with in the foregoing chapter. However, it also illustrates how to implement real-world secondary message handlers for the Windows common dialogs, and how to modify the COMMDLG.DLL resource templates. The complete source code for DEMO5.CPP is listed in Fig. 4-11. In addition to DEMO5.CPP, you'll need DEMO5.RC, as

shown in Fig. 4-12. Suitable DEF and project files for DEMO5 are
included with the source code on the companion disk for this book.

Figure 4-11 *The DEMO5.CPP source code.*

```
/*
    Dialog Demo 5
    Copyright (c) 1993 Alchemy Mindworks Inc.
*/

#include <windows.h>
#include <stdio.h>
#include <stdlib.h>
#include <ctype.h>
#include <alloc.h>
#include <string.h>
#include <dos.h>
#include <time.h>
#include <dir.h>
#include <commdlg.h>
#include <bwcc.h>

#define say(s)      MessageBox(NULL,s,"Yo...",MB_OK | MB_ICONSTOP);
#define saynumber(f,s)    {char b[128]; sprintf((LPSTR)b,(LPSTR)f,s); \
    MessageBox(NULL,b,"Debug Message",MB_OK | MB_ICONSTOP); }

#define STRINGSIZE        129        /* how big is a string? */

#ifndef IDHELP
#define IDHELP            998
#endif

#define MESSAGE_STRING    101        /* message box object */

#define MAIN_EDIT         401

#define FILE_OPEN         101
#define FILE_SAVE         102
#define FILE_SAVEAS       103
#define FILE_FONT         104
#define FILE_PRINT        105
#define FILE_COLOUR       106
#define FILE_EXIT         199

#define EDIT_UNDO         201
#define EDIT_CUT          202
#define EDIT_COPY         203
#define EDIT_PASTE        204

#define HELPM_INDEX       901
#define HELPM_USING       905
#define HELPM_ABOUT       999
```

```
#define HELPFILE            "DEMO.HLP"

#define FILEOPEN_BITMAP     "FileOpenBitmap"
#define FILESAVE_BITMAP     "FileSaveBitmap"
#define PRINT_BITMAP        "PrintBitmap"

#define DIALOG_KEY          "DialogDemo"

#define MESSAGE_ABOUT       0
#define MESSAGE_HELP        1
#define MESSAGE_TEXTFILES   2
#define MESSAGE_ALLFILES    3
#define MESSAGE_BADREAD     4
#define MESSAGE_BADWRITE    5
#define MESSAGE_BADPRINT    6

#define LIGHTGRAY           RGB(193,193,193)
#define BLACK               RGB(0,0,0)

#define BACKGROUND          RGB(0,64,0)
#define DARKBACKGROUND      RGB(128,128,0)

#define TEXTCOLOUR          RGB(255,255,0)
#define DARKTEXTCOLOUR      RGB(0,0,0)

#define CreateControlFont()     if(ControlFontName[0]) \
                controlfont=CreateFont(16,0,0,0,0,0,0,0,\
                ANSI_CHARSET,OUT_DEFAULT_PRECIS,CLIP_DEFAULT_PRECIS,\
                DEFAULT_QUALITY,DEFAULT_PITCH | FF_DONTCARE,\
                ControlFontName)

#define SetControlFont(hwnd,id) {HWND dlgH;\
                if(controlfont != NULL) {\
                    dlgH=GetDlgItem(hwnd,id);\
                    SendMessage(dlgH,WM_SETFONT,(WORD)controlfont,FALSE);\
                }\
                }

#define DestroyControlFont()    if(controlfont != NULL) \
        DeleteObject(controlfont)

#define CheckOn(item)       SendDlgItemMessage(hwnd,item,BM_SETCHECK,1,0L);
#define CheckOff(item)      SendDlgItemMessage(hwnd,item,BM_SETCHECK,0,0L);
#define ItemOn(item)      { dlgH=GetDlgItem(hwnd,item); EnableWindow(dlgH,TRUE); }
#define ItemOff(item)     { dlgH=GetDlgItem(hwnd,item); EnableWindow(dlgH,FALSE); }
#define IsItemChecked(item)     SendDlgItemMessage(hwnd,item,BM_GETCHECK,0,0L)
#define ItemName(item,string)   { dlgH=GetDlgItem(hwnd,item); \
        SetWindowText(dlgH,(LPSTR)string); }
#define GetItemName(item,string) { dlgH=GetDlgItem(hwnd,item); \
        GetWindowText(dlgH,(LPSTR)string,BIGSTRINGSIZE); }

/* bad memory management techniques... conveniently packaged */
#define FixedGlobalAlloc(n)     MAKELONG(0,GlobalAlloc(GPTR,(DWORD)n))
```

4-11 *Continued*

```
#define FixedGlobalFree(p)     GlobalFree((GLOBALHANDLE)HIWORD((LONG)p));

#ifndef max
#define max(a,b)                (((a)>(b))?(a):(b))
#endif
#ifndef min
#define min(a,b)                (((a)<(b))?(a):(b))
#endif

/* prototypes */
DWORD FAR PASCAL SelectProc(HWND hwnd,WORD message,WORD wParam,LONG lParam);
DWORD FAR PASCAL AboutDlgProc(HWND hwnd,WORD message,WORD wParam,LONG lParam);
DWORD FAR PASCAL MessageDlgProc(HWND hwnd,WORD message,WORD wParam,LONG lParam);
DWORD CALLBACK FileOpenHookProc(HWND hwnd,unsigned int msg,
    unsigned int wParam,unsigned long lParam);
DWORD CALLBACK FileSaveHookProc(HWND hwnd,unsigned int msg,
    unsigned int wParam,unsigned long lParam);
DWORD CALLBACK FontHookProc(HWND hwnd,unsigned int msg,
    unsigned int wParam,unsigned long lParam);
DWORD CALLBACK PrintHookProc(HWND hwnd,unsigned int msg,
    unsigned int wParam,unsigned long lParam);
DWORD CALLBACK PrintSetupHookProc(HWND hwnd,unsigned int msg,
    unsigned int wParam,unsigned long lParam);

void DoMessage(HWND hwnd,LPSTR message);
void SetHelpSize(HWND hwnd);
void DoHelp(HWND hwnd,LPSTR keyword);
void MakeHelpPathName(LPSTR szFileName);
void CentreWindow(HWND hwnd);
void SetFileOpen(HWND hwnd);
void DrawImage(HDC hdc,int x,int y,HBITMAP image,DWORD op);

int GetFileName(HWND hwnd,LPSTR path);
int GetNewFileName(HWND hwnd,LPSTR path);
int LoadFile(HWND hwnd,int listbox,char *path);
int SaveFile(HWND hwnd,int listbox,char *path);
int SelectFont(HWND hwnd,HFONT FAR *hfont);
int SelectColour(HWND hwnd,COLORREF FAR *clr);
int SelectFind(HWND hwnd,LPSTR text);
int DoPrint(HWND hwnd,int listbox);
int DoPaste(HWND hwnd,int listbox);
int DoCopy(HWND hwnd,int listbox);
int DoCut(HWND hwnd,int listbox);
int DoUndo(HWND hwnd,int listbox);
int GetBitmapDimensions(LPSTR name,LPINT x,LPINT y,LPINT bits);

LPSTR FetchString(unsigned int n);

/* globals*/
char szAppName[]="DialogDemoFive";
char ControlFontName[STRINGSIZE+1]="Arial";
```

```
LPSTR messagehook=NULL;
HANDLE hInst;
HFONT controlfont=NULL;

#pragma warn -par
int PASCAL WinMain(HANDLE hInstance,HANDLE hPrevInstance,
    LPSTR lpszCmdParam,int nCmdShow)
{
    FARPROC dlgProc;
    int r=0;

    BWCCGetVersion();
    hInst=hInstance;

    if(lstrlen(lpszCmdParam)) messagehook=lpszCmdParam;
    else messagehook=NULL;

    dlgProc=MakeProcInstance((FARPROC)SelectProc,hInst);
    r=DialogBox(hInst,"MainScreen",NULL,dlgProc);

    FreeProcInstance(dlgProc);

    return(r);
}

DWORD FAR PASCAL SelectProc(HWND hwnd,WORD message,WORD wParam,LONG lParam)
{
    static HBRUSH hBrush;
    static HFONT hFont;
    static COLORREF colour;
    HFONT oldFont;
    FARPROC lpfnDlgProc;
    PAINTSTRUCT ps;
    RECT mainrect;
    static HICON hIcon;
    char b[STRINGSIZE+1],name[16],ext[8];
    HWND dlgH;
    POINT point;

    switch(message) {
        case WM_SYSCOMMAND:
            switch(wParam & 0xfff0) {
                case SC_CLOSE:
                    SendMessage(hwnd,WM_COMMAND,FILE_EXIT,0L);
                    break;
            }
            break;
        case WM_INITDIALOG:
            colour=BACKGROUND;
            hBrush=CreateSolidBrush(colour);
            hFont=CreateFont(16,0,0,0,0,0,0,0,ANSI_CHARSET,
                    OUT_DEFAULT_PRECIS,CLIP_DEFAULT_PRECIS,
                    DEFAULT_QUALITY,DEFAULT_PITCH | FF_DONTCARE,\
```

4-11 *Continued*

```
        ControlFontName);

    SetHelpSize(hwnd);

    GetProfileString(DIALOG_KEY,"ControlFont",
        ControlFontName,b,STRINGSIZE);
    if(lstrlen(b)) lstrcpy(ControlFontName,b);
    CreateControlFont();

    hIcon=LoadIcon(hInst,szAppName);
    SetClassWord(hwnd,GCW_HICON,(WORD)hIcon);
    CentreWindow(hwnd);
    SetControlFont(hwnd,MAIN_EDIT);

    if(messagehook != NULL) {
        lstrcpy(b,messagehook);
        if(!LoadFile(hwnd,MAIN_EDIT,b))
            DoMessage(hwnd,FetchString(MESSAGE_BADREAD));
        else {
            SetWindowText(hwnd,strlwr(b));
            SetFileOpen(hwnd);
        }
    }
case WM_SIZE:
    GetClientRect(hwnd,&mainrect);

    dlgH=GetDlgItem(hwnd,MAIN_EDIT);
    MoveWindow(dlgH,mainrect.left+16,mainrect.top+16,mainrect.right-
        mainrect.left-32,mainrect.bottom-mainrect.top-32,TRUE);

    break;
      case WM_CTLCOLOR:
    if(HIWORD(lParam)==CTLCOLOR_STATIC ||
        HIWORD(lParam)==CTLCOLOR_DLG) {
        SetBkColor(wParam,DARKBACKGROUND);
        SetTextColor(wParam,TEXTCOLOUR);

        ClientToScreen(hwnd,&point);
        UnrealizeObject(hBrush);
        SetBrushOrg(wParam,point.x,point.y);

        return((DWORD)hBrush);

    }
    if(HIWORD(lParam)==CTLCOLOR_BTN) {
        SetBkColor(wParam,DARKBACKGROUND);
        SetTextColor(wParam,TEXTCOLOUR);

        ClientToScreen(hwnd,&point);
        UnrealizeObject(hBrush);
        SetBrushOrg(wParam,point.x,point.y);
```

```
                    return((DWORD)hBrush);
            }
        break;
    case WM_PAINT:
        BeginPaint(hwnd,&ps);
        EndPaint(hwnd,&ps);
        break;
    case WM_COMMAND:
        switch(wParam) {
            case HELPM_INDEX:
                MakeHelpPathName(b);
                WinHelp(hwnd,b,HELP_INDEX,NULL);
                break;
            case HELPM_USING:
                WinHelp(hwnd,"",HELP_HELPONHELP,NULL);
                break;
            case HELPM_ABOUT:
                if((lpfnDlgProc=MakeProcInstance
                  ((FARPROC)AboutDlgProc,hInst)) != NULL) {
                    DialogBox(hInst,"AboutBox",hwnd,lpfnDlgProc);
                    FreeProcInstance(lpfnDlgProc);
                }
                break;
            case EDIT_UNDO:
                DoUndo(hwnd,MAIN_EDIT);
                break;
            case EDIT_CUT:
                DoCut(hwnd,MAIN_EDIT);
                break;
            case EDIT_COPY:
                DoCopy(hwnd,MAIN_EDIT);
                break;
            case EDIT_PASTE:
                DoPaste(hwnd,MAIN_EDIT);
                break;
            case FILE_COLOUR:
                if(SelectColour(hwnd,&colour)) {
                    DeleteObject(hBrush);
                    hBrush=CreateSolidBrush(colour);
                    InvalidateRect(hwnd,NULL,TRUE);
                }
                break;
            case FILE_FONT:
                oldFont=hFont;
                if(SelectFont(hwnd,&hFont)) {
                    if(oldFont != NULL) DeleteObject(oldFont);
                    dlgH=GetDlgItem(hwnd,MAIN_EDIT);
                    SendMessage(dlgH,WM_SETFONT,(WORD)hFont,TRUE);
                }
                break;
            case FILE_OPEN:
                if(GetFileName(hwnd,b)) {
                    if(!LoadFile(hwnd,MAIN_EDIT,b))
```

4-11 *Continued*

```
                            DoMessage(hwnd,FetchString(MESSAGE_BADREAD));
                    else {
                        SetWindowText(hwnd,strlwr(b));
                        SetFileOpen(hwnd);
                    }
                }
                break;
            case FILE_PRINT:
                if(!DoPrint(hwnd,MAIN_EDIT))
                    DoMessage(hwnd,FetchString(MESSAGE_BADPRINT));
                break;
            case FILE_SAVE:
                fnsplit(b,NULL,NULL,name,ext);
                lstrcat(name,ext);
                lstrcpy(b,name);
                if(!SaveFile(hwnd,MAIN_EDIT,b))
                    DoMessage(hwnd,FetchString(MESSAGE_BADWRITE));
                break;
            case FILE_SAVEAS:
                GetWindowText(hwnd,b,128);
                fnsplit(b,NULL,NULL,name,ext);
                lstrcat(name,ext);
                lstrcpy(b,name);
                if(GetNewFileName(hwnd,b)) {
                    if(!SaveFile(hwnd,MAIN_EDIT,b))
                        DoMessage(hwnd,FetchString(MESSAGE_BADWRITE));
                }
                break;
            case FILE_EXIT:
                if(hBrush != NULL) DeleteObject(hBrush);
                if(hFont != NULL) DeleteObject(hFont);
                MakeHelpPathName(b);
                WinHelp(hwnd,b,HELP_QUIT,NULL);

                FreeResource(hIcon);
                DestroyControlFont();
                PostQuitMessage(0);
                break;
        }
        break;

    }

    return(FALSE);
}

int SaveFile(HWND hwnd,int listbox,char *path)
{
    HCURSOR hSaveCursor,hHourGlass;
    LPSTR p;
    HWND dlgH;
```

```
        unsigned int size;
        int fh;

        hHourGlass=LoadCursor(NULL,IDC_WAIT);
        hSaveCursor=SetCursor(hHourGlass);

        if((fh=_lcreat(path,0))==-1) {
            SetCursor(hSaveCursor);
            return(FALSE);
        }

        dlgH=GetDlgItem(hwnd,listbox);
        size=GetWindowTextLength(dlgH);

        if((p=(LPSTR)FixedGlobalAlloc(size+1))==NULL) {
            SetCursor(hSaveCursor);
            _lclose(fh);
            return(FALSE);
        }

        GetWindowText(dlgH,p,size);

        --size;
        if(_lwrite(fh,p,size) != size) {
            SetCursor(hSaveCursor);
            FixedGlobalFree(p);
            _lclose(fh);
            return(FALSE);
        }

        FixedGlobalFree(p);

        _lclose(fh);
        SetCursor(hSaveCursor);
        return(TRUE);
}

int LoadFile(HWND hwnd,int listbox,char *path)
{
        HCURSOR hSaveCursor,hHourGlass;
        LPSTR p;
        HWND dlgH;
        long l;
        int fh;

        hHourGlass=LoadCursor(NULL,IDC_WAIT);
        hSaveCursor=SetCursor(hHourGlass);

        if((fh=_lopen(path,OF_READ))==-1) {
            SetCursor(hSaveCursor);
            return(FALSE);
        }
```

4-11 *Continued*

```
    l=_llseek(fh,OL,SEEK_END);
    _llseek(fh,OL,SEEK_SET);

    if(l > 0xfffOL) {
        _lclose(fh);
        SetCursor(hSaveCursor);
        return(FALSE);
    }

    if((p=(LPSTR)FixedGlobalAlloc(l))==NULL) {
        _lclose(fh);
        SetCursor(hSaveCursor);
        return(FALSE);
    }

    if(_lread(fh,p,(unsigned int)l) != (unsigned int)l) {
        FixedGlobalFree(p);
        _lclose(fh);
        SetCursor(hSaveCursor);
        return(FALSE);
    }

    ItemName(listbox,p);

    FixedGlobalFree(p);

    _lclose(fh);

    SetCursor(hSaveCursor);

    return(TRUE);
}

void DoMessage(HWND hwnd,LPSTR message)
{
    FARPROC lpfnDlgProc;

    messagehook=message;

    if((lpfnDlgProc=MakeProcInstance((FARPROC)MessageDlgProc,hInst)) != NULL) {
        DialogBox(hInst,"MessageBox",hwnd,lpfnDlgProc);
        FreeProcInstance(lpfnDlgProc);
    }
}

DWORD FAR PASCAL MessageDlgProc(HWND hwnd,WORD message,WORD wParam,LONG lParam)
{
    static HBRUSH hBrush;
    POINT point;
    HWND dlgH;
```

```
        switch(message) {
            case WM_INITDIALOG:
                hBrush=CreateSolidBrush(LIGHTGRAY);
                ItemName(MESSAGE_STRING,messagehook);
                CentreWindow(hwnd);
                SetControlFont(hwnd,MESSAGE_STRING);
                return(FALSE);
            case WM_CTLCOLOR:
                if(HIWORD(lParam)==CTLCOLOR_STATIC ||
                    HIWORD(lParam)==CTLCOLOR_DLG) {
                    SetBkColor(wParam,LIGHTGRAY);
                    SetTextColor(wParam,BLACK);

                    ClientToScreen(hwnd,&point);
                    UnrealizeObject(hBrush);
                    SetBrushOrg(wParam,point.x,point.y);

                    return((DWORD)hBrush);

                }
                if(HIWORD(lParam)==CTLCOLOR_BTN) {
                    SetBkColor(wParam,LIGHTGRAY);
                    SetTextColor(wParam,BLACK);

                    ClientToScreen(hwnd,&point);
                    UnrealizeObject(hBrush);
                    SetBrushOrg(wParam,point.x,point.y);

                    return((DWORD)hBrush);
                }
                break;
            case WM_COMMAND:
                switch(wParam) {
                    case IDOK:
                        if(hBrush != NULL) DeleteObject(hBrush);
                        EndDialog(hwnd,wParam);
                        return(FALSE);
                }
                break;
        }

        return(FALSE);
}

DWORD FAR PASCAL AboutDlgProc(HWND hwnd,WORD message,WORD wParam,LONG lParam)
{
    static HBRUSH hBrush;
    POINT point;
    HWND dlgH;

    switch(message) {
        case WM_INITDIALOG:
            hBrush=CreateSolidBrush(LIGHTGRAY);
```

4-11   *Continued*

```
                ItemName(MESSAGE_STRING,FetchString(MESSAGE_ABOUT));
                CentreWindow(hwnd);
                SetControlFont(hwnd,MESSAGE_STRING);
                return(FALSE);
        case WM_CTLCOLOR:
                if(HIWORD(lParam)==CTLCOLOR_STATIC ||
                    HIWORD(lParam)==CTLCOLOR_DLG) {
                    SetBkColor(wParam,LIGHTGRAY);
                    SetTextColor(wParam,BLACK);

                    ClientToScreen(hwnd,&point);
                    UnrealizeObject(hBrush);
                    SetBrushOrg(wParam,point.x,point.y);

                    return((DWORD)hBrush);

                }
                if(HIWORD(lParam)==CTLCOLOR_BTN) {
                    SetBkColor(wParam,LIGHTGRAY);
                    SetTextColor(wParam,BLACK);

                    ClientToScreen(hwnd,&point);
                    UnrealizeObject(hBrush);
                    SetBrushOrg(wParam,point.x,point.y);

                    return((DWORD)hBrush);
                }

                break;
        case WM_COMMAND:
                switch(wParam) {
                    case IDOK:
                        if(hBrush != NULL) DeleteObject(hBrush);
                        EndDialog(hwnd,wParam);
                        return(FALSE);
                }
                break;
    }

    return(FALSE);
}

void CentreWindow(HWND hwnd)
{
    RECT rect;
    unsigned int x,y;

    GetWindowRect(hwnd,&rect);
    x=(GetSystemMetrics(SM_CXSCREEN)-(rect.right-rect.left))/2;
    y=(GetSystemMetrics(SM_CYSCREEN)-(rect.bottom-rect.top))/2;
    SetWindowPos(hwnd,NULL,x,y,rect.right-rect.left,rect.bottom-rect.top,
```

```
        SWP_NOSIZE);
}

LPSTR FetchString(unsigned int n)
{
    static char b[257];

    if(!LoadString(hInst,n,b,256))
        lstrcpy(b,"String table error - this application may be damaged");
    return(b);
}

void SetHelpSize(HWND hwnd)
{
    HELPWININFO helpinfo;
    char b[145];

    memset((char *)&helpinfo,0,sizeof(HELPWININFO));
    helpinfo.wStructSize=sizeof(HELPWININFO);
    helpinfo.x=10;
    helpinfo.y=10;
    helpinfo.dx=512;
    helpinfo.dy=1004;

    MakeHelpPathName(b);
    WinHelp(hwnd,b,HELP_SETWINPOS,(DWORD)&helpinfo);
}

void DoHelp(HWND hwnd,LPSTR keyword)
{
    char b[145];

    MakeHelpPathName(b);
    WinHelp(hwnd,b,HELP_KEY,(DWORD)keyword);
}

void MakeHelpPathName(LPSTR szFileName)
{
    LPSTR pcFileName;
    int nFileNameLen;

    nFileNameLen = GetModuleFileName(hInst,szFileName,144);
    pcFileName = szFileName+nFileNameLen;

    while(pcFileName > szFileName) {
        if(*pcFileName == '\\' || *pcFileName == ':') {
            *(++pcFileName) = '\0';
            break;
        }
        nFileNameLen--;
        pcFileName--;
    }
```

4-11 *Continued*

```
    if((nFileNameLen+13) < 144) lstrcat(szFileName,HELPFILE);
    else lstrcat(szFileName, "?");
}

#pragma warn -par
DWORD CALLBACK FileOpenHookProc(HWND hwnd,unsigned int msg,
    unsigned int wParam,unsigned long lParam)
{
    RECT rect;
    PAINTSTRUCT ps;
    POINT point;
    HDC hdc;
    HBITMAP hBitmap;
    int x,y,i;

    switch(msg) {
        case WM_INITDIALOG:
            CentreWindow(hwnd);
            _DS=_SS;
            SetControlFont(hwnd,1088);    //path
            SetControlFont(hwnd,1089);    //List files of type
            SetControlFont(hwnd,1090);    //File name
            SetControlFont(hwnd,1091);    //Drives
            SetControlFont(hwnd,2001);    //Directories
            return(FALSE);
        case WM_CTLCOLOR:
            if(HIWORD(lParam)==CTLCOLOR_STATIC ||
               HIWORD(lParam)==CTLCOLOR_DLG) {
                SetBkColor(wParam,LIGHTGRAY);
                SetTextColor(wParam,BLACK);

                ClientToScreen(hwnd,&point);
                UnrealizeObject(GetStockObject(LTGRAY_BRUSH));
                SetBrushOrg(wParam,point.x,point.y);

                return((DWORD)GetStockObject(LTGRAY_BRUSH));
            }
            if(HIWORD(lParam)==CTLCOLOR_BTN) {
                SetBkColor(wParam,LIGHTGRAY);
                SetTextColor(wParam,BLACK);

                ClientToScreen(hwnd,&point);
                UnrealizeObject(GetStockObject(BLACK_BRUSH));
                SetBrushOrg(wParam,point.x,point.y);

                return((DWORD)GetStockObject(BLACK_BRUSH));
            }
            break;
        case WM_PAINT:
            hdc=BeginPaint(hwnd,&ps);
```

```
            _DS=_SS;        //How to juggle live polecats in six easy steps
            if(GetBitmapDimensions(FILEOPEN_BITMAP,&x,&y,&i)) {
                GetClientRect(hwnd,&rect);
                if((hBitmap=LoadResource(hInst,
                  FindResource(hInst,FILEOPEN_BITMAP,RT_BITMAP))) != NULL) {
                    DrawImage(hdc,0,0,hBitmap,SRCAND);
                    FreeResource(hBitmap);
                }
            }
            EndPaint(hwnd,&ps);
            break;
    }
    return(FALSE);
}

DWORD CALLBACK FileSaveHookProc(HWND hwnd,unsigned int msg,
    unsigned int wParam,unsigned long lParam)
{
    RECT rect;
    PAINTSTRUCT ps;
    POINT point;
    HDC hdc;
    HBITMAP hBitmap;
    int x,y,i;

    switch(msg) {
        case WM_INITDIALOG:
            CentreWindow(hwnd);
            _DS=_SS;
            SetControlFont(hwnd,1088);      //path
            SetControlFont(hwnd,1089);      //List files of type
            SetControlFont(hwnd,1090);      //File name
            SetControlFont(hwnd,1091);      //Drives
            SetControlFont(hwnd,2001);      //Directories
            return(FALSE);
        case WM_CTLCOLOR:
            if(HIWORD(lParam)==CTLCOLOR_STATIC ||
                HIWORD(lParam)==CTLCOLOR_DLG) {
                SetBkColor(wParam,LIGHTGRAY);
                SetTextColor(wParam,BLACK);

                ClientToScreen(hwnd,&point);
                UnrealizeObject(GetStockObject(LTGRAY_BRUSH));
                SetBrushOrg(wParam,point.x,point.y);

                return((DWORD)GetStockObject(LTGRAY_BRUSH));
            }
            if(HIWORD(lParam)==CTLCOLOR_BTN) {
                SetBkColor(wParam,LIGHTGRAY);
                SetTextColor(wParam,BLACK);

                ClientToScreen(hwnd,&point);
                UnrealizeObject(GetStockObject(BLACK_BRUSH));
```

4-11 *Continued*

```
                SetBrushOrg(wParam,point.x,point.y);

                return((DWORD)GetStockObject(BLACK_BRUSH));
            }
            break;
        case WM_PAINT:
            hdc=BeginPaint(hwnd,&ps);

            _DS=_SS;
            if(GetBitmapDimensions(FILESAVE_BITMAP,&x,&y,&i)) {
                GetClientRect(hwnd,&rect);
                if((hBitmap=LoadResource(hInst,
                  FindResource(hInst,FILESAVE_BITMAP,RT_BITMAP))) != NULL) {
                    DrawImage(hdc,0,rect.bottom-y,hBitmap,SRCAND);
                    FreeResource(hBitmap);
                }
            }
            EndPaint(hwnd,&ps);
            break;
    }
    return(FALSE);
}

DWORD CALLBACK FontHookProc(HWND hwnd,unsigned int msg,
    unsigned int wParam,unsigned long lParam)
{
    POINT point;

    switch(msg) {
        case WM_INITDIALOG:
            CentroWindow(hwnd);
            _DS=_SS;
            SetControlFont(hwnd,1088);      //Font
            SetControlFont(hwnd,1089);      //Font style
            SetControlFont(hwnd,1090);      //Size
            SetControlFont(hwnd,1072);      //Effects
            SetControlFont(hwnd,1040);      //Strikeout
            SetControlFont(hwnd,1041);      //Underline
            SetControlFont(hwnd,1091);      //Colour
            SetControlFont(hwnd,IDOK);      //OK button
            SetControlFont(hwnd,IDCANCEL);//Cancel button
            return(FALSE);
        case WM_CTLCOLOR:
            if(HIWORD(lParam)==CTLCOLOR_STATIC ||
                HIWORD(lParam)==CTLCOLOR_DLG) {
                SetBkColor(wParam,LIGHTGRAY);
                SetTextColor(wParam,BLACK);

                ClientToScreen(hwnd,&point);
                UnrealizeObject(GetStockObject(LTGRAY_BRUSH));
                SetBrushOrg(wParam,point.x,point.y);
```

```
                    return((DWORD)GetStockObject(LTGRAY_BRUSH));
            }
            if(HIWORD(lParam)==CTLCOLOR_BTN) {
                SetBkColor(wParam,LIGHTGRAY);
                SetTextColor(wParam,BLACK);

                ClientToScreen(hwnd,&point);
                UnrealizeObject(GetStockObject(BLACK_BRUSH));
                SetBrushOrg(wParam,point.x,point.y);

                return((DWORD)GetStockObject(BLACK_BRUSH));
            }
            break;
    }
    return(FALSE);
}

DWORD CALLBACK PrintHookProc(HWND hwnd,unsigned int msg,
    unsigned int wParam,unsigned long lParam)
{
    static HBITMAP sBitmap[3];
    RECT rect;
    PAINTSTRUCT ps;
    POINT point;
    HDC hdc;
    HWND dlgH;
    HBITMAP hBitmap;
    int x,y,i;

    switch(msg) {
        case WM_INITDIALOG:
            CentreWindow(hwnd);
            _DS=_SS;
            SetControlFont(hwnd,1093);      //Printer
            SetControlFont(hwnd,1088);      //System Default
            SetControlFont(hwnd,1089);      //From
            SetControlFont(hwnd,1152);      //From edit
            SetControlFont(hwnd,1090);      //To
            SetControlFont(hwnd,1053);      //To edit
            SetControlFont(hwnd,1091);      //Print quality
            SetControlFont(hwnd,1092);      //Copies
            SetControlFont(hwnd,1072);      //Print range
            SetControlFont(hwnd,1056);      //All
            SetControlFont(hwnd,1057);      //Selection
            SetControlFont(hwnd,1058);      //Pages
            SetControlFont(hwnd,1040);      //Print to file
            SetControlFont(hwnd,1041);      //Collate copies

            sBitmap[0]=LoadBitmap(hInst,"SetupButtonNormal");
            sBitmap[1]=LoadBitmap(hInst,"SetupButtonHighlight");
            sBitmap[2]=LoadBitmap(hInst,"SetupButtonFocus");

            dlgH=GetDlgItem(hwnd,1024);
```

4-11 *Continued*

```
            SendMessage(dlgH,BBM_SETBITS,0,(LONG)(LPSTR)sBitmap);

        return(FALSE);
    case WM_CTLCOLOR:
        if(HIWORD(lParam)==CTLCOLOR_STATIC ||
           HIWORD(lParam)==CTLCOLOR_DLG) {
            SetBkColor(wParam,LIGHTGRAY);
            SetTextColor(wParam,BLACK);

            ClientToScreen(hwnd,&point);
            UnrealizeObject(GetStockObject(LTGRAY_BRUSH));
            SetBrushOrg(wParam,point.x,point.y);

            return((DWORD)GetStockObject(LTGRAY_BRUSH));
        }
        if(HIWORD(lParam)==CTLCOLOR_BTN) {
            SetBkColor(wParam,LIGHTGRAY);
            SetTextColor(wParam,BLACK);

            ClientToScreen(hwnd,&point);
            UnrealizeObject(GetStockObject(BLACK_BRUSH));
            SetBrushOrg(wParam,point.x,point.y);

            return((DWORD)GetStockObject(BLACK_BRUSH));
        }
        break;
    case WM_PAINT:
        hdc=BeginPaint(hwnd,&ps);

        _DS=_SS;
        if(GetBitmapDimensions(PRINT_BITMAP,&x,&y,&i)) {
            GetClientRect(hwnd,&rect);
            if((hBitmap=LoadResource(hInst,
              FindResource(hInst,PRINT_BITMAP,RT_BITMAP))) != NULL) {
                DrawImage(hdc,0,rect.bottom-y,hBitmap,SRCCOPY);
                FreeResource(hBitmap);
            }
        }
        EndPaint(hwnd,&ps);
        break;
    case WM_DESTROY:
        _DS=_SS;
        if(sBitmap[0] != NULL) DeleteObject(sBitmap[0]);
        if(sBitmap[1] != NULL) DeleteObject(sBitmap[1]);
        if(sBitmap[2] != NULL) DeleteObject(sBitmap[2]);
        break;
    }
    return(FALSE);
}

DWORD CALLBACK PrintSetupHookProc(HWND hwnd,unsigned int msg,
```

```
            unsigned int wParam,unsigned long lParam)
{
    POINT point;
    PAINTSTRUCT ps;

    switch(msg) {
        case WM_INITDIALOG:
            CentreWindow(hwnd);
            _DS=_SS;
            SetControlFont(hwnd,1074);      //Printer
            SetControlFont(hwnd,1088);      //Default
            SetControlFont(hwnd,1058);      //Default printer
            SetControlFont(hwnd,1059);      //Specific printer
            SetControlFont(hwnd,1072);      //Orientation
            SetControlFont(hwnd,1056);      //Portrait
            SetControlFont(hwnd,1057);      //Landscape
            SetControlFont(hwnd,1073);      //Paper
            SetControlFont(hwnd,1089);      //Size
            SetControlFont(hwnd,1090);      //Source
            SetControlFont(hwnd,1024);      //Options
            SetControlFont(hwnd,1036);      //Combo
            SetControlFont(hwnd,1037);      //Combo
            SetControlFont(hwnd,1038);      //Combo
            return(FALSE);
        case WM_CTLCOLOR:
            if(HIWORD(lParam)==CTLCOLOR_STATIC ||
               HIWORD(lParam)==CTLCOLOR_DLG) {
                SetBkColor(wParam,LIGHTGRAY);
                SetTextColor(wParam,BLACK);

                ClientToScreen(hwnd,&point);
                UnrealizeObject(GetStockObject(LTGRAY_BRUSH));
                SetBrushOrg(wParam,point.x,point.y);

                return((DWORD)GetStockObject(LTGRAY_BRUSH));
            }
            if(HIWORD(lParam)==CTLCOLOR_BTN) {
                SetBkColor(wParam,LIGHTGRAY);
                SetTextColor(wParam,BLACK);

                ClientToScreen(hwnd,&point);
                UnrealizeObject(GetStockObject(BLACK_BRUSH));
                SetBrushOrg(wParam,point.x,point.y);

                return((DWORD)GetStockObject(BLACK_BRUSH));
            }
            break;
        case WM_PAINT:
            BeginPaint(hwnd,&ps);
            EndPaint(hwnd,&ps);
            break;
    }
    return(FALSE);
```

4-11 *Continued*

```
}

#pragma warn +par
int GetFileName(HWND hwnd,LPSTR path)
{
    FARPROC lpfnDlgProc;
    OPENFILENAME ofn;
    char szDirName[257],szFile[256],szFileTitle[256],szFilter[768],*p;
    int r;

    getcwd(szDirName,256);
    if(szDirName[lstrlen(szDirName)-1] != '\\') lstrcat(szDirName,"\\");

    lstrcpy(szFile,"*.TXT");

    p=szFilter;
    lstrcpy(p,FetchString(MESSAGE_ALLFILES));
    p+=lstrlen(p)+1;
    lstrcpy(p,szFile);
    p+=lstrlen(p)+1;

    lstrcpy(p,FetchString(MESSAGE_TEXTFILES));
    p+=lstrlen(p)+1;
    lstrcpy(p,"*.*");
    p+=lstrlen(p)+1;
        *p=0;

    memset((char *)&ofn,0,sizeof(OPENFILENAME));

    szFileTitle[0]=0;

    lpfnDlgProc=MakeProcInstance((FARPROC)FileOpenHookProc,hInst);

    ofn.lStructSize=sizeof(OPENFILENAME);
    ofn.hwndOwner=hwnd;
    ofn.hInstance=hInst;
    ofn.lpstrFilter=szFilter;
    ofn.nFilterIndex=0;
    ofn.lpstrFile=szFile;
    ofn.nMaxFile=sizeof(szFile);
    ofn.lpstrFileTitle=szFileTitle;
    ofn.nMaxFileTitle=sizeof(szFileTitle);
    ofn.lpstrInitialDir=szDirName;
    ofn.Flags=OFN_PATHMUSTEXIST | OFN_FILEMUSTEXIST |
            OFN_ENABLETEMPLATE | OFN_ENABLEHOOK;
    ofn.lpstrTitle="Open";
    ofn.nFileExtension=0;
    ofn.lpstrDefExt=NULL;
    ofn.lpTemplateName=(LPSTR)"FileOpen";
    ofn.lpfnHook=(UINT (CALLBACK *)(unsigned int,unsigned int,
            unsigned int,long))lpfnDlgProc;
```

```
        r=GetOpenFileName(&ofn);

        lstrcpy(path,ofn.lpstrFile);

        FreeProcInstance(lpfnDlgProc);

        return(r);
}

int GetNewFileName(HWND hwnd,LPSTR path)
{
        FARPROC lpfnDlgProc;
        OPENFILENAME ofn;
        char szDirName[257],szFile[256],szFileTitle[256],szFilter[768],*p;
        int r;

        getcwd(szDirName,256);
        if(szDirName[lstrlen(szDirName)-1] != '\\') lstrcat(szDirName,"\\");

        lstrcpy(szFile,path);

        p=szFilter;
        lstrcpy(p,FetchString(MESSAGE_ALLFILES));
        p+=lstrlen(p)+1;
        lstrcpy(p,szFile);
        p+=lstrlen(p)+1;

        lstrcpy(p,FetchString(MESSAGE_TEXTFILES));
        p+=lstrlen(p)+1;
        lstrcpy(p,"*.*");
        p+=lstrlen(p)+1;
        *p=0;

        memset((char *)&ofn,0,sizeof(OPENFILENAME));

        szFileTitle[0]=0;

        lpfnDlgProc=MakeProcInstance((FARPROC)FileSaveHookProc,hInst);

        ofn.lStructSize=sizeof(OPENFILENAME);
        ofn.hwndOwner=hwnd;
        ofn.hInstance=hInst;
        ofn.lpstrFilter=szFilter;
        ofn.nFilterIndex=0;
        ofn.lpstrFile=szFile;
        ofn.nMaxFile=sizeof(szFile);
        ofn.lpstrFileTitle=szFileTitle;
        ofn.nMaxFileTitle=sizeof(szFileTitle);
        ofn.lpstrInitialDir=szDirName;
        ofn.Flags=OFN_PATHMUSTEXIST | OFN_OVERWRITEPROMPT |
                OFN_ENABLETEMPLATE | OFN_ENABLEHOOK;
        ofn.lpstrTitle="Save As";
            ofn.nFileExtension=0;
```

4-11 *Continued*

```
    ofn.lpstrDefExt=NULL;
    ofn.lpTemplateName=(LPSTR)"FileSave";
    ofn.lpfnHook=(UINT (CALLBACK *)(unsigned int,unsigned int,
            unsigned int,long))lpfnDlgProc;
    r=GetSaveFileName(&ofn);

    lstrcpy(path,ofn.lpstrFile);

    FreeProcInstance(lpfnDlgProc);

    return(r);
}

int SelectFont(HWND hwnd,HFONT FAR *hfont)
{
    FARPROC lpfnDlgProc;
    LOGFONT lf;
    CHOOSEFONT cf;
    int r;

    memset((char *)&cf,0,sizeof(CHOOSEFONT));
    GetObject((HFONT)*hfont,sizeof(LOGFONT),(LPSTR)&lf);

    lpfnDlgProc=MakeProcInstance((FARPROC)FontHookProc,hInst);

    cf.lStructSize=sizeof(CHOOSEFONT);
    cf.hwndOwner=hwnd;
    cf.hInstance=hInst;
    cf.lpLogFont=&lf;
    cf.Flags=CF_TTONLY | CF_SCREENFONTS | CF_ENABLETEMPLATE |
            CF_ENABLEHOOK | CF_INITTOLOGFONTSTRUCT | CF_ANSIONLY;
    cf.rgbColors=BACKGROUND;
    cf.nFontType=REGULAR_FONTTYPE;
    cf.lpTemplateName=(LPSTR)"FontBox";
    cf.lpfnHook=(UINT (CALLBACK *)(unsigned int,unsigned int,
            unsigned int,long))lpfnDlgProc;

    if((r=ChooseFont(&cf)) != FALSE)
        *hfont=CreateFontIndirect(cf.lpLogFont);

    FreeProcInstance(lpfnDlgProc);

    return(r);
}

int SelectColour(HWND hwnd,COLORREF FAR *clr)
{
    CHOOSECOLOR cc;
    COLORREF pclr[16];
    int i,r;
```

```
        for(i=0;i<16;++i) pclr[i]=RGB(i<<4,i<<4,i<<4);

        memset((char *)&cc,0,sizeof(CHOOSECOLOR));

        cc.lStructSize=sizeof(CHOOSECOLOR);
        cc.hwndOwner=hwnd;
        cc.hInstance=hInst;
        cc.rgbResult=*clr;
        cc.lpCustColors=pclr;
        cc.Flags=CC_FULLOPEN | CC_RGBINIT;

        r=ChooseColor(&cc);

        *clr=cc.rgbResult;

        return(r);
}

int DoPrint(HWND hwnd,int listbox)
{
        FARPROC lpfnDlgPrintProc,lpfnDlgSetupProc;
        HCURSOR hSaveCursor,hHourGlass;
        TEXTMETRIC tm;
        HWND dlgH;
        PRINTDLG pd;
        LPSTR p,pr;
        unsigned int i,size,length,pagesize,textdeep,top;
        char b[STRINGSIZE+1];
        int r;

        memset((char *)&pd,0,sizeof(PRINTDLG));
        GetWindowText(hwnd,b,STRINGSIZE);

        lpfnDlgPrintProc=MakeProcInstance((FARPROC)PrintHookProc,hInst);
        lpfnDlgSetupProc=MakeProcInstance((FARPROC)PrintSetupHookProc,hInst);

        pd.lStructSize=sizeof(PRINTDLG);
        pd.hwndOwner=hwnd;
        pd.hInstance=hInst;
        pd.Flags=PD_RETURNDC | PD_NOPAGENUMS | PD_NOSELECTION |
            PD_ENABLEPRINTTEMPLATE | PD_ENABLEPRINTHOOK | PD_ENABLESETUPTEMPLATE |
            PD_ENABLESETUPHOOK;
        pd.lpPrintTemplateName=(LPSTR)"PrintBox";
        pd.lpSetupTemplateName=(LPSTR)"PrintSetupBox";
        pd.lpfnPrintHook=(UINT (CALLBACK *)(unsigned int,unsigned int,
            unsigned int,long))lpfnDlgPrintProc;
        pd.lpfnSetupHook=(UINT (CALLBACK *)(unsigned int,unsigned int,
            unsigned int,long))lpfnDlgSetupProc;

        r=PrintDlg(&pd);

        FreeProcInstance(lpfnDlgPrintProc);
        FreeProcInstance(lpfnDlgSetupProc);
```

4-11 *Continued*

```
if(!r) return(TRUE);

hHourGlass=LoadCursor(NULL,IDC_WAIT);
hSaveCursor=SetCursor(hHourGlass);

dlgH=GetDlgItem(hwnd,listbox);
size=GetWindowTextLength(dlgH);

if((p=(LPSTR)FixedGlobalAlloc(size+1))==NULL) {
    SetCursor(hSaveCursor);
    return(FALSE);
}

GetWindowText(dlgH,p,size);

--size;

GetTextMetrics(pd.hDC,&tm);
textdeep=tm.tmHeight+tm.tmExternalLeading;
pagesize=GetDeviceCaps(pd.hDC,VERTRES)/textdeep;

Escape(pd.hDC,STARTDOC,strlen(b),b,NULL);

pr=p;
top=i=0;
    do {
    while(*pr < 32 && size) {
        if(*pr==13) {
            top+=textdeep;
            ++i;
        }
        ++pr;
        --size;
    }

    if(++i >= pagesize) {
        Escape(pd.hDC,NEWFRAME,0,NULL,NULL);
        top=i=0;
    }

    if(size) {
        for(length=0;pr[length]>=32;++length);
        TextOut(pd.hDC,0,top,pr,length);
        pr+=length;
        size-=length;
    }

} while(size);

Escape(pd.hDC,NEWFRAME,0,NULL,NULL);
```

```
        Escape(pd.hDC,ENDDOC,0,NULL,NULL);

        DeleteDC(pd.hDC);

        FixedGlobalFree(p);
        SetCursor(hSaveCursor);
        return(TRUE);
}

int DoPaste(HWND hwnd,int listbox)
{
        GLOBALHANDLE gh;
        LPSTR p;

        if(!IsClipboardFormatAvailable(CF_TEXT)) return(FALSE);

        OpenClipboard(hwnd);

        gh=GetClipboardData(CF_TEXT);

        if((p=GlobalLock(gh)) != NULL) {
            SendDlgItemMessage(hwnd,listbox,EM_REPLACESEL,0,(DWORD)p);
            GlobalUnlock(gh);
        }

        CloseClipboard();
        return(TRUE);
}

int DoCopy(HWND hwnd,int listbox)
{
        GLOBALHANDLE gh;
        LPSTR p,pr;
        HWND dlgH;
        unsigned long l;
        unsigned int i,start,end,size;

        l=SendDlgItemMessage(hwnd,listbox,EM_GETSEL,0,0L);
        start=LOWORD(l);
        end=HIWORD(l);

        dlgH=GetDlgItem(hwnd,listbox);
        size=GetWindowTextLength(dlgH);

        if((p=(LPSTR)FixedGlobalAlloc(size+1))==NULL) return(FALSE);

        GetWindowText(dlgH,p,size);

        size=end-start;

        if((gh=GlobalAlloc(GHND,size+1)) != NULL) {
            if((pr=GlobalLock(gh)) != NULL) {
                for(i=0;i<size;++i) pr[i]=p[start+i];
```

4-11 *Continued*

```
            pr[i]=0;
            GlobalUnlock(gh);

            OpenClipboard(hwnd);
            EmptyClipboard();
            SetClipboardData(CF_TEXT,gh);
            CloseClipboard();
        }
    }

    FixedGlobalFree(p);

    return(TRUE);
}

int DoCut(HWND hwnd,int listbox)
{
    DoCopy(hwnd,listbox);
    SendDlgItemMessage(hwnd,listbox,EM_REPLACESEL,0,(DWORD)"");
}

int DoUndo(HWND hwnd,int listbox)
{
    SendDlgItemMessage(hwnd,listbox,EM_UNDO,0,0L);
}

void SetFileOpen(HWND hwnd)
{
    HMENU hmenu;

    hmenu=GetMenu(hwnd);
    EnableMenuItem(hmenu,FILE_SAVE,MF_BYCOMMAND | MF_ENABLED);
    EnableMenuItem(hmenu,FILE_SAVEAS,MF_BYCOMMAND | MF_ENABLED);
    EnableMenuItem(hmenu,FILE_FONT,MF_BYCOMMAND | MF_ENABLED);
    EnableMenuItem(hmenu,FILE_PRINT,MF_BYCOMMAND | MF_ENABLED);
    EnableMenuItem(hmenu,EDIT_UNDO,MF_BYCOMMAND | MF_ENABLED);
    EnableMenuItem(hmenu,EDIT_CUT,MF_BYCOMMAND | MF_ENABLED);
    EnableMenuItem(hmenu,EDIT_COPY,MF_BYCOMMAND | MF_ENABLED);
    EnableMenuItem(hmenu,EDIT_PASTE,MF_BYCOMMAND | MF_ENABLED);
}

void DrawImage(HDC hdc,int x,int y,HBITMAP image,DWORD op)
{
    LPSTR p,pi;
    HDC hMemoryDC;
    HBITMAP hBitmap,hOldBitmap;
    LPBITMAPINFO bh;
    HANDLE hPal;
    LOGPALETTE *pLogPal;
    int i,n;
```

```
        if(image==NULL) return;

        if((p=LockResource(image))==NULL) return;

        bh=(LPBITMAPINFO)p;
        if(bh->bmiHeader.biBitCount > 8) n=256;
        else n=(1<<bh->bmiHeader.biBitCount);

        pi=p+sizeof(BITMAPINFOHEADER)+n*sizeof(RGBQUAD);

        if((pLogPal=(LOGPALETTE *)LocalAlloc(LMEM_FIXED,
          sizeof(LOGPALETTE)+n*sizeof(PALETTEENTRY))) != NULL) {
            pLogPal->palVersion=0x0300;
            pLogPal->palNumEntries=n;

            for(i=0;i<n;i++) {
                pLogPal->palPalEntry[i].peRed=bh->bmiColors[i].rgbRed;
                pLogPal->palPalEntry[i].peGreen=bh->bmiColors[i].rgbGreen;
                pLogPal->palPalEntry[i].peBlue=bh->bmiColors[i].rgbBlue;
                pLogPal->palPalEntry[i].peFlags=0;
            }

            hPal=CreatePalette(pLogPal);
            LocalFree((HANDLE)pLogPal);

            SelectPalette(hdc,hPal,0);
            RealizePalette(hdc);
        }

        if((hBitmap=CreateDIBitmap(hdc,(LPBITMAPINFOHEADER)p,CBM_INIT,pi,
            (LPBITMAPINFO)p,DIB_RGB_COLORS)) != NULL) {
            if((hMemoryDC=CreateCompatibleDC(hdc)) != NULL) {
                hOldBitmap=SelectObject(hMemoryDC,hBitmap);
                if(hOldBitmap) {
                    BitBlt(hdc,x,y,(int)bh->bmiHeader.biWidth,
                        (int)bh->bmiHeader.biHeight,hMemoryDC,0,0,op);
                    SelectObject(hMemoryDC,hOldBitmap);
                }
                DeleteDC(hMemoryDC);
            }
            DeleteObject(hBitmap);
        }

    UnlockResource(image);
}

int GetBitmapDimensions(LPSTR name,LPINT x,LPINT y,LPINT bits)
{
    HBITMAP hBitmap;
    LPBITMAPINFO bh;

    if((hBitmap=LoadResource(hInst,FindResource(hInst,name,RT_BITMAP))) != NULL) {
        if((bh=(LPBITMAPINFO)LockResource(hBitmap))!=NULL) {
```

4-11 *Continued*

```
            *x=(int)bh->bmiHeader.biWidth;
            *y=(int)bh->bmiHeader.biHeight;
            *bits=bh->bmiHeader.biBitCount;
            UnlockResource(hBitmap);
        } else return(FALSE);
        FreeResource(hBitmap);
    } else return(FALSE);
    return(TRUE);
}
```

Figure 4-12   *The DEMO5.RC resource script.*

```
MainScreen DIALOG 29, 28, 300, 208
STYLE WS_POPUP | WS_CAPTION | WS_SYSMENU | WS_THICKFRAME | WS_MINIMIZEBOX |
    WS_MAXIMIZEBOX
CAPTION "Dialog Demo Five"
MENU MainMenu
BEGIN
    CONTROL "", 401, "EDIT", ES_LEFT | ES_MULTILINE | ES_AUTOVSCROLL |
    ES_WANTRETURN | WS_CHILD | WS_VISIBLE | WS_BORDER | WS_VSCROLL |
    WS_TABSTOP, 8, 8, 284, 192

END


AboutBox DIALOG 72, 72, 224, 128
STYLE WS_POPUP | WS_CAPTION
CAPTION "About"
BEGIN
    CTEXT "", 101, 16, 16, 192, 72, WS_CHILD | WS_VISIBLE | WS_GROUP
    CONTROL "OK", IDOK, "BorBtn", BS_DEFPUSHBUTTON | WS_CHILD |
      WS_VISIBLE | WS_TABSTOP, 96, 100, 32, 20
    CONTROL "", 102, "BorShade", 32769 | WS_CHILD | WS_VISIBLE,
      12, 12, 200, 80
END


FileOpen DIALOG 36, 24, 293, 178
STYLE DS_MODALFRAME | WS_POPUP | WS_CAPTION
CAPTION "Open"
FONT 8, "Helv"
BEGIN
    LTEXT "File &Name:", 1090, 24, 24, 92, 9
    CONTROL "", 1152, "EDIT", ES_LEFT | ES_AUTOHSCROLL | ES_OEMCONVERT |
      WS_CHILD | WS_VISIBLE | WS_BORDER | WS_TABSTOP, 24, 36, 92, 12
    CONTROL "", 1120, "LISTBOX", LBS_STANDARD | LBS_OWNERDRAWFIXED |
      LBS_HASSTRINGS | LBS_DISABLENOSCROLL | WS_CHILD | WS_VISIBLE |
      WS_TABSTOP, 24, 52, 92, 68
    LTEXT "&Directories:", 2001, 128, 24, 92, 9
    CONTROL "", 1088, "STATIC", SS_LEFT | SS_NOPREFIX | WS_CHILD |
      WS_VISIBLE | WS_GROUP, 128, 36, 92, 12
    CONTROL "", 1121, "LISTBOX", LBS_STANDARD | LBS_OWNERDRAWFIXED |
      LBS_HASSTRINGS | LBS_DISABLENOSCROLL | WS_CHILD | WS_VISIBLE |
```

```
        WS_TABSTOP, 128, 52, 92, 68
    LTEXT "List Files of &Type:", 1089, 24, 124, 92, 9
    CONTROL "", 1136, "COMBOBOX", CBS_DROPDOWNLIST ¦ CBS_AUTOHSCROLL ¦
        WS_CHILD ¦ WS_VISIBLE ¦ WS_BORDER ¦ WS_VSCROLL ¦
        WS_TABSTOP, 24, 136, 92, 36
    LTEXT "Dri&ves:", 1091, 128, 124, 92, 9
    CONTROL "", 1137, "COMBOBOX", CBS_DROPDOWNLIST ¦ CBS_OWNERDRAWFIXED ¦
        CBS_AUTOHSCROLL ¦ CBS_SORT ¦ CBS_HASSTRINGS ¦ WS_CHILD ¦
        WS_VISIBLE ¦ WS_BORDER ¦ WS_VSCROLL ¦ WS_TABSTOP, 128, 136, 92, 64
    CONTROL "Button", 1, "BorBtn", BS_DEFPUSHBUTTON ¦ WS_CHILD ¦
        WS_VISIBLE ¦ WS_TABSTOP, 232, 124, 36, 24
    CONTROL "Button", 2, "BorBtn", BS_PUSHBUTTON ¦ WS_CHILD ¦ WS_VISIBLE ¦
        WS_TABSTOP, 232, 92, 36, 24
END


FileSave DIALOG 36, 24, 264, 236
STYLE DS_MODALFRAME ¦ WS_POPUP ¦ WS_CAPTION
CAPTION "Open"
FONT 8, "Helv"
BEGIN
    LTEXT "File &Name:", 1090, 8, 4, 92, 9
    CONTROL "", 1152, "EDIT", ES_LEFT ¦ ES_AUTOHSCROLL ¦ ES_OEMCONVERT ¦
        WS_CHILD ¦ WS_VISIBLE ¦ WS_BORDER ¦ WS_TABSTOP, 8, 16, 92, 12
    CONTROL "", 1120, "LISTBOX", LBS_STANDARD ¦ LBS_OWNERDRAWFIXED ¦
        LBS_HASSTRINGS ¦ LBS_DISABLENOSCROLL ¦ WS_CHILD ¦ WS_VISIBLE ¦
        WS_TABSTOP, 8, 32, 92, 68
    LTEXT "&Directories:", 2001, 112, 4, 92, 9
    CONTROL "", 1088, "STATIC", SS_LEFT ¦ SS_NOPREFIX ¦ WS_CHILD ¦
        WS_VISIBLE ¦ WS_GROUP, 112, 16, 92, 12
    CONTROL "", 1121, "LISTBOX", LBS_STANDARD ¦ LBS_OWNERDRAWFIXED ¦
        LBS_HASSTRINGS ¦ LBS_DISABLENOSCROLL ¦ WS_CHILD ¦ WS_VISIBLE ¦
        WS_TABSTOP, 112, 32, 92, 68
    LTEXT "List Files of &Type:", 1089, 8, 104, 92, 9
    CONTROL "", 1136, "COMBOBOX", CBS_DROPDOWNLIST ¦ CBS_AUTOHSCROLL ¦
        WS_CHILD ¦ WS_VISIBLE ¦ WS_BORDER ¦ WS_VSCROLL ¦ WS_TABSTOP, 8, 116, 92, 36
    LTEXT "Dri&ves:", 1091, 112, 104, 92, 9
    CONTROL "", 1137, "COMBOBOX", CBS_DROPDOWNLIST ¦ CBS_OWNERDRAWFIXED ¦
        CBS_AUTOHSCROLL ¦ CBS_SORT ¦ CBS_HASSTRINGS ¦ WS_CHILD ¦ WS_VISIBLE ¦
        WS_BORDER ¦ WS_VSCROLL ¦ WS_TABSTOP, 112, 116, 92, 64
    CONTROL "Button", 1, "BorBtn", BS_DEFPUSHBUTTON ¦ WS_CHILD ¦
        WS_VISIBLE ¦ WS_TABSTOP, 220, 104, 36, 24
    CONTROL "Button", 2, "BorBtn", BS_PUSHBUTTON ¦ WS_CHILD ¦
        WS_VISIBLE ¦ WS_TABSTOP, 220, 72, 36, 24
END


FontBox DIALOG 13, 54, 264, 147
STYLE DS_MODALFRAME ¦ WS_POPUP ¦ WS_CAPTION ¦ WS_SYSMENU
CAPTION "Font"
FONT 8, "Helv"
BEGIN
    LTEXT "&Font:", 1088, 6, 3, 40, 9
    CONTROL "", 1136, "COMBOBOX", CBS_SIMPLE ¦ CBS_OWNERDRAWFIXED ¦
        CBS_AUTOHSCROLL ¦ CBS_SORT ¦ CBS_HASSTRINGS ¦ CBS_DISABLENOSCROLL ¦
```

4-12 *Continued·*

```
        WS_CHILD | WS_VISIBLE | WS_VSCROLL | WS_TABSTOP, 6, 13, 94, 54
    LTEXT "Font St&yle:", 1089, 108, 3, 44, 9
    CONTROL "", 1137, "COMBOBOX", CBS_SIMPLE | CBS_DISABLENOSCROLL |
        WS_CHILD | WS_VISIBLE | WS_VSCROLL | WS_TABSTOP, 108, 13, 64, 54
    LTEXT "&Size:", 1090, 179, 3, 30, 9
    CONTROL "", 1138, "COMBOBOX", CBS_SIMPLE | CBS_OWNERDRAWFIXED |
        CBS_SORT | CBS_HASSTRINGS | CBS_DISABLENOSCROLL | WS_CHILD |
        WS_VISIBLE | WS_VSCROLL | WS_TABSTOP, 179, 13, 32, 54
    CONTROL "OK", 1, "BUTTON", BS_DEFPUSHBUTTON | WS_CHILD | WS_VISIBLE |
        WS_GROUP | WS_TABSTOP, 220, 8, 36, 24
    CONTROL "Cancel", 2, "BUTTON", BS_PUSHBUTTON | WS_CHILD | WS_VISIBLE |
        WS_GROUP | WS_TABSTOP, 220, 40, 36, 24
    CONTROL "Effects", 1072, "BUTTON", BS_GROUPBOX | WS_CHILD | WS_VISIBLE |
        WS_GROUP, 6, 72, 84, 34
    CONTROL "Stri&keout", 1040, "BUTTON", BS_AUTOCHECKBOX | WS_CHILD |
        WS_VISIBLE | WS_TABSTOP, 10, 82, 49, 10
    CONTROL "&Underline", 1041, "BUTTON", BS_AUTOCHECKBOX | WS_CHILD |
        WS_VISIBLE, 10, 94, 51, 10
    LTEXT "&Color:", 1091, 6, 110, 30, 9
    CONTROL "", 1139, "COMBOBOX", CBS_DROPDOWNLIST | CBS_OWNERDRAWFIXED |
        CBS_AUTOHSCROLL | CBS_HASSTRINGS | WS_CHILD | WS_VISIBLE | WS_BORDER |
        WS_VSCROLL | WS_TABSTOP, 4, 120, 84, 100
    CONTROL "", 1093, "STATIC", SS_CENTER | SS_NOPREFIX | WS_CHILD |
        WS_VISIBLE, 100, 124, 160, 20
    CONTROL "AaBbYyZz", 1092, "STATIC", SS_CENTER | SS_NOPREFIX |
        WS_CHILD | NOT WS_VISIBLE | WS_GROUP, 104, 80, 152, 37
    CONTROL "", 1073, "BUTTON", BS_GROUPBOX | WS_CHILD | WS_VISIBLE |
        WS_GROUP, 100, 72, 160, 49
END

PrintBox DIALOG 36, 52, 224, 184
STYLE DS_MODALFRAME | WS_POPUP | WS_CAPTION | WS_SYSMENU
CAPTION "Print"
FONT 8, "Helv"
BEGIN
    LTEXT "Printer:", 1093, 12, 8, 32, 8
    LTEXT "System Default", 1088, 48, 8, 120, 18
    RTEXT "&From:", 1089, 24, 80, 24, 9
    CONTROL "", 1152, "EDIT", ES_RIGHT | WS_CHILD | WS_VISIBLE |
        WS_BORDER | WS_TABSTOP, 52, 78, 26, 12
    RTEXT "&To:", 1090, 82, 80, 16, 9
    CONTROL "", 1153, "EDIT", ES_RIGHT | WS_CHILD | WS_VISIBLE |
        WS_BORDER | WS_TABSTOP, 102, 78, 26, 12
    LTEXT "Print &Quality:", 1091, 136, 100, 80, 9
    CONTROL "", 1136, "COMBOBOX", CBS_DROPDOWNLIST | WS_CHILD |
        WS_VISIBLE | WS_BORDER | WS_VSCROLL | WS_GROUP, 136, 112, 81, 32
    LTEXT "&Copies:", 1092, 136, 132, 29, 9
    CONTROL "", 1154, "EDIT", ES_RIGHT | WS_CHILD | WS_VISIBLE |
        WS_BORDER | WS_TABSTOP, 172, 132, 44, 12
    CONTROL "OK", IDOK, "BorBtn", BS_DEFPUSHBUTTON | WS_CHILD |
        WS_VISIBLE | WS_TABSTOP, 180, 8, 36, 24
```

```
        CONTROL "Cancel", IDCANCEL, "BorBtn", BS_PUSHBUTTON | WS_CHILD |
            WS_VISIBLE | WS_TABSTOP, 180, 36, 36, 24
        CONTROL "", 1024, "BorBtn", BS_PUSHBUTTON | WS_CHILD | WS_VISIBLE |
            WS_TABSTOP, 180, 64, 36, 24
        CONTROL "Print Range", 1072, "BorShade", 32769 | WS_CHILD |
            WS_VISIBLE, 8, 28, 128, 68
        CONTROL "&All", 1056, "BorRadio", BS_AUTORADIOBUTTON | WS_CHILD |
            WS_VISIBLE, 12, 44, 72, 10
        CONTROL "S&election", 1057, "BorRadio", BS_AUTORADIOBUTTON |
            WS_CHILD | WS_VISIBLE, 12, 56, 72, 10
        CONTROL "&Pages", 1058, "BorRadio", BS_AUTORADIOBUTTON | WS_CHILD |
            WS_VISIBLE, 12, 68, 72, 10
        CONTROL "Print to Fi&le", 1040, "BorCheck", BS_AUTOCHECKBOX |
            WS_CHILD | WS_VISIBLE | WS_TABSTOP, 136, 168, 64, 10
        CONTROL "Collate Cop&ies", 1041, "BorCheck", BS_AUTOCHECKBOX |
            WS_CHILD | WS_VISIBLE | WS_TABSTOP, 136, 152, 64, 10
END

PrintSetupBox DIALOG 30, 23, 288, 132
STYLE DS_MODALFRAME | WS_POPUP | WS_CAPTION | WS_SYSMENU
CAPTION "Print Setup"
FONT 8, "Helv"
BEGIN
        LTEXT "(No Default Printer)", 1088, 18, 30, 208, 9
        CONTROL "", 1136, "COMBOBOX", CBS_DROPDOWNLIST | WS_CHILD |
            WS_VISIBLE | WS_BORDER | WS_VSCROLL | WS_GROUP, 18, 56, 208, 80
        ICON "", 1084, 12, 92, 18, 20
        LTEXT "Si&ze:", 1089, 104, 96, 26, 9
        CONTROL "", 1137, "COMBOBOX", CBS_DROPDOWNLIST | WS_CHILD |
            WS_VISIBLE | WS_BORDER | WS_VSCROLL | WS_TABSTOP, 136, 96, 92, 80
        LTEXT "&Source:", 1090, 104, 112, 28, 9
        CONTROL "", 1138, "COMBOBOX", CBS_DROPDOWNLIST | WS_CHILD |
            WS_VISIBLE | WS_BORDER | WS_VSCROLL | WS_TABSTOP, 136, 112, 92, 80
        CONTROL "OK", IDOK, "BorBtn", BS_DEFPUSHBUTTON | WS_CHILD |
            WS_VISIBLE | WS_TABSTOP, 240, 8, 36, 24
        CONTROL "Cancel", IDCANCEL, "BorBtn", BS_PUSHBUTTON | WS_CHILD |
            WS_VISIBLE | WS_TABSTOP, 240, 40, 36, 24
        CONTROL "&Options", 1024, "BorBtn", BS_PUSHBUTTON | WS_CHILD |
            WS_VISIBLE | WS_TABSTOP, 240, 72, 36, 24
        CONTROL "Paper", 1073, "BorShade", 32769 | WS_CHILD |
            WS_VISIBLE, 100, 76, 132, 52
        CONTROL "Orientation", 1072, "BorShade", 32769 | WS_CHILD |
            WS_VISIBLE, 4, 76, 92, 52
        CONTROL "Printer", 1074, "BorShade", 32769 | WS_CHILD |
            WS_VISIBLE, 4, 4, 228, 68
        CONTROL "Po&rtrait", 1056, "BorRadio", BS_AUTORADIOBUTTON |
            WS_CHILD | WS_VISIBLE, 40, 96, 52, 10
        CONTROL "&Landscape", 1057, "BorRadio", BS_AUTORADIOBUTTON |
            WS_CHILD | WS_VISIBLE, 40, 112, 52, 10
        CONTROL "&Default printer", 1058, "BorRadio", BS_AUTORADIOBUTTON |
            WS_CHILD | WS_VISIBLE, 10, 16, 216, 10
        CONTROL "Specific &Printer", 1059, "BorRadio", BS_AUTORADIOBUTTON |
            WS_CHILD | WS_VISIBLE, 12, 44, 212, 10
```

4-12 *Continued*

```
END

MessageBox DIALOG 72, 72, 224, 128
STYLE WS_POPUP | WS_CAPTION
CAPTION "Message"
BEGIN
    CTEXT "", 101, 16, 16, 192, 72, WS_CHILD | WS_VISIBLE | WS_GROUP
    CONTROL "OK", IDOK, "BorBtn", BS_DEFPUSHBUTTON | WS_CHILD |
      WS_VISIBLE | WS_TABSTOP, 96, 100, 32, 20
    CONTROL "", 102, "BorShade", 32769 | WS_CHILD |
      WS_VISIBLE, 12, 12, 200, 80
END

MainMenu MENU
BEGIN
    POPUP "File"
    BEGIN
        MENUITEM "&Open..", 101
        MENUITEM "&Save", 102, GRAYED
        MENUITEM "Save &as..", 103, GRAYED
        MENUITEM SEPARATOR
        MENUITEM "&Font", 104, GRAYED
        MENUITEM "&Print", 105, GRAYED
        MENUITEM "&Colour", 106
        MENUITEM SEPARATOR
        MENUITEM "E&xit", 199
    END

    POPUP "&Edit"
    BEGIN
        MENUITEM "&Undo", 201, GRAYED
        MENUITEM "&Cut\tShift+Del", 202, GRAYED
        MENUITEM "&Copy\tCtrl+Ins", 203, GRAYED
        MENUITEM "&Paste\tShift+Ins", 204, GRAYED
    END

    POPUP "&Help"
    BEGIN
        MENUITEM "&Index", 901
        MENUITEM "&Using help", 905
        MENUITEM SEPARATOR
        MENUITEM "&About...", 999
    END

END

STRINGTABLE
BEGIN
    0,"Dialog Demo Five\nCopyright \251 1993 Alchemy Mindworks Inc.\n
        From the book Windows Dialog Construction Set\rby Steven William Rimmer\r
        Published by Windcrest/McGraw Hill"
```

```
    1,"Help"
    2,"All files "
    3,"Text files "
    4,"There has been an error loading your file.\n\n\nKick your computer."
    5,"There has been an error saving your file.\n\n\n
        Must be elevator music at work."
    6,"There has been an error printing your file.\n\n\nWindows is haunted."
END


DialogDemoFive ICON
BEGIN
    '00 00 01 00 01 00 20 20 10 00 00 00 00 00 E8 02'
    '00 00 16 00 00 00 28 00 00 00 20 00 00 00 40 00'
    '00 00 01 00 04 00 00 00 00 00 80 02 00 00 00 00'
    '00 00 00 00 00 00 00 00 00 00 00 00 00 00 00 00'
    '00 00 00 00 80 00 00 00 80 00 00 00 80 80 00 80 00'
    '00 00 80 00 80 00 80 80 00 00 80 80 80 00 C0 C0'
    'C0 00 00 00 FF 00 00 FF 00 00 00 FF FF 00 FF 00'
    '00 00 FF 00 FF 00 FF FF 00 00 FF FF FF 00 2A 2A'
    '2A 2A 2A 2A 2A 2A 2A 22 77 70 00 00 00 00 A2 A2'
    'A2 A2 A2 A2 A2 A2 A2 A2 22 70 00 00 00 00 2A 2A'
    '2A 2A 2A 2A 2A 2A AA AA A2 70 00 00 00 00 A2 A2'
    'A2 A2 AA AA AA AA B2 AA AA 77 77 77 77 00 2A 2A'
    'AA AA 2A 2A AA 2A AA A9 19 19 19 19 17 77 AA A2'
    'A2 AA AB AB AB AA 91 91 91 91 91 91 91 97 2A AA'
    'BA BA 2A AA A9 19 19 19 19 99 99 99 99 19 AB AB'
    'A2 AA AA 11 11 91 99 99 99 90 00 00 00 09 99 BA BA'
    'AA A1 01 11 19 19 19 19 90 00 00 00 00 09 AA A2'
    '00 10 10 11 11 91 91 00 00 00 00 00 70 00 00 2A 00'
    '00 00 01 01 11 17 77 00 00 00 09 70 00 00 A2 22'
    '22 22 22 22 22 22 27 77 77 70 09 70 00 00 2A 2A'
    '2A 2A AA AA AA AA 22 22 22 77 09 77 00 00 A2 AA'
    'AA AA A2 AA AA AA A2 A2 A2 27 79 17 70 00 2A AA'
    'AA 2A 22 22 2A 2A AA AA AA 2A 79 91 77 00 A2 A2'
    'A2 22 70 70 22 A2 A2 AB A2 A2 00 99 17 77 2A 2A'
    '22 87 07 07 02 2A 2A AA AA 27 00 09 91 91 A2 A2'
    'F8 88 77 70 72 A2 AB AB AB A0 00 00 99 99 2A 22'
    '8F 88 00 77 07 2A 2A AA AA 70 00 00 00 00 A2 28'
    'F8 F0 00 08 70 22 22 A2 A2 00 00 00 00 00 2A 2F'
    '8F 80 00 07 07 2A 2A AA A7 00 00 00 00 00 A7 28'
    'F8 FF 00 88 82 22 A2 A2 A0 00 00 00 00 00 22 7F'
    '8F FF FF 8F 82 2A 2A 2A 70 00 00 00 00 00 A7 0F'
    'FF FF F8 F8 F2 A2 A2 A2 00 00 00 00 00 00 A2 70'
    'FF FF 8F 8F 2A 2A 2A 20 00 00 00 00 00 00 A7 07'
    'FF FF F8 F8 22 A2 A2 00 00 00 00 00 00 00 A2 70'
    '70 FF 8F 22 2A 2A 20 00 00 00 00 00 00 00 AA 07'
    '07 07 02 02 A2 A2 00 00 00 00 00 00 00 00 BA A0'
    '70 70 72 2A 2A 20 00 00 00 00 00 00 00 00 BB AA'
    'A7 A7 AA AA A0 00 00 00 00 00 00 00 00 00 AA BA'
    'AA AA AA 00 00 00 00 00 00 00 00 00 00 00 AA A0'
    '00 00 00 00 00 00 00 00 00 00 00 00 00 00 00 00'
    '01 FF 00 00 01 FF 00 00 01 FF 00 00 00 03 00 00'
    '00 00 00 00 00 00 00 00 00 00 00 00 00 01 F8 00 00'
```

4-12 *Continued*

```
        '07 FE 00 00 3F DF 00 00 3F 9F 00 00 01 9F 00 00'
        '00 8F 00 00 00 07 00 00 00 03 00 00 00 C0 00 00'
        '00 E0 00 00 01 F0 00 00 01 FF 00 00 03 FF 00 00'
        '03 FF 00 00 07 FF 00 00 07 FF 00 00 0F FF 00 00'
        '1F FF 00 00 3F FF 00 00 7F FF 00 00 FF FF 00 01'
        'FF FF 00 07 FF FF 00 3F FF FF 1F FF FF FF'
END

FileOpenBitmap BITMAP "border1.bmp"

FileSaveBitmap BITMAP "dragon1.bmp"

PrintBitmap BITMAP "print.bmp"

SetupButtonNormal BITMAP "sb-norm.bmp"

SetupButtonFocus BITMAP "sb-focs.bmp"

SetupButtonHighlight BITMAP "sb-pres.bmp"
```

In working through DEMO5.CPP, you'll find that all the functions of
DEMO4.CPP exist, along with some new ones, these being the
common dialog secondary message handlers. They all have function
names that end in HookProc. Note also that each of the common
dialogs that have secondary message handlers and custom templates
have flags to indicate this.

The Open and Save dialogs, as managed by FileOpenHookProc and
FileSaveHookProc, have been discussed to some degree earlier in this
section. Their message handlers don't do anything all that remarkable,
except for making the dialog backgrounds gray and painting a few
bitmaps. The dialog templates themselves have actually been the
recipients of considerable fiddling to make these pictures appear as
they should.

The Print dialog and its PrintHookProc function are also fairly tame
as secondary message handlers go. The 256-color bitmap in the
customized Print dialog required a bit of cunning. A color image can't
be knocked out of a gray background like a black-and-white one can,
that is, by painting it with the SRCAND raster operation code. In
order to make the girl's face in the Print dialog appear to be matted
against the gray background, the original bitmap was retouched in a

paint program so that the area behind the subject was flat gray—the same flat gray as returned by the LTGRAY_BRUSH stock object. This color is actually RGB(192,192,192).

Note that there are two secondary message handlers for the print dialog—PrintHookProc and PrintSetupHookProc respectively—and two dialog templates in DEMO5.RC—PrintBox and PrintSetupBox. Even though it's the Print dialog that will be called up from the Print item of DEMO5, you might still have recourse to the Print Setup dialog from within it.

The PrintDlg function allows you to define secondary message handlers and template names for both dialogs. Doing so will make the Print Setup dialog look consistent with the Print dialog—sadly, this will fall apart if someone clicks on the Options button in the Print Setup dialog. There are no hooks provided in a PRINTDLG object for the dialogs subsequent to Print Setup. This issue will be touched on again in a moment when we look at the automatic subclassing of CTL3D.DLL.

Note that there's no custom template or secondary message handler for the Colors dialog in DEMO5.CPP. The Colors dialog takes very unkindly to attempts to change its appearance or, at least, it can. If the full dialog is used and the dialog is given a background color other than white, the sliders that set the color percentages will turn out to leave white trails behind them as they move. While the dialog works properly this way, it looks pretty unprofessional.

If you prevent the Colors dialog from opening past the default color tiles, you can use a custom template and secondary message handler because the cosmetically nasty color sliders won't appear.

The Fonts dialog behaves like the other custom dialogs, with two catches. You can't put a Borland custom drop shadow around the font sample control, as Borland's lines and frames get drawn last. As the interior of a drop shadow is flat gray, rather than hollow, doing so would obscure the font sample. You also can't use Borland buttons in the Font dialog.

 # More custom Borland buttons

The Print dialog back in Fig. 4-9 included three Borland buttons—the traditional OK and Cancel buttons, and the Setup button that appeared in the Buttons dialog for DEMO2 in the previous chapter. This isn't a standard BWCC.DLL button, and its appearance in this dialog requires a bit of additional sorcery.

The standard Windows Print dialog has a Setup button with a resource ID of 1024. This value can't be changed, as the message handler in COMMDLG.DLL expects to see a WM_COMMAND message appear with this value as its wParam argument when the Setup button is clicked. As discussed in the previous chapter, however, the facility that BWCC.DLL possesses for automatically adding bitmaps to Borland buttons assumes that the buttons have resource IDs no higher than 999. This would seem to be an insurmountable problem, except that the bitmapped Setup button unquestionably appears in this dialog.

The way around this problem is to create the Setup button as a Borland button having the correct resource ID of 1024 and leave its caption blank. Store the three bitmaps for it in the resource script of your application and then add them to the button when they're required. The bitmaps are stored like this in DEMO5.RC:

```
SetupButtonNormal BITMAP "sb-norm.bmp"
SetupButtonFocus BITMAP "sb-focs.bmp"
SetupButtonHighlight BITMAP "sb-pres.bmp"
```

These bitmaps have names, rather than numbers, so they can't become confused with any numbered bitmaps that might appear for other Borland buttons, were any in fact defined. The following code appears in the WM_INITDIALOG case for the Print dialog's secondary message handler:

```
sBitmap[0]=LoadBitmap(hInst,"SetupButtonNormal");
sBitmap[1]=LoadBitmap(hInst,"SetupButtonHighlight");
sBitmap[2]=LoadBitmap(hInst,"SetupButtonFocus");

dlgH=GetDlgItem(hwnd,1024);

SendMessage(dlgH,BBM_SETBITS,0,(LONG)(LPSTR)sBitmap);
```

The three calls to LoadBitmap fetch the three bitmaps for the Setup button from the resource list of DEMO5. Handles to the bitmaps must be stored in an array of three HBITMAP objects. Because these must be deleted later, they should be declared static. The bitmaps are assigned to the HWND for the Setup button through the BBM_SETBITS message, a custom message defined in BWCC.H. Its lParam argument should be a far pointer to the array of bitmap handles.

You can use this facility both to take care of resource ID problems for bitmapped buttons, as illustrated here, and to manage bitmapped buttons that are to have different bitmaps for different occasions.

Microsoft CTL3D and common dialogs

Figure 4-13 illustrates the DEMO6 application. Another variation on DEMO4, this program illustrates how you can customize the Windows common dialogs when you're using the CTL3D custom control library—or, perhaps more to the point, how you can't customize them. While you can use custom dialog templates to move the controls and other elements of the common dialogs around if you want to, some of the things done in DEMO5 will cause CTL3D.DLL to take umbrage and crash. Specifically, returning brush handles in response to WM_CTLCOLOR messages will thoroughly annoy it, as was discussed in the previous chapter.

There's one decidedly useful feature of CTL3D when it's applied to the Windows common dialogs, actually. It performs automatic subclassing. This essentially means that there's no need to return brush handles from a secondary message handler to make the backgrounds of the common dialogs gray, nor need you explicitly tell CTL3D to make the controls therein three-dimensional. Once installed—and once Ctl3dAutoSubclass has been called—all the dialogs in your application will be drawn with the three-dimensional controls and gray backgrounds of the CTL3D library. This includes common dialogs and any dependent dialogs they happen to generate.

Figure 4-13

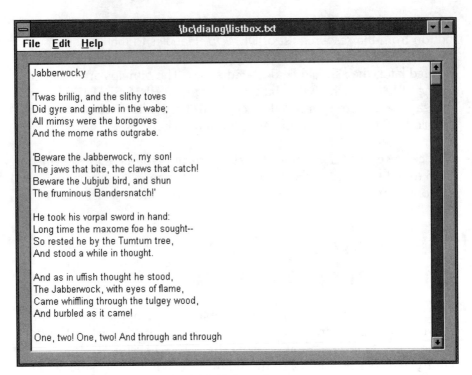

The DEMO6 application.

While arguably of little importance in the grand cosmic scheme of things, this is a minor failing of using Borland's BWCC controls with common dialogs. If the Save dialog pops up a child dialog to announce that the filename you want to write to already exists, it will have a white background and Microsoft controls even if you've modified the Save dialog itself to have a gray background and Borland controls. Windows purists will no doubt guffaw and chide you for this sort of thing, although most of them will have long since written you off for lost over the dragon in the Save dialog in any case.

There's no way around this minor faux pas if you use Borland's custom controls and the techniques discussed in the previous section of this chapter. You can't do much about it in an application with gray dialogs and no custom controls either. The CTL3D library takes care of it, however, as it subclasses all the dialogs in an application,

even the ones generated by COMMDLG.DLL. This means that all dialogs will look the same.

Having said this, if you use secondary message handlers to change the font used by the controls of a common dialog, note that these fonts won't be automatically subclassed. The conventional chunky Windows font will turn up in any dependent dialogs.

The complete source code for DEMO6.CPP is listed in Fig. 4-14. In addition to DEMO6.CPP, you'll need DEMO6.RC, as in Fig. 4-15. Suitable DEF and project files for DEMO6 are included with the source code on the companion disk for this book.

The DEMO6.CPP source code. Figure 4-14

```
/*
    Dialog Demo 6
    Copyright (c) 1993 Alchemy Mindworks Inc.
*/

#include <windows.h>
#include <stdio.h>
#include <stdlib.h>
#include <ctype.h>
#include <alloc.h>
#include <string.h>
#include <dos.h>
#include <time.h>
#include <dir.h>
#include <commdlg.h>
#include "ctl3d.h"
#include "draw3d.h"

#define say(s)      MessageBox(NULL,s,"Yo...",MB_OK | MB_ICONSTOP);
#define saynumber(f,s)      {char b[128]; sprintf((LPSTR)b,(LPSTR)f,s); \
    MessageBox(NULL,b,"Debug Message",MB_OK | MB_ICONSTOP); }

#define STRINGSIZE          129         /* how big is a string? */

#ifndef IDHELP
#define IDHELP              998
#endif

#define MESSAGE_STRING      101         /* message box object */

#define MAIN_EDIT           401

#define FILE_OPEN           101
#define FILE_SAVE           102
```

4-14 *Continued*

```
#define FILE_SAVEAS      103
#define FILE_FONT        104
#define FILE_PRINT       105
#define FILE_EXIT        199

#define EDIT_UNDO        201
#define EDIT_CUT         202
#define EDIT_COPY        203
#define EDIT_PASTE       204

#define HELPM_INDEX      901
#define HELPM_USING      905
#define HELPM_ABOUT      999

#define HELPFILE         "DEMO.HLP"

#define DIALOG_KEY       "DialogDemo"

#define MESSAGE_ABOUT     0
#define MESSAGE_HELP      1
#define MESSAGE_TEXTFILES 2
#define MESSAGE_ALLFILES  3
#define MESSAGE_BADREAD   4
#define MESSAGE_BADWRITE  5
#define MESSAGE_BADPRINT  6

#define CreateControlFont()    if(ControlFontName[0]) \
             controlfont=CreateFont(16,0,0,0,0,0,0,0,\
             ANSI_CHARSET,OUT_DEFAULT_PRECIS,CLIP_DEFAULT_PRECIS,\
             DEFAULT_QUALITY,DEFAULT_PITCH : FF_DONTCARE,\
             ControlFontName)

#define SetControlFont(hwnd,id) {HWND dlgH;\
             if(controlfont != NULL) {\
                 dlgH=GetDlgItem(hwnd,id);\
                 SendMessage(dlgH,WM_SETFONT,(WORD)controlfont,FALSE);\
             }\
             }

#define DestroyControlFont()    if(controlfont != NULL) \
     DeleteObject(controlfont)

#define CheckOn(item)      SendDlgItemMessage(hwnd,item,BM_SETCHECK,1,0L);
#define CheckOff(item)     SendDlgItemMessage(hwnd,item,BM_SETCHECK,0,0L);
#define ItemOn(item)      { dlgH=GetDlgItem(hwnd,item); EnableWindow(dlgH,TRUE); }
#define ItemOff(item)     { dlgH=GetDlgItem(hwnd,item); EnableWindow(dlgH,FALSE); }
#define IsItemChecked(item)   SendDlgItemMessage(hwnd,item,BM_GETCHECK,0,0L)
#define ItemName(item,string)    { dlgH=GetDlgItem(hwnd,item); \
     SetWindowText(dlgH,(LPSTR)string); }
#define GetItemName(item,string) { dlgH=GetDlgItem(hwnd,item); \
     GetWindowText(dlgH,(LPSTR)string,BIGSTRINGSIZE); }
```

```
/* bad memory management techniques... conveniently packaged */
#define FixedGlobalAlloc(n)     MAKELONG(0,GlobalAlloc(GPTR,(DWORD)n))
#define FixedGlobalFree(p)     GlobalFree((GLOBALHANDLE)HIWORD((LONG)p));

#ifndef max
#define max(a,b)               (((a)>(b))?(a):(b))
#endif
#ifndef min
#define min(a,b)               (((a)<(b))?(a):(b))
#endif

/* prototypes */
DWORD FAR PASCAL SelectProc(HWND hwnd,WORD message,WORD wParam,LONG lParam);
DWORD FAR PASCAL AboutDlgProc(HWND hwnd,WORD message,WORD wParam,LONG lParam);
DWORD FAR PASCAL MessageDlgProc(HWND hwnd,WORD message,WORD wParam,LONG lParam);

void DoMessage(HWND hwnd,LPSTR message);
void SetHelpSize(HWND hwnd);
void DoHelp(HWND hwnd,LPSTR keyword);
void MakeHelpPathName(LPSTR szFileName);
void CentreWindow(HWND hwnd);
void SetFileOpen(HWND hwnd);

int GetFileName(HWND hwnd,LPSTR path);
int GetNewFileName(HWND hwnd,LPSTR path);
int LoadFile(HWND hwnd,int listbox,char *path);
int SaveFile(HWND hwnd,int listbox,char *path);
int SelectFont(HWND hwnd,HFONT FAR *hfont);
int SelectFind(HWND hwnd,LPSTR text);
int DoPrint(HWND hwnd,int listbox);
int DoPaste(HWND hwnd,int listbox);
int DoCopy(HWND hwnd,int listbox);
int DoCut(HWND hwnd,int listbox);
int DoUndo(HWND hwnd,int listbox);

LPSTR FetchString(unsigned int n);

/* globals*/
char szAppName[]="DialogDemoSix";
char ControlFontName[STRINGSIZE+1]="Arial";

LPSTR messagehook=NULL;
HANDLE hInst;
HFONT controlfont=NULL;

#pragma warn -par
int PASCAL WinMain(HANDLE hInstance,HANDLE hPrevInstance,
     LPSTR lpszCmdParam,int nCmdShow)
{
    FARPROC dlgProc;
    int r=0;

    hInst=hInstance;
```

313

4-14 *Continued*

```
    Ctl3dRegister(hInstance);
    Ctl3dAutoSubclass(hInstance);

    if(lstrlen(lpszCmdParam)) messagehook=lpszCmdParam;
    else messagehook=NULL;

    dlgProc=MakeProcInstance((FARPROC)SelectProc,hInst);
    r=DialogBox(hInst,"MainScreen",NULL,dlgProc);

    FreeProcInstance(dlgProc);

    Ctl3dUnregister(hInstance);

    return(r);
}

DWORD FAR PASCAL SelectProc(HWND hwnd,WORD message,WORD wParam,LONG lParam)
{
    static HFONT hFont;
    HFONT oldFont;
    FARPROC lpfnDlgProc;
    PAINTSTRUCT ps;
    RECT mainrect;
    static HICON hIcon;
    char b[STRINGSIZE+1],name[16],ext[8];
    HWND dlgH;

    switch(message) {
        case WM_SYSCOMMAND:
            switch(wParam & 0xfff0) {
                case SC_CLOSE:
                    SendMessage(hwnd,WM_COMMAND,FILE_EXIT,0L);
                    break;
            }
            break;
        case WM_CTLCOLOR:
            return(Ctl3dCtlColorEx(message,wParam,lParam));
        case WM_INITDIALOG:
            hFont=CreateFont(16,0,0,0,0,0,0,0,ANSI_CHARSET,
                OUT_DEFAULT_PRECIS,CLIP_DEFAULT_PRECIS,
                DEFAULT_QUALITY,DEFAULT_PITCH | FF_DONTCARE,\
                ControlFontName);

            SetHelpSize(hwnd);

            GetProfileString(DIALOG_KEY,"ControlFont",
                ControlFontName,b,STRINGSIZE);
            if(lstrlen(b)) lstrcpy(ControlFontName,b);
            CreateControlFont();

            hIcon=LoadIcon(hInst,szAppName);
```

```
        SetClassWord(hwnd,GCW_HICON,(WORD)hIcon);
        CentreWindow(hwnd);
        SetControlFont(hwnd,MAIN_EDIT);

        if(messagehook != NULL) {
            lstrcpy(b,messagehook);
            if(!LoadFile(hwnd,MAIN_EDIT,b))
                DoMessage(hwnd,FetchString(MESSAGE_BADREAD));
            else {
                SetWindowText(hwnd,strlwr(b));
                SetFileOpen(hwnd);
            }
        }
    case WM_SIZE:
        GetClientRect(hwnd,&mainrect);

        dlgH=GetDlgItem(hwnd,MAIN_EDIT);
        MoveWindow(dlgH,mainrect.left+16,mainrect.top+16,mainrect.right-
            mainrect.left-32,mainrect.bottom-mainrect.top-32,TRUE);

        break;
    case WM_PAINT:
        BeginPaint(hwnd,&ps);
        EndPaint(hwnd,&ps);
        break;
    case WM_COMMAND:
        switch(wParam) {
            case HELPM_INDEX:
                MakeHelpPathName(b);
                WinHelp(hwnd,b,HELP_INDEX,NULL);
                break;
            case HELPM_USING:
                WinHelp(hwnd,"",HELP_HELPONHELP,NULL);
                break;
            case HELPM_ABOUT:
                if((lpfnDlgProc=MakeProcInstance((FARPROC)
                  AboutDlgProc,hInst)) != NULL) {
                    DialogBox(hInst,"AboutBox",hwnd,lpfnDlgProc);
                    FreeProcInstance(lpfnDlgProc);
                }
                break;
            case EDIT_UNDO:
                DoUndo(hwnd,MAIN_EDIT);
                break;
            case EDIT_CUT:
                DoCut(hwnd,MAIN_EDIT);
                break;
            case EDIT_COPY:
                DoCopy(hwnd,MAIN_EDIT);
                break;
            case EDIT_PASTE:
                DoPaste(hwnd,MAIN_EDIT);
                break;
```

4-14 *Continued*

```
            case FILE_FONT:
                oldFont=hFont;
                if(SelectFont(hwnd,&hFont)) {
                    if(oldFont != NULL) DeleteObject(oldFont);
                    dlgH=GetDlgItem(hwnd,MAIN_EDIT);
                    SendMessage(dlgH,WM_SETFONT,(WORD)hFont,TRUE);
                }
                break;
            case FILE_OPEN:
                if(GetFileName(hwnd,b)) {
                    if(!LoadFile(hwnd,MAIN_EDIT,b))
                        DoMessage(hwnd,FetchString(MESSAGE_BADREAD));
                    else {
                        SetWindowText(hwnd,strlwr(b));
                        SetFileOpen(hwnd);
                    }
                }
                break;
            case FILE_PRINT:
                if(!DoPrint(hwnd,MAIN_EDIT))
                    DoMessage(hwnd,FetchString(MESSAGE_BADPRINT));
                break;
            case FILE_SAVE:
                fnsplit(b,NULL,NULL,name,ext);
                lstrcat(name,ext);
                lstrcpy(b,name);
                if(!SaveFile(hwnd,MAIN_EDIT,b))
                    DoMessage(hwnd,FetchString(MESSAGE_BADWRITE));
                break;
            case FILE_SAVEAS:
                GetWindowText(hwnd,b,128);
                fnsplit(b,NULL,NULL,name,ext);
                lstrcat(name,ext);
                lstrcpy(b,name);
                if(GetNewFileName(hwnd,b)) {
                    if(!SaveFile(hwnd,MAIN_EDIT,b))
                        DoMessage(hwnd,FetchString(MESSAGE_BADWRITE));
                }
                break;
            case FILE_EXIT:
                if(hFont != NULL) DeleteObject(hFont);
                MakeHelpPathName(b);
                WinHelp(hwnd,b,HELP_QUIT,NULL);

                FreeResource(hIcon);
                DestroyControlFont();
                PostQuitMessage(0);
                break;
        }
        break;
```

```
        }

        return(FALSE);
    }

int SaveFile(HWND hwnd,int listbox,char *path)
{
    HCURSOR hSaveCursor,hHourGlass;
    LPSTR p;
    HWND dlgH;
    unsigned int size;
    int fh;

    hHourGlass=LoadCursor(NULL,IDC_WAIT);
    hSaveCursor=SetCursor(hHourGlass);

    if((fh=_lcreat(path,0))==-1) {
        SetCursor(hSaveCursor);
        return(FALSE);
    }

    dlgH=GetDlgItem(hwnd,listbox);
    size=GetWindowTextLength(dlgH);

    if((p=(LPSTR)FixedGlobalAlloc(size+1))==NULL) {
        SetCursor(hSaveCursor);
        _lclose(fh);
        return(FALSE);
    }

    GetWindowText(dlgH,p,size);

    --size;
    if(_lwrite(fh,p,size) != size) {
        SetCursor(hSaveCursor);
        FixedGlobalFree(p);
        _lclose(fh);
        return(FALSE);
    }

    FixedGlobalFree(p);

    _lclose(fh);
    SetCursor(hSaveCursor);
    return(TRUE);
}

int LoadFile(HWND hwnd,int listbox,char *path)
{
    HCURSOR hSaveCursor,hHourGlass;
    LPSTR p;
    HWND dlgH;
    long l;
```

4-14 *Continued*

```
    int fh;

    hHourGlass=LoadCursor(NULL,IDC_WAIT);
    hSaveCursor=SetCursor(hHourGlass);

    if((fh=_lopen(path,OF_READ))==-1) {
        SetCursor(hSaveCursor);
        return(FALSE);
    }

    l=_llseek(fh,0L,SEEK_END);
    _llseek(fh,0L,SEEK_SET);

    if(l > 0xfff0L) {
        _lclose(fh);
        SetCursor(hSaveCursor);
        return(FALSE);
    }

    if((p=(LPSTR)FixedGlobalAlloc(l))==NULL) {
        _lclose(fh);
        SetCursor(hSaveCursor);
        return(FALSE);
    }

    if(_lread(fh,p,(unsigned int)l) != (unsigned int)l) {
        FixedGlobalFree(p);
        _lclose(fh);
        SetCursor(hSaveCursor);
        return(FALSE);
    }

    ItemName(listbox,p);

    FixedGlobalFree(p);

    _lclose(fh);

    SetCursor(hSaveCursor);

    return(TRUE);
}

void DoMessage(HWND hwnd,LPSTR message)
{
    FARPROC lpfnDlgProc;

    messagehook=message;

    if((lpfnDlgProc=MakeProcInstance((FARPROC)MessageDlgProc,hInst)) != NULL) {
        DialogBox(hInst,"MessageBox",hwnd,lpfnDlgProc);
```

```
            FreeProcInstance(lpfnDlgProc);
    }
}

DWORD FAR PASCAL MessageDlgProc(HWND hwnd,WORD message,WORD wParam,LONG lParam)
{
    HWND dlgH;

    switch(message) {
        case WM_INITDIALOG:
            ItemName(MESSAGE_STRING,messagehook);
            CentreWindow(hwnd);
            SetControlFont(hwnd,MESSAGE_STRING);
            SetControlFont(hwnd,IDOK);
            return(FALSE);
        case WM_CTLCOLOR:
            return(Ctl3dCtlColorEx(message,wParam,lParam));
        case WM_COMMAND:
            switch(wParam) {
                case IDOK:
                    EndDialog(hwnd,wParam);
                    return(FALSE);
            }
            break;
    }

    return(FALSE);
}

DWORD FAR PASCAL AboutDlgProc(HWND hwnd,WORD message,WORD wParam,LONG lParam)
{
    HWND dlgH;

    switch(message) {
        case WM_INITDIALOG:
            ItemName(MESSAGE_STRING,FetchString(MESSAGE_ABOUT));
            CentreWindow(hwnd);
            SetControlFont(hwnd,MESSAGE_STRING);
            SetControlFont(hwnd,IDOK);
            return(FALSE);
        case WM_CTLCOLOR:
            return(Ctl3dCtlColorEx(message,wParam,lParam));
        case WM_COMMAND:
            switch(wParam) {
                case IDOK:
                    EndDialog(hwnd,wParam);
                    return(FALSE);
            }
            break;
    }

    return(FALSE);
}
```

4-14 *Continued*

```
void CentreWindow(HWND hwnd)
{
    RECT rect;
    unsigned int x,y;

    GetWindowRect(hwnd,&rect);
    x=(GetSystemMetrics(SM_CXSCREEN)-(rect.right-rect.left))/2;
    y=(GetSystemMetrics(SM_CYSCREEN)-(rect.bottom-rect.top))/2;
    SetWindowPos(hwnd,NULL,x,y,rect.right-rect.left,rect.bottom-rect.top,
        SWP_NOSIZE);
}

LPSTR FetchString(unsigned int n)
{
    static char b[257];

    if(!LoadString(hInst,n,b,256))
        lstrcpy(b,"String table error - this application may be damaged");
    return(b);
}

void SetHelpSize(HWND hwnd)
{
    HELPWININFO helpinfo;
    char b[145];

    memset((char *)&helpinfo,0,sizeof(HELPWININFO));
    helpinfo.wStructSize=sizeof(HELPWININFO);
    helpinfo.x=10;
    helpinfo.y=10;
    helpinfo.dx=512;
    helpinfo.dy=1004;

    MakeHelpPathName(b);
    WinHelp(hwnd,b,HELP_SETWINPOS,(DWORD)&helpinfo);
}

void DoHelp(HWND hwnd,LPSTR keyword)
{
    char b[145];

    MakeHelpPathName(b);
    WinHelp(hwnd,b,HELP_KEY,(DWORD)keyword);
}

void MakeHelpPathName(LPSTR szFileName)
{
    LPSTR pcFileName;
    int nFileNameLen;

    nFileNameLen = GetModuleFileName(hInst,szFileName,144);
```

```
        pcFileName = szFileName+nFileNameLen;

    while(pcFileName > szFileName) {
        if(*pcFileName == '\\' || *pcFileName == ':') {
            *(++pcFileName) = '\0';
            break;
        }
        nFileNameLen--;
        pcFileName--;
    }

    if((nFileNameLen+13) < 144) lstrcat(szFileName,HELPFILE);
    else lstrcat(szFileName, "?");
}

int GetFileName(HWND hwnd,LPSTR path)
{
    OPENFILENAME ofn;
    char szDirName[257],szFile[256],szFileTitle[256],szFilter[768],*p;
    int r;

    getcwd(szDirName,256);
    if(szDirName[lstrlen(szDirName)-1] != '\\') lstrcat(szDirName,"\\");

    lstrcpy(szFile,"*.TXT");

    p=szFilter;
    lstrcpy(p,FetchString(MESSAGE_ALLFILES));
    p+=lstrlen(p)+1;
    lstrcpy(p,szFile);
    p+=lstrlen(p)+1;

    lstrcpy(p,FetchString(MESSAGE_TEXTFILES));
    p+=lstrlen(p)+1;
    lstrcpy(p,"*.*");
    p+=lstrlen(p)+1;
    *p=0;

    memset((char *)&ofn,0,sizeof(OPENFILENAME));

    szFileTitle[0]=0;

    ofn.lStructSize=sizeof(OPENFILENAME);
    ofn.hwndOwner=hwnd;
    ofn.hInstance=hInst;
    ofn.lpstrFilter=szFilter;
    ofn.nFilterIndex=0;
    ofn.lpstrFile=szFile;
    ofn.nMaxFile=sizeof(szFile);
    ofn.lpstrFileTitle=szFileTitle;
    ofn.nMaxFileTitle=sizeof(szFileTitle);
    ofn.lpstrInitialDir=szDirName;
    ofn.Flags=OFN_PATHMUSTEXIST | OFN_FILEMUSTEXIST;
```

4-14 *Continued*

```
    ofn.lpstrTitle="Open";
    ofn.nFileExtension=0;
    ofn.lpstrDefExt=NULL;
    r=GetOpenFileName(&ofn);

    lstrcpy(path,ofn.lpstrFile);

    return(r);
}

int GetNewFileName(HWND hwnd,LPSTR path)
{
    OPENFILENAME ofn;
    char szDirName[257],szFile[256],szFileTitle[256],szFilter[768],*p;
    int r;

    getcwd(szDirName,256);
    if(szDirName[lstrlen(szDirName)-1] != '\\') lstrcat(szDirName,"\\");

    lstrcpy(szFile,path);

    p=szFilter;
    lstrcpy(p,FetchString(MESSAGE_ALLFILES));
    p+=lstrlen(p)+1;
    lstrcpy(p,szFile);
    p+=lstrlen(p)+1;

    lstrcpy(p,FetchString(MESSAGE_TEXTFILES));
    p+=lstrlen(p)+1;
    lstrcpy(p,"*.*");
    p+=lstrlen(p)+1;
    *p=0;

    memset((char *)&ofn,0,sizeof(OPENFILENAME));

    szFileTitle[0]=0;

    ofn.lStructSize=sizeof(OPENFILENAME);
    ofn.hwndOwner=hwnd;
    ofn.hInstance=hInst;
    ofn.lpstrFilter=szFilter;
    ofn.nFilterIndex=0;
    ofn.lpstrFile=szFile;
    ofn.nMaxFile=sizeof(szFile);
    ofn.lpstrFileTitle=szFileTitle;
    ofn.nMaxFileTitle=sizeof(szFileTitle);
    ofn.lpstrInitialDir=szDirName;
    ofn.Flags=OFN_PATHMUSTEXIST | OFN_OVERWRITEPROMPT;
    ofn.lpstrTitle="Save As";
    ofn.nFileExtension=0;
    ofn.lpstrDefExt=NULL;
```

```
        r=GetSaveFileName(&ofn);

        lstrcpy(path,ofn.lpstrFile);

        return(r);
}

int SelectFont(HWND hwnd,HFONT FAR *hfont)
{
        LOGFONT lf;
        CHOOSEFONT cf;
        int r;

        memset((char *)&cf,0,sizeof(CHOOSEFONT));
        GetObject((HFONT)*hfont,sizeof(LOGFONT),(LPSTR)&lf);

        cf.lStructSize=sizeof(CHOOSEFONT);
        cf.hwndOwner=hwnd;
        cf.hInstance=hInst;
        cf.lpLogFont=&lf;
        cf.Flags=CF_TTONLY | CF_SCREENFONTS | CF_INITTOLOGFONTSTRUCT | CF_ANSIONLY;
        cf.nFontType=REGULAR_FONTTYPE;
        if((r=ChooseFont(&cf)) != FALSE)
        *hfont=CreateFontIndirect(cf.lpLogFont);

        return(r);
}

int DoPrint(HWND hwnd,int listbox)
{
        HCURSOR hSaveCursor,hHourGlass;
        TEXTMETRIC tm;
        HWND dlgH;
        PRINTDLG pd;
        LPSTR p,pr;
        unsigned int i,size,length,pagesize,textdeep,top;
        char b[STRINGSIZE+1];

        memset((char *)&pd,0,sizeof(PRINTDLG));
        GetWindowText(hwnd,b,STRINGSIZE);

        pd.lStructSize=sizeof(PRINTDLG);
        pd.hwndOwner=hwnd;
        pd.hInstance=hInst;
        pd.Flags=PD_RETURNDC | PD_NOPAGENUMS | PD_NOSELECTION;

        if(!PrintDlg(&pd)) return(FALSE);

        hHourGlass=LoadCursor(NULL,IDC_WAIT);
        hSaveCursor=SetCursor(hHourGlass);

        dlgH=GetDlgItem(hwnd,listbox);
        size=GetWindowTextLength(dlgH);
```

4-14 *Continued*

```
if((p=(LPSTR)FixedGlobalAlloc(size+1))==NULL) {
    SetCursor(hSaveCursor);
    return(FALSE);
}

GetWindowText(dlgH,p,size);

--size;

GetTextMetrics(pd.hDC,&tm);
textdeep=tm.tmHeight+tm.tmExternalLeading;
pagesize=GetDeviceCaps(pd.hDC,VERTRES)/textdeep;

Escape(pd.hDC,STARTDOC,strlen(b),b,NULL);

pr=p;
top=i=0;
do {
    while(*pr < 32 && size) {
        if(*pr==13) {
            top+=textdeep;
            ++i;
        }
        ++pr;
        --size;
    }

    if(++i >= pagesize) {
        Escape(pd.hDC,NEWFRAME,0,NULL,NULL);
        top=i=0;
    }

    if(size) {
        for(length=0;pr[length]>=32;++length);
        TextOut(pd.hDC,0,top,pr,length);
        pr+=length;
        size-=length;
    }

} while(size);

Escape(pd.hDC,NEWFRAME,0,NULL,NULL);

Escape(pd.hDC,ENDDOC,0,NULL,NULL);

DeleteDC(pd.hDC);

FixedGlobalFree(p);
SetCursor(hSaveCursor);
return(TRUE);
}
```

```
int DoPaste(HWND hwnd,int listbox)
{
    GLOBALHANDLE gh;
    LPSTR p;

    if(!IsClipboardFormatAvailable(CF_TEXT)) return(FALSE);

    OpenClipboard(hwnd);

    gh=GetClipboardData(CF_TEXT);

    if((p=GlobalLock(gh)) != NULL) {
        SendDlgItemMessage(hwnd,listbox,EM_REPLACESEL,0,(DWORD)p);
        GlobalUnlock(gh);
    }

    CloseClipboard();
    return(TRUE);
}

int DoCopy(HWND hwnd,int listbox)
{
    GLOBALHANDLE gh;
    LPSTR p,pr;
    HWND dlgH;
    unsigned long l;
    unsigned int i,start,end,size;

    l=SendDlgItemMessage(hwnd,listbox,EM_GETSEL,0,0L);
    start=LOWORD(l);
    end=HIWORD(l);

    dlgH=GetDlgItem(hwnd,listbox);
    size=GetWindowTextLength(dlgH);

    if((p=(LPSTR)FixedGlobalAlloc(size+1))==NULL) return(FALSE);

    GetWindowText(dlgH,p,size);

    size=end-start;

    if((gh=GlobalAlloc(GHND,size+1)) != NULL) {
        if((pr=GlobalLock(gh)) != NULL) {
            for(i=0;i<size;++i) pr[i]=p[start+i];
            pr[i]=0;
            GlobalUnlock(gh);

            OpenClipboard(hwnd);
            EmptyClipboard();
            SetClipboardData(CF_TEXT,gh);
            CloseClipboard();
        }
    }
```

4-14 *Continued*

```
    FixedGlobalFree(p);

    return(TRUE);
}

int DoCut(HWND hwnd,int listbox)
{
    DoCopy(hwnd,listbox);
    SendDlgItemMessage(hwnd,listbox,EM_REPLACESEL,0,(DWORD)"");
}

int DoUndo(HWND hwnd,int listbox)
{
    SendDlgItemMessage(hwnd,listbox,EM_UNDO,0,0L);
}

void SetFileOpen(HWND hwnd)
{
    HMENU hmenu;

    hmenu=GetMenu(hwnd);
    EnableMenuItem(hmenu,FILE_SAVE,MF_BYCOMMAND | MF_ENABLED);
    EnableMenuItem(hmenu,FILE_SAVEAS,MF_BYCOMMAND | MF_ENABLED);
    EnableMenuItem(hmenu,FILE_FONT,MF_BYCOMMAND | MF_ENABLED);
    EnableMenuItem(hmenu,FILE_PRINT,MF_BYCOMMAND | MF_ENABLED);
    EnableMenuItem(hmenu,EDIT_UNDO,MF_BYCOMMAND | MF_ENABLED);
    EnableMenuItem(hmenu,EDIT_CUT,MF_BYCOMMAND | MF_ENABLED);
    EnableMenuItem(hmenu,EDIT_COPY,MF_BYCOMMAND | MF_ENABLED);
    EnableMenuItem(hmenu,EDIT_PASTE,MF_BYCOMMAND | MF_ENABLED);
}
```

Figure 4-15 *The DEMO6.RC resource script.*

```
MainScreen DIALOG 29, 28, 300, 208
STYLE WS_POPUP | WS_CAPTION | WS_SYSMENU | WS_THICKFRAME |
    WS_MINIMIZEBOX | WS_MAXIMIZEBOX
CAPTION "Dialog Demo Six"
MENU MainMenu
BEGIN
    CONTROL "", 401, "EDIT", ES_LEFT | ES_MULTILINE | ES_AUTOVSCROLL |
    ES_WANTRETURN | WS_CHILD | WS_VISIBLE | WS_BORDER | WS_VSCROLL |
    WS_TABSTOP, 8, 8, 284, 192
END

AboutBox DIALOG 72, 72, 220, 128
STYLE WS_POPUP | WS_CAPTION
CAPTION "About"
BEGIN
    CTEXT "", 101, 16, 16, 188, 72, WS_CHILD | WS_VISIBLE | WS_GROUP
    DEFPUSHBUTTON "OK", IDOK, 96, 104, 28, 16, WS_CHILD | WS_VISIBLE |
```

```
    WS_TABSTOP
    CONTROL "", -1, "static", SS_BLACKFRAME | WS_CHILD | WS_VISIBLE,
        8, 8, 204, 88
END

MainMenu MENU
BEGIN
    POPUP "File"
    BEGIN
        MENUITEM "&Open..", 101
        MENUITEM "&Save", 102, GRAYED
        MENUITEM "Save &as..", 103, GRAYED
        MENUITEM SEPARATOR
        MENUITEM "&Font", 104, GRAYED
        MENUITEM "&Print", 105, GRAYED
        MENUITEM SEPARATOR
        MENUITEM "E&xit", 199
    END

    POPUP "&Edit"
    BEGIN
        MENUITEM "&Undo", 201, GRAYED
        MENUITEM "&Cut\tShift+Del", 202, GRAYED
        MENUITEM "&Copy\tCtrl+Ins", 203, GRAYED
        MENUITEM "&Paste\tShift+Ins", 204, GRAYED
    END

    POPUP "&Help"
    BEGIN
        MENUITEM "&Index", 901
        MENUITEM "&Using help", 905
        MENUITEM SEPARATOR
        MENUITEM "&About...", 999
    END

END

STRINGTABLE
BEGIN
    0,"Dialog Demo Six\nCopyright \251 1993 Alchemy Mindworks Inc.\n
        From the book Windows Dialog Construction Set\r
        by Steven William Rimmer\rPublished by Windcrest/McGraw Hill"
    1,"Help"
    2,"All files "
    3,"Text files "
    4,"There has been an error loading your file.\n\n\nKick your computer."
    5,"There has been an error saving your file.\n\n\n
        Must be elevator music at work."
    6,"There has been an error printing your file.\n\n\nWindows is haunted."
END

DialogDemoSix ICON
BEGIN
```

4-15 *Continued*

```
'00 00 01 00 01 00 20 20 10 00 00 00 00 00 E8 02'
'00 00 16 00 00 00 28 00 00 00 20 00 00 00 40 00'
'00 00 01 00 04 00 00 00 00 00 80 02 00 00 00 00'
'00 00 00 00 00 00 00 00 00 00 00 00 00 00 00 00'
'00 00 00 00 80 00 00 80 00 00 00 80 80 00 80 00'
'00 00 80 00 80 00 80 80 00 00 80 80 80 00 C0 C0'
'C0 00 00 00 FF 00 00 FF 00 00 00 FF FF 00 FF 00'
'00 00 FF 00 FF 00 FF FF 00 00 FF FF FF 00 2A 2A'
'2A 2A 2A 2A 2A 2A 2A 22 77 70 00 00 00 00 A2 A2'
'A2 A2 A2 A2 A2 A2 A2 A2 22 70 00 00 00 00 2A 2A'
'2A 2A 2A 2A 2A 2A AA AA A2 70 00 00 00 00 A2 A2'
'A2 A2 AA AA AA AA B2 AA AA 77 77 77 77 00 2A 2A'
'AA AA 2A 2A AA 2A AA A9 19 19 19 19 17 77 AA A2'
'A2 AA AB AB AB AA 91 91 91 91 91 91 91 97 2A AA'
'BA BA 2A AA A9 19 19 19 19 99 99 99 99 19 AB AB'
'A2 AA AA 11 11 91 99 99 99 90 00 00 09 99 BA BA'
'AA A1 01 11 19 19 19 19 90 00 00 00 00 09 AA A2'
'00 10 10 11 11 91 91 00 00 00 00 70 00 00 2A 00'
'00 00 01 01 11 17 77 00 00 00 09 70 00 00 A2 22'
'22 22 22 22 22 22 27 77 77 70 09 70 00 00 2A 2A'
'2A 2A AA AA AA AA 22 22 22 77 09 77 00 00 A2 AA'
'AA AA A2 AA AA AA A2 A2 A2 27 79 17 70 00 2A AA'
'AA 2A 22 22 2A 2A AA AA AA 2A 79 91 77 00 A2 A2'
'A2 22 70 70 22 A2 A2 AB A2 A2 00 99 17 77 2A 2A'
'22 87 07 07 02 2A 2A AA AA 27 00 09 91 91 A2 A2'
'F8 88 77 70 72 A2 AB AB AB A0 00 00 99 99 2A 22'
'8F 88 00 77 07 2A 2A AA AA 70 00 00 00 00 A2 28'
'F8 F0 00 08 70 22 22 A2 A2 00 00 00 00 00 2A 2F'
'8F 80 00 07 07 2A 2A AA A7 00 00 00 00 00 A7 28'
'F8 FF 00 88 82 22 A2 A2 A0 00 00 00 00 00 22 7F'
'8F FF FF 8F 82 2A 2A 2A 70 00 00 00 00 00 A7 0F'
'FF FF F8 F8 F2 A2 A2 A2 00 00 00 00 00 00 A2 70'
'FF FF 8F 8F 2A 2A 2A 20 00 00 00 00 00 00 A7 07'
'FF FF F8 F8 22 A2 A2 00 00 00 00 00 00 00 A2 70'
'70 FF 8F 22 2A 2A 20 00 00 00 00 00 00 00 AA 07'
'07 07 02 02 A2 A2 00 00 00 00 00 00 00 00 BA A0'
'70 70 72 2A 2A 20 00 00 00 00 00 00 00 00 BB AA'
'A7 A7 AA AA A0 00 00 00 00 00 00 00 00 00 AA BA'
'AA AA AA 00 00 00 00 00 00 00 00 00 00 00 AA A0'
'00 00 00 00 00 00 00 00 00 00 00 00 00 00 00 00'
'01 FF 00 00 01 FF 00 00 01 FF 00 00 00 03 00 00'
'00 00 00 00 00 00 00 00 00 00 00 00 00 01 F8 00 00'
'07 FE 00 00 3F DF 00 00 3F 9F 00 00 01 9F 00 00'
'00 8F 00 00 00 07 00 00 00 03 00 00 00 C0 00 00'
'00 E0 00 00 01 F0 00 00 01 FF 00 00 03 FF 00 00'
'03 FF 00 00 07 FF 00 00 07 FF 00 00 0F FF 00 00'
'1F FF 00 00 3F FF 00 00 7F FF 00 00 FF FF 00 01'
'FF FF 00 07 FF FF 00 3F FF FF 1F FF FF FF'
END

MessageBox DIALOG 72, 72, 220, 128
```

```
STYLE WS_POPUP ¦ WS_CAPTION
CAPTION "Message"
BEGIN
    CTEXT "", 101, 16, 16, 188, 72, WS_CHILD ¦ WS_VISIBLE ¦ WS_GROUP
    DEFPUSHBUTTON "OK", IDOK, 96, 104, 28, 16, WS_CHILD ¦ WS_VISIBLE ¦
      WS_TABSTOP
    CONTROL "", -1, "static", SS_BLACKFRAME ¦ WS_CHILD ¦
      WS_VISIBLE, 8, 8, 204, 88
END
```

The DEMO6 application doesn't have a Colors item in its File menu.
There are actually two good reasons for this. The first, as was
touched on earlier, is that it would be impossible to change the color
of the main window of DEMO6 in any case. The second is that the
color dialog's sliders don't behave themselves any better against the
gray background of a CTL3D-based dialog than they do against a
dialog painted gray in the conventional way.

The CTL3D library is inherently more limited in the sorts of things
you can make it do, and it will prove to be somewhat fragile if you
attempt to make it perform tricks it wasn't taught by its creators.
However, especially for applications that have many common dialogs,
its automatic subclassing feature is exceedingly convenient. It does a
lot of work for you, and can reduce the amount of code you need to
write considerably.

This is especially worthwhile in that secondary message handlers for
the Windows common dialogs are among the trickier sorts of code to
write.

Adding multimedia
to dialogs

CHAPTER 5

"Anarchy is better than no government at all."

There's a lot to be said for the argument that multimedia, as it presently exists under Windows, is a brilliant solution in search of a problem to solve. To be sure, it offers a lot of promise. Finding something that the promise can be applied to, however, might take some head scratching, especially if you're bent on writing a complete application wrapped around multimedia. (Talking kids' books and noisy reference works seem to be the measure of the technology at the moment.)

On a smaller scale, multimedia can be useful to add special effects and attention-getting devices to ordinarily silent Windows software. You might not want your programs to speak at every opportunity—a menu that says "thank you for opening this menu" every time you click on it is both difficult to program and certain to get intensely irritating within about 20 minutes. However, having the option of generating sounds other than the default Windows message beep can be a genuinely useful element of a Windows application.

This chapter will discuss three specific multimedia elements that are common under Windows: wave files, MIDI files, and AVI Video for Windows files. Should you not have encountered these things face to face until now, wave files are bites of digitized sound, MIDI files are sequences of instrumental music, and AVI files are short video clips.

There are a number of catches and caveats to using the information in this chapter. The first is that it is, of necessity, somewhat abbreviated. There's a lot more to say about multimedia than there's room to say it in the context of this book. If you want to explore the area in greater detail, you might want to have a look at my book *Windows Multimedia Programming*, also published by Windcrest/McGraw-Hill.

Secondly, you'll need some additional software to really make the most of multimedia—specifically, the Microsoft Windows Multimedia Development Kit. This is a fairly extensive package that offers a complete reference guide and interface code for the Windows multimedia extensions.

If you don't have the Multimedia Development Kit you'll still be able to apply the facilities of this chapter, although only the second half of it will be of immediate use. In the second half of this chapter, you'll see a dynamic link library that will allow you to use some multimedia facilities in your applications without having to plunge into the somewhat turgid waters of the Multimedia Development Kit.

Depending on your applications for multimedia, you might also require some additional hardware. Windows wave and MIDI files require a sound card installed in your system to play them. Something along the lines of an AdLib card will do—the AdLib card has the advantage of being available from Radio Shack, which seems to have them on sale every other week as of this writing.

Wave files can actually be played through the Windows speaker driver, a subject that will be discussed in greater detail later in this chapter. This obviates the requirement for a sound card, but it imposes some heavy penalties on any computer that uses it. Specifically, only very short sounds can be played, they'll sound like a mouse in a milk bottle, and your entire system will come to a stuttering halt for the duration of any sound handled by the speaker driver.

If the Windows speaker driver hadn't been written by Microsoft, it almost certainly would have been written by the manufacturer of one of the more popular sound cards to illustrate why a sound card is necessary for anything more than speaker beeps.

Note that MIDI files—even short MIDI files of elevator music—can't be played through the Windows speaker driver at all.

Video for Windows AVI movies don't require any specific hardware in their simplest sense, but they too have their restrictions. Figure 5-1 illustrates a Video for Windows movie in action.

Creating real-time video on your monitor requires that a lot of bitmap information be updated to a window in a very short time. This, in turn, requires a fast computer and an accelerated video card. The Video for Windows protocol is fairly clever— if things begin to bog down, it doesn't slow the movie being played. Rather, it begins to

Figure 5-1

A Windows AVI movie.

skip frames, with the result that the movie in question plays at the correct speed but gets jumpy in places.

Most AVI files include sound tracks, which are essentially wave files embedded in the AVI files they're part of. You'll need a sound card to be able to hear these.

In reading through all this discussion of hardware, you might have spotted an obvious problem with multimedia in general when it turns up in Windows applications. Having run out and sprung for a sound card yourself, it's hard to compel everyone else who might use your software to do the same. And someone without a sound card won't be able to hear the audible parts of an application that uses these facilities.

In some cases, this could be fairly crippling. For example, if you were to write a multimedia application to explain the history of baroque music in which most of the interesting parts were MIDI files, the phrase "requires a Windows-compatible sound card" should probably be displayed prominently on its packaging. However, most software authors who use multimedia elements do so for effect. If you create a dialog that speaks when it opens or pleads when you click on Quit, your application will work well enough whether its sound is heard or not.

In this latter sort of software, multimedia elements can be included in an application under the premise that they'll be audible on systems equipped to play them and never even suspected on systems that aren't.

Multimedia on five dollars a day

The Windows multimedia interface offers a plethora of options, system calls, accessories, techniques, functions, flags, structures, and venomous digital cavern dwellers with unpleasant habits. There are at least six ways to do everything worth doing. In working with the Multimedia Development Kit in its entirety, you might have the sense of trying to find one particular rattlesnake out of many while dancing barefoot in a whole box of them.

As a bit of preventive snakebite technique, this chapter will deal with a single stratum of the Windows multimedia interface. While it won't avail you of everything multimedia can do for you—it won't allow you to play a wave file backwards, for example—it's dead easy to use and even less involved to understand.

This section will discuss the Windows MCI interface. An attractive feature of MCI is that it treats all the multimedia elements it supports—even fairly complex ones, such as AVI movies—as black boxes. Rather than having to know how a wave file is structured in order to play it, MCI allows you to hand the whole works over to Windows and think no more of it.

Among other things, MCI provides complete support for wave, MIDI, and AVI files. Under Windows these have the file extensions WAV, MID, and AVI, respectively. You can find example WAV files in the \WINDOWS directory of your hard drive. The Multimedia Workshop shareware application on the companion disk for this book offers an example MIDI file as well. Example AVI files will typically require rather more disk space—small ones start at three quarters of a megabyte, with two to five megabytes being about average for a movie of reasonable length and dimensions. The *Windows Multimedia Programming* book mentioned earlier in this chapter includes several on a companion CD-ROM.

Each of the three multimedia file types to be discussed in this chapter are handled using essentially the same MCI calls. We'll look at how a wave file would be played in this example, but almost identical code would be used to handle MIDI or AVI files.

Before you can play anything through the MCI interface, however, the appropriate MCI driver must be installed in Windows. Drivers are handled through the Drivers applet of the Windows Control Panel. The Control Panel drivers list should include the drivers that appear in Fig. 5-2. It will probably have other entries as well.

Figure 5-2

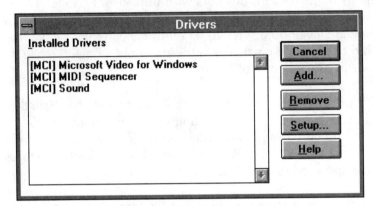

The MCI drivers required by the applications in this chapter.

If the MCI drivers aren't installed in your system, click on the Add button in the Control Panel applet. The wave and MIDI drivers should be available in the list of available drivers. The AVI Video for Windows driver might be. If it isn't, unpack the Multimedia Workshop application from the companion disk for this book onto a floppy disk. It includes the AVI driver, and you can install it from the floppy you create.

To play a wave file you must use MCI calls to open the MCI sound driver, play the sound, and then wait for it to terminate. When it terminates, the driver should be closed. Because waiting for things isn't something Windows does particularly elegantly, the MCI interface will send a special message to the message handler of your choice to indicate that a sound—or any other sort of file MCI supports—has finished playing. While a bit more complex to implement, this approach to dealing with sounds and movies, which can take a while to run, means that your application can start something playing and then get on with whatever it would normally be doing. It need not take any more notice of what MCI is up to until the message signifying that it's no longer up to anything at all appears.

The actual code that implements all this isn't a lot more complex than a discussion of the procedure. To begin with, here's what's involved in opening an MCI device. The device in this case is called waveaudio.

```
MCI_OPEN_PARMS mciopen;
DWORD rtrn;
char b[STRINGSIZE=1];

mciopen.lpstrDeviceType="waveaudio";
mciopen.lpstrElementName=path;
if((rtrn=mciSendCommand(0,MCI_OPEN,MCI_OPEN_TYPE |
 MCI_OPEN_ELEMENT,(DWORD)(LPVOID)&mciopen)) != 0L) {
   mciGetErrorString(rtrn,b,STRINGSIZE);
   DoMessage(hwnd,b);
   return(-1);
}
```

The MCI_OPEN_PARMS object is defined by the Multimedia Development Kit's header files. It tells MCI everything it needs to know about opening a driver and a sound file. The call to mciSendCommand attempts to open the wave file defined by path and reconcile it with the facilities of the current waveaudio driver. It will return 0L if all is well, or an error code.

The mciGetErrorString call will fetch a text string that describes the error code returned by mciSendCommand.

If the request to open the waveaudio driver and the wave file in question went well, the wDeviceID element of the MCI_OPEN_PARMS object used to open the file will contain an ID value for the open device. The following call starts the wave file in question playing:

```
MCI_PLAY_PARMS mciplay;

mciplay.dwCallback=(DWORD)hwnd;
if((rtrn=mciSendCommand(id,MCI_PLAY,
 MCI_NOTIFY,(DWORD)(LPVOID)&mciplay)) != 0L) {
   mciSendCommand(id,MCI_CLOSE,0,NULL);
   mciGetErrorString(rtrn,message,STRINGSIZE);
   return(-1);
}
```

The hwnd value assigned to the dwCallback element of the mciplay object is the window handle of the window you'd like to receive notification of the termination of the wave file being played. Once

again, the mciSendCommand call will return 0L if the function was successful or an error code. Note that if an error is returned, the mciSendCommand function must be used to close the previously opened waveaudio driver.

That's all there is to playing a wave file through MCI. The only other bit of code that's required is a case in the message handler that will receive notification of the termination of the wave file being played. It works like this:

```
case MM_MCINOTIFY:
  mciSendCommand(LOWORD(lParam),MCI_CLOSE,MCI_WAIT,NULL);
  break;
```

An MM_MCINOTIFY message is sent by the MCI extensions to the window indicated by the dwCallback value in the mciplay object used when the wave was initially set up to play. When this message appears, the low-order word of its lParam argument will contain the device ID value of the waveaudio driver being used to play the wave file. It should be closed using a call to mciSendCommand.

Because MCI can be counted on to send an MM_MCINOTIFY message when a wave file stops playing, your application can pretty well ignore the issue of waiting for the sound to stop. It can get on with whatever else it would normally be up to, and let the sound largely take care of itself.

With MCI being prepared to tell you when a wave file stops playing, however, you can arrange to have something happen at the moment of silence. The Multimedia Workshop application on the companion disk for this book, for example, uses the MM_MCINOTIFY message from the end of one wave file in a list of wave files to queue up the next file in the list. In more involved applications you could use this facility to string words or discrete sounds together.

What Multimedia Workshop does when it runs one wave file after another is to have the MM_MCINOTIFY message case call PostMessage. The PostMessage function posts a message to the message handler for the main window to tell it to play the next file in its list. As was touched on earlier, it's important that you use PostMessage rather than SendMessage in this situation. The

PostMessage function places a message in the message queue, and as such allows the current invocation of the message handler it's called from to complete its work and return before the message it posts is received and handled. The SendMessage function, by comparison, sends the message in question directly to the specified message handler. In this sort of application— having SendMessage repeatedly sending a message to the same message handler it's part of—SendMessage would in effect become recursive. Used enough times it would overflow your application's stack and crash.

The handy thing about all this wave playing code is that it's almost exactly the same code you'll require to play MIDI and AVI files. The only important difference is that the device names must change: for wave files to waveaudio, for MIDI files to sequencer, and for AVI files to avivideo.

There are a few catches to using MCI to play wave files. It works gloriously well with a sound card, and not at all if the only sound device in your system is a Windows speaker driver. It can play only wave files that reside on disk. Finally, it represents a fairly complex way to play simple noises if all you're interested in doing is attracting attention. There's an alternate approach to playing sounds, however, and in some respects you might find it preferable to the MCI calls we've just looked at.

Playing wave files with sndPlaySound

The sndPlaySound function of the Windows multimedia extension represents a very simple way to play wave files of moderate size. The official upper limit for sndPlaySound is 100 kilobytes of sound data. In reality, you can usually exceed this somewhat on a system with lots of free memory, although it's inadvisable to do so.

The sndPlaySound function will drive the Windows speaker driver as well as a sound card. There's a great deal less to worry about in using sndPlaySound. Here's how to play a wave file with it:

```
sndPlaySound("C:\\WINDOWS\\DING.WAV",SND_ASYNC | SND_NODEFAULT);
```

The first argument to sndPlaySound is a path to the wave file to be played. The second one is a set of flags telling it how to treat the wave file. The SND_ASYNC flag tells it to play asynchronously, that is, to return immediately and make noise in the background. The SND_NODEFAULT flag tells it not to play a default sound from your \WINDOWS directory directly if it can't play the sound you've asked for.

The sndPlaySound function will return a true value if it has successfully started playing the wave file you've asked for, and a false value otherwise. The first argument to sndPlaySound can also be a far pointer to a wave file that has previously been loaded into memory. In this case, the flags in the second argument must include the SND_MEMORY flag.

There's no particular advantage to loading a sound explicitly and then playing it from memory rather than allowing sndPlaySound to load it for you. The really useful aspect of playing wave files from memory with sndPlaySound is that it allows you to store them as resources in the resource list of your application, and fetch them with a call to LoadResource.

To begin with, this is how you'd add a wave file to the RC source file for an application:

```
AboutWave RCDATA PLAYME.WAV
```

This line will include a file called PLAYME.WAV and call it AboutWave in your application's resource list.

One of the obvious applications of wave files called from resources is as dedicated sounds to be used when a dialog opens. This is fairly easy to accomplish—you must fetch the wave file data in question in the WM_INITDIALOG case of the message handler for your dialog and start it playing. The resource should be freed when your dialog terminates. Here's how to load and play a wave file stored as a resource:

```
static GLOBALHANDLE handle;
static LPSTR p;

if((handle=LoadResource(hInst,
  FindResource(hInst,"AboutWave",RT_RCDATA))) != NULL) {
    if((p=(LPSTR)LockResource(handle))!=NULL)
```

```
        sndPlaySound(p,SND_ASYNC | SND_MEMORY | SND_NODEFAULT);
   }
```

You'll probably want to handle closing down a wave file in the IDOK and IDCANCEL cases of the WM_COMMAND section of your dialog's message handler. Here's how to take care of this:

```
sndPlaySound(NULL,SND_SYNC);
if(p != NULL) UnlockResource(handle);
FreeResource(handle);
```

The second call to SndPlaySound shuts off the wave file being played, should someone attempt to close the dialog in question before the sound stops. This is very important, because after you call UnlockResource the sound data will no longer reside in memory that your application owns. Continuing to play it will usually cause sndPlaySound to throw a protected-mode fault.

Note that there's no equivalent to sndPlaySound for playing MIDI and AVI files. It might be argued that none is really needed; it's unlikely that you'd want to store a five-megabyte movie as a resource in your application's EXE file and play it whenever a dialog opens.

Trapping system events

One of the features of Windows 3.1 that enables itself in the presence of a sound card—or if you install the Windows speaker driver—is Windows' ability to play canned sounds whenever certain system events take place. The list of events is mercifully short—it includes such things as Windows itself starting up and closing down, dialogs opening, and so on.

A number of commercial and shareware packages have appeared to allow you to "attach" wave file sounds to a much larger range of system events, such as clicking on buttons and pulling down menus. The Windows Multimedia Programming book mentioned earlier in this chapter includes the source code for one such program.

Of all the Windows applications capable of provoking normally rational, even-tempered souls into shooting holes in their computers with small tactical nuclear missiles, this seems to be the most likely.

Creating an application capable of attaching wave files to all the applications running under Windows is somewhat beyond the scope of this book. Trapping individual messages and making noises in response to some of them in one application is somewhat less involved. The programs discussed in this chapter will use this facility.

The easiest way to play wave files in response to mouse clicks and such is to watch the message stream passing through the message handler of a dialog and initiate wave files as a result of specific messages. In this chapter, an event to be responded to with a wave file sound is defined like this:

```
typedef struct {
WORD message;
WORD wParam;
char path[STRINGSIZE+1];
} EVENT;
```

The message element of an EVENT object is the message to be responded to. The wParam element is the NOPARAM constant if a sound is to be played whenever the message in question appears or a particular wParam value for the message. For example, if the message element were WM_COMMAND and the wParam were IDOK, the sound in question would be played whenever an OK button was clicked. The path element of an EVENT object is the path to a wave file to be associated with the particular event in question.

Here's an example list of initialized EVENT objects. This list uses the default wave files included in the \WINDOWS directory of your hard drive—you would probably want to use a more adventurous set of sounds. Some of the wParam values are resource ID constants for buttons and menu items. They'll turn up in a moment in the DEMO7 application.

```
EVENT eventlist[]= {
WM_COMMAND,IDOK,"C:\\WINDOWS\\CHIMES.WAV",
WM_COMMAND,MAIN_AVI,"C:\\WINDOWS\\CHIMES.WAV",
WM_COMMAND,MAIN_WAVE,"C:\\WINDOWS\\TADA.WAV",
WM_COMMAND,MAIN_MIDI,"C:\\WINDOWS\\DING.WAV",
WM_INITDIALOG,NOPARAM,"C:\\WINDOWS\\DING.WAV",
};
```

With all this data set up, it's possible to trap specific messages. The TrapMessageHook function should be called at the beginning of the

message handler for any dialog that's to make noises as a result of
things happening while it's active.

```
void TrapMessageHook(HWND hwnd,WORD message,WORD wParam,
 EVENT FAR *event,int number)
{
 int i=0;
 for(i=0;i<number;++i) {
  if(event[i].message==message) {
   if(event[i].wParam==NOPARAM ||
    event[i].wParam==wParam) {
     sndPlaySound(event[i].path,SND_ASYNC);
     break;
   }
  }
 }
}
```

The hwnd, message and wParam arguments to TrapMessageHook
are the same values passed to the message handler it's called from.
The event argument is a far pointer to a table of initialized EVENT
objects. The number argument is the number of events in the table.

There's not much to TrapMessageHook. Every time it's called, it
looks through the list of events passed to it to see if one of them
matches the event it's been called to respond to. If a match is found,
it calls sndPlaySound to play the wave file in question.

There are a few obvious caveats to using TrapMessageHook. If it finds
itself being used on a system with a Windows speaker driver installed,
it will effectively lock up the system for as long as the wave file in
question takes to play. Short wave files are preferable. Further to this,
most people won't want to hear the entire last act of Macbeth, the
parrot sketch in its completeness or fifteen minutes of the best of ZZ
Top's guitar riffs played every time they pull down a menu, even if
they do have an asynchronous sound card installed in their systems.

While not the case in the programs to be discussed in this chapter,
real world Windows software should probably make this feature user
configurable if it's implemented at all, such that it can be disabled—lest
the users of your applications start fishing around in their respective
desks for the aforementioned small tactical nuclear missiles.

→ Playing multimedia files

Figure 5-3 illustrates the DEMO7 application: a browser for wave, MIDI, and AVI files. If you've tried the Multimedia Workshop application from the companion disk for this book you'll probably notice some similarity between them—Multimedia Workshop was derived from the DEMO7.CPP code.

Figure 5-3

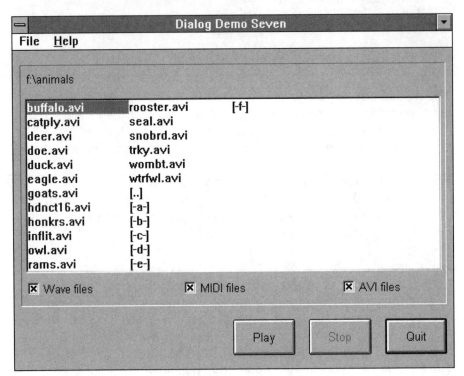

The DEMO7 application.

The DEMO7 program will display a large multiple-column list control with the file names of wave, MIDI, and AVI files in it. Select one and click on the Play button—or just double click on a filename—and it will be played through the MCI interface. By default, if the MCI calls to play a wave file fail, DEMO7 will reattempt the function using sndPlaySound.

You can determine which of the file types should appear in the list box through the three check boxes below the main list control.

Note that the main list control also provides for moving between directories and drives. Double click on the [..] entry to move up one step in your current directory tree. Double click on one of the directory entries in square brackets to move down the tree and double click on a drive letter to change drives. This arrangement won't work all that well if you're running under a Novell network, which suppresses the [..] entry. Graphic Workshop gets around this by providing a Change Directory function in its File menu, something you might want to consider if you implement a big list box like this in your own applications.

The structure of DEMO7 should be fairly obvious, even before you look at the source code. Every time a filename is selected, its type is determined by its extension and the appropriate MCI calls are performed to play it. As was touched on earlier, the calls for the three file types DEMO7 knows how to deal with are almost identical, save for the actual MCI devices to be used.

The complete source code for DEMO7.CPP is listed in Fig. 5-4. In addition to DEMO7.CPP, you'll need DEMO7.RC, as shown in Fig. 5-5. Suitable DEF and project files for DEMO7 are included with the source code on the companion disk for this book.

The DEMO7.CPP source code.　　　　　　　　　　　　　　　　Figure 5-4

```
/*
    Dialog Demo 7
    Copyright (c) 1993 Alchemy Mindworks Inc.
*/

#include <windows.h>
#include <stdio.h>
#include <stdlib.h>
#include <ctype.h>
#include <alloc.h>
#include <string.h>
#include <dos.h>
#include <time.h>
#include <dir.h>
#include <errno.h>
#include <commdlg.h>
```

5-4 *Continued*

```
#include "ctl3d.h"
#include "draw3d.h"
#include <mmsystem.h>
#include <mciavi.h>
#include <digitalv.h>

#define say(s)     MessageBox(NULL,s,"Yo...",MB_OK | MB_ICONSTOP);
#define saynumber(f,s)   {char b[128]; sprintf((LPSTR)b,(LPSTR)f,s);
     MessageBox(NULL,b,"Debug Message",MB_OK | MB_ICONSTOP); }

#define STRINGSIZE        129        /* how big is a string? */

#ifndef IDHELP
#define IDHELP          998
#endif

#define MESSAGE_STRING   101        /* message box object */

#define MAIN_LIST        401
#define MAIN_PATH        402
#define MAIN_PLAY        101
#define MAIN_STOP        102

#define MAIN_WAVE        201
#define MAIN_MIDI        202
#define MAIN_AVI         203

#define FILE_PLAY        101
#define FILE_STOP        102
#define FILE_EXIT        199

#define HELPM_INDEX      901
#define HELPM_USING      905
#define HELPM_ABOUT      999

#define HELPFILE         "DEMO.HLP"
#define ABOUT_WAVE       "AboutWave"

#define DIALOG_KEY       "DialogDemo"

#define MESSAGE_ABOUT    0
#define MESSAGE_HELP     1
#define MESSAGE_NODISK   2

#define NOPARAM          0xffff

#define CreateControlFont()     if(ControlFontName[0]) \
             controlfont=CreateFont(16,0,0,0,0,0,0,0,\
             ANSI_CHARSET,OUT_DEFAULT_PRECIS,CLIP_DEFAULT_PRECIS,\
             DEFAULT_QUALITY,DEFAULT_PITCH | FF_DONTCARE,\
             ControlFontName)
```

```
#define SetControlFont(hwnd,id) {HWND dlgH;\
            if(controlfont != NULL) {\
                dlgH=GetDlgItem(hwnd,id);\
                SendMessage(dlgH,WM_SETFONT,(WORD)controlfont,FALSE);\
            }\
            }

#define DestroyControlFont()    if(controlfont != NULL) \
    DeleteObject(controlfont)

#define CheckOn(item)     SendDlgItemMessage(hwnd,item,BM_SETCHECK,1,0L);
#define CheckOff(item)     SendDlgItemMessage(hwnd,item,BM_SETCHECK,0,0L);
#define ItemOn(item)    { dlgH=GetDlgItem(hwnd,item); EnableWindow(dlgH,TRUE); }
#define ItemOff(item)     { dlgH=GetDlgItem(hwnd,item); EnableWindow(dlgH,FALSE); }
#define IsItemChecked(item)     SendDlgItemMessage(hwnd,item,BM_GETCHECK,0,0L)
#define ItemName(item,string)    { dlgH=GetDlgItem(hwnd,item); \
    SetWindowText(dlgH,(LPSTR)string); }
#define GetItemName(item,string) { dlgH=GetDlgItem(hwnd,item); \
    GetWindowText(dlgH,(LPSTR)string,BIGSTRINGSIZE); }
#define TrapMessage(hwnd,message,wParam,event) \
    TrapMessageHook(hwnd,message,wParam,&event[0],sizeof(event)/sizeof(EVENT))

//This macro enables using sndPlaySound if the MCI call fails...
//this takes care of the Windows speaker driver, if it's in use.
//To disable this feature, comment out this macro.
#define PLAYSOUND(p,f)        sndPlaySound(p,f)

/* bad memory management techniques... conveniently packaged */
#define FixedGlobalAlloc(n)     MAKELONG(0,GlobalAlloc(GPTR,(DWORD)n))
#define FixedGlobalFree(p)     GlobalFree((GLOBALHANDLE)HIWORD((LONG)p));

#ifndef max
#define max(a,b)         (((a)>(b))?(a):(b))
#endif
#ifndef min
#define min(a,b)         (((a)<(b))?(a):(b))
#endif

/* structures */
typedef struct {
    WORD message;
    WORD wParam;
    char path[STRINGSIZE+1];
    } EVENT;

/* prototypes */
DWORD FAR PASCAL SelectProc(HWND hwnd,WORD message,WORD wParam,LONG lParam);
DWORD FAR PASCAL AboutDlgProc(HWND hwnd,WORD message,WORD wParam,LONG lParam);
DWORD FAR PASCAL MessageDlgProc(HWND hwnd,WORD message,WORD wParam,LONG lParam);

void DoMessage(HWND hwnd,LPSTR message);
void SetHelpSize(HWND hwnd);
void DoHelp(HWND hwnd,LPSTR keyword);
```

5-4 *Continued*

```
void MakeHelpPathName(LPSTR szFileName);
void ResetSelectorList(HWND hwnd);
void CentreWindow(HWND hwnd);
void TrapMessageHook(HWND hwnd,WORD message,WORD wParam,\
    EVENT FAR *event,int number);

int testdisk(int n);
int PlayEffect(HWND hwnd,LPSTR path,LPSTR message);
int PlayFlick(LPSTR path,HWND hwnd,LPSTR message);
int PlaySound(LPSTR path,HWND hwnd,LPSTR message);
int PlayMusic(LPSTR path,HWND hwnd,LPSTR message);

LPSTR FetchString(unsigned int n);

/* globals*/
char szAppName[]="DialogDemoSeven";
char ControlFontName[STRINGSIZE+1]="Arial";

LPSTR messagehook=NULL;
HANDLE hInst;
HFONT controlfont=NULL;

EVENT eventlist[]= {
    WM_COMMAND,IDOK,"C:\\WINDOWS\\CHIMES.WAV",
    WM_COMMAND,MAIN_AVI,"C:\\WINDOWS\\CHIMES.WAV",
    WM_COMMAND,MAIN_WAVE,"C:\\WINDOWS\\TADA.WAV",
    WM_COMMAND,MAIN_MIDI,"C:\\WINDOWS\\DING.WAV",
    WM_INITDIALOG,NOPARAM,"C:\\WINDOWS\\DING.WAV",
    };

#pragma warn -par
int PASCAL WinMain(HANDLE hInstance,HANDLE hPrevInstance,
    LPSTR lpszCmdParam,int nCmdShow)
{
    FARPROC dlgProc;
    int r=0;

    hInst=hInstance;

    Ctl3dRegister(hInstance);
    Ctl3dAutoSubclass(hInstance);

    dlgProc=MakeProcInstance((FARPROC)SelectProc,hInst);
    r=DialogBox(hInst,"MainScreen",NULL,dlgProc);

    FreeProcInstance(dlgProc);

    Ctl3dUnregister(hInstance);

    return(r);
}
```

```
DWORD FAR PASCAL SelectProc(HWND hwnd,WORD message,WORD wParam,LONG lParam)
{
    MCI_GENERIC_PARMS mcigen;
    static HFONT hFont;
    FARPROC lpfnDlgProc;
    PAINTSTRUCT ps;
    HMENU hmenu;
    static HICON hIcon;
    char b[STRINGSIZE+1];
    static id;
    HWND dlgH;
    long l;
    int i;

    TrapMessage(hwnd,message,wParam,eventlist);

    switch(message) {
        case MM_MCINOTIFY:
            mciSendCommand(LOWORD(lParam),MCI_CLOSE,MCI_WAIT,NULL);
            ItemOff(MAIN_STOP);
            ItemOn(MAIN_PLAY);

            ItemOn(MAIN_WAVE);
            ItemOn(MAIN_MIDI);
            ItemOn(MAIN_AVI);
            ItemOn(MAIN_LIST);

            hmenu=GetMenu(hwnd);
            EnableMenuItem(hmenu,FILE_PLAY,MF_ENABLED);
            EnableMenuItem(hmenu,FILE_STOP,MF_GRAYED);

            id=-1;
            break;
        case WM_SYSCOMMAND:
            switch(wParam & 0xfff0) {
                case SC_CLOSE:
                    SendMessage(hwnd,WM_COMMAND,FILE_EXIT,0L);
                    break;
            }
            break;
        case WM_CTLCOLOR:
                return(Ctl3dCtlColorEx(message,wParam,lParam));
        case WM_INITDIALOG:
            hFont=CreateFont(16,0,0,0,0,0,0,0,ANSI_CHARSET,
                    OUT_DEFAULT_PRECIS,CLIP_DEFAULT_PRECIS,
                    DEFAULT_QUALITY,DEFAULT_PITCH | FF_DONTCARE,\
                    ControlFontName);

            SetHelpSize(hwnd);

            GetProfileString(DIALOG_KEY,"ControlFont",
                ControlFontName,b,STRINGSIZE);
            if(lstrlen(b)) lstrcpy(ControlFontName,b);
```

5-4 *Continued*

```
    CreateControlFont();

    hIcon=LoadIcon(hInst,szAppName);
    SetClassWord(hwnd,GCW_HICON,(WORD)hIcon);
    CentreWindow(hwnd);
    CheckOn(MAIN_WAVE);
    CheckOn(MAIN_MIDI);
    CheckOn(MAIN_AVI);
    ItemOff(MAIN_STOP);

    ResetSelectorList(hwnd);
    id=-1;

    SetControlFont(hwnd,MAIN_WAVE);
    SetControlFont(hwnd,MAIN_MIDI);
    SetControlFont(hwnd,MAIN_AVI);
    SetControlFont(hwnd,MAIN_PATH);
    SetControlFont(hwnd,FILE_PLAY);
    SetControlFont(hwnd,FILE_STOP);
    SetControlFont(hwnd,FILE_EXIT);

    break;
case WM_PAINT:
    BeginPaint(hwnd,&ps);
    EndPaint(hwnd,&ps);
    break;
case WM_COMMAND:
    switch(wParam) {
        case HELPM_INDEX:
            MakeHelpPathName(b);
            WinHelp(hwnd,b,HELP_INDEX,NULL);
            break;
        case HELPM_USING:
            WinHelp(hwnd,"",HELP_HELPONHELP,NULL);
            break;
        case HELPM_ABOUT:
            if((lpfnDlgProc=MakeProcInstance
              ((FARPROC)AboutDlgProc,hInst)) != NULL) {
                DialogBox(hInst,"AboutBox",hwnd,lpfnDlgProc);
                FreeProcInstance(lpfnDlgProc);
            }
            break;
        case MAIN_LIST:
            switch(HIWORD(lParam)) {
                case LBN_DBLCLK:
                    if(DlgDirSelect(hwnd,b,MAIN_LIST)) {
                        i=lstrlen(b);
                        if(b[i-1]=='\\') {
                            b[i-1]=0;
                            chdir(b);
                        }
```

```
                    else {
                        if(!testdisk(b[0]-'A'))
                            setdisk(toupper(b[0])-'A');
                        else DoMessage(hwnd,FetchString
                            (MESSAGE_NODISK));
                    }
                    ResetSelectorList(hwnd);
                }
                else SendMessage(hwnd,WM_COMMAND,FILE_PLAY,OL);
                break;
        }
        break;
    case FILE_PLAY:
        if((l=SendDlgItemMessage(hwnd,MAIN_LIST,
          LB_GETCURSEL,0,OL)) != LB_ERR) {
            SendDlgItemMessage(hwnd,MAIN_LIST,LB_GETTEXT,
              (unsigned int)l,(long)b);
            if(b[0]!='[') {
                if((id=PlayEffect(hwnd,b,b)) == -1) {
                    if(b[0]) DoMessage(hwnd,b);
                }
                else {
                    ItemOn(MAIN_STOP);
                    ItemOff(MAIN_PLAY);

                    ItemOff(MAIN_WAVE);
                    ItemOff(MAIN_MIDI);
                    ItemOff(MAIN_AVI);
                    ItemOff(MAIN_LIST);

                    hmenu=GetMenu(hwnd);
                    EnableMenuItem(hmenu,FILE_PLAY,MF_GRAYED);
                    EnableMenuItem(hmenu,FILE_STOP,MF_ENABLED);
                }
            }
        }
        break;
    case FILE_STOP:
        if(id != -1) {
            mcigen.dwCallback=hwnd;
            mciSendCommand(id,MCI_STOP,MCI_NOTIFY | MCI_WAIT,
              (DWORD)(LPVOID)&mcigen);
        }
        sndPlaySound(NULL,SND_SYNC);
        break;
    case FILE_EXIT:
        SendMessage(hwnd,WM_COMMAND,FILE_STOP,OL);
        if(hFont != NULL) DeleteObject(hFont);
        MakeHelpPathName(b);
        WinHelp(hwnd,b,HELP_QUIT,NULL);

        FreeResource(hIcon);
        DestroyControlFont();
```

5-4 *Continued*

```
                PostQuitMessage(0);
                break;
            case MAIN_AVI:
            case MAIN_WAVE:
            case MAIN_MIDI:
                if(IsItemChecked(wParam)) {
                    CheckOff(wParam);
                }
                else {
                    CheckOn(wParam);
                }
                ResetSelectorList(hwnd);
                break;
        }
        break;
    }

    return(FALSE);
}

void DoMessage(HWND hwnd,LPSTR message)
{
    FARPROC lpfnDlgProc;

    messagehook=message;

    if((lpfnDlgProc=MakeProcInstance((FARPROC)MessageDlgProc,hInst)) != NULL) {
        DialogBox(hInst,"MessageBox",hwnd,lpfnDlgProc);
        FreeProcInstance(lpfnDlgProc);
    }
}

DWORD FAR PASCAL MessageDlgProc(HWND hwnd,WORD message,WORD wParam,LONG lParam)
{
    HWND dlgH;

    TrapMessage(hwnd,message,wParam,eventlist);

    switch(message) {
        case WM_INITDIALOG:
            ItemName(MESSAGE_STRING,messagehook);
            CentreWindow(hwnd);
            SetControlFont(hwnd,MESSAGE_STRING);
            SetControlFont(hwnd,IDOK);
            return(FALSE);
        case WM_CTLCOLOR:
            return(Ctl3dCtlColorEx(message,wParam,lParam));
        case WM_COMMAND:
            switch(wParam) {
                case IDOK:
                    EndDialog(hwnd,wParam);
```

```
                         return(FALSE);
                }
                break;
        }

        return(FALSE);
}

DWORD FAR PASCAL AboutDlgProc(HWND hwnd,WORD message,WORD wParam,LONG lParam)
{
        static GLOBALHANDLE handle;
        static LPSTR p;
        HWND dlgH;

        TrapMessage(hwnd,message,wParam,eventlist);

        switch(message) {
            case WM_INITDIALOG:
                if((handle=LoadResource(hInst,FindResource(hInst,
                  ABOUT_WAVE,RT_RCDATA))) != NULL) {
                    if((p=(LPSTR)LockResource(handle))!=NULL)
                        sndPlaySound(p,SND_ASYNC | SND_MEMORY | SND_NODEFAULT);
                }
                ItemName(MESSAGE_STRING,FetchString(MESSAGE_ABOUT));
                CentreWindow(hwnd);
                SetControlFont(hwnd,MESSAGE_STRING);
                SetControlFont(hwnd,IDOK);
                return(FALSE);
            case WM_CTLCOLOR:
                return(Ctl3dCtlColorEx(message,wParam,lParam));
            case WM_COMMAND:
                switch(wParam) {
                    case IDOK:
                        if(handle != NULL) {
                            sndPlaySound(NULL,SND_SYNC);
                            if(p != NULL) UnlockResource(handle);
                            FreeResource(handle);
                        }
                        EndDialog(hwnd,wParam);
                        return(FALSE);
                }
                break;
        }

        return(FALSE);
}

void CentreWindow(HWND hwnd)
{
        RECT rect;
        unsigned int x,y;

        GetWindowRect(hwnd,&rect);
```

353

5-4 *Continued*

```
    x=(GetSystemMetrics(SM_CXSCREEN)-(rect.right-rect.left))/2;
    y=(GetSystemMetrics(SM_CYSCREEN)-(rect.bottom-rect.top))/2;
    SetWindowPos(hwnd,NULL,x,y,rect.right-rect.left,rect.bottom-rect.top,
        SWP_NOSIZE);
}

LPSTR FetchString(unsigned int n)
{
    static char b[257];

    if(!LoadString(hInst,n,b,256))
        lstrcpy(b,"String table error - this application may be damaged");
    return(b);
}

void SetHelpSize(HWND hwnd)
{
    HELPWININFO helpinfo;
    char b[145];

    memset((char *)&helpinfo,0,sizeof(HELPWININFO));
    helpinfo.wStructSize=sizeof(HELPWININFO);
    helpinfo.x=10;
    helpinfo.y=10;
    helpinfo.dx=512;
    helpinfo.dy=1004;

    MakeHelpPathName(b);
    WinHelp(hwnd,b,HELP_SETWINPOS,(DWORD)&helpinfo);
}

void DoHelp(HWND hwnd,LPSTR keyword)
{
    char b[145];

    MakeHelpPathName(b);
    WinHelp(hwnd,b,HELP_KEY,(DWORD)keyword);
}

void MakeHelpPathName(LPSTR szFileName)
{
    LPSTR pcFileName;
    int nFileNameLen;

    nFileNameLen = GetModuleFileName(hInst,szFileName,144);
    pcFileName = szFileName+nFileNameLen;

    while(pcFileName > szFileName) {
        if(*pcFileName == '\\' || *pcFileName == ':') {
            *(++pcFileName) = '\0';
            break;
```

```
        }
        nFileNameLen--;
        pcFileName--;
    }

    if((nFileNameLen+13) < 144) lstrcat(szFileName,HELPFILE);
    else lstrcat(szFileName, "?");
}

void ResetSelectorList(HWND hwnd)
{
    HWND dlgH;
    HCURSOR hSaveCursor,hHourGlass;
    char b[STRINGSIZE+1];

    hHourGlass=LoadCursor(NULL,IDC_WAIT);
    hSaveCursor=SetCursor(hHourGlass);

    dlgH=GetDlgItem(hwnd,MAIN_LIST);
    SendDlgItemMessage(hwnd,MAIN_LIST,LB_RESETCONTENT,0,0L);
    SendMessage(dlgH,WM_SETREDRAW,FALSE,0L);

    if(IsItemChecked(MAIN_WAVE)) {
        SendDlgItemMessage(hwnd,MAIN_LIST,LB_DIR,0x0000,(long )"*.WAV");
    }
    if(IsItemChecked(MAIN_MIDI)) {
        SendDlgItemMessage(hwnd,MAIN_LIST,LB_DIR,0x0000,(long )"*.MID");
    }
    if(IsItemChecked(MAIN_AVI)) {
        SendDlgItemMessage(hwnd,MAIN_LIST,LB_DIR,0x0000,(long )"*.AVI");
    }

    SendDlgItemMessage(hwnd,MAIN_LIST,LB_DIR,0xc010,(long )"*.*");

    SendDlgItemMessage(hwnd,MAIN_LIST,LB_SETCURSEL,0,0L);
    SendDlgItemMessage(hwnd,MAIN_LIST,LB_GETTEXT,0,(long)b);

    SendMessage(dlgH,WM_SETREDRAW,TRUE,0L);

    getcwd(b,STRINGSIZE);
    strlwr(b);
    ItemName(MAIN_PATH,b);

    SetCursor(hSaveCursor);
}

int testdisk(int n)
{
    FILE *fp;
    char b[32];
    int r;

    SetErrorMode(1);
```

5-4 *Continued*

```
        sprintf(b,"%c:\\TEMP.DAT",n+'A');
        if((fp=fopen(b,"r")) != NULL) fclose(fp);

        if(_doserrno==ENOPATH) r=1;
        else r=0;

        SetErrorMode(0);
        return(r);
}

int PlayEffect(HWND hwnd,LPSTR path,LPSTR message)
{
        char s[144],b[16];

        lstrcpy(s,path);
        fnsplit(s,NULL,NULL,NULL,b);
        if(!stricmp(b,".WAV")) return(PlaySound(path,hwnd,message));
        else if(!stricmp(b,".MID")) return(PlayMusic(path,hwnd,message));
        else if(!stricmp(b,".AVI")) return(PlayFlick(path,hwnd,message));
        else return(-1);
}

int PlayMusic(LPSTR path,HWND hwnd,LPSTR message)
{
        MCI_OPEN_PARMS mciOpen;
        MCI_PLAY_PARMS mciPlay;
        unsigned long rtrn;
        int id=-1;

        mciOpen.wDeviceID=NULL;
        mciOpen.lpstrDeviceType="sequencer";
        mciOpen.lpstrElementName=path;
        if((rtrn=mciSendCommand(NULL,MCI_OPEN,MCI_OPEN_TYPE :
          MCI_OPEN_ELEMENT,(DWORD)(LPVOID)&mciOpen)) != 0L) {
            mciGetErrorString(rtrn,message,STRINGSIZE);
            return(-1);
        }

        id=mciOpen.wDeviceID;

        mciPlay.dwCallback=hwnd;
        if((rtrn=mciSendCommand(id,MCI_PLAY,MCI_NOTIFY,
          (DWORD)(LPVOID)&mciPlay)) != 0L) {
            mciSendCommand(id,MCI_CLOSE,0,NULL);
            mciGetErrorString(rtrn,message,STRINGSIZE);
            return(-1);
        }

        return(id);
}
```

```c
int PlaySound(LPSTR path,HWND hwnd,LPSTR message)
{
    MCI_OPEN_PARMS mciopen;
    MCI_PLAY_PARMS mciplay;
    DWORD rtrn;
    int id=-1;

    mciopen.lpstrDeviceType="waveaudio";
    mciopen.lpstrElementName=path;
    if((rtrn=mciSendCommand(0,MCI_OPEN,MCI_OPEN_TYPE |
      MCI_OPEN_ELEMENT,(DWORD)(LPVOID)&mciopen)) != 0L) {
        mciGetErrorString(rtrn,message,STRINGSIZE);
        return(-1);
    }

    id=mciopen.wDeviceID;

    mciplay.dwCallback=(DWORD)hwnd;
    if((rtrn=mciSendCommand(id,MCI_PLAY,MCI_NOTIFY,
      (DWORD)(LPVOID)&mciplay)) != 0L) {

        #ifdef PLAYSOUND
        if(PLAYSOUND(path,SND_ASYNC | SND_NODEFAULT)) {
            message[0]=0;
            mciSendCommand(id,MCI_CLOSE,MCI_WAIT,NULL);
            return(-1);
        }
        #endif

        mciSendCommand(id,MCI_CLOSE,0,NULL);
        mciGetErrorString(rtrn,message,STRINGSIZE);
        return(-1);
    }

    return(id);
}

int PlayFlick(LPSTR path,HWND hwnd,LPSTR message)
{
    MCI_DGV_OPEN_PARMS mciopen;
    MCI_DGV_PLAY_PARMS mciplay;
    MCI_DGV_STATUS_PARMS mcistat;
    DWORD rtrn;
    int id=-1;

    mciopen.lpstrDeviceType="avivideo";
    mciopen.lpstrElementName=path;
    if((rtrn=mciSendCommand(0,MCI_OPEN,MCI_OPEN_TYPE |
      MCI_OPEN_ELEMENT,(DWORD)(LPVOID)&mciopen)) != 0L) {
        mciGetErrorString(rtrn,message,STRINGSIZE);
        return(-1);
    }
```

5-4 *Continued*

```
        id=mciopen.wDeviceID;

        //this call centres the window...
        //comment it out to let the flick play where it wants to
        mcistat.dwItem=MCI_DGV_STATUS_HWND;
        if((rtrn=mciSendCommand(id,MCI_STATUS,MCI_STATUS_ITEM,
            (DWORD)(LPVOID)&mcistat)) == 0)
            CentreWindow((HWND)mcistat.dwReturn);

        mciplay.dwCallback=(DWORD)hwnd;
        if((rtrn=mciSendCommand(id,MCI_PLAY,MCI_NOTIFY,
            (DWORD)(LPVOID)&mciplay)) != 0L) {
            mciSendCommand(id,MCI_CLOSE,0,NULL);
            mciGetErrorString(rtrn,message,STRINGSIZE);
            return(-1);
        }

        return(id);
}

void TrapMessageHook(HWND hwnd,WORD message,
        WORD wParam,EVENT FAR *event,int number)
{
        int i=0;

        for(i=0;i<number;++i) {
            if(event[i].message==message) {
                if(event[i].wParam==NOPARAM || event[i].wParam==wParam) {
                    sndPlaySound(event[i].path,SND_ASYNC);
                    break;
                }

            }
        }
}
```

Figure 5-5   *The DEMO7.RC resource script.*

```
MainScreen DIALOG 29, 28, 256, 180
STYLE WS_POPUP | WS_CAPTION | WS_SYSMENU | WS_MINIMIZEBOX
CAPTION "Dialog Demo Seven"
MENU MainMenu
BEGIN
    CONTROL "", 401, "LISTBOX", LBS_STANDARD | LBS_MULTICOLUMN |
      WS_CHILD | WS_VISIBLE, 8, 28, 240, 100
    CONTROL "", -1, "static", SS_BLACKFRAME | WS_CHILD | WS_VISIBLE, 4, 8, 248, 136
    CHECKBOX "Wave files", 201, 8, 128, 56, 12, WS_CHILD | WS_VISIBLE | WS_TABSTOP
    CHECKBOX "MIDI files", 202, 100, 128, 56, 12, WS_CHILD | WS_VISIBLE | WS_TABSTOP
    CHECKBOX "AVI files", 203, 192, 128, 56, 12, WS_CHILD | WS_VISIBLE | WS_TABSTOP
    PUSHBUTTON "Play", 101, 128, 152, 36, 20, WS_CHILD | WS_VISIBLE | WS_TABSTOP
```

```
        DEFPUSHBUTTON "Quit", 199, 216, 152, 36, 20, WS_CHILD ¦ WS_VISIBLE ¦ WS_TABSTOP
        PUSHBUTTON "Stop", 102, 172, 152, 36, 20, WS_CHILD ¦ WS_VISIBLE ¦ WS_TABSTOP
        LTEXT "", 402, 8, 12, 240, 10, WS_CHILD ¦ WS_VISIBLE ¦ WS_GROUP
END

AboutBox DIALOG 72, 72, 220, 128
STYLE WS_POPUP ¦ WS_CAPTION
CAPTION "About"
BEGIN
        CTEXT "", 101, 16, 16, 188, 72, WS_CHILD ¦ WS_VISIBLE ¦ WS_GROUP
        DEFPUSHBUTTON "OK", IDOK, 96, 104, 28, 16, WS_CHILD ¦ WS_VISIBLE ¦ WS_TABSTOP
        CONTROL "", -1, "static", SS_BLACKFRAME ¦ WS_CHILD ¦ WS_VISIBLE, 8, 8, 204, 88
END

MainMenu MENU
BEGIN
        POPUP "File"
        BEGIN
            MENUITEM "&Play", 101
            MENUITEM "&Stop", 102, GRAYED
            MENUITEM SEPARATOR
            MENUITEM "E&xit", 199
        END

        POPUP "&Help"
        BEGIN
            MENUITEM "&Index", 901
            MENUITEM "&Using help", 905
            MENUITEM SEPARATOR
            MENUITEM "&About...", 999
        END

END

STRINGTABLE
BEGIN
        0,"Dialog Demo Seven\nCopyright \251 1993 Alchemy Mindworks Inc.\n
           From the book Windows Dialog Construction Set\r
           by Steven William Rimmer\rPublished by Windcrest/McGraw Hill"
        1,"Help"
        2,"That drive is off line. Please check to see that there's a disk in it."
END

DialogDemoSeven ICON
BEGIN
        '00 00 01 00 01 00 20 20 10 00 00 00 00 00 E8 02'
        '00 00 16 00 00 00 28 00 00 00 20 00 00 00 40 00'
        '00 00 01 00 04 00 00 00 00 00 80 02 00 00 00 00'
        '00 00 00 00 00 00 00 00 00 00 00 00 00 00 00 00'
        '00 00 00 00 80 00 00 00 80 00 00 00 80 80 00 80'
        '00 00 80 00 80 00 80 80 00 00 80 80 80 00 C0 C0'
        'C0 00 00 00 FF 00 00 FF 00 00 00 FF FF 00 FF 00'
        '00 00 FF 00 FF 00 FF FF 00 00 FF FF FF 00 2A 2A'
```

5-5 *Continued*

```
    '2A 2A 2A 2A 2A 2A 2A 22 77 70 00 00 00 00 A2 A2'
    'A2 A2 A2 A2 A2 A2 A2 A2 22 70 00 00 00 00 2A 2A'
    '2A 2A 2A 2A 2A 2A AA AA A2 70 00 00 00 00 A2 A2'
    'A2 A2 AA AA AA AA B2 AA AA 77 77 77 77 00 2A 2A'
    'AA AA 2A 2A AA 2A AA A9 19 19 19 19 17 77 AA A2'
    'A2 AA AB AB AB AA 91 91 91 91 91 91 91 97 2A AA'
    'BA BA 2A AA A9 19 19 19 19 99 99 99 99 19 AB AB'
    'A2 AA AA 11 11 91 99 99 99 90 00 00 09 99 BA BA'
    'AA A1 01 11 19 19 19 19 90 00 00 00 09 AA A2'
    '00 10 10 11 11 91 91 00 00 00 00 70 00 00 2A 00'
    '00 00 01 01 11 17 77 00 00 00 09 70 00 00 A2 22'
    '22 22 22 22 22 22 27 77 77 70 09 70 00 00 2A 2A'
    '2A 2A AA AA AA AA 22 22 22 77 09 77 00 00 A2 AA'
    'AA AA A2 AA AA AA A2 A2 A2 27 79 17 70 00 2A AA'
    'AA 2A 22 22 2A 2A AA AA AA 2A 79 91 77 00 A2 A2'
    'A2 22 70 70 22 A2 A2 AB A2 A2 00 99 17 77 2A 2A'
    '22 87 07 07 02 2A 2A AA AA 27 00 09 91 91 A2 A2'
    'F8 88 77 70 72 A2 AB AB AB A0 00 00 99 99 2A 22'
    '8F 88 00 77 07 2A 2A AA AA 70 00 00 00 00 A2 28'
    'F8 F0 00 08 70 22 22 A2 A2 00 00 00 00 00 2A 2F'
    '8F 80 00 07 07 2A 2A AA A7 00 00 00 00 00 A7 28'
    'F8 FF 00 88 82 22 A2 A2 A0 00 00 00 00 00 22 7F'
    '8F FF FF 8F 82 2A 2A 2A 70 00 00 00 00 00 A7 0F'
    'FF FF F8 F8 F2 A2 A2 A2 00 00 00 00 00 00 A2 70'
    'FF FF 8F 8F 2A 2A 2A 20 00 00 00 00 00 00 A7 07'
    'FF FF F8 F8 22 A2 A2 00 00 00 00 00 00 00 A2 70'
    '70 FF 8F 22 2A 2A 20 00 00 00 00 00 00 00 AA 07'
    '07 07 02 02 A2 A2 00 00 00 00 00 00 00 00 BA A0'
    '70 70 72 2A 2A 20 00 00 00 00 00 00 00 00 BB AA'
    'A7 A7 AA AA A0 00 00 00 00 00 00 00 00 00 AA BA'
    'AA AA AA 00 00 00 00 00 00 00 00 00 00 00 AA A0'
    '00 00 00 00 00 00 00 00 00 00 00 00 00 00 00 00'
    '01 FF 00 00 01 FF 00 00 01 FF 00 00 00 03 00 00'
    '00 00 00 00 00 00 00 00 00 00 00 00 01 F8 00 00'
    '07 FE 00 00 3F DF 00 00 3F 9F 00 00 01 9F 00 00'
    '00 8F 00 00 00 07 00 00 00 03 00 00 00 C0 00 00'
    '00 E0 00 00 01 F0 00 00 01 FF 00 00 03 FF 00 00'
    '03 FF 00 00 07 FF 00 00 07 FF 00 00 0F FF 00 00'
    '1F FF 00 00 3F FF 00 00 7F FF 00 00 FF FF 00 01'
    'FF FF 00 07 FF FF 00 3F FF FF 1F FF FF FF'
END

MessageBox DIALOG 72, 72, 220, 128
STYLE WS_POPUP | WS_CAPTION
CAPTION "Message"
BEGIN
    CTEXT "", 101, 16, 16, 188, 72, WS_CHILD | WS_VISIBLE | WS_GROUP
    DEFPUSHBUTTON "OK", IDOK, 96, 104, 28, 16, WS_CHILD | WS_VISIBLE | WS_TABSTOP
    CONTROL "", -1, "static", SS_BLACKFRAME | WS_CHILD | WS_VISIBLE, 8, 8, 204, 88
END

AboutWave RCDATA demo.wav
```

In order to compile DEMO7, you'll require the Microsoft Multimedia Development Kit, which includes the extra headers and such the program uses. If the Multimedia Development Kit isn't installed on your hard drive, DEMO7 won't compile. As mentioned earlier, we'll look at an alternate approach to this later in this chapter.

The SelectProc message handler for the main window of DEMO7 does little more than manage the main list box. If you select an item in the list box, a WM_COMMAND message with MAIN_LIST as its wParam argument will appear. The high-order word of its lParam argument will be the constant LBN_DBLCLK if the item has been double clicked. The MAIN_LIST case of the WM_COMMAND handler illustrates how this is used to change drives and directories or to send a FILE_PLAY command to SelectProc if the entry is a filename.

The FILE_PLAY case of the SelectProc message handler calls PlayEffect, which will in turn call the appropriate function to play the file in question, based on its file extension. It will return a true value if the file passed to it has begun playing. Keep in mind that multimedia files play asynchronously—the PlayEffects function will return as soon as your file starts playing. If it returns a true value, some of the controls and menu items in the main window of DEMO7 will be disabled.

In fact, the PlayEffect function has been cooked a bit to deal with the possibility of playing sounds through sndPlaySound rather than using the appropriate MCI calls. The second argument to PlayEffect is the name of the file to be played. The third argument is a buffer in which it will return an error message should a problem occur. As was touched on earlier, the MCI interface can provide text error messages when it fails to do something that's asked of it.

The PlayEffect function will fill in the string passed as its third argument if it encounters an error, unless the error is in playing a wave file and the sndPlaySound function subsequently takes care of the task. Note, however, that because sndPlaySound won't send an MM_MCINOTIFY message at the end of a sound, the main window controls can't be disabled and then re-enabled when the sound terminates if the sound was initiated by sndPlaySound.

There are two other functions called from SelectProc that aren't contained in earlier applications in this book. The first is testdisk, which checks to see if the drive you select from the main list box in DEMO7 actually exists, and is on line. The latter case is important, as you might select a floppy drive with no disk in it, for example. The testdisk function, as declared in DEMO7.CPP, temporarily prohibits Windows from complaining about an off-line drive, attempts to access the drive in question, checks the resulting error code, and returns an appropriate value.

The other new function, ResetSelectorList, adds the names of the wave, MIDI, and AVI files in the current directory to the main list control. It also adds the appropriate drive and directory entries. The main list control has its sort flag set, so anything added to it will be automatically sorted alphabetically. Note that the redraw flag is turned off for the main list control before its contents are updated and then turned on again when the update is complete by sending it WM_SETREDRAW messages. This looks a lot more attractive than having the list re-sort itself several times, and reduces the time it takes to add entries to it.

The PlayEffect function is exceedingly simple; it figures out whether the file it's been asked to play is a wave, MIDI, or AVI file by having a look at its file extension. It then calls the appropriate dedicated playing function accordingly. While the PlaySound, PlayMusic and PlayFlick functions are all similar—using the MCI calls discussed earlier in this chapter—it's convenient to have them as separate bits of code rather than as a single function with a spaghetti dinner of if statements.

The PlayMusic function, which takes care of playing MIDI files, is actually the simplest of the three. It gets by with nothing more than the MCI calls dealt with previously. The PlaySound function, which handles wave files, adds a bit of code to call sndPlaySound if the MCI calls fail. You might not want this capability—I didn't use it in the Multimedia Workshop application, for example. If you undefine the PLAYSOUND macro up at the top of DEMO7.CPP, it won't be enabled.

Finally, the PlayFlick function uses the MCI calls I've discussed, plus an additional one that invokes the MCI_DGV_STATUS_HWND MCI command. This rather mysterious-sounding incantation causes the

mciSendCommand to fetch the HWND window handle of a Video for Windows display window. In fact, strategically placed—as it is in the PlayFlick function—it will fetch it just before the window actually appears. You can do anything you would do to a conventional window with this HWND, including moving it, resizing it, and adding controls to it. In this case DEMO7 calls CentreWindow to position it in the center of your screen.

There's a more complete discussion of the various ancillary functions the MCI interface can perform in *Windows Multimedia Programming*, and a still more complete reference in the Windows Multimedia Development Kit and Video for Windows packages, both from Microsoft. Having said this, be warned that as of this writing the latter two sources have some pretty insidious errors in them.

Multimedia without multimedia— the PLAY.DLL library

Writing a dynamic link library would seem to be a rather complex and esoteric undertaking, and one worth staying away from. In fact, this isn't really the case. Writing a DLL is only slightly more involved than writing a conventional Windows application in C. At least, it can be. There are a few shortcuts to be observed if you're new to the craft.

The first thing that can make writing a DLL in Borland C++ obscenely complicated is setting up all the compiler options correctly. Simply clicking on the DLL option in the Application Options dialog won't begin to do it. To this end, you should keep in mind one of the unspoken-of axioms of writing software—if you can't find a solution that works yourself, steal one.

In the case of writing a DLL of your own, you can begin with all the compiler options correctly set up by taking a copy of a working project file for a DLL, deleting all the entries in it, and adding your own items. The PLAY.PRJ file, as used to compile the PLAY.DLL library to be discussed in this section, is a perfect example.

To this end, it's also worth noting that the skeletal structure of a C language source file for a dynamic link library is also a bit more complex than would be the case for a Windows application. You can use the PLAY.CPP file to be discussed in a moment as the basis of your own DLLs.

This section doesn't require that you go to these lengths, however, as the complete source code and a working project file for a dynamic link library are included on the companion disk for this book. The completed DLL is also included, as is an import library to link to it. Import libraries were discussed earlier in this book—they allow an application to call the functions in a DLL as if they were native to Windows.

The PLAY.DLL library will give you access to a few basic Windows multimedia functions even if you don't own a copy of the Multimedia Development Kit. While it's exceedingly limited compared to what the Windows multimedia extensions are capable of, it will allow you to implement the functionality discussed thus far in this chapter. Specifically, you'll be able to play wave, MIDI, and AVI files.

The next section of this chapter will present an application that performs the same tasks as DEMO7, but does so entirely through the PLAY.DLL library.

Once you understand how PLAY.DLL works you'll be able to use it to add multimedia features to your own applications. Note the copyright restrictions for PLAY.DLL—or rather, the lack of them—as discussed in the disclaimer at the end of this book.

The PLAY.DLL library is also a great deal easier to use than are the MCI calls from the previous section. Finally, once you've had a look at how it's put together you'll be able to write your own dynamic link libraries.

Once again, you won't be able to compile PLAY.DLL from the PLAY.CPP source code unless you have the Microsoft Multimedia Development Kit and Video for Windows packages. However, because the compiled DLL file is included with this book, you don't really have to.

The complete source code for PLAY.CPP is listed in Fig. 5-6. In addition to PLAY.CPP, you'll need PLAY.H, which is illustrated in Fig. 5-7. There's no PLAY.RC, as PLAY.DLL requires no resources. Suitable DEF and project files for PLAY.DLL are included with the source code on the companion disk for this book.

The PLAY.CPP source code.

Figure 5-6

```
/*
    PLAY - main module
    Copyright (c) 1993 Alchemy Mindworks Inc.
*/

#include <windows.h>
#include <string.h>
#include <dir.h>
#include <mmsystem.h>
#include <mciavi.h>
#include <digitalv.h>
#include "play.h"

int PlayMusic(LPSTR path,HWND hwnd,LPSTR message,WORD flags);
int PlaySound(LPSTR path,HWND hwnd,LPSTR message,WORD flags);
int PlayFlick(LPSTR path,HWND hwnd,LPSTR message,WORD flags);
void CentreWindow(HWND hwnd);

#pragma argsused
extern "C" int FAR PASCAL LibMain(HANDLE hInstance,WORD wDataSeg,
    WORD wHeapSize, LPSTR lpCmdLine)
{
    if (wHeapSize > 0) UnlockData(0);
        return (1);
}

#pragma argsused
extern "C" int FAR PASCAL _export WEP(int nParameter)
{
    return (1);
}

#pragma argsused
extern "C" int FAR PASCAL _export PLAYTrapMessage(HWND hwnd,
    WORD message,WORD wParam,DWORD lParam)
{
    if(message==MM_MCINOTIFY) {
        mciSendCommand(LOWORD(lParam),MCI_CLOSE,MCI_WAIT,NULL);
        return(TRUE);
    }
    return(FALSE);
}
```

5-6 *Continued*

```
#pragma argsused
extern "C" int FAR PASCAL _export PLAYStop(HWND hwnd,int id,WORD flags)
{
    MCI_GENERIC_PARMS mcigen;
        int r=FALSE;

    if(id != PLF_ERROR) {
        mcigen.dwCallback=hwnd;
        mciSendCommand(id,MCI_STOP,MCI_NOTIFY |
          MCI_WAIT,(DWORD)(LPVOID)&mcigen);
        r=TRUE;
    }
    if(flags & PLF_SNDPLAYSOUND) sndPlaySound(NULL,SND_SYNC);
    return(r);
}

extern "C" int FAR PASCAL _export PLAYPlayEffect(HWND hwnd,
    LPSTR path,LPSTR message,WORD flags)
{
    char s[STRINGSIZE+1],b[16];

    lstrcpy(s,path);
    fnsplit(s,NULL,NULL,NULL,b);

    if(flags & PLF_WAVE) return(PlaySound(path,hwnd,message,flags));
    if(flags & PLF_MIDI) return(PlayMusic(path,hwnd,message,flags));
    if(flags & PLF_AVI) return(PlayFlick(path,hwnd,message,flags));

    if(!stricmp(b,".WAV")) return(PlaySound(path,hwnd,message,flags));
    if(!stricmp(b,".MID")) return(PlayMusic(path,hwnd,message,flags));
    if(!stricmp(b,".AVI")) return(PlayFlick(path,hwnd,message,flags));

    else return(PLF_ERROR);
}

extern "C" int FAR PASCAL _export PLAYPlaySound(LPSTR path)
{
    return(sndPlaySound(path,SND_ASYNC | SND_NODEFAULT));
}

extern "C" int FAR PASCAL _export PLAYPlayMemorySound(LPSTR sound)
{
    return(sndPlaySound(sound,SND_ASYNC | SND_NODEFAULT | SND_MEMORY));
}

extern "C" int FAR PASCAL _export PLAYGetVersion(void)
{
        return((VERSION << 8) | SUBVERSION);
}

extern "C" LPSTR FAR PASCAL _export PLAYGetCopyright(void)
```

```
{
    return("PLAY.DLL -- Copyright \251 1993 Alchemy Mindworks Inc.");
}

#pragma argsused
int PlayMusic(LPSTR path,HWND hwnd,LPSTR message,WORD flags)
{
    MCI_OPEN_PARMS mciOpen;
    MCI_PLAY_PARMS mciPlay;
    unsigned long rtrn;
    int id=PLF_ERROR;

    mciOpen.wDeviceID=NULL;
    mciOpen.lpstrDeviceType="sequencer";
    mciOpen.lpstrElementName=path;
    if((rtrn=mciSendCommand(NULL,MCI_OPEN,MCI_OPEN_TYPE |
      MCI_OPEN_ELEMENT,(DWORD)(LPVOID)&mciOpen)) != 0L) {
        mciGetErrorString(rtrn,message,STRINGSIZE);
        return(PLF_ERROR);
    }

    id=mciOpen.wDeviceID;

    mciPlay.dwCallback=hwnd;
    if((rtrn=mciSendCommand(id,MCI_PLAY,MCI_NOTIFY,
      (DWORD)(LPVOID)&mciPlay)) != 0L) {
        mciSendCommand(id,MCI_CLOSE,0,NULL);
        mciGetErrorString(rtrn,message,STRINGSIZE);
        return(PLF_ERROR);
    }

    return(id);
}

#pragma argsused
int PlaySound(LPSTR path,HWND hwnd,LPSTR message,WORD flags)
{
    MCI_OPEN_PARMS mciopen;
    MCI_PLAY_PARMS mciplay;
    DWORD rtrn;
    int id=PLF_ERROR;

    mciopen.lpstrDeviceType="waveaudio";
    mciopen.lpstrElementName=path;
    if((rtrn=mciSendCommand(0,MCI_OPEN,MCI_OPEN_TYPE |
      MCI_OPEN_ELEMENT,(DWORD)(LPVOID)&mciopen)) != 0L) {
        mciGetErrorString(rtrn,message,STRINGSIZE);
        return(PLF_ERROR);
    }

    id=mciopen.wDeviceID;

    mciplay.dwCallback=(DWORD)hwnd;
```

5-6 *Continued*

```
    if((rtrn=mciSendCommand(id,MCI_PLAY,MCI_NOTIFY,
      (DWORD)(LPVOID)&mciplay)) != 0L) {
        mciSendCommand(id,MCI_CLOSE,0,NULL);

        if(flags & PLF_SNDPLAYSOUND) {
            if(sndPlaySound(path,SND_ASYNC ¦ SND_NODEFAULT)) {
                message[0]=0;
                return(PLF_ERROR);
            }
        }

        mciGetErrorString(rtrn,message,STRINGSIZE);
        return(PLF_ERROR);
    }

    return(id);
}

#pragma argsused
int PlayFlick(LPSTR path,HWND hwnd,LPSTR message,WORD flags)
{
    MCI_DGV_OPEN_PARMS mciopen;
    MCI_DGV_PLAY_PARMS mciplay;
    MCI_DGV_STATUS_PARMS mcistat;
    DWORD rtrn;
    int id=PLF_ERROR;

    mciopen.lpstrDeviceType="avivideo";
    mciopen.lpstrElementName=path;
    if((rtrn=mciSendCommand(0,MCI_OPEN,MCI_OPEN_TYPE ¦
      MCI_OPEN_ELEMENT,(DWORD)(LPVOID)&mciopen)) != 0L) {
        mciGetErrorString(rtrn,message,STRINGSIZE);
        return(PLF_ERROR);
    }

    id=mciopen.wDeviceID;

    if(flags & PLF_CENTRE) {
        mcistat.dwItem=MCI_DGV_STATUS_HWND;
        if((rtrn=mciSendCommand(id,MCI_STATUS,MCI_STATUS_ITEM,
          (DWORD)(LPVOID)&mcistat)) == 0)
            CentreWindow((HWND)mcistat.dwReturn);
    }

    mciplay.dwCallback=(DWORD)hwnd;
    if((rtrn=mciSendCommand(id,MCI_PLAY,MCI_NOTIFY,
      (DWORD)(LPVOID)&mciplay)) != 0L) {
        mciSendCommand(id,MCI_CLOSE,0,NULL);
        mciGetErrorString(rtrn,message,STRINGSIZE);
        return(PLF_ERROR);
    }
```

```
        return(id);
}

void CentreWindow(HWND hwnd)
{
    RECT rect;
    unsigned int x,y;

    GetWindowRect(hwnd,&rect);
    x=(GetSystemMetrics(SM_CXSCREEN)-(rect.right-rect.left))/2;
    y=(GetSystemMetrics(SM_CYSCREEN)-(rect.bottom-rect.top))/2;
    SetWindowPos(hwnd,NULL,x,y,rect.right-rect.left,rect.bottom-rect.top,
      SWP_NOSIZE);
}
```

The PLAY.H file.

Figure 5-7

```
/*
    IFMT defines
*/

/* defines */
#define    APPLICATION       "PLAY$DLL"
#define    VERSION           1
#define    SUBVERSION        0

#define    STRINGSIZE        128

#define    PLF_WAVE          0x0001
#define    PLF_MIDI          0x0002
#define    PLF_AVI           0x0004
#define    PLF_CENTRE        0x0008
#define    PLF_SNDPLAYSOUND  0x0010
#define    PLF_ERROR         -1
#define    PLF_NORMAL        (PLF_SNDPLAYSOUND | PLF_CENTRE)

#ifndef max
#define max(a,b)            (((a)>(b))?(a):(b))
#endif
#ifndef min
#define min(a,b)            (((a)<(b))?(a):(b))
#endif

extern "C" int FAR PASCAL _export PLAYTrapMessage(HWND hwnd,
    WORD message,WORD wParam,DWORD lParam);
extern "C" int FAR PASCAL _export PLAYStop(HWND hwnd,int id,WORD flags);
extern "C" int FAR PASCAL _export PLAYPlayEffect(HWND hwnd,LPSTR path,
    LPSTR message,WORD flags);
extern "C" int FAR PASCAL _export PLAYPlaySound(LPSTR path);
extern "C" int FAR PASCAL _export PLAYPlayMemorySound(LPSTR sound);
extern "C" int FAR PASCAL _export PLAYGetVersion(void);
extern "C" LPSTR FAR PASCAL _export PLAYGetCopyright(void);
```

There are a number of basic considerations for creating a dynamic link library. As was touched on earlier in this book when the problem of addressing global data from within a function called from a DLL was encountered, a dynamic link library has its own local data segment but no private stack. For this reason, you should always use far pointers when you're working with data in a DLL, so that the data segment involved will be explicitly referenced in every pointer. For this reason, a DLL should always be compiled using the large memory model.

An import library, PLAY.LIB, is also included with the companion disk for this book. You should add it to the project of any application that will call functions from PLAY.DLL. If you have cause to recompile PLAY.DLL, you should also rebuild its import library. This is handled with the Import Library application included with Borland C++ for Windows. Open the File Select dialog from the File menu of Import Library. Select the DLL file you want to create an import library for and click on OK. The procedure is typically so fast as to make you wonder if anything really happened.

There are two functions that must be declared in a DLL. They are LibMain and WEP. They're called when a DLL is first linked and initialized, and when it shuts down, respectively. They can be found at the top of PLAY.CPP back in Fig. 5-6. This is usually what they look like in all dynamic link libraries.

The rest of PLAY.CPP will probably look reassuringly familiar—it consists of functions lifted bodily from DEMO7 and some interface code. The functions that are declared with the rather wordy prefix extern "C" int FAR PASCAL _export and extern "C" LPSTR FAR PASCAL _export are the ones that are externally callable, that is, they're what your applications will call to use the functions of PLAY.DLL. They all start with PLAY. Here's a list of the callable functions offered by PLAY.DLL:

✳ **PLAYTrapMessage** This call should be placed at the beginning of any message handler that makes calls to PLAY.DLL. It takes care of MM_MCINOTIFY messages sent back from terminating wave, MIDI, and AVI files. Its arguments are:

HWND hwnd The HWND of the window it's called from.

WORD _message_ The message to be processed.

WORD _wParam_ The _wParam_ argument of the message.

DWORD _lParam_ The _lParam_ argument of the message.

The return value will be true if the message has been processed and false otherwise.

✳ **PLAYStop** This function stops the current file playing. Its arguments are:

HWND _hwnd_ The HWND of the window it's called from.

int _id_ The ID of the sound to be terminated.

WORD _flags_ Flags, as discussed in a following section.

The return value will be true if the current file has been stopped.

✳ **PLAYPlayEffect** This function plays a wave, MIDI, or AVI file. Its arguments are:

HWND _hwnd_ The HWND of the window it's called from.

LPSTR _path_ The path to the file to be played.

LPSTR _message_ A string to hold text messages. It should be at least STRINGSIZE+1 bytes long, as defined in PLAY.H.

WORD _flags_ Flags, as discussed in a following section.

The return value will be the ID of the device being used to play the file in question, or the constant PLF_ERROR if something's amiss.

✳ **PLAYPlaySound** This function will play a wave file through sndPlaySound. Its argument is:

LPSTR _path_ The path to the file to be played.

The return value will be true if the sound has been played, and false otherwise.

✳ **PLAYMemoryPlaySound** This function will play a wave file in memory through sndPlaySound. Its argument is:

LPSTR *sound* A far pointer to the loaded and locked buffer that contains the sound to be played.

The return value will be true if the sound has been played, and false otherwise.

✳ **PLAYGetVersion** This function will return a word with the version number of the PLAY.DLL library in its high-order byte and the subversion number in its low-order byte. You should call this function from the WinMain function of your application to make sure PLAY.DLL is loaded.

✳ **PLAYGetCopyright** This function returns a string that defines the copyright of PLAY.DLL. This should be displayed in the About box of any application that uses PLAY.DLL.

The flags and constants associated with PLAY.DLL are as follows:

✳ **PLF_WAVE** If this flag is passed in the flags argument to PLAYPlayEffect, the file passed as the path argument will be assumed to be a wave file, whatever its extension is.

✳ **PLF_MIDI** If this flag is passed in the flags argument to PLAYPlayEffect, the file passed as the path argument will be assumed to be a MIDI file, whatever its extension is.

✳ **PLF_AVI** If this flag is passed in the flags argument to PLAYPlayEffect, the file passed as the path argument will be assumed to be an AVI file, whatever its extension is.

✳ **PLF_CENTER** If this flag is passed in the flags argument to PLAYPlayEffect and an AVI file is played, the window it appears in will be centered.

✳ **PLF_SNDPLAYSOUND** If this flag is passed in the flags argument to PLAYPlayEffect and a wave file is played, the sndPlaySound function will be used if the MCI interface fails. This will allow short sounds to be played through the Windows speaker driver, however badly. This flag should be used with PLAYStop if it was used with PLAYPlayEffect.

✳ **PLF_NORMAL** This is a set of flags that will usually be appropriate for passing to PLAYPlayEffect. It consists of PLF_SNDPLAYSOUND and PLF_CENTER.

✳ **PLF_ERROR** This value will be returned by PLAYPlayEffect if the request to play a file was not successful. An error message will be stored in the buffer pointed to by its message argument in this case.

Multiple flags can be ORed together. The prototypes for the external functions and the definitions for the previous flags are stored in PLAY.H. You should include this in the C language source code files for any application that makes calls to the functions in PLAY.DLL.

Finally, you must be sure to have the PLAY.DLL file itself where Windows can find it—either in your \WINDOWS\SYSTEM subdirectory, somewhere along your DOS path, or in the same subdirectory as the EXE files for your application.

⇨ Calling PLAY.DLL

The DEMO8 application is both cosmetically and functionally identical to DEMO7. It works a bit differently, though, in that it uses PLAY.DLL to do all the work formerly accomplished by the PlayEffect function and the things it called. The DEMO8 application itself uses nothing that isn't part of Borland C++ for Windows, with the exception of PLAY.DLL and PLAY.LIB.

The complete source code for DEMO8.CPP is listed in Fig. 5-8. In addition to DEMO8.CPP, you'll need DEMO8.RC, as shown in Fig. 5-9. Suitable DEF and project files for DEMO8 are included with the source code on the companion disk for this book. Note that the project file includes a reference to PLAY.LIB, the import library for PLAY.DLL.

The DEMO8.CPP source code.

Figure 5-8

```
/*
    Dialog Demo 8
    Copyright (c) 1993 Alchemy Mindworks Inc.
*/
```

5-8 *Continued*

```c
#include <windows.h>
#include <stdio.h>
#include <stdlib.h>
#include <ctype.h>
#include <alloc.h>
#include <string.h>
#include <dos.h>
#include <time.h>
#include <dir.h>
#include <errno.h>
#include <commdlg.h>
#include "ctl3d.h"
#include "draw3d.h"
#include "play.h"

#define say(s)      MessageBox(NULL,s,"Yo...",MB_OK | MB_ICONSTOP);
#define saynumber(f,s)   {char b[128]; sprintf((LPSTR)b,(LPSTR)f,s); \
     MessageBox(NULL,b,"Debug Message",MB_OK | MB_ICONSTOP); }

#ifndef IDHELP
#define IDHELP          998
#endif

#define MESSAGE_STRING   101        /* message box object */

#define MAIN_LIST        401
#define MAIN_PATH        402
#define MAIN_PLAY        101
#define MAIN_STOP        102

#define MATN_WAVE        201
#define MAIN_MIDI        202
#define MAIN_AVI         203

#define FILE_PLAY        101
#define FILE_STOP        102
#define FILE_EXIT        199

#define HELPM_INDEX      901
#define HELPM_USING      905
#define HELPM_ABOUT      999

#define HELPFILE         "DEMO.HLP"
#define ABOUT_WAVE       "AboutWave"

#define DIALOG_KEY       "DialogDemo"

#define MESSAGE_ABOUT    0
#define MESSAGE_HELP     1
#define MESSAGE_NODISK   2
```

```
#define NOPARAM              0xffff

#define CreateControlFont()     if(ControlFontName[0]) \
              controlfont=CreateFont(16,0,0,0,0,0,0,0,\
              ANSI_CHARSET,OUT_DEFAULT_PRECIS,CLIP_DEFAULT_PRECIS,\
              DEFAULT_QUALITY,DEFAULT_PITCH : FF_DONTCARE,\
              ControlFontName)

#define SetControlFont(hwnd,id) {HWND dlgH;\
              if(controlfont != NULL) {\
                  dlgH=GetDlgItem(hwnd,id);\
                  SendMessage(dlgH,WM_SETFONT,(WORD)controlfont,FALSE);\
              }\
              }

#define DestroyControlFont()    if(controlfont != NULL) \
     DeleteObject(controlfont)

#define CheckOn(item)     SendDlgItemMessage(hwnd,item,BM_SETCHECK,1,0L);
#define CheckOff(item)    SendDlgItemMessage(hwnd,item,BM_SETCHECK,0,0L);
#define ItemOn(item)     { dlgH=GetDlgItem(hwnd,item); EnableWindow(dlgH,TRUE); }
#define ItemOff(item)    { dlgH=GetDlgItem(hwnd,item); EnableWindow(dlgH,FALSE); }
#define IsItemChecked(item)     SendDlgItemMessage(hwnd,item,BM_GETCHECK,0,0L)
#define ItemName(item,string)    { dlgH=GetDlgItem(hwnd,item); \
     SetWindowText(dlgH,(LPSTR)string); }
#define GetItemName(item,string) { dlgH=GetDlgItem(hwnd,item); \
     GetWindowText(dlgH,(LPSTR)string,BIGSTRINGSIZE); }
#define TrapMessage(hwnd,message,wParam,event) \
     TrapMessageHook(hwnd,message,wParam,&event[0],sizeof(event)/sizeof(EVENT))

/* structures */
typedef struct {
    WORD message;
    WORD wParam;
    char path[STRINGSIZE+1];
    } EVENT;

/* prototypes */
DWORD FAR PASCAL SelectProc(HWND hwnd,WORD message,WORD wParam,LONG lParam);
DWORD FAR PASCAL AboutDlgProc(HWND hwnd,WORD message,WORD wParam,LONG lParam);
DWORD FAR PASCAL MessageDlgProc(HWND hwnd,WORD message,WORD wParam,LONG lParam);

void DoMessage(HWND hwnd,LPSTR message);
void SetHelpSize(HWND hwnd);
void DoHelp(HWND hwnd,LPSTR keyword);
void MakeHelpPathName(LPSTR szFileName);
void ResetSelectorList(HWND hwnd);
void CentreWindow(HWND hwnd);
void TrapMessageHook(HWND hwnd,WORD message,
     WORD wParam,EVENT FAR *event,int number);

int testdisk(int n);
```

5-8 *Continued*

```
LPSTR FetchString(unsigned int n);

/* globals*/
char szAppName[]="DialogDemoEight";
char ControlFontName[STRINGSIZE+1]="Arial";

LPSTR messagehook=NULL;
HANDLE hInst;
HFONT controlfont=NULL;

EVENT eventlist[]= {
    WM_COMMAND,IDOK,"C:\\WINDOWS\\CHIMES.WAV",
    WM_COMMAND,MAIN_AVI,"C:\\WINDOWS\\CHIMES.WAV",
    WM_COMMAND,MAIN_WAVE,"C:\\WINDOWS\\TADA.WAV",
    WM_COMMAND,MAIN_MIDI,"C:\\WINDOWS\\DING.WAV",
    WM_INITDIALOG,NOPARAM,"C:\\WINDOWS\\DING.WAV",
    };

#pragma warn -par
int PASCAL WinMain(HANDLE hInstance,HANDLE hPrevInstance,
    LPSTR lpszCmdParam,int nCmdShow)
{
    FARPROC dlgProc;
    int r=0;

    hInst=hInstance;

    PLAYGetVersion();
    Ctl3dRegister(hInstance);
    Ctl3dAutoSubclass(hInstance);

    dlgProc=MakeProcInstance((FARPROC)SelectProc,hInst);
    r=DialogBox(hInst,"MainScreen",NULL,dlgProc);

    FreeProcInstance(dlgProc);

    Ctl3dUnregister(hInstance);

    return(r);
}

DWORD FAR PASCAL SelectProc(HWND hwnd,WORD message,WORD wParam,LONG lParam)
{
    static HFONT hFont;
    FARPROC lpfnDlgProc;
    PAINTSTRUCT ps;
    HMENU hmenu;
    static HICON hIcon;
    char b[STRINGSIZE+1];
    static id;
    HWND dlgH;
```

```
long l;
int i;

TrapMessage(hwnd,message,wParam,eventlist);

if(PLAYTrapMessage(hwnd,message,wParam,lParam)) {
    ItemOff(MAIN_STOP);
    ItemOn(MAIN_PLAY);

    ItemOn(MAIN_WAVE);
    ItemOn(MAIN_MIDI);
    ItemOn(MAIN_AVI);
    ItemOn(MAIN_LIST);

    hmenu=GetMenu(hwnd);
    EnableMenuItem(hmenu,FILE_PLAY,MF_ENABLED);
    EnableMenuItem(hmenu,FILE_STOP,MF_GRAYED);

    id=PLF_ERROR;
}

switch(message) {
    case WM_SYSCOMMAND:
        switch(wParam & 0xfff0) {
            case SC_CLOSE:
                SendMessage(hwnd,WM_COMMAND,FILE_EXIT,0L);
                break;
        }
        break;
    case WM_CTLCOLOR:
        return(Ctl3dCtlColorEx(message,wParam,lParam));
    case WM_INITDIALOG:
        hFont=CreateFont(16,0,0,0,0,0,0,0,ANSI_CHARSET,
            OUT_DEFAULT_PRECIS,CLIP_DEFAULT_PRECIS,
            DEFAULT_QUALITY,DEFAULT_PITCH | FF_DONTCARE,\
            ControlFontName);

        SetHelpSize(hwnd);

        GetProfileString(DIALOG_KEY,"ControlFont",
            ControlFontName,b,STRINGSIZE);
        if(lstrlen(b)) lstrcpy(ControlFontName,b);
        CreateControlFont();

        hIcon=LoadIcon(hInst,szAppName);
        SetClassWord(hwnd,GCW_HICON,(WORD)hIcon);
        CentreWindow(hwnd);
        CheckOn(MAIN_WAVE);
        CheckOn(MAIN_MIDI);
        CheckOn(MAIN_AVI);
        ItemOff(MAIN_STOP);

        ResetSelectorList(hwnd);
```

5-8 *Continued*

```
            id=PLF_ERROR;
            SetControlFont(hwnd,MAIN_WAVE);
            SetControlFont(hwnd,MAIN_MIDI);
            SetControlFont(hwnd,MAIN_AVI);
            SetControlFont(hwnd,MAIN_PATH);
            SetControlFont(hwnd,FILE_PLAY);
            SetControlFont(hwnd,FILE_STOP);
            SetControlFont(hwnd,FILE_EXIT);

        break;
    case WM_PAINT:
        BeginPaint(hwnd,&ps);
        EndPaint(hwnd,&ps);
        break;
    case WM_COMMAND:
        switch(wParam) {
            case HELPM_INDEX:
                MakeHelpPathName(b);
                WinHelp(hwnd,b,HELP_INDEX,NULL);
                break;
            case HELPM_USING:
                WinHelp(hwnd,"",HELP_HELPONHELP,NULL);
                break;
            case HELPM_ABOUT:
                if((lpfnDlgProc=MakeProcInstance((FARPROC)
                  AboutDlgProc,hInst)) != NULL) {
                    DialogBox(hInst,"AboutBox",hwnd,lpfnDlgProc);
                    FreeProcInstance(lpfnDlgProc);
                }
                break;
            case MAIN_LIST:
                switch(HIWORD(lParam)) {
                    case LBN_DBLCLK:
                        if(DlgDirSelect(hwnd,b,MAIN_LIST)) {
                            i=lstrlen(b);
                            if(b[i-1]=='\\') {
                                b[i-1]=0;
                                chdir(b);
                            }
                            else {
                                if(!testdisk(b[0]-'A'))
                                    setdisk(toupper(b[0])-'A');
                                else DoMessage(hwnd,FetchString
                                    (MESSAGE_NODISK));
                            }
                            ResetSelectorList(hwnd);
                        }
                        else SendMessage(hwnd,WM_COMMAND,FILE_PLAY,OL);
                        break;
                }
                break;
```

```
            case FILE_PLAY:
                if((l=SendDlgItemMessage(hwnd,
                  MAIN_LIST,LB_GETCURSEL,0,0L)) != LB_ERR) {
                    SendDlgItemMessage(hwnd,MAIN_LIST,LB_GETTEXT,
                      (unsigned int)l,(long)b);
                    if(b[0]!='[') {
                        if((id=PLAYPlayEffect(hwnd,b,
                          b,PLF_NORMAL)) == PLF_ERROR) {
                            if(b[0]) DoMessage(hwnd,b);
                        }
                        else {
                            ItemOn(MAIN_STOP);
                            ItemOff(MAIN_PLAY);

                            ItemOff(MAIN_WAVE);
                            ItemOff(MAIN_MIDI);
                            ItemOff(MAIN_AVI);
                            ItemOff(MAIN_LIST);

                            hmenu=GetMenu(hwnd);
                            EnableMenuItem(hmenu,FILE_PLAY,MF_GRAYED);
                            EnableMenuItem(hmenu,FILE_STOP,MF_ENABLED);
                        }
                    }
                }
                break;
            case FILE_STOP:
                PLAYStop(hwnd,id,PLF_NORMAL);
                break;
            case FILE_EXIT:
                SendMessage(hwnd,WM_COMMAND,FILE_STOP,0L);
                if(hFont != NULL) DeleteObject(hFont);
                MakeHelpPathName(b);
                WinHelp(hwnd,b,HELP_QUIT,NULL);

                FreeResource(hIcon);
                DestroyControlFont();
                PostQuitMessage(0);
                break;
            case MAIN_AVI:
            case MAIN_WAVE:
            case MAIN_MIDI:
                if(IsItemChecked(wParam)) {
                    CheckOff(wParam);
                }
                else {
                    CheckOn(wParam);
                }
                ResetSelectorList(hwnd);
                break;
        }
    break;
}
```

5-8 *Continued*

```
    return(FALSE);
}

void DoMessage(HWND hwnd,LPSTR message)
{
    FARPROC lpfnDlgProc;

    messagehook=message;

    if((lpfnDlgProc=MakeProcInstance((FARPROC)MessageDlgProc,hInst)) != NULL) {
        DialogBox(hInst,"MessageBox",hwnd,lpfnDlgProc);
        FreeProcInstance(lpfnDlgProc);
    }
}

DWORD FAR PASCAL MessageDlgProc(HWND hwnd,WORD message,WORD wParam,LONG lParam)
{
    HWND dlgH;

    TrapMessage(hwnd,message,wParam,eventlist);

    switch(message) {
        case WM_INITDIALOG:
            ItemName(MESSAGE_STRING,messagehook);
            CentreWindow(hwnd);
            SetControlFont(hwnd,MESSAGE_STRING);
            SetControlFont(hwnd,IDOK);
            return(FALSE);
        case WM_CTLCOLOR:
            return(Ctl3dCtlColorEx(message,wParam,lParam));
        case WM_COMMAND:
            switch(wParam) {
                case IDOK:
                    EndDialog(hwnd,wParam);
                    return(FALSE);
            }
            break;
    }

    return(FALSE);
}

DWORD FAR PASCAL AboutDlgProc(HWND hwnd,WORD message,WORD wParam,LONG lParam)
{
    static GLOBALHANDLE handle;
    static LPSTR p;
    HWND dlgH;
    char b[STRINGSIZE*3+1];
    int i;

    TrapMessage(hwnd,message,wParam,eventlist);
```

```
        switch(message) {
            case WM_INITDIALOG:
                if((handle=LoadResource(hInst,FindResource(hInst,
                    ABOUT_WAVE,RT_RCDATA))) != NULL) {
                    if((p=(LPSTR)LockResource(handle))!=NULL)
                        PLAYPlayMemorySound(p);
                }
                i=PLAYGetVersion();
                wsprintf(b,"%s\n\n%s\nPLAY.DLL version %u.%u",
                    (LPSTR)FetchString(MESSAGE_ABOUT),
                    (LPSTR)PLAYGetCopyright(),
                    HIBYTE(i),LOBYTE(i));

                ItemName(MESSAGE_STRING,b);
                CentreWindow(hwnd);
                SetControlFont(hwnd,MESSAGE_STRING);
                SetControlFont(hwnd,IDOK);
                return(FALSE);
            case WM_CTLCOLOR:
                return(Ctl3dCtlColorEx(message,wParam,lParam));
            case WM_COMMAND:
                switch(wParam) {
                    case IDOK:
                        if(handle != NULL) {
                            PLAYStop(hwnd,PLF_ERROR,PLF_SNDPLAYSOUND);
                            if(p != NULL) UnlockResource(handle);
                            FreeResource(handle);
                        }
                        EndDialog(hwnd,wParam);
                        return(FALSE);
                }
                break;
        }

    return(FALSE);
}

void CentreWindow(HWND hwnd)
{
    RECT rect;
    unsigned int x,y;

    GetWindowRect(hwnd,&rect);
    x=(GetSystemMetrics(SM_CXSCREEN)-(rect.right-rect.left))/2;
    y=(GetSystemMetrics(SM_CYSCREEN)-(rect.bottom-rect.top))/2;
    SetWindowPos(hwnd,NULL,x,y,rect.right-rect.left,rect.bottom-rect.top,
        SWP_NOSIZE);
}

LPSTR FetchString(unsigned int n)
{
    static char b[257];
```

5-8 *Continued*

```
    if(!LoadString(hInst,n,b,256))
        lstrcpy(b,"String table error - this application may be damaged");
    return(b);
}

void SetHelpSize(HWND hwnd)
{
    HELPWININFO helpinfo;
    char b[145];

    memset((char *)&helpinfo,0,sizeof(HELPWININFO));
    helpinfo.wStructSize=sizeof(HELPWININFO);
    helpinfo.x=10;
    helpinfo.y=10;
    helpinfo.dx=512;
    helpinfo.dy=1004;

    MakeHelpPathName(b);
    WinHelp(hwnd,b,HELP_SETWINPOS,(DWORD)&helpinfo);
}

void DoHelp(HWND hwnd,LPSTR keyword)
{
    char b[145];

    MakeHelpPathName(b);
    WinHelp(hwnd,b,HELP_KEY,(DWORD)keyword);
}

void MakeHelpPathName(LPSTR szFileName)
{
    LPSTR pcFileName;
    int nFileNameLen;

    nFileNameLen = GetModuleFileName(hInst,szFileName,144);
    pcFileName = szFileName+nFileNameLen;

    while(pcFileName > szFileName) {
        if(*pcFileName == '\\' || *pcFileName == ':') {
            *(++pcFileName) = '\0';
            break;
        }
        nFileNameLen--;
        pcFileName--;
    }

    if((nFileNameLen+13) < 144) lstrcat(szFileName,HELPFILE);
    else lstrcat(szFileName, "?");
}

void ResetSelectorList(HWND hwnd)
```

```
{
    HWND dlgH;
    HCURSOR hSaveCursor,hHourGlass;
    char b[STRINGSIZE+1];

    hHourGlass=LoadCursor(NULL,IDC_WAIT);
    hSaveCursor=SetCursor(hHourGlass);

    dlgH=GetDlgItem(hwnd,MAIN_LIST);
    SendDlgItemMessage(hwnd,MAIN_LIST,LB_RESETCONTENT,0,0L);
    SendMessage(dlgH,WM_SETREDRAW,FALSE,0L);

    if(IsItemChecked(MAIN_WAVE)) {
        SendDlgItemMessage(hwnd,MAIN_LIST,LB_DIR,0x0000,(long )"*.WAV");
    }
    if(IsItemChecked(MAIN_MIDI)) {
        SendDlgItemMessage(hwnd,MAIN_LIST,LB_DIR,0x0000,(long )"*.MID");
    }
    if(IsItemChecked(MAIN_AVI)) {
        SendDlgItemMessage(hwnd,MAIN_LIST,LB_DIR,0x0000,(long )"*.AVI");
    }

    SendDlgItemMessage(hwnd,MAIN_LIST,LB_DIR,0xc010,(long )"*.*");

    SendDlgItemMessage(hwnd,MAIN_LIST,LB_SETCURSEL,0,0L);
    SendDlgItemMessage(hwnd,MAIN_LIST,LB_GETTEXT,0,(long)b);

    SendMessage(dlgH,WM_SETREDRAW,TRUE,0L);

    getcwd(b,STRINGSIZE);
    strlwr(b);
    ItemName(MAIN_PATH,b);

    SetCursor(hSaveCursor);
}

int testdisk(int n)
{
    FILE *fp;
    char b[32];
    int r;

    SetErrorMode(1);
    sprintf(b,"%c:\\TEMP.DAT",n+'A');
    if((fp=fopen(b,"r")) != NULL) fclose(fp);

    if(_doserrno==ENOPATH) r=1;
    else r=0;

    SetErrorMode(0);
    return(r);
}
```

5-8 *Continued*

```
void TrapMessageHook(HWND hwnd,WORD message,
    WORD wParam,EVENT FAR *event,int number)
{
    int i=0;

    for(i=0;i<number;++i) {
        if(event[i].message==message) {
            if(event[i].wParam==NOPARAM || event[i].wParam==wParam) {
                PLAYPlaySound(event[i].path);
                break;
            }

        }
    }
}
```

Figure 5-9   *The DEMO8.RC resource script.*

```
MainScreen DIALOG 29, 28, 256, 180
STYLE WS_POPUP | WS_CAPTION | WS_SYSMENU | WS_MINIMIZEBOX
CAPTION "Dialog Demo Eight"
MENU MainMenu
BEGIN
    CONTROL "", 401, "LISTBOX", LBS_STANDARD | LBS_MULTICOLUMN |
      WS_CHILD | WS_VISIBLE, 8, 28, 240, 100
    CONTROL "", -1, "static", SS_BLACKFRAME | WS_CHILD |
      WS_VISIBLE, 4, 8, 248, 136
    CHECKBOX "Wave files", 201, 8, 128, 56, 12, WS_CHILD |
      WS_VISIBLE | WS_TABSTOP
    CHECKBOX "MIDI files", 202, 100, 128, 56, 12, WS_CHILD |
      WS_VISIBLE | WS_TABSTOP
    CHECKBOX "AVI files", 203, 192, 128, 56, 12, WS_CHILD |
      WS_VISIBLE | WS_TABSTOP
    PUSHBUTTON "Play", 101, 128, 152, 36, 20, WS_CHILD |
      WS_VISIBLE | WS_TABSTOP
    DEFPUSHBUTTON "Quit", 199, 216, 152, 36, 20, WS_CHILD |
      WS_VISIBLE | WS_TABSTOP
    PUSHBUTTON "Stop", 102, 172, 152, 36, 20, WS_CHILD |
      WS_VISIBLE | WS_TABSTOP
    LTEXT "", 402, 8, 12, 240, 10, WS_CHILD | WS_VISIBLE | WS_GROUP
END

AboutBox DIALOG 72, 72, 220, 128
STYLE WS_POPUP | WS_CAPTION
CAPTION "About"
BEGIN
    CTEXT "", 101, 16, 16, 188, 72, WS_CHILD | WS_VISIBLE | WS_GROUP
    DEFPUSHBUTTON "OK", IDOK, 96, 104, 28, 16, WS_CHILD | WS_VISIBLE | WS_TABSTOP
    CONTROL "", -1, "static", SS_BLACKFRAME | WS_CHILD | WS_VISIBLE, 8, 8, 204, 88
END
```

```
MainMenu MENU
BEGIN
    POPUP "File"
    BEGIN
        MENUITEM "&Play", 101
        MENUITEM "&Stop", 102, GRAYED
        MENUITEM SEPARATOR
        MENUITEM "E&xit", 199
    END

    POPUP "&Help"
    BEGIN
        MENUITEM "&Index", 901
        MENUITEM "&Using help", 905
        MENUITEM SEPARATOR
        MENUITEM "&About...", 999
    END

END


STRINGTABLE
BEGIN
    0,"Dialog Demo Eight\nCopyright \251 1993 Alchemy Mindworks Inc.\n
        From the book Windows Dialog Construction Set\r
        by Steven William Rimmer\rPublished by Windcrest/McGraw Hill"
    1,"Help"
    2,"That drive is off line. Please check to see that there's a disk in it."
END


DialogDemoEight ICON
BEGIN
    '00 00 01 00 01 00 20 20 10 00 00 00 00 00 E8 02'
    '00 00 16 00 00 00 28 00 00 00 20 00 00 00 40 00'
    '00 00 01 00 04 00 00 00 00 00 80 02 00 00 00 00'
    '00 00 00 00 00 00 00 00 00 00 00 00 00 00 00 00'
    '00 00 00 00 80 00 00 80 00 00 00 80 80 00 80 00'
    '00 00 80 00 80 00 80 80 00 00 80 80 80 00 C0 C0'
    'C0 00 00 00 FF 00 00 FF 00 00 00 FF FF 00 FF 00'
    '00 00 FF 00 FF 00 FF FF 00 00 FF FF FF 00 2A 2A'
    '2A 2A 2A 2A 2A 2A 2A 22 77 70 00 00 00 00 A2 A2'
    'A2 A2 A2 A2 A2 A2 A2 A2 22 70 00 00 00 00 2A 2A'
    '2A 2A 2A 2A 2A 2A AA AA A2 70 00 00 00 00 A2 A2'
    'A2 A2 AA AA AA AA B2 AA AA 77 77 77 77 00 2A 2A'
    'AA AA 2A 2A AA 2A AA A9 19 19 19 19 17 77 AA A2'
    'A2 AA AB AB AB AA 91 91 91 91 91 91 91 97 2A AA'
    'BA BA 2A AA A9 19 19 19 19 99 99 99 99 19 AB AB'
    'A2 AA AA 11 11 91 99 99 99 90 00 00 09 99 BA BA'
    'AA A1 01 11 19 19 19 19 90 00 00 00 00 09 AA A2'
    '00 10 10 11 11 91 91 00 00 00 00 70 00 00 2A 00'
    '00 00 01 01 11 17 77 00 00 00 09 70 00 00 A2 22'
    '22 22 22 22 22 22 22 27 77 77 70 09 70 00 00 2A 2A'
    '2A 2A AA AA AA AA 22 22 22 77 09 77 00 00 A2 AA'
    'AA AA A2 AA AA AA A2 A2 A2 27 79 17 70 00 2A AA'
END
```

5-9 *Continued*

```
    'AA 2A 22 22 2A 2A AA AA AA 2A 79 91 77 00 A2 A2'
    'A2 22 70 70 22 A2 A2 AB A2 A2 00 99 17 77 2A 2A'
    '22 87 07 07 02 2A 2A AA AA 27 00 09 91 91 A2 A2'
    'F8 88 77 70 72 A2 AB AB AB A0 00 00 99 99 2A 22'
    '8F 88 00 77 07 2A 2A AA AA 70 00 00 00 00 A2 28'
    'F8 F0 00 08 70 22 22 A2 A2 00 00 00 00 00 2A 2F'
    '8F 80 00 07 07 2A 2A AA A7 00 00 00 00 00 A7 28'
    'F8 FF 00 88 82 22 A2 A2 A0 00 00 00 00 00 22 7F'
    '8F FF FF 8F 82 2A 2A 2A 70 00 00 00 00 00 A7 0F'
    'FF FF F8 F8 F2 A2 A2 A2 A0 00 00 00 00 00 A2 70'
    'FF FF 8F 8F 2A 2A 2A 20 00 00 00 00 00 00 A7 07'
    'FF FF F8 F8 22 A2 A2 00 00 00 00 00 00 00 A2 70'
    '70 FF 8F 22 2A 2A 20 00 00 00 00 00 00 00 AA 07'
    '07 07 02 02 A2 A2 00 00 00 00 00 00 00 00 BA A0'
    '70 70 72 2A 2A 20 00 00 00 00 00 00 00 00 BB AA'
    'A7 A7 AA AA A0 00 00 00 00 00 00 00 00 00 AA BA'
    'AA AA AA 00 00 00 00 00 00 00 00 00 00 00 AA A0'
    '00 00 00 00 00 00 00 00 00 00 00 00 00 00 00 00'
    '01 FF 00 00 01 FF 00 00 01 FF 00 00 00 03 00 00'
    '00 00 00 00 00 00 00 00 00 00 00 00 00 01 F8 00 00'
    '07 FE 00 00 3F DF 00 00 3F 9F 00 00 01 9F 00 00'
    '00 8F 00 00 00 07 00 00 00 03 00 00 00 C0 00 00'
    '00 E0 00 00 01 F0 00 00 01 FF 00 00 03 FF 00 00'
    '03 FF 00 00 07 FF 00 00 07 FF 00 00 0F FF 00 00'
    '1F FF 00 00 3F FF 00 00 7F FF 00 00 FF FF 00 01'
    'FF FF 00 07 FF FF 00 3F FF FF 1F FF FF FF'
END

MessageBox DIALOG 72, 72, 220, 128
STYLE WS_POPUP ¦ WS_CAPTION
CAPTION "Message"
BEGIN
    CTEXT "", 101, 16, 16, 188, 72, WS_CHILD ¦ WS_VISIBLE ¦ WS_GROUP
    DEFPUSHBUTTON "OK", IDOK, 96, 104, 28, 16, WS_CHILD ¦ WS_VISIBLE ¦ WS_TABSTOP
    CONTROL "", -1, "static", SS_BLACKFRAME ¦ WS_CHILD ¦ WS_VISIBLE, 8, 8, 204, 88
END

AboutWave RCDATA DEMO.WAV
```

The source code for DEMO8 is considerably simpler than that of
DEMO7. The FILE_PLAY case of the WM_COMMAND handler in the
SelectProc function makes a direct call to PLAYPlayEffect in PLAY.DLL.
You can see how to use the PLAYGetVersion and PLAYGetCopyright
functions in the AboutDlgProc function. There's also an example of
using PLAYPlayMemorySound therein—when the About box of DEMO8
opens, a canned sound from the resource list of DEMO8.EXE will play.

Finally, the TrapMessageHook function at the bottom of the DEMO8.CPP listing illustrates PLAYPlaySound at work.

 Applying multimedia

There's a lot you can do with the Windows multimedia extensions— they offer both an interesting tool to add special effects to conventional Windows applications and a resource for creating an entirely new sort of software. Your applications need not be wholly visual any longer, nor wholly static.

From a practical perspective, however, it's worth noting that sound cards and the other hardware required to make multimedia get up and dance aren't quite as common as mice—a situation that's likely to remain so for some time to come.

If your application uses multimedia elements merely to enhance its functions, it won't restrict its market unduly when confronted by users for whom a sound card is right up there with a large, habitually inebriated African elephant as high-priority purchases. On the other hand, boldly applying multimedia tools to software—speaking encyclopedias, interactive explorations of music that actually play, or histories that really show you how things looked back when—offers a really powerful new medium for software authors.

They also offer software authors an almost mandatory introduction to another powerful new medium—that of CD-ROMs. Unless you feel that including a pickup truck with your application to hold all the floppy disks required to install it is a viable packaging option, multimedia software of any scope pretty well always calls for a recourse to CD-ROMs.

Creating custom controls

CHAPTER 6

"Reciprocity works both ways."

In the quest for more interesting Windows controls—or perhaps in the quest for more functional ones—there comes a time when no howling swarm of messages, no insidious manipulation of dialog templates and no clever use of hidden features will coerce Windows into doing what you're after. In these most extreme of circumstances there is but one resort. You'll require a custom control library of your own devising.

Writing Windows custom controls seems as if it should be one of those things only even considered by the bravest and most noble of software authors, those with pure hearts and perfect teeth flashing in the morning sunlight before a great battle. Curiously, while poorly documented, writing custom controls isn't actually all that difficult. At least, it isn't once you know how the whole affair works.

Unlike everything else that's been discussed in this book, writing custom control libraries is largely a work of imagination. They can be as simple or as complex as you like, depending upon your requirements. The most difficult aspect of the craft is in figuring out what sort of custom controls you require, and then how they should behave. This is, by its nature, something a book can't provide for you.

This chapter will discuss a very simple custom control library and an application that exercises it. The AMCC.DLL library generates panic buttons, a hitherto unheard of type of Windows controls. They're illustrated in Fig. 6-1—this is the DEMO9 application, the program to be dealt with over the next few pages.

The buttons in DEMO9 are custom controls. Clicked once they display a green "go" symbol. Clicked again they display a red "stop" symbol. In effect, they behave like check boxes, which is actually what they are to some extent.

The simplest way to write custom controls is to subclass them from existing controls provided by Windows. In this case, the panic button controls are derived from the generic control class button, and the specific control style checkbox. In fact, because these controls

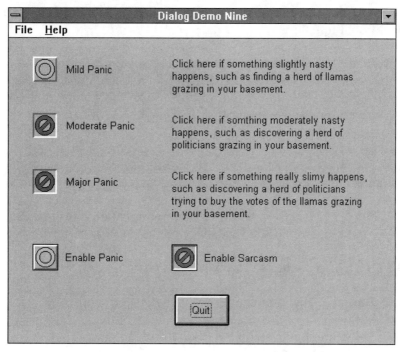

Figure 6-1

The DEMO9 application, replete with panic buttons.

behave like check boxes, even if they don't actually look like them, they can be dealt with using the same techniques you'd use in working with conventional check boxes. The CheckOn, CheckOff and IsItemChecked macros that have turned up throughout this book are applicable to panic button controls as well.

About the only difference between a check box and a panic button from the point of view of an application that uses the latter is the resource script statement required to create a panic button. Here's an example:

```
CONTROL "Mild Panic", 101, "PanicButton", BSS_PANICBUTTON,
16, 12, 17, 17
```

Thus far it hasn't been necessary to deal with resource script statements directly, as Resource Workshop has managed them pretty handily. You can have it work with panic buttons, too, although it's a lot easier to create one panic button RC statement by hand, and then duplicate it as you require. Resource Workshop's management of

custom controls other than its own isn't quite as seamless as its more conventional functions.

As an aside, if you're prepared to complicate your custom control libraries somewhat, you can construct them in such a way as to become compatible with Resource Workshop. This means that you will be able to see your custom controls in Resource Workshop just as you can the custom controls of BWCC.DLL. Creating such a library is by no means a trivial undertaking, however. A discussion of doing so is included in the \BC\DOC directory of the Borland C++ for Windows package, should you be feeling particularly adventurous one day.

The Windows CONTROL resource statement is fairly easy to use. In the foregoing example, the fields work as follows:

CONTROL This defines the object as a custom control.

"Mild Panic" This is the caption for the custom control.

101 This is the resource ID for the control.

"PanicButton" This is the class for the control.

BSS_PANICBUTTON This is the style of the control.

16, 12 This is the location of the control.

17, 17 This is the width and depth of the frame of the control.

There are a few things to note about this. The BSS_PANICBUTTON constant isn't a predefined value for the resource compiler. You must add the line #include amcc.h to any RC file that will be invoking the panic button custom control type. Secondly, it's important that the width and depth values for a panic button control always be seventeen.

You can OR the WM_BORDER constant with the style value for a panic button to provide it with a black border if you like.

You should also include the amcc.h header in the C language source files of applications that use panic button controls, and you should

call PANICGetVersion, a function from the AMCC.DLL library, in the WinMain of your applications. As has been touched on earlier in this book, doing so makes sure that the AMCC.DLL library is available and loaded when your application starts up.

The complete source code for DEMO9.CPP is listed in Fig. 6-2. In addition to DEMO9.CPP, you'll need DEMO9.RC, as shown in Fig. 6-3. Suitable DEF and project files for DEMO9 are included with the source code on the companion disk for this book.

The DEMO9.CPP source code.   Figure 6-2

```
/*
    Dialog Demo 9
    Copyright (c) 1993 Alchemy Mindworks Inc.
*/

#include <windows.h>
#include <stdio.h>
#include <stdlib.h>
#include <ctype.h>
#include <alloc.h>
#include <string.h>
#include <dos.h>
#include <time.h>
#include <dir.h>
#include <errno.h>
#include "amcc.h"

#define say(s)     MessageBox(NULL,s,"Yo...",MB_OK | MB_ICONSTOP);
#define saynumber(f,s)    {char b[128]; sprintf((LPSTR)b,(LPSTR)f,s); \
    MessageBox(NULL,b,"Debug Message",MB_OK | MB_ICONSTOP); }

#define STRINGSIZE         129        /* how big is a string? */

#ifndef IDHELP
#define IDHELP             998
#endif

#define MILDPANIC          101
#define MODERATEPANIC      102
#define SERIOUSPANIC       103
#define ENABLEPANIC        104
#define ENABLESARCASM      105

#define MILDPANIC_TEXT     201
#define MODERATEPANIC_TEXT 202
#define SERIOUSPANIC_TEXT  203

#define MESSAGE_STRING     101        /* message box object */
```

6-2 *Continued*

```
#define FILE_EXIT            199

#define HELPM_INDEX          901
#define HELPM_USING          905
#define HELPM_ABOUT          999

#define HELPFILE             "DEMO.HLP"

#define DIALOG_KEY           "DialogDemo"

#define MESSAGE_ABOUT        0
#define MESSAGE_HELP         1

#define BACKGROUND           RGB(192,192,192)
#define DARKBACKGROUND       RGB(128,128,0)

#define TEXTCOLOUR           RGB(0,0,0)
#define DARKTEXTCOLOUR       RGB(0,0,0)

#define CreateControlFont()      if(ControlFontName[0]) \
                controlfont=CreateFont(16,0,0,0,0,0,0,0,\
                ANSI_CHARSET,OUT_DEFAULT_PRECIS,CLIP_DEFAULT_PRECIS,\
                DEFAULT_QUALITY,DEFAULT_PITCH | FF_DONTCARE,\
                ControlFontName)

#define SetControlFont(hwnd,id) {HWND dlgH;\
                if(controlfont != NULL) {\
                    dlgH=GetDlgItem(hwnd,id);\
                    SendMessage(dlgH,WM_SETFONT,(WORD)controlfont,FALSE);\
                }\
                }

#define DestroyControlFont()     if(controlfont != NULL) \
        DeleteObject(controlfont)

#define CheckOn(item)        SendDlgItemMessage(hwnd,item,BM_SETCHECK,1,0L);
#define CheckOff(item)       SendDlgItemMessage(hwnd,item,BM_SETCHECK,0,0L);
#define ItemOn(item)      { dlgH=GetDlgItem(hwnd,item); EnableWindow(dlgH,TRUE); }
#define ItemOff(item)     { dlgH=GetDlgItem(hwnd,item); EnableWindow(dlgH,FALSE); }
#define IsItemChecked(item)      SendDlgItemMessage(hwnd,item,BM_GETCHECK,0,0L)
#define ItemName(item,string)    { dlgH=GetDlgItem(hwnd,item); \
        SetWindowText(dlgH,(LPSTR)string); }
#define GetItemName(item,string) { dlgH=GetDlgItem(hwnd,item); \
        GetWindowText(dlgH,(LPSTR)string,BIGSTRINGSIZE); }

/* prototypes */
DWORD FAR PASCAL SelectProc(HWND hwnd,WORD message,WORD wParam,LONG lParam);
DWORD FAR PASCAL AboutDlgProc(HWND hwnd,WORD message,WORD wParam,LONG lParam);
DWORD FAR PASCAL MessageDlgProc(HWND hwnd,WORD message,WORD wParam,LONG lParam);

void DoMessage(HWND hwnd,LPSTR message);
```

```
    void SetHelpSize(HWND hwnd);
    void DoHelp(HWND hwnd,LPSTR keyword);
    void MakeHelpPathName(LPSTR szFileName);
    void CentreWindow(HWND hwnd);

    LPSTR FetchString(unsigned int n);

    /* globals*/
    char szAppName[]="DialogDemoNine";
    char ControlFontName[STRINGSIZE+1]="Arial";

    LPSTR messagehook=NULL;
    HANDLE hInst;
    HFONT controlfont=NULL;

    #pragma warn -par
    int PASCAL WinMain(HANDLE hInstance,HANDLE hPrevInstance,
        LPSTR lpszCmdParam,int nCmdShow)
    {
        FARPROC dlgProc;
        int r=0;

        PANICGetVersion();

        hInst=hInstance;

        dlgProc=MakeProcInstance((FARPROC)SelectProc,hInst);
        r=DialogBox(hInst,"MainScreen",NULL,dlgProc);

        FreeProcInstance(dlgProc);

        return(r);
    }

    DWORD FAR PASCAL SelectProc(HWND hwnd,WORD message,WORD wParam,LONG lParam)
    {
        static HBRUSH hBrush;
        static HFONT hFont;
        FARPROC lpfnDlgProc;
        PAINTSTRUCT ps;
        POINT point;
        HWND dlgH;
        static HICON hIcon;
        char b[STRINGSIZE+1];

        switch(message) {
            case WM_SYSCOMMAND:
                switch(wParam & 0xfff0) {
                    case SC_CLOSE:
                        SendMessage(hwnd,WM_COMMAND,FILE_EXIT,OL);
                        break;
                }
                break;
```

6-2 *Continued*

```
case WM_INITDIALOG:
    hBrush=CreateSolidBrush(BACKGROUND);
    hFont=CreateFont(16,0,0,0,0,0,0,0,ANSI_CHARSET,
            OUT_DEFAULT_PRECIS,CLIP_DEFAULT_PRECIS,
            DEFAULT_QUALITY,DEFAULT_PITCH | FF_DONTCARE,\
            ControlFontName);

    SetHelpSize(hwnd);

    GetProfileString(DIALOG_KEY,"ControlFont",
        ControlFontName,b,STRINGSIZE);
    if(lstrlen(b)) lstrcpy(ControlFontName,b);
    CreateControlFont();

    hIcon=LoadIcon(hInst,szAppName);
    SetClassWord(hwnd,GCW_HICON,(WORD)hIcon);
    CentreWindow(hwnd);

    CheckOn(MILDPANIC);
    CheckOn(ENABLEPANIC);

    SetControlFont(hwnd,MILDPANIC);
    SetControlFont(hwnd,MODERATEPANIC);
    SetControlFont(hwnd,SERIOUSPANIC);
    SetControlFont(hwnd,ENABLEPANIC);
    SetControlFont(hwnd,ENABLESARCASM);

    SetControlFont(hwnd,MILDPANIC_TEXT);
    SetControlFont(hwnd,MODERATEPANIC_TEXT);
    SetControlFont(hwnd,SERIOUSPANIC_TEXT);
    SetControlFont(hwnd,FTIF_FXTT);

    break;
case WM_CTLCOLOR:
    if(HIWORD(lParam)==CTLCOLOR_STATIC ||
        HIWORD(lParam)==CTLCOLOR_DLG) {
        SetBkColor(wParam,BACKGROUND);
        SetTextColor(wParam,TEXTCOLOUR);

        ClientToScreen(hwnd,&point);
        UnrealizeObject(hBrush);
        SetBrushOrg(wParam,point.x,point.y);

        return((DWORD)hBrush);

    }
    if(HIWORD(lParam)==CTLCOLOR_BTN) {
        SetBkColor(wParam,BACKGROUND);
        SetTextColor(wParam,TEXTCOLOUR);

        ClientToScreen(hwnd,&point);
```

```
            UnrealizeObject(hBrush);
            SetBrushOrg(wParam,point.x,point.y);

            return((DWORD)hBrush);
        }
        break;
    case WM_PAINT:
        BeginPaint(hwnd,&ps);
        EndPaint(hwnd,&ps);
        break;
    case WM_COMMAND:
        switch(wParam) {
            case HELPM_INDEX:
                MakeHelpPathName(b);
                WinHelp(hwnd,b,HELP_INDEX,NULL);
                break;
            case HELPM_USING:
                WinHelp(hwnd,"",HELP_HELPONHELP,NULL);
                break;
            case HELPM_ABOUT:
                if((lpfnDlgProc=MakeProcInstance((FARPROC)
                  AboutDlgProc,hInst)) != NULL) {
                    DialogBox(hInst,"AboutBox",hwnd,lpfnDlgProc);
                    FreeProcInstance(lpfnDlgProc);
                }
                break;
            case FILE_EXIT:
                if(hBrush != NULL) DeleteObject(hBrush);
                MakeHelpPathName(b);
                WinHelp(hwnd,b,HELP_QUIT,NULL);

                FreeResource(hIcon);
                DestroyControlFont();
                PostQuitMessage(0);
                break;
            case ENABLEPANIC:
                if(IsItemChecked(wParam)) {
                    ItemOn(MILDPANIC);
                    ItemOn(MODERATEPANIC);
                    ItemOn(SERIOUSPANIC);
                }
                else{
                    ItemOff(MILDPANIC);
                    ItemOff(MODERATEPANIC);
                    ItemOff(SERIOUSPANIC);
                }
                break;
            case ENABLESARCASM:
                break;
            default:
                if(IsItemChecked(ENABLESARCASM)) {
                    if(IsItemChecked(wParam))
                        DoMessage(hwnd,FetchString(wParam));
```

6-2 *Continued*

```
                    }
                    break;
            }
        break;
    }
    return(FALSE);
}

void DoMessage(HWND hwnd,LPSTR message)
{
    FARPROC lpfnDlgProc;

    messagehook=message;

    if((lpfnDlgProc=MakeProcInstance((FARPROC)MessageDlgProc,hInst)) != NULL) {
        DialogBox(hInst,"MessageBox",hwnd,lpfnDlgProc);
        FreeProcInstance(lpfnDlgProc);
    }
}

DWORD FAR PASCAL MessageDlgProc(HWND hwnd,WORD message,WORD wParam,LONG lParam)
{
    static HBRUSH hBrush;
    HWND dlgH;
    POINT point;

    switch(message) {
        case WM_INITDIALOG:
            hBrush=CreateSolidBrush(DARKBACKGROUND);
            ItemName(MESSAGE_STRING,messagehook);
            CentreWindow(hwnd);
            SetControlFont(hwnd,MESSAGE_STRING);
            SetControlFont(hwnd,IDOK);
            return(FALSE);
        case WM_CTLCOLOR:
            if(HIWORD(lParam)==CTLCOLOR_STATIC ||
               HIWORD(lParam)==CTLCOLOR_DLG) {
                SetBkColor(wParam,DARKBACKGROUND);
                SetTextColor(wParam,DARKTEXTCOLOUR);

                ClientToScreen(hwnd,&point);
                UnrealizeObject(hBrush);
                SetBrushOrg(wParam,point.x,point.y);

                return((DWORD)hBrush);

            }
            if(HIWORD(lParam)==CTLCOLOR_BTN) {
                SetBkColor(wParam,DARKBACKGROUND);
                SetTextColor(wParam,DARKBACKGROUND);
```

```
                    ClientToScreen(hwnd,&point);
                    UnrealizeObject(hBrush);
                    SetBrushOrg(wParam,point.x,point.y);

                    return((DWORD)hBrush);
                }
                break;
            case WM_COMMAND:
                switch(wParam) {
                    case IDOK:
                        if(hBrush != NULL) DeleteObject(hBrush);
                        EndDialog(hwnd,wParam);
                        return(FALSE);
                }
                break;
        }

        return(FALSE);
}

DWORD FAR PASCAL AboutDlgProc(HWND hwnd,WORD message,WORD wParam,LONG lParam)
{
        static HBRUSH hBrush;
        HWND dlgH;
        POINT point;

        switch(message) {
            case WM_INITDIALOG:
                hBrush=CreateSolidBrush(DARKBACKGROUND);
                CentreWindow(hwnd);
                ItemName(MESSAGE_STRING,FetchString(MESSAGE_ABOUT));
                SetControlFont(hwnd,MESSAGE_STRING);
                SetControlFont(hwnd,IDOK);
                return(FALSE);
            case WM_CTLCOLOR:
                if(HIWORD(lParam)==CTLCOLOR_STATIC ||
                   HIWORD(lParam)==CTLCOLOR_DLG) {
                    SetBkColor(wParam,DARKBACKGROUND);
                    SetTextColor(wParam,DARKTEXTCOLOUR);

                    ClientToScreen(hwnd,&point);
                    UnrealizeObject(hBrush);
                    SetBrushOrg(wParam,point.x,point.y);

                    return((DWORD)hBrush);

                }
                if(HIWORD(lParam)==CTLCOLOR_BTN) {
                    SetBkColor(wParam,DARKBACKGROUND);
                    SetTextColor(wParam,DARKBACKGROUND);

                    ClientToScreen(hwnd,&point);
                    UnrealizeObject(hBrush);
```

6-2 *Continued*

```
                SetBrushOrg(wParam,point.x,point.y);

                return((DWORD)hBrush);
            }
            break;
        case WM_COMMAND:
            switch(wParam) {
                case IDOK:
                    if(hBrush != NULL) DeleteObject(hBrush);
                    EndDialog(hwnd,wParam);
                    return(FALSE);
            }
            break;
    }

    return(FALSE);
}

void CentreWindow(HWND hwnd)
{
    RECT rect;
    unsigned int x,y;

    GetWindowRect(hwnd,&rect);
    x=(GetSystemMetrics(SM_CXSCREEN)-(rect.right-rect.left))/2;
    y=(GetSystemMetrics(SM_CYSCREEN)-(rect.bottom-rect.top))/2;
    SetWindowPos(hwnd,NULL,x,y,rect.right-rect.left,rect.bottom-rect.top,
      SWP_NOSIZE);
}

LPSTR FetchString(unsigned int n)
{
    static char b[257];

    if(!LoadString(hInst,n,b,256))
        lstrcpy(b,"String table error - this application may be damaged");
    return(b);
}

void SetHelpSize(HWND hwnd)
{
    HELPWININFO helpinfo;
    char b[145];

    memset((char *)&helpinfo,0,sizeof(HELPWININFO));
    helpinfo.wStructSize=sizeof(HELPWININFO);
    helpinfo.x=10;
    helpinfo.y=10;
    helpinfo.dx=512;
    helpinfo.dy=1004;
```

```
        MakeHelpPathName(b);
        WinHelp(hwnd,b,HELP_SETWINPOS,(DWORD)&helpinfo);
}

void DoHelp(HWND hwnd,LPSTR keyword)
{
    char b[145];

    MakeHelpPathName(b);
    WinHelp(hwnd,b,HELP_KEY,(DWORD)keyword);
}

void MakeHelpPathName(LPSTR szFileName)
{
    LPSTR pcFileName;
    int nFileNameLen;

    nFileNameLen = GetModuleFileName(hInst,szFileName,144);
    pcFileName = szFileName+nFileNameLen;

    while(pcFileName > szFileName) {
        if(*pcFileName == '\\' || *pcFileName == ':') {
            *(++pcFileName) = '\0';
            break;
        }
        nFileNameLen--;
        pcFileName--;
    }

    if((nFileNameLen+13) < 144) lstrcat(szFileName,HELPFILE);
    else lstrcat(szFileName, "?");
}
```

The DEMO9.RC resource script.

Figure 6-3

```
#include "amcc.h"

MainScreen DIALOG 29, 28, 256, 196
STYLE WS_POPUP | WS_CAPTION | WS_SYSMENU | WS_MINIMIZEBOX
CAPTION "Dialog Demo Nine"
MENU MainMenu
BEGIN
    DEFPUSHBUTTON "Quit", 199, 110, 164, 36, 20, WS_CHILD | WS_VISIBLE | WS_TABSTOP
    CONTROL "Mild Panic", 101, "PanicButton", BSS_PANICBUTTON, 16, 12, 17, 17
    CONTROL "Moderate Panic", 102, "PanicButton", BSS_PANICBUTTON, 16, 48, 17, 17
    CONTROL "Major Panic", 103, "PanicButton", BSS_PANICBUTTON, 16, 84, 17, 17
    CONTROL "Enable Panic", 104, "PanicButton", WS_BORDER |
      BSS_PANICBUTTON, 16, 132, 17, 17
    LTEXT "Click here if something slightly nasty happens, such as finding a
      herd of llamas grazing in your basement.", 201, 108, 12, 132, 32,
      WS_CHILD | WS_VISIBLE | WS_GROUP
    LTEXT "Click here if somthing moderately nasty happens, such as
```

6-3 *Continued*

```
            discovering a herd of politicians grazing in your basement.",
        202, 108, 48, 132, 32, WS_CHILD | WS_VISIBLE | WS_GROUP
        LTEXT "Click here if something really slimy happens, such as discovering
        a herd of politicians trying to buy the votes of the llamas grazing in
        your basement.", 203, 108, 84, 132, 32, WS_CHILD | WS_VISIBLE | WS_GROUP
        CONTROL "Enable Sarcasm", 105, "PanicButton", WS_BORDER |
        BSS_PANICBUTTON, 108, 132, 17, 17
END

AboutBox DIALOG 72, 72, 220, 128
STYLE WS_POPUP | WS_CAPTION
CAPTION "About"
BEGIN
    CTEXT "", 101, 16, 16, 188, 72, WS_CHILD | WS_VISIBLE | WS_GROUP
    DEFPUSHBUTTON "OK", IDOK, 96, 104, 28, 16, WS_CHILD | WS_VISIBLE | WS_TABSTOP
    CONTROL "", -1, "static", SS_BLACKFRAME | WS_CHILD | WS_VISIBLE, 8, 8, 204, 88
END

MainMenu MENU
BEGIN
    POPUP "File"
    BEGIN
        MENUITEM SEPARATOR
        MENUITEM "E&xit", 199
    END

    POPUP "&Help"
    BEGIN
        MENUITEM "&Index", 901
        MENUITEM "&Using help", 905
        MENUITEM SEPARATOR
        MENUITEM "&About...", 999
    END

END

STRINGTABLE
BEGIN
    0,"Dialog Demo Nine\nCopyright \251 1993 Alchemy Mindworks Inc.\n
      From the book Windows Dialog Construction Set\rby Steven William Rimmer\rPublished by Windcrest/McGraw Hill
    1,"Help"
    101,"Mild panic\n\nGo to Sears and buy some llama traps."
    102,"Moderate panic\n\nGo to Sears and buy some shark repellant."
    103,"Serious panic\n\nGo to Sears, buy an unobtrusive camcorder, call CNN."
END

DialogDemoNine ICON
BEGIN
    '00 00 01 00 01 00 20 20 10 00 00 00 00 00 E8 02'
    '00 00 16 00 00 00 28 00 00 00 20 00 00 00 40 00'
    '00 00 01 00 04 00 00 00 00 00 80 02 00 00 00 00'
    '00 00 00 00 00 00 00 00 00 00 00 00 00 00 00 00'
```

```
    '00 00 00 00 80 00 00 80 00 00 00 80 80 00 80 00'
    '00 00 80 00 80 00 80 80 00 00 80 80 80 00 C0 C0'
    'C0 00 00 00 FF 00 00 FF 00 00 00 FF FF 00 FF 00'
    '00 00 FF 00 FF 00 FF FF 00 00 FF FF FF 00 2A 2A'
    '2A 2A 2A 2A 2A 2A 2A 22 77 70 00 00 00 00 A2 A2'
    'A2 A2 A2 A2 A2 A2 A2 A2 22 70 00 00 00 00 2A 2A'
    '2A 2A 2A 2A 2A 2A AA AA A2 70 00 00 00 00 A2 A2'
    'A2 A2 AA AA AA AA B2 AA AA 77 77 77 77 00 2A 2A'
    'AA AA 2A 2A AA 2A AA A9 19 19 19 19 17 77 AA A2'
    'A2 AA AB AB AB AA 91 91 91 91 91 91 91 97 2A AA'
    'BA BA 2A AA A9 19 19 19 19 99 99 99 99 19 AB AB'
    'A2 AA AA 11 11 91 99 99 99 90 00 00 09 99 BA BA'
    'AA A1 01 11 19 19 19 19 90 00 00 00 00 09 AA A2'
    '00 10 10 11 11 91 91 00 00 00 00 70 00 00 2A 00'
    '00 00 01 01 11 17 77 00 00 00 00 09 70 00 A2 22'
    '22 22 22 22 22 22 27 77 77 70 09 70 00 00 2A 2A'
    '2A 2A AA AA AA AA 22 22 22 77 09 77 00 00 A2 AA'
    'AA AA A2 AA AA AA A2 A2 A2 27 79 17 70 00 2A AA'
    'AA 2A 22 22 2A 2A AA AA AA 2A 79 91 77 00 A2 A2'
    'A2 22 70 70 22 A2 A2 AB A2 A2 00 99 17 77 2A 2A'
    '22 87 07 07 02 2A 2A AA AA 27 00 09 91 91 A2 A2'
    'F8 88 77 70 72 A2 AB AB AB A0 00 00 99 99 2A 22'
    '8F 88 00 77 07 2A 2A AA AA 70 00 00 00 00 A2 28'
    'F8 F0 00 08 70 22 22 A2 A2 00 00 00 00 00 2A 2F'
    '8F 80 00 07 07 2A 2A AA A7 00 00 00 00 00 A7 28'
    'F8 FF 00 88 82 22 A2 A2 A0 00 00 00 00 00 22 7F'
    '8F FF FF 8F 82 2A 2A 2A 70 00 00 00 00 00 A7 0F'
    'FF FF F8 F8 F2 A2 A2 A2 00 00 00 00 00 00 A2 70'
    'FF FF 8F 8F 2A 2A 2A 20 00 00 00 00 00 00 A7 07'
    'FF FF F8 F8 22 A2 A2 00 00 00 00 00 00 00 A2 70'
    '70 FF 8F 22 2A 2A 20 00 00 00 00 00 00 00 AA 07'
    '07 07 02 02 A2 A2 00 00 00 00 00 00 00 00 BA A0'
    '70 70 72 2A 2A 20 00 00 00 00 00 00 00 00 BB AA'
    'A7 A7 AA AA A0 00 00 00 00 00 00 00 00 00 AA BA'
    'AA AA AA 00 00 00 00 00 00 00 00 00 00 00 AA A0'
    '00 00 00 00 00 00 00 00 00 00 00 00 00 00 00 00'
    '01 FF 00 00 01 FF 00 00 01 FF 00 00 00 03 00 00'
    '00 00 00 00 00 00 00 00 00 00 00 00 01 F8 00 00'
    '07 FE 00 00 3F DF 00 00 3F 9F 00 00 01 9F 00 00'
    '00 8F 00 00 00 07 00 00 00 03 00 00 00 C0 00 00'
    '00 E0 00 00 01 F0 00 00 01 FF 00 00 03 FF 00 00'
    '03 FF 00 00 07 FF 00 00 07 FF 00 00 0F FF 00 00'
    '1F FF 00 00 3F FF 00 00 7F FF 00 00 FF FF 00 01'
    'FF FF 00 07 FF FF 00 3F FF FF 1F FF FF FF'
END


MessageBox DIALOG 72, 72, 220, 128
STYLE WS_POPUP | WS_CAPTION
CAPTION "Message"
BEGIN
    CTEXT "", 101, 16, 16, 188, 72, WS_CHILD | WS_VISIBLE | WS_GROUP
    DEFPUSHBUTTON "OK", IDOK, 96, 104, 28, 16, WS_CHILD | WS_VISIBLE | WS_TABSTOP
    CONTROL "", -1, "static", SS_BLACKFRAME | WS_CHILD | WS_VISIBLE, 8, 8, 204, 88
END
```

With the exception of the call to PANICGetVersion in its WinMain function and the PanicButton controls defined in DEMO9.RC, there's nothing in the DEMO9 application that's at all new. Everything of interest happens in its SelectProc function, and there isn't really very much going on there, either. The first three panic button controls, having the resource IDs MILDPANIC, MODERATEPANIC and SERIOUSPANIC will be enabled or disabled depending on whether the ENABLEPANIC control is checked or not. The ENABLESARCASM control defines whether checking one of the former three controls will cause it to generate a call to DoMessage. These events are all handled just as you would WM_COMMAND messages for conventional check boxes.

Note that if you edit the main window of DEMO9 with Resource Workshop, the panic button controls will look somewhat inscrutable, as illustrated in Fig. 6-4. This is nothing to be concerned about.

Figure 6-4

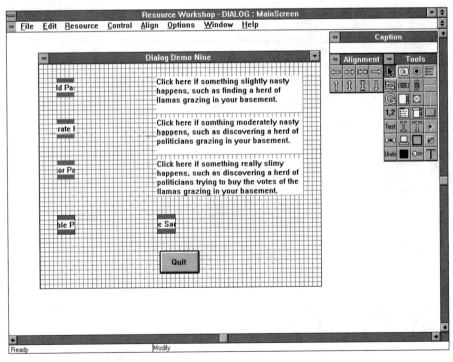

Resource Workshop editing the main window of DEMO9. It doesn't quite know what to make of the panic buttons.

The really interesting aspect of DEMO9 is actually how the AMCC.DLL library works. It implements the mechanism by which the panic button controls back in Fig. 6-1 could be so effortlessly displayed and managed.

⇨ A custom control library

A panic button is actually a set of four Windows icons. They're illustrated in Fig. 6-5. Icons are in one sense very small bitmaps, but they're convenient to work with in that Windows provides a dedicated function to display them. It doesn't offer anything called DrawImage, but it does support DrawIcon.

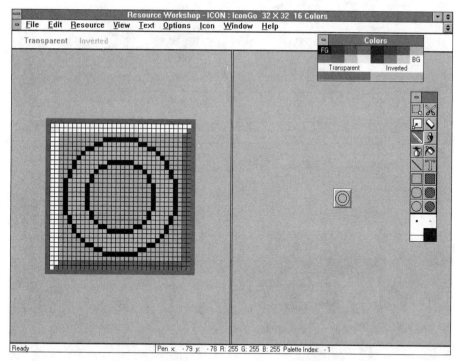

Figure 6-5A

The icons that comprise a panic button.

Figure 6-5B

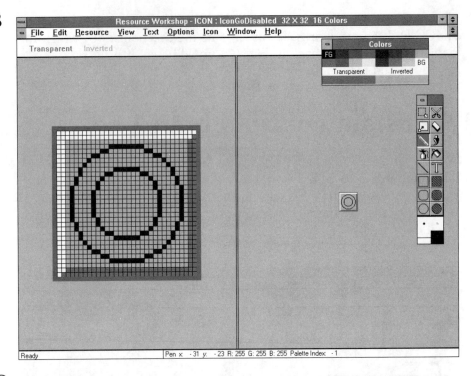

Figure 6-5C

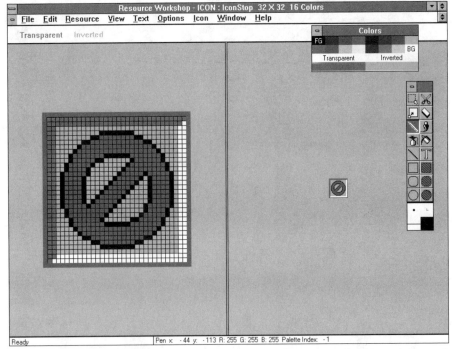

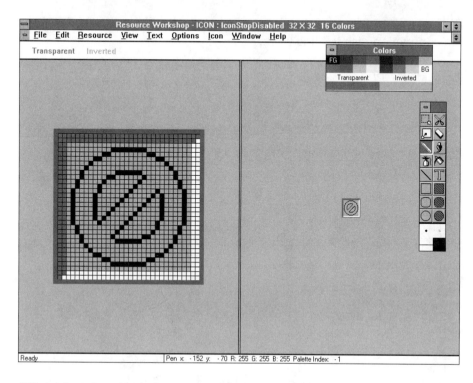

Figure 6-5D

While there's a bit more to AMCC.DLL than displaying icons, most of it is pretty conventional window dressing. The source code for the library is breathtakingly short, and is listed in Fig. 6-6. The accompanying AMC.H is as follows:

```
/*
    PANIC - header
    Copyright (c) 1993 Alchemy Mindworks Inc.
*/

#define VERSION            1
#define SUBVERSION         0

#define BSS_PANIC          0x1000L
#define BSS_BASECLASS      BS_AUTOCHECKBOX
#define BSS_PANICBUTTON    BSS_PANIC : BSS_BASECLASS

extern "C" int FAR PASCAL _export PANICGetVersion(void);
```

In addition to AMCC.CPP, you'll need AMCC.RC, as shown in Fig. 6-7. It's just the definition of the four icons shown back in Fig. 6-5. Suitable

DEF and project files for AMCC are included with the source code on the companion disk for this book.

Figure 6-6   *The AMCC.CPP source code.*

```cpp
/*
    PANIC - main module
    Copyright (c) 1993 Alchemy Mindworks Inc.

    With reference to Dan Brindle's VCR button custom control
    library, as seen in Dr. Dobbs Windows Sourcebook, Fall 1993
*/

#include <windows.h>
#include <string.h>
#include <stdio.h>
#include "amcc.h"

#define BM_SETBORDER            (WM_USER+5)

#define BTN_EXTRA               2
#define BTN_BORDER              0
#define DEFAULT_BTN_BORDER      2
#define STRINGSIZE              128

#define BACKGROUND              RGB(192,192,192)
#define TEXTCOLOUR              RGB(0,0,0)

#define TEXT_LEFT               10
#define TEXT_TOP                8

HANDLE hInst;
WNDPROC OldButtonProc;
int extra;
HICON hGoIcon,hStopIcon,hGoDisabledIcon,hStopDisabledIcon;

extern "C" int FAR PASCAL LibMain(HANDLE hInstance,
    WORD wDataSeg,WORD wHeapSize, LPSTR lpCmdLine);
extern "C" int FAR PASCAL _export WEP(int nParameter);

BOOL CTRLInit(HINSTANCE hInst);
LRESULT CALLBACK WndProcButton(HWND hwnd,UINT message,
    WORD wParam,DWORD lParam);

static int CheckStyle(HWND hwnd);
static void FocusBorder(HWND hwnd);

#pragma argsused
extern "C" int FAR PASCAL LibMain(HANDLE hInstance,
    WORD wDataSeg,WORD wHeapSize, LPSTR lpCmdLine)
{
    hInst=hInstance;
```

```
    if(!CTRLInit(hInst)) return(FALSE);
    else return(TRUE);
}

#pragma argsused
extern "C" int FAR PASCAL _export WEP(int nParameter)
{
    FreeResource(hGoIcon);
    FreeResource(hStopIcon);
    FreeResource(hGoDisabledIcon);
    FreeResource(hStopDisabledIcon);
    return(1);
}

extern "C" int FAR PASCAL _export PANICGetVersion(void)
{
        return((VERSION << 8) | SUBVERSION);
}

BOOL CTRLInit(HINSTANCE hInst)
{
    WNDCLASS WndClass;

    GetClassInfo(NULL,"button",&WndClass);

    OldButtonProc = WndClass.lpfnWndProc;

    WndClass.style |= CS_GLOBALCLASS;
    WndClass.lpfnWndProc = (WNDPROC)WndProcButton;
    extra = WndClass.cbWndExtra;
    WndClass.cbWndExtra += BTN_EXTRA;
    WndClass.hInstance = hInst;
    WndClass.hbrBackground = (HBRUSH)GetStockObject(BLACK_BRUSH);
    WndClass.lpszMenuName = NULL;
    WndClass.lpszClassName = (LPSTR)"PanicButton";

    hGoIcon=LoadIcon(hInst,"IconGo");
    hStopIcon=LoadIcon(hInst,"IconStop");
    hGoDisabledIcon=LoadIcon(hInst,"IconGoDisabled");
    hStopDisabledIcon=LoadIcon(hInst,"IconStopDisabled");

    return(RegisterClass(&WndClass));
}

LRESULT CALLBACK WndProcButton(HWND hwnd,UINT message,
    WORD wParam,DWORD lParam)
{
    PAINTSTRUCT ps;
    RECT rect,frect;
    HFONT hFont;
    WORD tmp_chk;
    DWORD dw;
```

6-6 *Continued*

```
HBRUSH oldbrush;
HPEN oldpen;
char text[STRINGSIZE+1];

switch(message) {
    case WM_CREATE:
        if(GetWindowLong(hwnd,GWL_STYLE) & BSS_PANIC) {
            if(CheckStyle(hwnd)== BSS_BASECLASS)
                SendMessage(hwnd,BM_SETBORDER,DEFAULT_BTN_BORDER,OL);
        }
        break;
    case WM_NCCALCSIZE:
        if(GetWindowLong(hwnd,GWL_STYLE) & BSS_PANIC) {
            if(CheckStyle(hwnd)==BSS_BASECLASS)
                return(DefWindowProc(hwnd,message,wParam,lParam));
        }
        break;
    case BM_SETCHECK:
        if(GetWindowLong(hwnd,GWL_STYLE) & BSS_PANIC) {
            if(CheckStyle(hwnd)==BSS_BASECLASS) {

                tmp_chk=GetWindowWord(hwnd,0);

                if(wParam) tmp_chk |= 0x0001;
                else tmp_chk &= ~0x0001;

                SetWindowWord(hwnd,0,tmp_chk);

                InvalidateRect(hwnd,NULL,FALSE);
                return(OL);
            }
        }
        break;
    case BM_SETSTATE:
        if(GetWindowLong(hwnd,GWL_STYLE) & BSS_PANIC) {
            if(CheckStyle(hwnd) == BSS_BASECLASS) {
                tmp_chk=GetWindowWord(hwnd,0);

                if(wParam) tmp_chk |= 0x0004;
                else tmp_chk &= ~0x0004;
                SetWindowWord(hwnd,0,tmp_chk);
                return(OL);
            }
        }
        break;
    case BM_SETBORDER:
        tmp_chk = GetWindowWord(hwnd,extra+BTN_BORDER);
        tmp_chk &= 0xFF00;
        if(wParam < 2) wParam=2;
        tmp_chk |= wParam & 0x0003F;
        SetWindowWord(hwnd,extra+BTN_BORDER,tmp_chk);
```

```
        return(OL);
    case WM_ENABLE:
        if(GetWindowLong(hwnd,GWL_STYLE) & BSS_PANIC) {
            if(CheckStyle(hwnd) == BSS_BASECLASS) {
                InvalidateRect(hwnd,NULL,FALSE);
                return(OL);
            }
        }
        break;
    case WM_SETFOCUS:
    case WM_KILLFOCUS:
        if(GetWindowLong(hwnd,GWL_STYLE) & BSS_PANIC) {
            if(CheckStyle(hwnd) == BSS_BASECLASS) {
                tmp_chk=GetWindowWord(hwnd,0);

                if(message==WM_SETFOCUS) tmp_chk |= 0x0008;
                else tmp_chk &= ~0x0008;

                SetWindowWord(hwnd,0,tmp_chk);

                FocusBorder(hwnd);

                return(OL);
            }
        }
        break;
    case WM_NCPAINT:
        if(GetWindowLong(hwnd,GWL_STYLE) & BSS_PANIC) {
            if(CheckStyle(hwnd) == BSS_BASECLASS) break;
        }
        break;
    case WM_PAINT:
        if(GetWindowLong(hwnd,GWL_STYLE) & BSS_PANIC) {
            if(CheckStyle(hwnd)==BSS_BASECLASS) {

                BeginPaint(hwnd,&ps);
                GetClientRect(hwnd,&rect);

                SetTextAlign(ps.hdc,TA_LEFT);

                if((hFont=(HFONT)LOWORD(SendMessage(hwnd,
                  WM_GETFONT,0,OL))) != OL)
                    hFont=SelectObject(ps.hdc,hFont);

                if(IsWindowEnabled(hwnd)==FALSE) {
                    if(GetWindowWord(hwnd,0) & 0x0001)
                        DrawIcon(ps.hdc,rect.left,rect.top,hGoDisabledIcon);
                    else
                        DrawIcon(ps.hdc,rect.left,rect.top,hStopDisabledIcon);
                }
                else {
                    if(GetWindowWord(hwnd,0) & 0x0001)
                        DrawIcon(ps.hdc,rect.left,rect.top,hGoIcon);
```

6-6 *Continued*

```
                else
                    DrawIcon(ps.hdc,rect.left,rect.top,hStopIcon);
            }

            GetWindowText(hwnd,text,STRINGSIZE);

            dw=GetTextExtent(ps.hdc,text,lstrlen(text));

            oldbrush=SelectObject(ps.hdc,GetStockObject(LTGRAY_BRUSH));
            oldpen=SelectObject(ps.hdc,GetStockObject(NULL_PEN));

            frect.top=rect.top+TEXT_TOP-4;
            frect.left=rect.right+TEXT_LEFT-8;
            frect.bottom=frect.top+HIWORD(dw)+12;
            frect.right=frect.left+LOWORD(dw)+18;

            Rectangle(ps.hdc,frect.left,frect.top,frect.right,
                frect.bottom);

            SelectObject(ps.hdc,oldpen);
            SelectObject(ps.hdc,oldbrush);

            SetBkColor(ps.hdc,BACKGROUND);
            SetTextColor(ps.hdc,TEXTCOLOUR);
            TextOut(ps.hdc,rect.right+TEXT_LEFT,
                rect.top+TEXT_TOP,text,lstrlen(text));

            if(hFont) hFont=SelectObject(ps.hdc,hFont);

            if(GetFocus()==hwnd) FocusBorder(hwnd);
            EndPaint(hwnd,&ps);

            return(0L);
            }
        }
        break;
    }

    return(CallWindowProc((int (CALLBACK *)())OldButtonProc,
        hwnd,message,wParam,lParam));
}

static void FocusBorder(HWND hwnd)
{
    RECT rect,frect;
    HDC hdc;
    HFONT hFont;
    char text[STRINGSIZE+1];
    DWORD dw;

    hdc = GetDC(hwnd);
```

```
    GetClientRect(hwnd,&rect);

    if((hFont=(HFONT)LOWORD(SendMessage(hwnd,WM_GETFONT,0,0L))) != 0L)
        hFont=SelectObject(hdc,hFont);

    GetWindowText(hwnd,text,STRINGSIZE);
    dw=GetTextExtent(hdc,text,lstrlen(text));

    frect.top=rect.top+TEXT_TOP-2;
    frect.left=rect.right+TEXT_LEFT-4;
    frect.bottom=frect.top+HIWORD(dw)+6;
    frect.right=frect.left+LOWORD(dw)+12;

    DrawFocusRect(hdc,&frect);

    if(hFont) hFont=SelectObject(hdc,hFont);

    ReleaseDC(hwnd,hdc);
}

static int CheckStyle(HWND hwnd)
{
    if((GetWindowLong(hwnd,GWL_STYLE) & BSS_BASECLASS) == BSS_BASECLASS)
      return(BSS_BASECLASS);
    else
      return(0);
}
```

The AMCC.RC resource script.

Figure 6-7

```
IconGo ICON
BEGIN
    '00 00 01 00 01 00 20 20 10 00 00 00 00 00 E8 02'
    '00 00 16 00 00 00 28 00 00 00 20 00 00 00 40 00'
    '00 00 01 00 04 00 00 00 00 00 80 02 00 00 00 00'
    '00 00 00 00 00 00 10 00 00 00 00 00 00 00 00 00'
    '00 00 00 00 BF 00 00 BF 00 00 00 BF BF 00 BF 00'
    '00 00 BF 00 BF 00 BF BF 00 00 C0 C0 C0 00 80 80'
    '80 00 00 00 FF 00 00 FF 00 00 00 FF FF 00 FF 00'
    '00 00 FF 00 FF 00 FF FF 00 00 FF FF FF 00 F8 88'
    '88 88 88 88 88 88 88 88 88 88 88 88 88 88 FF 88'
    '88 88 88 88 88 88 88 88 88 88 88 88 88 88 FF 77'
    '77 77 77 77 77 77 77 77 77 77 77 77 77 88 FF 77'
    '77 77 77 77 00 00 00 00 77 77 77 77 77 88 FF 77'
    '77 77 77 00 AA AA AA AA 00 77 77 77 77 88 FF 77'
    '77 77 00 AA AA AA AA AA AA 00 77 77 77 88 FF 77'
    '77 70 AA AA AA AA AA AA AA AA 07 77 77 88 FF 77'
    '77 0A AA AA AA AA AA AA AA AA A0 77 77 88 FF 77'
    '70 AA AA AA A0 00 00 0A AA AA AA 07 77 88 FF 77'
    '70 AA AA A0 07 77 77 70 0A AA AA 07 77 88 FF 77'
    '0A AA AA 07 77 77 77 77 70 AA AA A0 77 88 FF 77'
```

413

6-7 *Continued*

```
'0A AA A0 77 77 77 77 77 77 0A AA A0 77 88 FF 70'
'AA AA A0 77 77 77 77 77 77 0A AA AA 07 88 FF 70'
'AA AA 07 77 77 77 77 77 77 70 AA AA 07 88 FF 70'
'AA AA 07 77 77 77 77 77 77 70 AA AA 07 88 FF 70'
'AA AA 07 77 77 77 77 77 77 70 AA AA 07 88 FF 70'
'AA AA 07 77 77 77 77 77 77 70 AA AA 07 88 FF 70'
'AA AA 07 77 77 77 77 77 77 70 AA AA 07 88 FF 70'
'AA AA 07 77 77 77 77 77 77 70 AA AA 07 88 FF 70'
'AA AA A0 77 77 77 77 77 77 0A AA AA 07 88 FF 77'
'0A AA A0 77 77 77 77 77 77 0A AA A0 77 88 FF 77'
'0A AA AA 07 77 77 77 77 70 AA AA A0 77 88 FF 77'
'70 AA AA A0 07 77 77 70 0A AA AA 07 88 FF 77'
'70 AA AA AA A0 00 00 0A AA AA 07 77 88 FF 77'
'77 0A AA AA AA AA AA AA AA A0 77 77 88 FF 77'
'77 70 AA AA AA AA AA AA AA 07 77 77 88 FF 77'
'77 77 00 AA AA AA AA AA AA 00 77 77 77 88 FF 77'
'77 77 77 00 AA AA AA AA 00 77 77 77 77 88 FF 77'
'77 77 77 77 00 00 00 00 77 77 77 77 77 88 FF 77'
'77 77 77 77 77 77 77 77 77 77 77 77 77 88 FF FF'
'FF FF FF FF FF FF FF FF FF FF FF FF FF F8 FF FF'
'FF FF FF FF FF FF FF FF FF FF FF FF FF FF 00 00'
'00 00 00 00 00 00 00 00 00 00 00 00 00 00 00 00'
'00 00 00 00 00 00 00 00 00 00 00 00 00 00 00 00'
'00 00 00 00 00 00 00 00 00 00 00 00 00 00 00 00'
'00 00 00 00 00 00 00 00 00 00 00 00 00 00 00 00'
'00 00 00 00 00 00 00 00 00 00 00 00 00 00 00 00'
'00 00 00 00 00 00 00 00 00 00 00 00 00 00 00 00'
'00 00 00 00 00 00 00 00 00 00 00 00 00 00 00 00'
'00 00 00 00 00 00 00 00 00 00 00 00 00 00 00 00'
'00 00 00 00 00 00 00 00 00 00 00 00 00 00 00 00'
END

IconStop ICON
BEGIN
'00 00 01 00 01 00 20 20 10 00 00 00 00 00 E8 02'
'00 00 16 00 00 00 28 00 00 00 20 00 00 00 40 00'
'00 00 01 00 04 00 00 00 00 00 80 02 00 00 00 00'
'00 00 00 00 00 00 10 00 00 00 00 00 00 00 00 00'
'00 00 00 00 BF 00 00 BF 00 00 00 BF BF 00 BF 00'
'00 00 BF 00 BF 00 BF BF 00 00 C0 C0 C0 00 80 80'
'80 00 00 00 FF 00 00 FF 00 00 FF FF 00 FF 00'
'00 00 FF 00 FF 00 FF FF 00 00 FF FF FF 00 8F FF'
'FF FF FF FF FF FF FF FF FF FF FF FF FF FF 88 FF'
'FF FF FF FF FF FF FF FF FF FF FF FF FF FF 88 77'
'77 77 77 77 77 77 77 77 77 77 77 77 77 FF 88 77'
'77 77 77 77 00 00 00 00 77 77 77 77 77 FF 88 77'
'77 77 77 00 99 99 99 99 00 77 77 77 77 FF 88 77'
'77 77 00 99 99 99 99 99 99 00 77 77 77 FF 88 77'
'77 70 99 99 99 99 99 99 99 99 07 77 77 FF 88 77'
'77 09 99 99 99 99 99 99 99 99 90 77 77 FF 88 77'
'70 99 99 99 90 00 00 09 99 99 99 07 77 FF 88 77'
'70 99 99 99 07 77 77 70 09 99 99 07 77 FF 88 77'
END
```

```
        '09 99 99 99 90 77 77 77 70 99 99 90 77 FF 88 77'
        '09 99 99 99 99 07 77 77 77 09 99 90 77 FF 88 70'
        '99 99 90 99 99 90 77 77 77 09 99 99 07 FF 88 70'
        '99 99 07 09 99 99 07 77 77 70 99 99 07 FF 88 70'
        '99 99 07 70 99 99 90 77 77 70 99 99 07 FF 88 70'
        '99 99 07 77 09 99 99 07 77 70 99 99 07 FF 88 70'
        '99 99 07 77 70 99 99 90 77 70 99 99 07 FF 88 70'
        '99 99 07 77 77 09 99 99 07 70 99 99 07 FF 88 70'
        '99 99 07 77 77 70 99 99 90 70 99 99 07 FF 88 70'
        '99 99 90 77 77 77 09 99 99 09 99 99 07 FF 88 77'
        '09 99 90 77 77 77 70 99 99 99 99 90 77 FF 88 77'
        '09 99 99 07 77 77 77 09 99 99 99 90 77 FF 88 77'
        '70 99 99 90 07 77 77 70 99 99 99 07 77 FF 88 77'
        '70 99 99 99 90 00 00 09 99 99 99 07 77 FF 88 77'
        '77 09 99 99 99 99 99 99 99 99 99 90 77 77 FF 88 77'
        '77 70 99 99 99 99 99 99 99 99 07 77 77 FF 88 77'
        '77 77 00 99 99 99 99 99 99 00 77 77 77 FF 88 77'
        '77 77 77 00 99 99 99 99 00 77 77 77 77 FF 88 77'
        '77 77 77 77 00 00 00 00 77 77 77 77 77 FF 88 77'
        '77 77 77 77 77 77 77 77 77 77 77 77 77 FF 88 88'
        '88 88 88 88 88 88 88 88 88 88 88 88 88 8F 88 88'
        '88 88 88 88 88 88 88 88 88 88 88 88 88 88 00 00'
        '00 00 00 00 00 00 00 00 00 00 00 00 00 00 00 00'
        '00 00 00 00 00 00 00 00 00 00 00 00 00 00 00 00'
        '00 00 00 00 00 00 00 00 00 00 00 00 00 00 00 00'
        '00 00 00 00 00 00 00 00 00 00 00 00 00 00 00 00'
        '00 00 00 00 00 00 00 00 00 00 00 00 00 00 00 00'
        '00 00 00 00 00 00 00 00 00 00 00 00 00 00 00 00'
        '00 00 00 00 00 00 00 00 00 00 00 00 00 00 00 00'
        '00 00 00 00 00 00 00 00 00 00 00 00 00 00 00 00'
END

IconStopDisabled ICON
BEGIN
        '00 00 01 00 01 00 20 20 10 00 00 00 00 00 E8 02'
        '00 00 16 00 00 00 28 00 00 00 20 00 00 00 40 00'
        '00 00 01 00 04 00 00 00 00 00 80 02 00 00 00 00'
        '00 00 00 00 00 00 10 00 00 00 00 00 00 00 00 00'
        '00 00 00 00 BF 00 00 BF 00 00 00 BF BF 00 BF 00'
        '00 00 BF 00 BF 00 BF BF 00 00 C0 C0 C0 00 80 80'
        '80 00 00 00 FF 00 00 FF 00 00 00 FF FF 00 FF 00'
        '00 00 FF 00 FF 00 FF FF 00 00 FF FF FF 00 8F FF'
        'FF FF FF FF FF FF FF FF FF FF FF FF FF FF 88 FF'
        'FF FF FF FF FF FF FF FF FF FF FF FF FF FF 88 77'
        '77 77 77 77 77 77 77 77 77 77 77 77 77 FF 88 77'
        '77 77 77 77 00 00 00 00 77 77 77 77 77 FF 88 77'
        '77 77 77 00 77 77 77 77 00 77 77 77 77 FF 88 77'
        '77 77 00 77 77 77 77 77 77 00 77 77 77 FF 88 77'
        '77 70 77 77 77 77 77 77 77 77 07 77 77 FF 88 77'
        '77 07 77 77 77 77 77 77 77 77 70 77 77 FF 88 77'
        '70 77 77 77 70 00 00 07 77 77 77 07 77 FF 88 77'
        '70 77 77 77 07 77 77 70 07 77 77 07 77 FF 88 77'
        '07 77 77 77 70 77 77 77 70 77 77 70 77 FF 88 77'
```

6-7 *Continued*

```
'07 77 77 77 77 07 77 77 77 07 77 70 77 FF 88 70'
'77 77 70 77 77 70 77 77 77 07 77 77 07 FF 88 70'
'77 77 07 07 77 77 07 77 77 70 77 77 07 FF 88 70'
'77 77 07 70 77 77 70 77 77 70 77 77 07 FF 88 70'
'77 77 07 77 07 77 77 07 77 70 77 77 07 FF 88 70'
'77 77 07 77 70 77 77 70 77 70 77 77 07 FF 88 70'
'77 77 07 77 77 07 77 77 07 70 77 77 07 FF 88 70'
'77 77 07 77 77 70 77 77 70 70 77 77 07 FF 88 70'
'77 77 70 77 77 77 07 77 77 07 77 77 07 FF 88 77'
'07 77 70 77 77 77 70 77 77 77 77 70 77 FF 88 77'
'07 77 77 07 77 77 77 07 77 77 77 70 77 FF 88 77'
'70 77 77 70 07 77 77 77 70 77 77 07 77 FF 88 77'
'70 77 77 77 70 00 00 07 77 77 77 07 77 FF 88 77'
'77 07 77 77 77 77 77 77 77 77 70 77 77 FF 88 77'
'77 70 77 77 77 77 77 77 77 77 07 77 77 FF 88 77'
'77 77 00 77 77 77 77 77 77 00 77 77 77 FF 88 77'
'77 77 77 00 77 77 77 77 00 77 77 77 77 FF 88 77'
'77 77 77 77 00 00 00 00 77 77 77 77 77 FF 88 77'
'77 77 77 77 77 77 77 77 77 77 77 77 77 FF 88 88'
'88 88 88 88 88 88 88 88 88 88 88 88 88 8F 88 88'
'88 88 88 88 88 88 88 88 88 88 88 88 88 88 00 00'
'00 00 00 00 00 00 00 00 00 00 00 00 00 00 00 00'
'00 00 00 00 00 00 00 00 00 00 00 00 00 00 00 00'
'00 00 00 00 00 00 00 00 00 00 00 00 00 00 00 00'
'00 00 00 00 00 00 00 00 00 00 00 00 00 00 00 00'
'00 00 00 00 00 00 00 00 00 00 00 00 00 00 00 00'
'00 00 00 00 00 00 00 00 00 00 00 00 00 00 00 00'
'00 00 00 00 00 00 00 00 00 00 00 00 00 00 00 00'
'00 00 00 00 00 00 00 00 00 00 00 00 00 00 00 00'
END

IconGoDisabled ICON
BEGIN
'00 00 01 00 01 00 20 20 10 00 00 00 00 00 E8 02'
'00 00 16 00 00 00 28 00 00 00 20 00 00 00 40 00'
'00 00 01 00 04 00 00 00 00 00 80 02 00 00 00 00'
'00 00 00 00 00 00 10 00 00 00 00 00 00 00 00 00'
'00 00 00 00 BF 00 00 BF 00 00 00 BF BF 00 BF 00'
'00 00 BF 00 BF 00 BF BF 00 00 C0 C0 C0 00 80 80'
'80 00 00 00 FF 00 00 FF 00 00 00 FF FF 00 FF 00'
'00 00 FF 00 FF 00 FF FF 00 00 FF FF FF 00 F8 88'
'88 88 88 88 88 88 88 88 88 88 88 88 88 88 FF 88'
'88 88 88 88 88 88 88 88 88 88 88 88 88 88 FF 77'
'77 77 77 77 77 77 77 77 77 77 77 77 77 88 FF 77'
'77 77 77 77 00 00 00 00 77 77 77 77 77 88 FF 77'
'77 77 77 00 77 77 77 77 00 77 77 77 77 88 FF 77'
'77 77 00 77 77 77 77 77 77 00 77 77 77 88 FF 77'
'77 70 77 77 77 77 77 77 77 77 07 77 77 88 FF 77'
'77 07 77 77 77 77 77 77 77 77 70 77 77 88 FF 77'
'70 77 77 77 70 00 00 07 77 77 77 07 77 88 FF 77'
'70 77 77 70 07 77 77 70 07 77 77 07 77 88 FF 77'
```

```
'07 77 77 07 77 77 77 77 70 77 77 70 77 88 FF 77'
'07 77 70 77 77 77 77 77 77 07 77 70 77 88 FF 70'
'77 77 70 77 77 77 77 77 77 07 77 77 07 88 FF 70'
'77 77 07 77 77 77 77 77 77 70 77 77 07 88 FF 70'
'77 77 07 77 77 77 77 77 77 70 77 77 07 88 FF 70'
'77 77 07 77 77 77 77 77 77 70 77 77 07 88 FF 70'
'77 77 07 77 77 77 77 77 77 70 77 77 07 88 FF 70'
'77 77 07 77 77 77 77 77 77 70 77 77 07 88 FF 70'
'77 77 07 77 77 77 77 77 77 70 77 77 07 88 FF 70'
'77 77 70 77 77 77 77 77 77 07 77 77 07 88 FF 77'
'07 77 70 77 77 77 77 77 77 07 77 70 77 88 FF 77'
'07 77 77 07 77 77 77 77 70 77 77 70 77 88 FF 77'
'70 77 77 70 07 77 77 70 07 77 77 07 77 88 FF 77'
'70 77 77 77 70 00 00 07 77 77 77 07 77 88 FF 77'
'77 07 77 77 77 77 77 77 77 77 77 70 77 77 88 FF 77'
'77 70 77 77 77 77 77 77 77 77 77 07 77 77 88 FF 77'
'77 77 00 77 77 77 77 77 77 00 77 77 77 88 FF 77'
'77 77 77 00 77 77 77 77 00 77 77 77 77 88 FF 77'
'77 77 77 77 00 00 00 00 77 77 77 77 77 88 FF 77'
'77 77 77 77 77 77 77 77 77 77 77 77 77 88 FF FF'
'FF FF FF FF FF FF FF FF FF FF FF FF FF F8 FF FF'
'FF FF FF FF FF FF FF FF FF FF FF FF FF FF 00 00'
'00 00 00 00 00 00 00 00 00 00 00 00 00 00 00 00'
'00 00 00 00 00 00 00 00 00 00 00 00 00 00 00 00'
'00 00 00 00 00 00 00 00 00 00 00 00 00 00 00 00'
'00 00 00 00 00 00 00 00 00 00 00 00 00 00 00 00'
'00 00 00 00 00 00 00 00 00 00 00 00 00 00 00 00'
'00 00 00 00 00 00 00 00 00 00 00 00 00 00 00 00'
'00 00 00 00 00 00 00 00 00 00 00 00 00 00 00 00'
'00 00 00 00 00 00 00 00 00 00 00 00 00 00 00 00'
'00 00 00 00 00 00 00 00 00 00 00 00 00 00 00'
END
```

The AMCC.DLL library follows the rules for dynamic link libraries discussed earlier in this book. It's compiled using the large memory model, and must contain the two interface functions LibMain and WEP. The LibMain function calls CTRLInst, which initializes the library and registers the new PanicButton control class.

About half the tricky parts of AMCC.DLL take place in the CTRLInst function. It begins by fetching the class information of the control class on which the panic button controls will be based using a call to GetClassInfo. The message handler for the button class will be stored in the lpfnWndProc element of the WNDCLASS object it returns. This is the function that Windows normally calls to process messages to a button control. We'll store it in the global variable OldButtonProc and replace it with WndProcButton, the message handler in AMCC.DLL.

You might well ask what Windows will make of this should it have cause to respond to a conventional button control, as is the case for the Quit button in DEMO9. As will be discussed in a moment, the WndProcButton function will call the message handler stored in OldButtonProc if a message appears for something other than a panic button control.

Several other elements of the WNDCLASS object are modified in CTRLInst. The style value is augmented with the CS_GLOBALCLASS flag. The cbWndExtra element is adjusted to allow for some extra data storage along with each window object. The lpzsClassName is set to "PanicButton," the name of the custom control class.

The CTRLInit function also loads the four icons required to display the control. It might be argued that this is a bit wasteful of memory, and that the icons should probably be loaded dynamically as they're required. Certainly if you were to create a more elaborate library, with numerous bitmaps and other objects this would unquestionably be true. The amount of memory required by four icons, however, is pretty minimal. Having them in memory permanently makes the panic button controls they generate a lot more responsive.

The WndProcButton function is where all the work of AMCC.DLL really happens. It will be called to process any messages generated by button controls. It will, however, use the CallWindowsProc function to call OldButtonProc most of the time, that is, to handle messages sent to conventional button controls.

The WndProcButton function can determine whether a message it receives pertains to a panic button or to some other sort of button control by calling GetWindowLong to fetch the style value for the control in question and checking that for the presence of the BSS_PANIC flag. The BSS_PANIC flag is defined in AMCC.H, and is part of the BSS_PANICBUTTON control style. It's defined for a panic button control in its resource definition. If this flag is present in the style value returned by GetWindowsLong, the message can be processed by WndProcButton. If it isn't, the message pertains to a conventional button and should be passed along to the old message handler.

There are several messages that WndProcButton must process to display and maintain a panic button control. The BM_SETCHECK message will be sent to it when a panic button's state changes. The state is stored in the first bit of the first extra word of the window object that defines a panic button control.

The BM_SETSTATE message handles enabling and disabling a panic button. Its value is stored in the third bit of the first extra word of the window object of a panic button control. The focus, as managed by the WM_SETFOCUS and WM_KILLFOCUS messages, is stored in the fourth bit.

The majority of the work in WndProcButton is involved in responding to WM_PAINT messages. When a WM_PAINT message appears, the message handler must determine which of the four icons on a panic button is appropriate and display it. It must also update the text caption for the control and manage the focus rectangle accordingly.

Selecting and displaying an icon is relatively easy. The four icons are referenced by the following four handles:

hGoIcon The green "go" symbol.

hStopIcon The red "stop" symbol.

hGoDisabledIcon The hollow gray "go" symbol.

hStopDisabledIcon The hollow gray "stop" symbol.

If the control in question is enabled—as determined by a call to IsWindowEnabled—the choice is between the first two icons. If it's disabled, the choice is between the second two. If the panic button to be displayed is checked, as indicated by the state of the first bit of the first word of its extra window data, the appropriate "go" icon should be displayed.

The DrawIcon function handles displaying whichever icon is ultimately chosen.

The rest of the WM_PAINT handler in WndProcButton takes care of displaying the text caption for the panic button in question and then placing the focus rectangle around it if it has the focus. Note that panic buttons assume they'll be displayed against a light gray background.

The FocusBorder function can be called from several places within WndProcButton, and as such it fetches the current HDC rather than being passed it. It fetches the caption text for the control being displayed, measures it with a call to GetTextExtent and uses the DrawFocusRect function to place a rectangle around it.

Custom controls to go

The AMCC.DLL library is a very simple example of working with custom controls. You should have little difficulty in adapting it to your own applications—it makes a workable skeleton upon which to hang the rags and adornments of your own ideas for control classes. Windows custom controls can be comprised of pretty well anything that's turned up in this book, including bitmaps, conventional control types, windows and so on. They can be elaborate little applications in their own right.

Note that in creating a DLL to support custom controls, you must make use of the Import Library application that accompanies Borland C++ to create a LIB for your DLL. Make sure to rebuild the library if you add functions to your DLL, lest odd things happen when you go to call it.

In addition, make sure that the DLL itself remains accessible to its calling application, as has been discussed earlier in this book.

Index

About the author

When I'm not writing computer books, I write books. These other books are about as far removed from computer books as they can get, I imagine. The novels I write have thus far all been set in infrequently visited bits of Britain, mostly Wales and Scotland. I'm not certain what "genre" they'd fall into—they're typically concerned with witchcraft and fertility magic and such. That's real witchcraft, as opposed to Hollywood/Stephen King witchcraft. I'm pretty certain they're not horror novels, in any case. (There are those, of course, who will consider the phrase *real witchcraft* to be a contradiction in terms.)

My first novel was *Coven*, published by Ballantine a few years ago. My second novel, *The Order*, was recently published by Jam Ink Publishing.

One of the curious things about writing computer books is that everyone seems to think I write science fiction on the side. I'm not certain why this is—I rarely have any patience for it. A quick stroll through the science fiction section of most book stores suggests that half the books in the field are novelizations of episodes of Star Trek and the other half are works of would-be latter-day J.R.R. Tolkien.

One of the hardships of writing the sort of fiction I do is having to go over to Wales or Scotland *every* summer to do some research. This involves grueling afternoons and evenings spent in sundry pubs downing the local ale, tortuous walks through various towns and villages, and so on. The things one does for art frequently transcend the limits of human endurance . . . although I feel I'll manage to press on.

When I really can't face either computer books or lurid novels of debauchery, lust, and pagan excess, I play guitar in a band called Loftus. We started out doing traditional Irish instrumental music, although we've since diversified into bits of Breton and Elizabethan music and even a few left-over medieval tunes. The band's name is derived from the name of one of Turlough Carolan's fiddle tunes, "Loftus Jones."

I feel moved to point out that there's a distinction between traditional Irish music and the music that's traditionally played in pseudo-Irish bars on St. Patrick's day, when the beer has been dyed green. The latter group includes such favorites as "Danny Boy," "Black Velvet Band," and so on. I suspect that if any of the members of Loftus were to suggest playing one of these, it would be regarded as grounds for impeachment.

I'm not certain what else I do that would constitute a hobby. Megan thinks I collect cars as a sort of pastime. I'm not certain I'd agree with this. For example, Clive Cussler, who wrote *Raise the Titanic* and several other novels, has 86 of them. I have—I believe—only three. I used to build instruments for a while, until the cost of the wood involved in doing so made collecting cars cheaper.

Other Bestsellers

WINDOWS 3.1 PROGRAMMING
Takes novice C programmers into the next generation of Microsoft Windows Release 3.1 with the aid of numerous programming examples that are written in C/C++. Disk included. 832 pages.
07-881855-9 $39.95 paper only

WINDOWS 3.1:
The Complete Reference
2nd Edition
Contains information on every aspect of Windows including the use of Windows for Pen Computing, Windows for Workgroups, and Windows Connection. 826 pages.
07-881889-3 $29.95 paper only

WINDOWS 3.1: The Pocket
Reference
2nd Edition
A handy memory jogger to the newest release of Windows. A unique Task Reference, which clearly explains how to accomplish common tasks using Windows 3.1 is also included. 224 pages.
07-881824-9 $9.95 paper only

BIT-MAPPED GRAPHICS
2nd Edition
A programmer's guide to popular IBM PC and Macintosh graphics file formats. With updated coverage of Super VGA, TIFF 5.0, PC Paintbrush, GEM/IMG/GIF, and MacPaint standards. Ready-to-run source code and bit-mapped illustrations included. 520 pages.
8306-4208-0 $26.95 paper only

WINDOWS BIT-MAPPED GRAPHICS

Revised for Windows programmers. Covers Windows BMP, TIFF, PC Paintbrush, GEM/IMG, GIF, Targa, and MacPaint standards. Programmers have instant, fingertip access to all the practical information they need to work effectively with Windows-compatible graphics formats. 488 pages.

0-8306-4206-4   **$26.95 paper**
0-8306-4207-2   **$38.95 hard**

MULTIMEDIA PROGRAMMING FOR WINDOWS

A source of functions and complete programs for creating multimedia applications—fast. Complete source code for all applications, plus executable version of the programs, are included on CD-ROM. 400 pages.

0-8306-4539-X   **$39.95 paper**
0-8306-4538-1   **$49.95 hard**

Look for These and Other Windcrest/McGraw-Hill Books at Your Local Bookstore

---

To Order Call Toll Free 1-800-822-8158

(24-hour telephone service available.)

or write to Windcrest/McGraw-Hill, Blue Ridge Summit, PA 17294-0840.

- -

Title	Product No.	Quantity	Price

☐ Check or money order made payable to Windcrest/McGraw-Hill

Charge my ☐ VISA ☐ MasterCard ☐ American Express

Acct. No. _____ Exp. _____

Signature: _____

Name: _____

Address: _____

City: _____

State: _____ Zip: _____

Subtotal	$ _____
Postage and Handling ($3.00 in U.S., $5.00 outside U.S.)	$ _____
Add applicable state and local sales tax	$ _____
TOTAL	$ _____

Windcrest/McGraw-Hill catalog free with purchase; otherwise send $1.00 in check or money order and receive $1.00 credit on your next purchase.

Orders outside U.S. must pay with international money in U.S. dollars drawn on a U.S. bank.

Windcrest/McGraw-Hill Guarantee: If for any reason you are not satis-fied with the book(s) you order, simply return it (them) within 15 days and receive a full refund.

BC

431

DISK WARRANTY

This software is protected by both United States copyright law and international copyright treaty provision. You must treat this software just like a book, except that you may copy it into a computer in order to be used and you may make archival copies of the software for the sole purpose of backing up our software and protecting your investment from loss.

By saying "just like a book," McGraw-Hill means, for example, that this software may be used by any number of people and may be freely moved from one computer location to another, so long as there is no possibility of its being used at one location or on one computer while it also is being used at another. Just as a book cannot be read by two different people in two different places at the same time, neither can the software be used by two different people in two different places at the same time (unless, of course, McGraw-Hill's copyright is being violated).

LIMITED WARRANTY

Windcrest/McGraw-Hill takes great care to provide you with top-quality software, thoroughly checked to prevent virus infections. McGraw-Hill warrants the physical diskette(s) contained herein to be free of defects in materials and workmanship for a period of sixty days from the purchase date. If McGraw-Hill receives written notification within the warranty period of defects in materials or workmanship, and such notification is determined by McGraw-Hill to be correct, McGraw-Hill will replace the defective diskette(s). Send requests to:

Customer Service
Windcrest/McGraw-Hill
13311 Monterey Lane
Blue Ridge Summit, PA 17294-0850

The entire and exclusive liability and remedy for breach of this Limited Warranty shall be limited to replacement of defective diskette(s) and shall not include or extend to any claim for or right to cover any other damages, including but not limited to, loss of profit, data, or use of the software, or special, incidental, or consequential damages or other similar claims, even if McGraw-Hill has been specifically advised of the possibility of such damages. In no event will McGraw-Hill's liability for any damages to you or any other person ever exceed the lower of suggested list price or actual price paid for the license to use the software, regardless of any form of the claim.

McGRAW-HILL, INC. SPECIFICALLY DISCLAIMS ALL OTHER WARRANTIES, EXPRESS OR IMPLIED, INCLUDING, BUT NOT LIMITED TO, ANY IMPLIED WARRANTY OF MERCHANTABILITY OR FITNESS FOR A PARTICULAR PURPOSE.

Specifically, McGraw-Hill makes no representation or warranty that the software is fit for any particular purpose and any implied warranty of merchantability is limited to the sixty-day duration of the Limited Warranty covering the physical diskette(s) only (and not the software) and is otherwise expressly and specifically disclaimed.

This limited warranty gives you specific legal rights; you may have others which may vary from state to state. Some states do not allow the exclusion of incidental or consequential damages, or the limitation on how long an implied warranty lasts, so some of the above may not apply to you.

DISK INSTRUCTIONS

The companion disk for *Constructing Windows Dialogs*, includes the source code for each of the demonstration Windows applications presented in the book. You'll also find a compiled version of PLAY.DLL—its use is described in detail in chapter 5. Finally, you'll find two shareware applications: Graphic Workshop for Windows to help you with the graphics that turn up throughout the book, and Multimedia Workshop for Windows to assist in finding suitable crash-test dummies for the multimedia functions that appear in chapter 5. See the README.TXT file for more information.

DISCLAIMER

If you've bought this book and included disk, you've also bought the following rights to use the code herein for your applications:

- You're free to abstract code fragments for this book as you require and incorporate them into programs that you write. You can distribute these programs freely in their executable form so they can be run by other users but not readily decompiled, disassembled, or linked into other applications.

- You cannot distribute any of the source code from this book as source code, in either human- or machine-readable form.

- In distributing executable application files that contain functions or variations on function from this book, you aren't required to pay any additional royalties, nor do you require explicit written permission. No credit need be given to this book.

- You are free to distribute the PLAY.DLL dynamic link library included with this book with your applications, provided the copyright message provided by the *PLAYGetCopyright* function is displayed in the About box of your application, or somewhere equally prominent.

- You cannot distribute any of the applications, utilities, documentation, or complete packages on the companion disk for this book without explicit written permission from Alchemy Mindworks Inc.

In short, you can use the source code in any way that would not allow someone who has not bought this book to use the code.

IMPORTANT

Opening this package constitutes acceptance of the Disk Warranty terms and renders this entire book-disk package unreturnable except for replacement in kind due to material defect.